Politics and Leadership in North Korea

Politics and Leadership in North Korea, now fully updated in this second edition, presents an accessible and comprehensive account of North Korea's political, economic and foreign policies since its creation in 1945. Moving away from media representations of North Korea as dangerously erratic and dysfunctional, Adrian Buzo provides a thorough analysis of Kim Il Sung's vision for the DPRK and demonstrates the consistency of the successive leaderships' approach to politics, economics and international affairs.

This second edition has been fully revised and takes into account all the important events of the last fifteen years in North Korea, such as:

- endemic food shortages;
- the steady growth of military emphasis in both politics and ideology;
- the acquisition and continued development of nuclear capabilities;
- the implementation and eventual failure of South Korea's 'sunshine policy';
- the growth of private enterprise and a consumer economy.

As such, it will continue to be an essential resource for students of North Korea, East Asian Politics and International Politics.

Adrian Buzo is a lecturer at Macquarie University, Australia. He previously served in both Seoul and Pyongyang as a diplomat.

Politics and Leadership in North Korea

The Guerilla Dynasty

Second Edition

Adrian Buzo

LONDON AND NEW YORK

Second edition published 2018
by Routledge
2 Park Square, Milton Park, Abingdon, Oxon, OX14 4RN

and by Routledge
711 Third Avenue, New York, NY 10017

Routledge is an imprint of the Taylor & Francis Group, an informa business

© 2018 Adrian Buzo

The right of Adrian Buzo to be identified as author of this work has been asserted by him in accordance with sections 77 and 78 of the Copyright, Designs and Patents Act 1988.

All rights reserved. No part of this book may be reprinted or reproduced or utilised in any form or by any electronic, mechanical, or other means, now known or hereafter invented, including photocopying and recording, or in any information storage or retrieval system, without permission in writing from the publishers.

Trademark notice: Product or corporate names may be trademarks or registered trademarks, and are used only for identification and explanation without intent to infringe.

First edition published as *Guerilla Dynasty* by Allen & Unwin 1999

British Library Cataloguing-in-Publication Data
A catalogue record for this book is available from the British Library

Library of Congress Cataloging-in-Publication Data
Names: Buzo, Adrian, author.
Title: Politics and leadership in North Korea : the guerilla dynasty / Adrian Buzo.
Description: Milton Park, Abingdon, Oxon ; New York, NY : Routledge, 2018. | Includes bibliographical references and index.
Identifiers: LCCN 2017012166| ISBN 9781138187368 (hardback) | ISBN 9781138187375 (pbk.) | ISBN 9781315643090 (ebook)
Subjects: LCSH: Korea (North)—Politics and government. | Korea (North)—Economic policy. | Korea (North)—Foreign relations.
Classification: LCC JQ1729.5.A58 B89 2018 | DDC 320.95193—dc23
LC record available at https://lccn.loc.gov/2017012166

ISBN: 978-1-138–18736-8 (hbk)
ISBN: 978-1-138–18737-5 (pbk)
ISBN: 978-1-315–64309-0 (ebk)

Typeset in Bembo
by Florence Production Ltd, Stoodleigh, Devon, UK.
Printed and bound by CPI Group (UK) Ltd, Croydon, CR0 4YY

Contents

List of tables vi
Preface vii
List of abbreviations x

1 Approach March: 1912–50   1

2 The enemy on all sides: 1950–70   29

3 The tide turns: 1970–80   69

4 Dwindling options: 1980–6   93

5 Tactical retreat: 1987–94   117

6 Triage: 1994–2004   151

7 Regroup and strike: 2004–11   203

8 The young marshal takes command: 2011–16   231

9 Final perspective   271

   Index   289

Tables

3.1	Comparison of Fourth and Fifth KWP Congress Politburos	72
4.1	Comparison of Fifth and Sixth KWP Congress Politburos	96
4.2	DPRK foreign trade: 1980–3	98
5.1	DPRK trade with the ROK: 1989–92	122
6.1	Changes in the DPRK leadership rankings: 1994–8	160
7.1	National Defence Commission membership: 1998–2009	207
7.2	KWP Politburo elected, 28 September 2010	209
8.1	Comparison of KWP Politburos: 2010 and 2016	244
8.2	Members of the inaugural SPA State Affairs Commission, 2016	245
8.3	DPRK food production, 2009–15: FAO assessments	250

Preface

Reading a preface usually implies serious interest, and is usually restricted to those who may wonder how a work came into being and what it seeks to do. In this case, the responses are fairly straightforward: the first edition of *The Guerilla Dynasty* in 1999 seemed to fill a need, attracted enough attention to remain in people's memories and its basic analysis avoided becoming too dated in the eyes of many. This was motivation enough to revisit, substantially rewrite and update the original. In doing so, I have also not tried to belabour the 'guerilla' component. This is not a label, to be placed alongside the various other labels that people have attached to the DPRK, but more a simple observation that to me is useful in explaining a whole range of actions and phenomena which are so often put into the lazy, derogatory basket of the unknowable, the unpredictable and the bizarre. At all times I take DPRK decision-makers seriously. They are the products of a rigorous system and further back of a strong, advanced culture, but if they have traduced this heritage and perpetrated crimes against humanity on their own people, they are nevertheless just making their way through their grossly distorted political landscape, just as we are seeking to locate them in that same landscape.

In the first edition detailed coverage only really began in the 1970s, for the work of Scalapino and Lee provided extensive coverage of events before then. That is still largely the case, but attention should be drawn to the significant work done more recently on decisive events in the 1950s and 1960s, for they help us to understand more fully the establishment of the Kimist DPRK state. Andrei Lankov's work on the events of September 1956, Balasz Szalontai's work both on DPRK state formation and Kimist foreign policy in the 1960s, and Fyodor Tertitskiy's work on the 1967–8 period are just three of many examples. And, of course, the Wilson Centre International Cold War History Project has greatly enriched our understanding of these and many more topics.

More recently, the last twenty years have seen significant amounts of information about the DPRK become available, sometimes on the back of very fine scholarship, but at other times less so, and I have again tried to avoid analysing the analysts. This is sometimes hard to do because in their various ways they intrude into the story, as does the international media, and both parties often rearrange the political stage scenery in very inconvenient ways. Meanwhile, although I have learnt a lot from many more recent scholars, I have altered very little in matters of basic interpretation. That Kim Il Sung's guerilla experience and the DPRK's extended Stalinist tutelage have definitively shaped the nation remains not so much an argument but a common-sense and recurring theme, and it should become clear to the reader that I find reports of the death of Stalinism in the DPRK greatly exaggerated, for how one can say this with the country's personality cult politics, the fundamental structure of its governmental institutions, its *gulags*, and its state terror apparatus still thriving, and with the much-vaunted market economy serving the Kimist state much as Lenin's New Economic Policy served the Leninist state, continues to defeat me. In this I can only echo Brian Myers's lament at the passing of a generation of scholars who were deeply familiar with the history of the Soviet Union.

Comparison with the previous edition will nonetheless reveal some differences, mostly relating to degrees of relevance that shift with the passing of time. It seems less important now than it did fifteen years ago to present detailed evidence in support of the proposition that the DPRK was never interested in reform during the 1970s and 1980s, especially during the mid-1980s. The contrary proposition always rested on a flimsy base, is obviously disproved by subsequent events, and so it would only clutter the overarching narrative to maintain such a level of detail which is now unimportant. In addition, a detailed description of the political institutions of the DPRK in its Marxist–Leninist party heyday is obviously not quite so important for discussing the Kim Jong Il-Kim Jong Un era, and so such details have been pruned and dispersed throughout the book as part of the narrative. Of course, full discussion of both these topics and others such as DPRK 'traditionalism' that have now received only truncated coverage can still be found in the first edition.

I remain mindful of all the people who helped me complete the first edition of this work, and the fact that most of what I had to say is still relevant nearly twenty years later is a tribute to the quality of that support. More immediately, as an academic commuter between Sydney and Seoul I have made, and in some case remade, the acquaintance of a different, younger generation of North Korean scholars, and watchers and without this stimulus I don't think I would have prepared this current work. For such inspiration and companionship, among many others my special thanks go to Peter Sylvestre, Peter Ward, Chris Green, Andrei Lankov, Balazs Szalontai and Jacco Zwetsloot.

Concerning more technical matters, in referring to publications written in English, I have generally placed the author's family name last. In all cases, to avoid misunderstanding or ambiguity I have adopted a standard practice of inserting a hyphen between the two elements of the authors' personal names. Thus, 'Han Shik Park' becomes 'Han-Shik Park.'

For names, places, titles and terminology, I have followed the McCune–Reischauer (M–R) system of romanisation with the following modifications:

- For technical reasons I have omitted the diacritic marks.
- For Kim Il Sung, Kim Jong Il and Kim Jong Un, I have used the official DPRK romanisations as carried in English-language DPRK publications such as *The Pyongyang Times* since this is how they are known internationally.
- I have romanised DPRK place names and ideological terminology (e.g. 'Juche') according to DPRK practice.
- In the case of ROK public figures, I have used the spellings carried in Yonhap News Agency's *Korea Annual* since this is how these people are most widely known.

Abbreviations

AA	Australian Archives
CC	Central Committee
CCP	Chinese Communist Party
CMC	Central Military Committee (of the KWP)
CPSU	Communist Party of the Soviet Union
CPV	Chinese People's Volunteers
CRS	Commonwealth Record Series
DFAT	(Australian) Department of Foreign Affairs and Trade
DPRK	Democratic People's Republic of Korea
FAO	Food and Agricultural Organisation (of the United Nations)
FEER	*Far Eastern Economic Review*
FETZ	Free Economic and Trade Zone
HEU	Highly enriched uranium
IAEA	International Atomic Energy Agency
KCP	Korean Communist Party
KEDO	Korean Peninsula Energy Development Organization
KH	*Korea Herald*
KIZ	Kaesong Industrial Zone
KPA	Korean People's Army
KPAF	Korean People's Armed Forces
KWA	*Korea and World Affairs*
KWP	Korean Workers' Party
LWR	Light-water reactor
NAM	Non-Aligned Movement
NDC	National Defence Commission of the SPA
NEAJUA	Northeast Anti-Japanese United Army
NLL	Northern Limit Line
NPT	Nuclear Non-Proliferation Treaty
OGD	Organization and Guidance Department (of the KWP)
PDS	Public Distribution System
PT	*The Pyongyang Times*
ROK	Republic of Korea
SEZ	Special Economic Zone

SNCC	South–North Coordinating Committee
SPA	Supreme People's Assembly of the DPRK
THAAD	Terminal High Altitude Area Defence
UNC	United Nations Command
UNSC	United Nations Security Council

1 Approach March: 1912–50

Introduction

In a state governed by personal autocracy, the significance of the character, personality and life experiences of the leader is self-evident. His imprint on society is heavy, his shadow is long, he himself is an agent of transformation, and his likes, dislikes, biases and prejudices are relevant – often strangely so – in matters of state great and small. He does not seek to accommodate social forces but is oppressed by them, and so he in turn represses them and measures his success as a leader and a person accordingly. His achievements and failures are therefore usually measured on a grand scale, and this encourages considerable speculation on his personality and formative influences.

This is especially true when we consider the case of Kim Il Sung, for few individuals have shaped the character and destiny of a state in the modern world as thoroughly as he has, to the extent that the past history and present condition of the Democratic People's Republic of Korea (DPRK) cannot be understood apart from his life and career. Other shaping factors such as traditional Korean political culture, Japanese colonialism and militarism, Korean nationalism, Soviet hegemony and Cold War rivalry all have their place in the story of the DPRK, but the DPRK has been shaped and driven primarily by a vision of the nature of politics and indeed life itself which had profound meaning for Kim. This vision arose from his childhood and his experience as an anti-Japanese guerilla fighter in Manchuria during the 1930s, and then was given tangible shape through his subsequent ingestion of the Stalinist model of state building. Our search for an understanding of the DPRK therefore begins with an account of Kim Il Sung's background and his rise to power.

Kim Il Sung: the early years

Kim Il Sung was born Kim Song-ju in the village of Mangyongdae near Pyongyang on 15 April 1912.[1] The eldest of three sons, Kim is usually described as coming from a peasant background, but his actual social status defies exact definition since his father, Kim Hyong-jik (1894–1926), was partly educated at a missionary school and married the daughter of a school teacher from a prominent local Presbyterian family, while no members of the family ever appear to have directly engaged in farming. Kim's parents were Christians and were active in anti-Japanese activities in the immediate aftermath of the Japanese annexation of 1910. A maternal uncle died in prison while serving a long sentence for armed insurrection, and Kim's father himself took an active stance against the Japanese, participating in Christian-led nationalist groups and suffering imprisonment in 1917 for such activities. Released shortly before the 1919 March First Uprising, Kim Hyong-jik and his family left Korea in the wake of this upheaval for Manchuria, where the Japanese authorities had less reach and where nationalists in exile could conduct their activities with greater freedom but with, of course, less impact. At age 7, therefore, Kim Il Sung went with his parents to Manchuria and returned for only two years of schooling in 1923–4. From 1925 to 1941, from age 13 to 29, Kim lived in Manchuria. There the privations of immigrant life appear to have contributed to the deaths of his father in 1926 at the age of 32, his mother in 1932 at the age of 40, as well as a younger brother, Chol-ju, during the 1930s. His only other sibling, Kim Yong-ju, survived and had a long career, much of it spent within the inner circles of power in Pyongyang.

Again defying neat categorisation, in Manchuria Kim studied in the Chinese school system, even though Korean alternatives were available. Possibly the Chinese system was longer established and better developed. He left school in 1927, aged 14, while still a few months short of completing three years of Chinese middle school, and gradually became actively involved in Communist activities. This was to be his true *alma mater*. A contemporary Japanese police document records him as being present at a Communist youth group meeting in 1929 (Dae-Sook Suh, 1967: 266), and soon after this he was arrested after participating in various anti-Japanese activities and was imprisoned for eight months (Dae-Sook Suh, 1988: 7). The death of his mother in 1932 left him parentless at age 20, and soon afterwards he joined the Chinese Communist Party-led guerilla movement, which had become operational after the Japanese take-over of Manchuria in September 1931. The recollections of Kim's contemporaries place him under arms in early 1933 (Sung-Chul Yang, 1981: 81), while the earliest documentary record of Kim's military activities dates to early 1935 (Dae-Sook Suh, 1967: 268).

Kim's entry into anti-Japanese activism was part of a much broader nationalist movement which first arose with the steady Japanese penetration into Korea, beginning with the Treaty of Kanghwa in 1876 and culminating with the annexation of Korea as a Japanese colony in 1910. This penetration opened Korea to a wide range of modernising influences, and in the process members of the Korean intelligentsia began to see their country as an independent nation-state for the first time, after many centuries of self-identification as a state within the Chinese world order, usually described as a tributary state with laws of its own. Modern Korean nationalism dates from the growth of such perceptions and took form under the constant threat to Korean sovereignty posed by

Japanese imperialism. It developed at a time when the Choson Kingdom's efforts at self-strengthening were considerable but ultimately ineffective, and it grew to maturity under a harsh Japanese colonial regime. It was conditioned both by subsisting features of the traditional political culture and by the context of both a failing dynastic order and colonial exploitation. This nationalism also differed from the nationalism of most other colonised people across the world in that Korean nationalists did not have to manufacture a new nation out of heterogeneous parts. Korea had well-established geographical and cultural boundaries, a powerful sense of cultural distinctiveness, an advanced civilisation, and a long, discrete history as a unitary state. The major task of nationalist groups was not to convince people that 'Korea' existed, but to mobilise their countrymen and have them share their particular vision for the creation of a modern, independent nation-state – in other words, to have their countrymen believe that *their* Korea existed.

This was no simple matter, for despite this strong cultural identity, Korean nationalism under the Japanese was marked by lack of cohesion – and even outright hostility – between the nationalist groups themselves.[2] Many factors contributed to disunity, most obviously rigorous Japanese repression, but even when this repression was not present, it was always clear that while Korean nationalists had a strong sense of belonging to a single ethnic community, this did not mean that they perceived this community in a similar fashion. To individual Korean nationalists, 'Korea' was an abstract concept which they extrapolated from concrete experiences within particular groups, usually ordered around a dominant personality, a common education background, a common regional identity or a common clan affiliation.[3] The dire predicament of Koreans, faced as they were with cultural obliteration under Japanese assimilationist policies, may have cried out for leadership and action, but no section of the nationalist movement established a broad base of support that could cut across the boundaries of region, education and social status, and consequently Korean nationalism was never able to mount a sustained threat to Japanese rule.[4] They cohered, as the saying went, like grains of sand.

The efficiency and ruthlessness of the Japanese repressive apparatus confined most overtly political Korean nationalist activity to the exile sphere. Here Koreans generally found cold shoulders, for the Great Powers had tacitly accepted Japan's argument that Korea had lost the capacity to rule itself and that its people would somehow 'benefit' from Japanese colonisation.[5] While the Koreans managed to establish a Korean Provisional Government in Shanghai in 1919, this entity failed to rally a sizeable portion of the movement, and by the 1930s was virtually defunct (Dae-Sook Suh, 1967: 11). Elsewhere, the Soviets provided some assistance to the Korean Communist cause before killing off almost all their Korean assets during the Comintern Purge of 1937 (Lankov, 2002: 4), and the Chinese Nationalists were in the main sympathetic, except where Korean Communists became involved in the broader Nationalist–Communist civil war.

The net effect was that activities abroad remained sporadic, small-scale and uncoordinated, and only Manchuria, where for a while after 1931 sustained armed resistance became possible, was a partial exception to this. Not surprisingly, then, the Korean nationalist movement was a frustrated movement of limited influence. It was disadvantaged by many factors beyond its control, but whatever the contribution of individuals and groups, it was always a movement which added up to considerably less than the sum of its parts. Its level of actual achievement is symbolised somewhat sadly by the fact that in 1945 neither the US nor the USSR could find any compelling reason to include even a token Korean contingent in the first wave of their occupying forces, nor did they extend political recognition to any of the exile movements.

These characteristics of the nationalist movement as a whole also applied to the pre-1945 Korean Communist movement. The strong sense of cultural identity and the task of reclaiming the homeland from the Japanese meant that Korean Communists operated in an environment charged with nationalist sentiment. In practice, therefore, there was often little distinction between Communist and nationalist individuals as nationalists became Communists and Communists became nationalists with all manner of shadings in between.[6] However, this did not lead to effective united-front activities between the two movements, for while they could often appear to be similar in outlook, the Communists were strongly defined by a distinct ideology whose struggle against bourgeois nationalism was at least equal in importance to the main struggle against Japanese imperialism. Accordingly, relations between Communist and nationalist organisations and groups were often marked by hostility.

This Communist–nationalist overlap also reflected another key attribute of the pre-1945 Korean Communist movement – namely, its lack of ideological development. Although the movement attracted relatively educated urban dwellers, and although some Communists such as Pak Hon-yong, the leader of the Party in South Korea after 1945, had received training in the Soviet Union,[7] conditions for the development of serious interest in ideology and theory such as a stable, cosmopolitan learning environment were absent. As a result, theoretical issues played very little role in either attracting Koreans to Communist activism or to sustaining their interest in it. Not only did the movement lack any notable theoreticians or indeed any corpus of theoretical writing, but there were few internal party debates on theoretical issues. As far as the Soviet-led Communist International (Comintern) was concerned, the Korean Communist movement quickly acquired a reputation for falling into the heresy of bourgeois–nationalist deviationism, and for practising revolutionary violence of an adventurist or putschist variety (Dae-Sook Suh, 1967: 51–2).[8]

The Korean Communist movement was also hampered by the same strong traditions of localism and regionalism that afflicted the anti-Japanese movement as a whole. Moreover, the movement operated in a number of countries, and each section of the movement developed individual characteristics. These ranged from underground agitation and propaganda activities within the comparatively cosmopolitan, intellectual and internationalist environment of the Japanese Communist Party to the armed guerilla struggle in Manchuria, and to more regular politico-military activities in other areas of China. In matrix fashion, all these theatres of operation had their own subsets of regional and small-group affiliations which militated against unified command and activity.

The movement's diaspora-based character after 1928 therefore meant that each element acquired its own history, traditions, networks of association, tactical imperatives and ideological colouring. Poor communications and the distances involved meant that they rarely had contact with each other and could refer to no shared event or incident such as a Long March or an October Revolution. Even within Korea, the uneven impact of the Japanese colonial government's economic policies contributed to new forms of regional identity among domestic Communists and in the broader politicised community.[9] As members of a minority ethnic community who were subject to the discipline of foreign parties during 1928–45, the status of Korean Communists abroad remained insecure, their energies dissolving 'like salt in water', as Kim San put it (Kim and Wales, 1941: 208). This environment of poorly defined ideological and strategic priorities, poor communication and a steady diet of failure often directed thought inward toward issues of leadership and tactics, and internecine conflict was a constant problem.

The only significant source of foreign assistance to the Korean Communist movement was the Soviet Union through Comintern, which conducted liaison with foreign communist parties and movements, but here too the relationship was difficult. Because of the Korean Communist Party's minuscule size, its reputation for undisciplined or difficult behaviour and its lack of leaders and ideologues capable of making the right impression at the right level, it attracted little attention in Moscow. Comintern correspondence with the Koreans was sporadic, Korean participation in Comintern councils and conferences was infrequent, and although contacts between the Korean Communist (KCP) movement and Comintern had begun in the early 1920s, the KCP's admission to Comintern was not ratified until September 1928 (Dae-Sook Suh, 1970: 227), too late to encourage the Koreans because two months earlier, in July 1928, the KCP had officially dissolved itself after a fourth and final attempt to establish a KCP on Korean soil had ended in failure. Formal relations with Comintern therefore began with bitter analyses of the reasons for failure and wide-ranging Comintern criticisms of the Korean Communist movement. These included factionalism, failure to address agrarian issues, failure to build viable networks and cells, failure to broaden a membership base that was overwhelmingly petty bourgeois in background, and failure to preserve security in agitation and propaganda activities. The repeated tendency to jeopardise clandestine activities by premature public demonstrations was also highlighted (Suh, 1967: 178; Scalapino and Lee, 1972: 90–3, 106–11). The Korean Communist movement therefore derived little benefit from its Comintern relationship, and, as we shall see, the memory of this earlier, somewhat fraught relationship lingered to influence the judgements of the Soviet occupying authorities in 1945.

Like the nationalist movement as a whole, then, the Korean Communist movement functioned as a collection of different movements, each possessing distinct organisations, hierarchies, histories and personal networks. We risk distorting the nature of its activities, and hence the nature of its struggle, by conflating its activities and its significance, for by 1945 it had not attempted to hold a Party Congress, nor had it held any broadly representative meetings. It had no recognised headquarters or base, it had published no theoretical journals, and its platform and policies were poorly developed and articulated. It had no widely recognised leader or leadership group, nor indeed any individuals with reputations for providing ideological, theoretical or practical guidance to the movement as a whole. As a diaspora-based movement working mainly in an environment of efficient Japanese repression, it suffered high rates of attrition in armed struggle, and it was unable to build a viable grass-roots organisation within Korea itself. Few, if any, of its leading members had ever set foot in the settled areas of Korea and were therefore unknown to most Koreans.

The Korean Communist movement in Manchuria in which Kim Il Sung now made his way struggled with the same set of disabilities that afflicted the movement as a whole. After the final dissolution of the Korean Communist Party, Korean Communists in Manchuria faced the choice of either accepting a Comintern-directed merger with the Chinese Communist Party (CCP), which took effect in 1930, or else leaving the movement. Many chose to leave, for it was never easy working with the Chinese comrades, and beyond common commitment to anti-Japanese resistance, the Chinese and Korean political agendas did not easily overlap. But Kim Il Sung was one of those who stayed, becoming a member of the CCP, and for roughly ten years fighting in the Northeast Anti-Japanese United Army (NEAJUA), a Chinese Communist guerilla army which brought a number of scattered Chinese and Korean guerilla bands under unified CCP command after the Japanese annexation of Manchuria in 1931. From 1933 on, the NEAJUA came under extreme pressure from a sustained Japanese offensive and by the end of 1935 it had been driven out of settled areas. According to official Japanese estimates, at this time it consisted of six armies with a total of about 15,000 men, mostly under arms, conducting anti-Japanese guerilla activities deep in the rugged countryside (Dae-Sook Suh, 1988: 17).

During 1936–8, the remnants of the NEAJUA armies were reorganised into three route armies. The Korean guerillas were concentrated into the First Route army, whose area of operation was closest to the east Manchuria–northeast Korea border, and it was in this army that Kim attained prominence, rising to become one of the dozen or so top-ranking Koreans in the command structure. By this time, organised operations of any description had either ceased or else were being conducted by isolated guerilla units whose only link to the Party was the presence of a political commissar in their ranks (Scalapino and

Lee, 1972: 162; Dae-Sook Suh, 1967: 277–8). Kim's command varied from 50 to 300 men engaged in hit-and-run operations with the enemy and in extracting supplies from the local population, mostly by means of kidnapping, robbery and extortion (Dae-Sook Suh, 1988: 39).[10] His largest and most famous operation was the June 1937 attack on the Japanese garrison at the border village of Bochonbo, in which he led a company of about 200 men. Kim continued to conduct operations under extremely adverse conditions before retreating from Manchuria to the Soviet Far East in late 1940, whereupon a new phase in his career began.

In the Soviet Union, Kim was transported into the midst of an immense socialist state where, after the Nazi invasion in July 1941, the air rang with appeals not to socialist internationalism but to Russian nationalism, and he was given a role to play, albeit a small one, in a massive mobilisation effort for a great and desperate military struggle against Nazi Germany, an effort which ended in a glorious victory. For Kim, the Soviet Union must have been a startling and exhilarating revelation, especially as a model for the effective mobilisation of human and material resources for war. After routine internment by border security guards and a period of recovery from the extended period of privation he had endured, Kim was assigned to the Khabarovsk Infantry Officers School, and in August 1942 he was assigned to the 88th Brigade, which had absorbed the Chinese and Korean remnants of the Manchurian guerillas who had retreated to the Soviet Far East. This brigade, which functioned within the Soviet Army command structure with a guerilla training regimen centred on reconnaissance and infiltration, consisted of four battalions, each with a strength of about 150 men, and did not involve actual combat training. Kim commanded one battalion with the rank of captain.[11] The extent to which Kim was able to travel within the Soviet Union and observe its society and economy is not clear, but as a foreign soldier in wartime it would obviously have been limited. He appears to have made at least two extended trips to Moscow (Seiler, 1994: 35–6), but given his duties, he would have remained within military circles. He also appears to have been well liked by his Soviet superiors and quickly gained a reputation for strict discipline. In particular, Soviet officers recalled his strict rules against heavy drinking (Goncharev *et al.*, 1993: 131ff.).

The Soviets entered the Pacific War on 8 August 1945, but the Japanese surrender seven days later meant that the Korean elements in the 88th Brigade saw no active service. Surplus to requirements, they were excluded from even symbolic participation in the actual Soviet entry and occupation of Korea north of the 38th parallel, which began with the occupation of Pyongyang on 24 August. The brigade returned to Korea some three weeks later on 19 September and was disbanded shortly afterwards. However, another door soon opened as Kim and sixty-six other former Korean officers of the 88th brigade were reassigned to assist the Soviet occupation authorities in liaison and interpreting roles. This placed them in strategically important positions throughout the occupation forces *apparat*.

The Soviets come to Korea

In both North and South Korea political activity in the immediate post-liberation period proceeded amid strong popular expectations of the immediate restoration of Korean independence and of wide-ranging social and political change, but also amid the chaos created by the abrupt withdrawal of the Japanese colonial administration after thirty-five years of intensive rule. There were Korean exile movements, but there was no broad-based government-in-exile waiting to assume power. There were Korean politicians, but no mass political movements or parties waiting to re-emerge. Instead, political allegiance was largely claimed by prominent individuals who derived their authority from their social standing in Korean society and from their record of nationalist resistance to the Japanese. There were few such figures in the North, and among them the standing of Cho Man-sik, a Christian leader and long-time activist, was nonpareil (Scalapino and Lee, 1972: 314ff.). There was also intense expectation in both the Soviet zone of occupation north of the 38th parallel and the US zone in the south that immediate restoration of Korean sovereignty would take place, but there was no coherent political centre capable of pressing this issue. In both occupation zones, military governments adjusted to their new and unaccustomed role as de facto governments in accordance with their orders, which were to receive the Japanese surrender, not to pave the way for Korean sovereignty, an issue that was to be decided elsewhere. There were many points of contrast between the US and Soviet approaches, but in confronting an unfamiliar local political culture, both were united in the need to empower Korean political allies who shared their respective political philosophies and who could become reliable instruments for their rule until broader issues affecting Korea's future were resolved.

How, then, did the Soviets see their role in North Korea? There is general agreement that the Soviets had only sketchy plans prior to August 1945 (Scalapino and Lee, 1972: 317; Weathersby, 1990: 184; Hak-Soon Paik, 1995; van Ree, 1989: 50–1; Lankov, 2002: 5).[12] Their major objective was to secure their vulnerable, sparsely populated eastern Siberian flank against any revival of Japanese military aggression, but when it became clear that the US would not allow them any real influence in shaping post-war Japan, they opted for the alternative of a foothold on the Korean Peninsula, built around a Korean regime compatible with this objective.[13] If such a regime controlled the entire Korean Peninsula, well and good, but if not, then a friendly Korean state north of the 38th parallel was acceptable.

In addition to entering North Korea ill-prepared and at short notice, like the Americans in the South the Soviets were called upon to fill an administrative and political vacuum caused by the suddenness of the Japanese capitulation, and, again like the Americans, the search for reliable local clients presented serious problems. The background here was that the Communist Party of the Soviet Union (CPSU) had changed radically during the 1930s under Stalin, and was now a very different entity from the CPSU of the 1920s. Stalin had abandoned the organisational pattern of the Party as an elitist, internationalist revolutionary vanguard in favour of a mass party headed by an autocratic genius-leader, and in the process had made far more stringent demands on foreign parties for loyalty to the Soviet Union than the Bolsheviks with their commitment to proletarian internationalism had ever done. One notable feature of Stalin's personal autocracy was an attitude of deep suspicion towards national Communist movements, and wherever possible he sought to replace them with cadres who were more directly dependent upon Moscow. This was the circumstance that underlay the near-total annihilation of the old Comintern as part of the Great Purge of 1937, and it also meant that local Communists were very much seen as part of a problem, not a solution, for they were largely remnants left over from the pre-Purge Comintern. The Soviets may not have had clear objectives in the early stages of their occupation, but they were guided by strong principles laid down from the very top, and these did not include automatically empowering local Communists or encouraging new or independent forms of Communism to flourish.[14]

The classic Soviet formula for occupation government was the united front, in which non-communist but acceptable 'progressive' political elements were teamed with leftists and especially Communists in a power-sharing arrangement which could then bring the political combat skills of the latter to bear in order to subdue and emasculate the former. Thus, for several months until towards the end of 1945 the Soviets endeavoured to co-opt the nationalist leader Cho Man-sik and his Democratic Party into such an arrangement. However, Cho proved to be too wary of such potential bedfellows and too confident of his own political strength to respond with much enthusiasm, and as impasse grew, and as the Japanese colonial prisons emptied and as exiles returned, local Communist assets grew, and Soviet attention turned away from Cho to alternative formulae for leadership that were more compatible with their own aims and objectives.[15]

A brief profile of the field of Communist groupings in North Korea helps us to appreciate further the difficulties faced by the Soviets in this endeavour, and also the opportunities that it opened up for Kim Il Sung. Here we find four distinct elements – the domestic Communists, the Korean soldier-guerillas of the so-called Yan'an group, the Soviet-Koreans, and the former Manchurian guerilla group led by Kim Il Sung, each defined by a mix of common background, interest, spheres of operation, and long association and friendship, and each having little in common with each other. The most significant group, the domestic Communist group, comprised Communists who had conducted operations within Korea for much of the Japanese colonial period. Their major assets were their established record as anti-Japanese agitators and their pre-1945 organisational remnants, which they now sought to revive and extend in the South. Their major weaknesses began with the fact that many were in essence chance survivors of the 1937 Comintern purge, and so they still looked over their shoulder at the equally mistrustful Soviets. Moreover, to little effect they had long advocated an esoteric, doctrinaire urban proletariat-based political ideology that associated political activity with small-group political conspiracy, agitation and violence. Although they were present in the North throughout the 1930s, where they had attempted to build networks through the tiny industrial proletariat that existed in the Hamhung-Hungnam area in the north-east, they had focused their activities on Seoul, where there was a far greater concentration of workers, predominantly in light industry. Accordingly, as many domestic Communists emerged from prison or hiding, they re-established the Korean Communist Party in Seoul immediately after liberation and stayed there during the crucial early period of regime formation in the North. They established close links with the Soviet authorities in the North and worked in concert with them, but the centre of their political world remained in the South.

The second major group in the oligarchy, the Yan'an group, comprised Korean Communists who had fought in China proper against the Japanese and the Chinese Nationalists under the leadership of the Chinese Communist Party.[16] As a group, the Yan'an veterans were generally older, better educated, and also more sophisticated than most other Korean Communists by reason of their exposure to large-scale military and political activities in China. In post-liberation North Korea, they initially maintained their distinct identity by establishing the New People's Party (*Sinmin-dang*) in February 1946, but their strategic position was weak. Long years in exile had left them with tenuous roots in Korea, they had no big power patron, their service in China was grounds for deep Soviet suspicion, and many of their number continued to fight in China until the victory of the CCP in 1949. In order to compensate for these weaknesses, they soon entered into a loose strategic alliance with the Manchurian guerilla group, with whom they merged to form the North Korean Workers' Party in August 1946. Lacking grass-roots organisation or support, their survival hinged upon recognition of their predominantly military-based skills, and upon the emergence of a broad-based Communist party, capable of accepting distinct groupings within its ranks. This, of course, was not to be.

The third group in the oligarchy, the Soviet-Koreans, had no affiliation with the pre-war Korean Communist movement. This group consisted of a cadre of Soviet bureaucrats and Party officials of Korean background who were dispatched to the North to perform essential administrative and bureaucratic tasks. Much as they did in Eastern Europe, the Soviets drew on the valuable resource of CPSU cadres of ethnic Korean origin, who possessed what were described as special 'national characteristics' for organisation and guidance skills at appropriate levels of government.[17] Beginning in earnest in late 1945, an estimated two hundred CPSU cadres of Korean background were deployed in senior positions in the bureaucracy up to Vice Minister level and were also in overall charge of Party organisation and propaganda.[18] To occupy such positions in a government established under Leninist party auspices was, of course, to play an active role in support of Soviet objectives. In fact, so seamless was the relationship between the North Korean Party and the CPSU that the Soviet-Koreans who were CPSU members automatically became North Korean Party members in Korea while retaining their Soviet citizenship and CPSU party membership.[19] By contrast, Korean members of the Chinese Communist Party had to relinquish their membership and reapply to the Korean party (Lee and Oh, 1968: 287). One can only guess how local Korean Communists must have felt as they saw so many choice jobs go to such outsiders, but meanwhile the Soviet-Koreans played senior and influential policy roles within the new Party well into the 1950s.

The fourth major group in the oligarchy, the former Manchurian guerillas, was led by Kim Il Sung. Like Kim, most members of this group were in their twenties and early thirties, of limited education, and of low social status. They had fought under CCP command and were virtually unknown to the rest of the Korean Communist movement, as well as to the population at large. Numerically small, this group was, for the most part, highly disciplined and tightly knit after long years of shared danger and privation. The Manchurian guerillas entered Korea in October 1945 after some four years of training in the Soviet Union, and although its members lacked political stature, and had no semblance of a political organisation on Korean soil beyond intermittent liaison in the far north during the 1930s, they possessed the decisive advantages of close ties and clear compatibility with the Soviet modus operandi.

As a ruling oligarchy, these Communist groupings were far from united, but they were bound together by the opportunities of power and suffered from the common problem of popular indifference, if not hostility. Their esoteric ideology had little obvious relevance to the material problems of an overwhelmingly backward, rural society, and their pre-war record was not impressive. Liberation in 1945 brought vigorous grass-roots political activity in the form of local People's Committees, which reflected the turbulence of the times in their advocacy of wide-ranging transformations in Korean society, but this activity included little or no specific reference to the Korean Communist movement or to Marxism-Leninism.[20] As Kim Il Sung himself observed in 1955, 'If we had yelled about building socialism in the period of construction directly after liberation, who would have accepted it?' (Hale, 2002: 286).[21]

Another problem shared by all Communist groups was that between them they had few individuals recognised as political leaders by the general population. Despite social upheaval and dislocation on the peninsula during the final stages of the Japanese occupation, there is no compelling evidence that core features of the Korean political tradition had been significantly set aside. The four key attributes of age, social status, educational background and place of origin were still important determinants of credibility for political leadership, and the Communists had to contend with better credentialed rivals in all these categories. This was especially the case with Kim Il Sung and his Manchurian guerilla colleagues, who typically were at least a generation younger than veteran nationalist leaders such as Cho Man-sik, were almost all from poor rural backgrounds, had received little education past the middle-school level, and mostly came from remote hinterland areas.

Nor were the guerillas known for their deeds. They had a more than respectable record of anti-Japanese resistance, but while anti-Japanese nationalism translated into public respect and even formed the basis for a prominent political role in many parts of East and Southeast Asia after the Japanese surrender, the work of such nationalists had, of course, to be widely known if a major political dividend were to be reaped. Here it needs to be borne in mind that Korean Communist activities had been mainly sporadic, low-level armed clashes carried out in remote regions on foreign soil, or in otherwise obscure circumstances. Moreover, Japanese censorship was such that there was little public awareness of their deeds. The Communist campaigns lacked the power on the public imagination that might have come through eminent leadership, large-scale, sustained campaigns or notable battlefield accomplishments.

A further serious problem for the Communists after August 1945 was that they did not gain access to power as a result of any mass-based political or military campaign within Korea, but were handed power by coercive foreign occupation authorities. This, of course, had its benefits, for Soviet backing meant control of the political centre, and hence a means of building and consolidating a power base that bypassed the intense localism of Korean political culture and the rough local-level democracy of the politically diverse People's Committees. The Soviets proceeded to hand over agitprop assets such as printing presses and radio stations, as well as provide practical bureaucratic expertise through the Soviet-Koreans – invaluable for an inexperienced movement. However, the Soviets also had exacting standards of loyalty, and these required the Communists to offer regular and fulsome public praise for a liberator who, like the US in the south, gradually acquired tarnish as a coercive foreign occupier.[22] Over time, constant public praise for the Soviets in the lavish style dictated by Stalinist political culture served to underscore the Communists' status as a marginal political movement with strong external linkages,[23] while unquestioning support for unpopular policies in the Soviet interest, such as the December 1945 Moscow Agreement on trusteeship, not immediate independence, for Korea, also placed a heavy political burden on the Communist oligarchy.[24]

Nevertheless, many Communists were prepared to accept close and public identification with the Soviet Union. This was despite undoubted feelings of resentment at the overbearing nature of Soviet control, because most North Korean Communists in 1945 considered themselves in some sense to be members of an international brotherhood of socialist parties which freely acknowledged the pre-eminence of the Soviet Union and the CPSU, and which deeply admired the achievements of Stalin as an individual leader. Being a good Communist meant proudly and closely identifying oneself with a friendly major world power which had a long history of support for anti-colonialist movements and which had just expelled the Japanese from the North

– and of course, one didn't necessarily have to be a Communist Party member to be supportive on this score. Korean Communists also owed much to the Soviet Union, and were they to compare their prospects in 1945 to their situation only five or ten years previously, they would have much reason to give thanks to their big brother, for the occupation was enabling action to implement their specific political agenda.

It was in these circumstances that Soviet methodology quickly narrowed the field of potential Korean Communist proxies down to Kim Il Sung. They orchestrated his public emergence in Pyongyang at a rally on 14 October, where he spoke from a text provided by the Soviets (Lankov, 2002: 19), and by January 1946 he was established as the first among equals in the emergent Korean Communist oligarchy. Why Kim? First, amid a fluent situation, once Cho Man-sik was discarded, the Soviets had few other 'safe' options in what was, after all, not a very competitive field. Second, although it could hardly be said that they embraced him with enthusiasm, Kim at least appeared to the Soviets as a known quality. He and his guerilla group had come of age politically in the post-Bolshevik late 1930s, and had spent four years training in the Soviet Union during 1941–5. They had become familiar with the Stalinist system and the Soviets had had the opportunity to become familiar with them.[25] Third, far from being seen by ordinary Koreans as a leader, the fact that Kim had no vestige of a local, independent power base was a perverse strength in the eyes of the Soviets since it meant that he would remain their client. Finally, while at the time the Soviets would certainly have noted Kim's youth and inexperience, they seem to have been attracted by other qualities relevant to their limited strategic aims – self-discipline, the ability to command men, a strong work ethic and little intellectual interest in ideological matters. In short, he possessed all the desirable attributes of the subordinate client and of the typical Stalinist cadre. This quality of outward conformity to type helps us to understand how the Soviets could have come to smooth the path to leadership for a man who was to spend most of the rest of his life confounding their expectations and working counter to their interests.

The socialist North takes shape

Consolidating the framework for indigenous leadership enabled the Soviet authorities to concentrate on the broader issues of establishing coherent, responsive government. Thus, in February 1946 they oversaw the establishment of the North's first transitional governmental structure, the North Korean Provisional People's Committee, chaired by Kim Il Sung. The Committee succeeded the Soviet military occupation administration, but since realities had not changed, and since the country was still desperately short of bureaucratic and technocratic talent, the North continued to be ruled by an admixture of Soviet advisers, Soviet-Korean cadres and local Koreans operating under firm Soviet guidance and applying strong Stalinist precedents in the Party, government and military spheres. This arrangement ensured that, as in the Soviet

Union, the Party held strong drive reins over the population, and that only such grass-roots political activity as was favoured by the central authorities could flourish.

Throughout 1946 a series of economic and social measures began to transform North Korean society. The overwhelming priority in the highly ruralised and impoverished country was land reform, which was proclaimed on 5 March 1946 and then rapidly carried out. This was followed up on 23 March with a broader proclamation covering policies on health, education and commerce. In the latter field, the rights of small private businesses were guaranteed, while only larger enterprises were to be nationalised. Other measures followed within months, covering a number of issues including workers' rights, gender equality and nationalisation of the commanding heights of industry, including transportation, banking and major industries such as forestry and mining. These were introduced to the public under the name of Kim Il Sung himself, and his authority was further buttressed by continuing praise in the official media. One thus measures his rise from the political wilderness to leadership in months, not years.

Land reform was effected within a month of proclamation, according to the government, and in one stroke it eliminated the landlord class, a major class enemy and a source of hostility at the local level. Unlike the South, though, farmers in the North acquired not land itself but the right to cultivation as determined by local political committees (Mitchell, 1949: 150). In pursuit of ideological objectives, one does not necessarily look for economic dividends, and so it is not surprising to find that by 1948 grain production had only barely moved ahead of production under the Japanese a decade earlier (Scalapino and Lee, 1972: 345, 384), which meant that the economic lot for the vast majority of North Koreans had barely changed. Moreover, farmers now paid a flat 25 per cent of their produce to the government, which was probably a better deal for many, but not an unalloyed benefit, for while tenants in some parts of Korea had paid up to 50 per cent under the old system, quite a few had paid considerably less. In addition, the prices they received for their crops were now centrally fixed and often artificially depressed to support other economic sectors, while farmers were also subject to other forms of intervention such as requisition and 'patriotic' contributions.[26] Collectivisation, the definitive form of North Korean agriculture, was far beyond the organisational capabilities of the government at this time, and would not be instituted until the mid-1950s.

Meanwhile, progress in building an industrial base remained slow. The Japanese had left behind a modest mineral processing and chemical base, whose contribution to the overall economy had grown substantially during the late 1930s, but it still contributed only marginally to the overwhelmingly agrarian economy. It was also geared to war production, and although this was not necessarily a drawback given the emerging priorities of the North Korea leadership, it offered little benefit to the civilian population. Moreover, in many cases it had been heavily degraded due to over-use of the final years of the Japanese occupation as well as last-minute Japanese sabotage. It was also focused on the relatively low-level semi-processing of raw materials as the higher technology industries remained quartered in Japan, and so Korea had gained little in the way of managerial or technical expertise. On the positive side, the Japanese were efficient infrastructure planners, they had left behind major mining, hydroelectricity and rail transportation assets, and the North now also had access to substantial Soviet technical expertise.

The 1945–50 period is therefore almost impossible to evaluate from an orthodox economic point of view. In addition to the paucity of statistics there is the issue – then as now – of determining just what success might look like. What were the government's economic goals? One should not overestimate the magnitude of the economic problems caused by the division in both North and South, nor discount the manifold distortions of the Japanese colonial order, but nor should one misconstrue the central objectives of the new DPRK economy. In addition to the creation of an effective distribution system to simply feed, clothe and house people amid the dislocation and chaos, the overwhelming priority for the North's leaders – then, as for decades after – was the creation of a strong military foundation in the North in order to complete the task of reunification. Thus, they themselves measured the effectiveness of economic policies in no small part by the extent to which the means of production were concentrated in the hands of the government from where other priorities, especially military priorities could be met. Established in the wake of the Soviet Union's experience in the Second World War, the structure of the North Korean economy began life with a pronounced military purpose.

Meanwhile, when we pan outward from economic statistics to view more broadly the new society taking shape, we find that there are many stories to be told about the North during 1945–50, of liberation and exhilaration at the sense of a new dawn and of release from bondage and colonial irrelevance – joining 'the ranks of men in the making of history together,' in Richard E. Kim's memorable phrase (Kim, 1970: 195), of the many Koreans who rallied to the visions of a socialist future, of the many who were filled with fear and loathing by what was taking place and who fled south,[27] and of the many who remained suspended between these two polarities. And while many North Koreans may not have consciously identified the new agenda in the North with socialism per se, in the ideology of the mother party under Stalin, the new recruits who now swelled the ranks of the Party in the north would have found much to inspire them. Like so many of the cadres who rose in the CPSU under Stalin, they too were relatively unsophisticated, recently educated young idealists who were not interested in cosmopolitan ideological debate, but instead were attracted by liberating calls to conduct class warfare against the established political and social orders, and by the discipline, intensity and violence of mobilised political life.

With time and experience, a more nationalistic brand of Communism would come to the fore, but in the atmosphere of 1945, to be a good Communist in North Korea was to be heir to the way in which Soviet-style

Communism had evolved ideologically and organisationally since 1917. In short, to be a good Korean Communist in 1945 was to praise the Soviet Union and to revere Stalin. Amid very imperfect visions of what a future modern Korean state might look like, Stalinism provided a model for modernisation at a time when the only pre-existing model of economic development and modernisation – the Japanese colonial model – had been emphatically rejected. Furthermore, this model was an organised, systematic and thorough blueprint for economic development that had been employed – with success in the eyes of true believers – in the Soviet Union for the best part of fifteen years, and was held to have spearheaded the victory over Nazi Germany.

Preparations for war

It is a truism, widely observed of politics, and useful in attempting to account for the otherwise unaccountable, that power holders tend to concentrate on what they believe they are good at and keep on doing it, often past the point of diminishing returns. This has obvious resonance for North Korea, and so we find that the militarism which later engulfed both state and society to the point of dysfunction, was not just a later, post-Korean War phenomenon but had strong antecedents. It was there in the recent experience of Japanese militarism, it was there in the Soviet Union's military occupation and its requirement for a buffer state capable of defending itself without undue cost to Moscow, it was there in the capacity of a still highly mobilised Soviet Union to arm and train North Koreans efficiently and in significant numbers, and most of all it was there in the siren call to arms to complete the glorious task of reunifying the country. The sum of these factors, when combined with the singular drives of Kim Il Sung and his followers, meant that in the late 1940s an irresistible tide towards war making was rising that the profoundly civilianised nature of traditional Korean society and culture could not withstand.

The high level of resources devoted to the military in a North Korea still desperately poor and underdeveloped emphasises the extent to which this was a core Soviet priority, with actual organisation and mobilisation defined and shaped by all groupings within the North Korean oligarchy itself. The contribution of the Kimists, the Yan'an group and the Soviet-Koreans was to be found within the Korean People's Army (KPA) itself, where Kim Il Sung and ex-guerilla colleagues such as Ch'oe Yong-kon, Kim Il and Ch'oe Hyon held dominant sway, while a Soviet-Korean, Kang Kon, was Chief of General Staff, and the Yan'an group military leader, Mu Chong, was a corps commander (Scalapino and Lee, 1972: 392). The domestic Communists led by Pak Hon-yong were strong and insistent advocates for invading the South, and claimed to have built a substantial Party structure there, capable of directing internal insurrection to complete the task of the regular military forces of the KPA. This turned out to be largely false, but the North was not to know this until after the war had begun. In the meantime, it accepted at face value the argument that in any drive for reunification this network would be valuable, if not indispensable.

Accordingly, the KPA itself underwent rapid growth during this period. Beginning as a modest domestic security force in 1945, but with strong recent practical experience of Japanese methods, it 'volunteered' young men under quotas allotted to local People's Committees, and by the end of 1948 it comprised a regular force of 60,000 soldiers, in turn backed up by a network of organisations and fronts that enrolled all males to the age of 50 in military support roles. Assets of leadership, weaponry and training were likewise built up, with thousands of Koreans receiving advanced and extended training in the Soviet Union, war surplus Soviet weaponry including tanks, aircraft and logistical support assets deployed to the North, and Soviet advisers assigned to assist KPA divisional commanders. An essential spine was then added as the Chinese civil war wound down during 1949 and an estimated 40,000 combat-hardened Korean veterans returned, giving the North a credible fighting force of over 100,000 men.

The tipping point came in early 1950, and it hinged on the thinking of Stalin. The Soviets had had to stand by and watch the reconstitution of Japan as a US ally with many of its pre-war features intact – except, of course, its military forces and its imperialist mission. This situation was further complicated by a sense of uncertainty created in Moscow by the October 1949 Communist victory in the Chinese civil war, and by mixed signals from the US which, with a certain admixture of wishful thinking, induced Stalin to believe the US was wavering in its commitment to defend the Republic of Korea.[28] In a fluid situation, the resolute man has an advantage, and Kim Il Sung, who had repeatedly advocated a strike against the South, now gained Stalin's ear, who in turn ascertained that the Chinese were in favour of an invasion, and so the calculus swung in favour of war.[29] Soviet military staff drew up military plans to be executed by the North, which duly occurred on 25 June 1950, whereupon Kim Il Sung's career entered a new phase.

Concluding remarks

At the heart of politics in Soviet-occupied Korea in 1945 was the clash between a Soviet-backed revolutionary ideology consecrated to class warfare and military conquest, and a strong traditional social fabric which expressed its profoundly civilianised political and cultural tradition through neo-Confucian values which were still functional and relevant despite Japanese depredations. From the outset, the degree of state violence employed in repressing this tradition was significant and sustained, and it duly prevailed, with Kim Il Sung quickly emerging in the role of spearhead. This role, so significant in the early shaping of the DPRK, owed much to the life he had led throughout his entire adolescent and adult life to this point.

When we examine Kim Il Sung's pre-1945 career, the strength of his basic convictions is immediately apparent. We may speculate on his inner drives, but his decision to join the Communist guerilla movement came early, before the age of 20, and struck a deep chord within, for no record survives of early role-modelling or mentoring, beyond an obvious commitment to the path laid down by his own family's anti-Japanese resistance activities. This was clearly his vocation and he never seems to have wavered in pursuing it, in good part because he entered this life before any other life experiences that might have given him pause, either then or later on, intruded.

Kim also lived in fractured times, and he rejected the political culture into which he had been born, for it gave him next to nothing, effectively denying him such basic forms of security and fulfilment as education, the gaining of a profession or trade, social security, emotional or peer support, and protection for loved ones or property, while he also saw the early deaths of his parents and his younger brother. It is therefore not surprising that these circumstances led Kim to a near-total, hostile rejection of the long-established norms of traditional Korean society, culture and politics, and the progressive adoption of an antithetically different set of norms quite alien to Korean tradition.

Within the guerilla movement, Kim demonstrated leadership qualities and was given command over significant numbers of men. Many of these men later formed the nucleus of his leadership circle after 1945, bound by durable personal ties of loyalty. In assessing Kim's rise to leadership at this time, we may speculate that this was not a highly competitive environment, and that Kim's education record of having nearly completed middle school compared well with his Korean comrades, many of whom were barely literate. Kim's own autobiography contains various references to his comrades' poor standard of education, in a matter-of-fact and not ungenerous manner.[30] In addition, his status as the eldest son in a family with respectable anti-Japanese credentials may have given him a certain bearing and innate self-confidence. His Chinese-language education may also have helped him to function as a go-between in the often difficult relationship between the Chinese command and the Korean guerillas. From Soviet accounts and from his post-1945 record, we may also surmise that while he was affable and a strict disciplinarian, he was ruthless and quick to resort to intimidation.

In understanding Kim, we should also take into account the surrounding environment of Japanese militarism, though here we are on more speculative ground, for Kim did not live directly under the Japanese, and so he knew them primarily as a faceless enemy. Clearly, though, strong familiarity with Japanese organisational and ideological norms was part of Korean experience by the 1930s, and while assessment of their direct influence on Kim is problematic, the efficacy of their norms could not but operate in the minds and consciousness of the Party intellectuals and propagandists as they filled in the outlines of Kim's ideology for him. Thus, we observe such shared features as sacred leader-worship, a mythologised history redolent with mysticism and cultural chauvinism but demanding acceptance as objective fact, strong emphasis on racial purity, proclamation and pursuit of a special national destiny through righteous war-making, insistence on organic unity between ruler and subjects which is based on a putatively sublime collective will, and definition of this will as transcending the sectional, divisive concerns of base politics and civil society interest groups. Central to both, of course, was also an all-embracing militarist vision, which helps us to explain how DPRK militarism came to far transcend the militarism of pre-1914 Europe or wartime Stalinism.[31]

However, perhaps the most striking feature at this stage of Kim's career is the extent of his isolation – physical, political, social and cultural. He went into virtual exile at the age of 7 and spent his formative years as a mobile guerilla operating in a harsh climate in remote areas. As a member of the CCP and of the NEAJUA, Kim operated outside the mainstream of the Korean Communist movement and was therefore all but unknown within it (Dae-Sook Suh, 1970: 429–30). He may have occasionally read newspapers and heard radio broadcasts, but he would rarely, if ever, have spent any significant time in a Korean or Chinese settlement of more than a few hundred people, let alone lived in a town or city. Until 1941 his exposure to the modern world was very limited, for during these years there were no trappings of government-in-exile, no liberated areas to administer, no intellectuals at his elbow and no foreign advisers.[32] This, of course, meant that he was cut off from the lives of ordinary people and had little cause to reflect on what they thought or might have wished from life, and so he arrived at his belief that they were there to be deployed as instruments of his will. More darkly, he had no cause to reflect on the ultimate objectives of the revolutionary violence he himself practised, and this constituted the roots of catastrophe for the North at the hands of an extraordinarily callous man who took weakened, dependent people and instilled into them a disastrous set of alien values.

When we move forward to consider Kim's post-1945 career, we find it difficult to underestimate the Soviet role in Kim's rise, for without it substantial political power and eventual political control of the country would not have passed to an obscure, patchily educated 33-year-old member of a tiny guerilla splinter group within an exclusivist, Leninist political subculture, who had not seen the settled areas of his country during his entire adult life. This notwithstanding, could Kim somehow have attracted significant support as a potential leader without such overt Soviet grooming? The immediate and obvious answer is that if he had shown any potential in this direction, the Soviets would never have backed him: Kim's first hurdle was the Soviet authorities, not public opinion or grass-roots support.

More broadly, the priorities of the embryonic North were not the priorities of peacetime nation-building, but of a continuing state of mobilisation for the purpose of completing the task of reunification. What was essentially a rhetorical commitment in the disorganised South was a real commitment in the North, it was compatible with Soviet strategy, and it proved an excellent fit for Kim's past experience, his talent and his temperament, and he was thus afforded the luxury of working from inside his comfort zone. He appears to have enthusiastically embraced his circumstances, and soon became a happy warrior for his cause, directing harsh, extreme language against all 'class enemies' in a manner that varied little in intensity or exaggeration from the gross rhetoric that raised eyebrows in the ensuing decades.[33]

In the political sphere, these years marked the first time that Kim had been called upon to work in harness with other Communists, mainly older, better educated and trained men, and it is not surprising that he did not embrace the experience, establishing few if any ties of substance with people outside his own tightly knit circle.[34] Power was poorly institutionalised, and in dealing with the often vicious factional warfare within the Party all actors fell back to rely on personal networks of loyalty. Here Kim was especially favoured by the intensity of the bonds between his guerilla comrades. Such loyalty in turn promoted a zero-sum approach to the handling of Party affairs, and again, this suited his instincts. He exploited the military expertise of the Yan'an group while keeping its leaders under careful political control. He was ruthless and forthright in purging domestic Communist leaders in the North such as O Ki-sop, and as the southern Communists gradually began to retreat north under pressure from the US military government from late 1946 on, he effectively screened them off from power. Thus, when the parting of the ways came during 1950–6, and the domestic, Yan'an and Soviet-Korean groups began to be purged, they were purged ruthlessly and utterly.

And yet, throughout this process, Kim does not appear to have been out of his depth among such men. We cannot gauge the precise calibre of rivals such as Pak Hon-yong, but, like Stalin before him, Kim appears to have got the better of a considerable number of more educated and credentialed people. People outside the movement cannot really know enough to judge with precision the skill-set required within an esoteric political organisation dedicated first and foremost to political combat. The wreck of a state, society and economy that Kim went on to create demonstrates the stringent limits that apply to the deployment of such a skill-set in the wider world, but within the Party and in times of intense mobilisation, such attributes as exceptional ruthlessness, the routine application of physical intimidation, a strong work ethic, self-discipline, fixed strategic purpose, ability to recognise and seize the moment, a well-honed sense of threat approaching paranoid proportions, and, of course, the ever-present factor of luck, are more than useful. We see all of these traits in Kim Il Sung during 1945–50, and North Koreans would see a lot more of them in the years ahead.

Notes

1 For English language accounts of Kim Il Sung's early life, see Scalapino and Lee (1972: 203–6), Dae-Sook Suh (1967: 261–6) and Sung-chul Yang (1981: 79–87). Also see Seiler (1994: 7–41) for a discussion of the various accounts of Kim's pre-1945 career. Lankov (2002: 49–76) provides a useful overview, including details of Kim's time in the Soviet Union 1940–5. The standard DPRK biography of Kim is by Baek Bong (1969). See also Kim's autobiography, the first volumes of which began to appear in 1992. Six were published in his lifetime, two more posthumously.

2 Dae-Sook Suh (1973: 190), for example, lists ten of the most prominent nationalist leaders in the 1920s and 1930s, and notes that establishing an organisation that could bring together more than two-thirds or even half of the forces of these men 'was an impossibility'. From inside the movement, Kim San observed that 'Our curse was that each individual wanted to be a leader and did not cooperate with the others, therefore every leader suspected every other' (Kim and Wales, 1941: 132). Such traits were also widely observed of the Communist oligarchy in North Korea and political groups in the South in the months and years after August 1945.

3 See Dae-Sook Suh (1967: 49): 'The habit of tightly organised regional groupings of the Koreans at home was reflected abroad in the Nationalist as well as the Communist groups. Many Nationalist groups were also identified as Kiho-p'a, Honamp'a, Sopukp'a, and other geographical groupings.'

4 It is interesting to pan back from an overtly political view of what motivated predominantly young Korean nationalists and see them come more to life in broader socio-cultural terms. This is the gift of Kim San in making the following comment: 'All Koreans wanted only two things really, though they differed in how to achieve these – independence and democracy. Really, they wanted only one thing – freedom. A golden word to those who know it not. Any kind of freedom looked divine to them. They wanted freedom from Japanese oppression, freedom in marriage and love, freedom to live a normal, happy life, freedom to rule their own lives. That is why anarchism had such an appeal. The urge toward a broad democracy was really very strong in Korea. This was one reason why we did not develop a centralised system of political parties. Each group defended its right to exist and its right to free expression. And each individual fought to the end for his own freedom of belief. There was plenty of democracy among us – but very little discipline' (Kim and Wales, 1941: 73).

5 See Ku Dae-yeol (1995) for a comprehensive account of the efforts of Korean nationalists to lay their case before the international community during the Japanese occupation.

6 On the Communist-nationalist overlap, see Scalapino and Lee (1972: 61) and Chong-sik Lee (1965: ix).

7 For information on Pak's pre-1945 activities, see van Ree (1989: 20–23) and Sung-Chul Yang (1981: 168).

8 Kim San relates an instructive anecdote from when Yi Tong-hwi, the pre-eminent Korean socialist leader in the early 1920s, met and briefed Lenin on the situation in Korea. Lenin quickly perceived that Yi offered little of practical value to the building of an underground movement within Korea and remarked to Grigory Zinoviev, then head of the Communist International, 'We must help Comrade Li here. He has hot blood for Korean independence but no method. This is a natural oriental condition. They have no revolutionary base but only a background of terrorism and military action' (Kim and Wales, 1941: 53).

9 A couple of examples of regional differentiation: tenancy rates tended to be higher in the export rice-growing regions in the south and west coast Kyongsang and Cholla provinces than the north-east Hamgyong provinces, intensifying pressure for land reform in those regions (Gragert, 1994: 141), while the concentration of industry on the north-east coast, especially in the Hamhung-Hungnam area, made those centres 'one of the very few points of sustained urban Communist activity inside northern Korea before 1945' (Scalapino and Lee, 1972: 319). In passing, we might note that under Japanese rule, fundamental socioeconomic (and therefore political) distinctions on the Peninsula tended to promote an east–west axis, rather than the north–south axis claimed by some as a contributing factor to the post-1945 divide. The fertile west coast plains were the focus of the export rice trade, and from the P'yong'an provinces in the north-east to the Chollas in the south-west, the socioeconomic impact of Japanese rule had many common features. This

contrasted with the pattern of development in the remote coastal areas east of the T'aebaek mountain ranges in Kangwon and Hamgyong provinces, where Japanese penetration was less intense. For a detailed anthropological account of a Hamgyong village in the late 1930s, which illuminates significant aspects of Hamgyong distinctiveness, see Han Chungnim [1949] 1987.

10 For the texts of extortion notes from this period, including one issued in the name of Ch'oe Hyon, later a high-ranking KWP cadre, see Dae-Sook Suh (1970: 449–51).

11 The extent to which this brigade brought together many cadres who rose to high office in the DPRK in the era of Kim Il-Sung's personal autocracy (1968–94) is worth noting. They included Chon Mun-sop, Ch'oe Hyon, Ch'oe Yong-gon, Han Ik-su, Kim Il, O Chin-u, Pak Song-ch'ol, So Ch'ol, Yi Ul-sol, Yi Tu-ik, and Yim Ch'un-ch'u (Seiler, 1994: 85–8).

12 Lankov notes that the initial Soviet forces to enter Korea did not bring Korean interpreters with them: their business was with the Japanese. Assessments of the actual role the Soviets proceeded to play vary from perceptions of Moscow enacting a classic takeover and creation of a client state with subordinate leadership, as was then occurring in Soviet-occupied Eastern Europe, to the Soviets essentially assisting the emergence of a grass-roots indigenous agrarian revolution. The classic study in the former vein is the 1961 State Department study *North Korea: A Case Study in the Techniques of Takeover*. Often dismissed as propaganda, a more objective assessment would acknowledge its obvious political purpose, but also note the detailed evidence and argumentation offered by trained observers who were close to the action. This is not to endorse the study's findings, nor the view that the North was in fact 'taken over.' See Szalontai (2005: 13–45) for a more nuanced account of Soviet occupation policy.

13 Regarding the grass-roots view, the theory of Soviet ideological pragmatism and flexibility suggested by Cumings (1981) and Armstrong (2003) must contend with rich evidence from both standard Soviet *modus operandi* as an occupying power in Europe in 1945, and with the contradicting, detailed materials of Soviet Bloc archives which have become available for study since the early 1990s. The latter in particular strongly supports the case for high levels of Soviet control in practically all facets of North Korean political life during the formative stages of the northern regime. For further discussion on this point, see Lankov (2004) and Szalontai (2005).

14 For a more detailed treatment of Soviet strategic objectives at this time, see Okonogi (1979). In fact, very similar objectives were still major considerations in Soviet policy decades later, and lay behind the major shift in Soviet policy toward Pyongyang that began in the early 1980s. See below, Chapter 4.

14 For an account of the Comintern purges, see Starkov (1994). On the purging of foreign party leaders within the Comintern during the Terror, also see Conquest (1973), Volkogonov (1991, 1999), Chase (2001) and Schlogel (2012). It is also worth noting that the Soviet occupation forces had with them strong, well-trained and well-connected political commissars who knew precisely what the Soviet leadership wanted. Chief among them was M. G. Lebedev, a protégé of leading CPSU Politburo member A. A. Zhdanov (Lankov, 2002: 2).

15 The final straw for the Soviets was Cho's refusal to back the idea of a trusteeship arrangement for Korea, agreed to by the US, Britain and the Soviet Union at the Moscow Conference in December 1945. Any position other than immediate independence was anathema to broad sections of Korean society, for they had lost sovereignty in 1910 with broad imperialist power complicity, and anything less than full, immediate restitution of this sovereignty was intolerable. Cho was arrested in January 1946, imprisoned and is believed to have been executed in September–October 1950 during the North Korean evacuation of Pyongyang after

the Inch'on landing (Lankov, 2002: 24). Also see Halberstam (2007: 78–9) for an interesting summary of Cho's dealings with the Soviets.
16 Dae-Sook Suh (1970: 379) notes that the term 'Yan'an' is misleading, because they were based not in the CCP heartland of Yan'an but in south-eastern Shaanxi province, where they fought on the front line, and sometimes behind enemy lines, against the Japanese. With few exceptions, the Chinese Communists appear to have remained largely indifferent to this group of Koreans. They evidently made little effort to either integrate them into the CCP during the war, or else to support them in the post-war period (Dae-Sook Suh, 1967: 230). Kim and Wales (1941) contains an interesting account of one Korean's somewhat fraught experience of struggle within the Communist movement in China during the 1920s and 1930s.
17 Koreans began to migrate to Russia in the 1860s. By 1917 they numbered approximately 60,000, including some 20,000 who had become Russian subjects. Numbers continued to grow in the 1920s and significant numbers – 7,884 in 1926 alone – were granted Soviet citizenship, many of them explicitly as a reward for the services they had rendered to the Soviet cause in the Far East. For accounts of the Korean community in Russia and the Soviet Union prior to 1945, see Chong-sik Lee and Ki-wan Oh (1968), Ginsbergs (1975) and Weathersby (1990). For Soviet policy, including personnel policy in Eastern Europe in the immediate post-war period, see Brus (1977), Skilling (1977) and Mastny (1996).
18 Ginsbergs (1976: 5) describes the policy of 'cadre export' as one where 'Soviet citizens with particular "national" attributes were systematically planted within the inner circles of the governing elites of countries gravitating in the Soviet orbit'. See Weathersby (1990: 196) and the US State Department study *North Korea: A Case Study in the Techniques of Takeover* (1961: 101) for its application in North Korea. Also see the brief biographies in Chong-sik Lee and Ki-wan Oh (1968) and Lankov (2002: 110ff.), both of which help us to grasp the extensive scale of Soviet control of DPRK party and government affairs. Perhaps the most egregious example is that of Pang Hak-se, a former NKVD officer in the Uzbekistan party *apparat* who, as Minister of Home Affairs (1951–1960), remained in control of all internal political security matters in the DPRK throughout the 1950s.
19 At this stage a word of clarification about Party titles is in order. Soon after liberation, the Korean Communist Party (KCP) divided into northern and southern bureaus and then into northern and southern parties, though under a single leadership. The exact date of the establishment of the North Korean Communist Party (NKCP) is not clear, although Scalapino and Lee (1972: 355) note Kim Il Sung's use of the term 'North Korean Communist Party organisation' at the Third Executive Committee meeting of the Bureau during 17–18 December 1945. The NKCP and SKCP became the North Korean Workers' Party (NKWP) and the South Korean Workers' Party (SKWP) after merger with the Yan'an group's New People's Party in August 1946. The SKWP effectively ceased to exist after its leadership went north in 1949, but the NKWP retained the fiction of a separate SKWP until after the outbreak of the Korean War.
20 Assessments of the Communists' popular support vary, as does the nature of the evidence on which these assessments are based, but a picture emerges of very limited popular support. Sung-Chul Yang (1990) quotes figures suggesting that the Communists comprised 4 per cent of the elected members of the first legislature in the South in December 1946, with left-wing members comprising a further 7 per cent. Given the coercive conditions under which they were operating, one could add further to this total. We can only speculate on their strength in the North in 1945. The east coast provinces of Hwanghae-do and P'yongan-do, where the bulk of the population lived, and where a strong tradition of conservative Christianity had long prevailed, shared many features in common with the southern

provinces, and Communist influence would have been limited accordingly. Higher, but still modest, levels of support probably existed in the eastern and northern provinces of Kangwon-do and Hamgyong-do, among the urban industrial populations of cities such as Hamhung, although it is easy to conflate this constituency. In 1945 Hamhung and Hungnam had populations of roughly 112,000 and 143,000 respectively.

21 Hale cites the 1960 edition of Kim's collected works for this quote. In a similar vein, Dae-Sook Suh (1970: 476–7) notes of the many surviving policy documents of Korean leftist groups from the immediate post-1945 era:

> These documents are generally repetitious in nature and they contain statements expressing exuberance accompanied by strong hatred toward the defeated Japanese. Surprisingly, no major statement of the party is available which discusses the general direction or policies of the party immediately after the liberation even when the operation of the Communist party was legal.

22 Initial widespread industrial pillage seems to have been countermanded once the Soviets fully assessed their role in the economic rehabilitation of the North. On Soviet behaviour more generally see, for example, Weathersby (1990: 190–2) and Lankov (2002: 6). There is also the evidence of a detailed internal Soviet occupation force report dated January 1946 which paints a detailed, somewhat alarming – though also possibly alarmist – picture. See http://digitalarchive.wilsoncenter.org/document/114893. Armstrong (2003: 44ff.) assesses that 'the period of widespread assaults on Korean women in the Soviet zone of occupation was relatively short-lived', which is neither very comforting in itself nor very likely, especially given the sustained predatory behaviour of Red Army troops in post-war Europe.

23 Both the First [North] Korean Workers' Party Congress in August 1946 and the Second NKWP Congress in August 1948 elected Stalin as honorary chairman. The basic laws and the constitution of the DPRK were written in Russian and then translated into Korean, and the agendas for significant conferences involving North Korean representatives were vetted by the Soviets. Both contemporary accounts and later studies have demonstrated in considerable detail how Soviet political and economic practices became the norm. See, for example, van Ree (1989), Weathersby (1990), Goncharov et al. (1993), Hak-Soon Paik (1993) and Myung-Lim Paik (1995).

24 On the negative effect of the Moscow conference on Korean Communist support, see Soon-Sung Cho (1967: 92–113) and Scalapino and Lee (1972: 273ff.).

25 Hak-Soon Paik (1993: 80) makes use of Soviet documents to provide a useful description of Kim's rise under the Soviets. In addition, Yu Song-ch'ol has given a valuable account of the precise movements and assignments of Kim and his group in which he stresses the significance of their roles as interpreters and liaison officers to the Soviet authorities in the establishment of their political organisation (Seiler, 1994: 122). Weathersby (1990: 196) makes a similar point: 'So important was the role of these Soviet Koreans that North Koreans refer to the immediate post-liberation period as the "Age of the Rule of the Interpreters."'

26 Joseph Chung (1974: 9) notes that 'A limited number of North Korean peasants interviewed during the Korean War indicated that they preferred ownership status'. We should also note in passing that assessing the institution of tenancy in rural Korea under the Japanese has its complexities, for it was not always exploitative and the rents in kind charged were not uniformly high. In places such as in the west and south, where the Japanese were more directly involved in growing for the export rice market, rents in kind could be extortionate, but in more isolated, marginal areas such as Hamgyong Province, tenancy rates were lower. Moreover, the prevalence of clan-based villages – in the majority of Korean villages at this time a single clan lineage dominated the population – meant that often the

landlord–tenant relationship was between fellow clan members, and the various non-commercial considerations that this brought into play resulted in lower rents as well. This common relationship is described by a number of anthropologists, including Osgood (1951), Brandt (1971), and Park and Gamble (1975), and especially by Han ([1949] 1987: 19), whose account is Hamgyong-specific.
27 Scalapino and Lee (1972: 313) quote 1944 Japanese census statistics in estimating the population south of the 38th parallel as 15.9 million, with 9.2 million to the north. They note that by September 1946 the figure for the south had risen to 19.4 million, the increase coming mainly from the northern exodus, some in transit from Manchuria, and from the repatriation of Koreans (mainly former Kyongsang Province residents) from Japan.
28 The best-known example of this was US Secretary of State Dean Acheson's speech to the National Press Club on 12 January 1950, which did not mention the Korean Peninsula in outlining the US 'defense perimeter' in East Asia.
29 For an absorbing report on Kim's mindset at the time by the Soviet Ambassador to Pyongyang, T. Shtykov, sent direct to Stalin on 19 January 1950, see Volkogonov (1999: 154).
30 Lankov (2002: 85) cites the work of Wada Haruki, who has analysed in detail the social and education background of members of the Manchuria guerilla movement to similar effect.
31 The resonances also extend to symbolism and ritual protocol. To witness Kim receive formal adulation from banquet attendees in 1975, who raised both arms high for the shout of 'Mansei!' was to witness an eerily precise reproduction of the Japanese imperial salutation '*Tenno heika banzai!*' One might have thought this would have been as anathematised in Korea after 1945 as the Hitlerite salute in the West has been.
32 See Dae-Sook Suh (1988: 340): 'The huge paintings depicting him as an ever-victorious general, well-equipped with binoculars and pistol and smartly dressed with leather boots and all, hardly match the haggard look in tattered partisan clothes, lugging an old Japanese rifle, in the original photographs.'
33 For some examples, see Scalapino and Lee (1972: 360).
34 This was, of course, true of the post-1945 factions in Pyongyang more generally, held together as they were by intensely personalised loyalties.

References

Armstrong, Charles (2003) *The North Korean Revolution, 1945–1950*. Cornell University Press: Ithaca, NY.
Baik, Bong (1969) *Kim Il Sung: Biography*. 3 volumes. Miraisha: Tokyo.
Brandt, Vincent S.R. (1971) *A Korean Village between Farm and Sea*. Harvard University Press: Cambridge, MA.
Brus, Wlodzimierz (1977) Stalinism and the 'people's democracies', in *Stalinism: Essays in Historical Interpretation*, Robert C. Tucker (ed.). W.W. Norton: New York, pp. 239–258.
Chase, William J. (2001) *Enemies within the Gates?: The Comintern and the Stalinist Repression, 1934–1939*. Yale University Press: New Haven, CT.
Cho, Soon-Sung (1967) *Korea in World Politics 1940–1950: An Evaluation of American Responsibility*. University of California Press: Berkeley, CA.
Chung, Joseph S. (1974) *The North Korean Economy: Structure and Development*. Hoover Institution Press: Stanford, CA.
Conquest, Robert (1973) *The Great Terror*. Collier: New York.

Cumings, Bruce (1981) *The Origins of the Korean War: Liberation and the Emergence of Separate Regimes 1945–1947*. Princeton University Press: Princeton, NJ.

Ginsbergs, George (1975) The citizenship status of Koreans in pre-revolutionary Russia and the early years of the Soviet regime, *Journal of Korean Affairs*, V(2): 1–19.

Ginsbergs, George (1976) The citizenship status of Koreans in the USSR: Post-World War II developments, *Journal of Korean Affairs*, VI(1): 1–18.

Goncharov, Sergei N., Lewis, John W. and Xue, Litai (1993) *Uncertain Partners: Stalin, Mao, and the Korean War*. Stanford University Press: Stanford, CA.

Gragert, Edwin (1994) *Land Ownership under Colonial Rule: Korea's Japanese Experience, 1900–1935*. University of Hawaii Press: Honolulu.

Halberstam, David (2007) *The Coldest Winter: America and the Korean War*. Hyperion: New York.

Hale, Christopher (2002) Multifunctional Juche: A study of the changing dynamic between Juche and the state constitution in North Korea, *Korea Journal*, 42(3): 283–308.

Han, Chungnim C. [1949] (1987) Social organization of Upper Han Hamlet in Korea. Dissertation thesis. University of Michigan, reprinted in *Transactions of the Royal Asiatic Society Korea Branch*, 62: 1–142.

Kim, Il Sung (1994) *Reminiscences with the Century 1*. 8 volumes. The Foreign Languages Publishing House: Pyongyang.

Kim, Richard E. (1970) *Lost Names: Scenes from a Korean Boyhood*. Sisayongo-sa Publishing Co.: Seoul.

Kim, San and Wales, Nym (1941) *Song of Ariran: The Life Story of a Korean Rebel*. The John Day Company: New York.

Ku, Dae-yeol (1995) *Han'guk Kuche kwangyesa yon'gu*. Yoksa pip'yonsa: Seoul.

Lankov, Andrei (2002) *From Stalin to Kim Il Sung: The Formation of North Korea 1945–1960*. Rutgers University Press: New Brunswick, NJ.

Lee, Chong-sik (1965) *The Politics of Korean Nationalism*. University of California Press: Berkeley, CA.

Lee, Chong-sik and Oh, Ki-wan (1968) The Russian faction in North Korea, *Asian Survey*, VIII(4): 270–88.

Mastny, Vojtech (1996) *The Cold War and Soviet Insecurity: The Stalin Years*. Oxford University Press: Oxford.

Mitchell, Clyde (1949) Land reform in South Korea, *Pacific Affairs*, 22(2): 144–54.

Okonogi, Masao (1979) The shifting strategic value of Korea, 1942–1950, *Korean Studies*, 3(1): 49–80.

Osgood, Cornelius (1951) *The Koreans and Their Culture*. The Ronald Press Company: New York.

Paik, Hak-Soon (1993) North Korean state formation 1945–50. Ph.D thesis. University of Pennsylvania, PA.

Paik, Hak-Soon (1995) The Soviet Union's objectives and policies in North Korea, 1945–50, *Korea and World Affairs*, 19(2): 269–93.

Park, Myung-Lim (1995) North Korea's Inner Leadership and the Decision to Launch the Korean War, *Korea and World Affairs*, 19(2): 240–68.

Park, Ki-hyuk and Gamble, Sidney D. (1975) *The Changing Korean Village*. The Royal Asiatic Society Korea Branch: Seoul.

Scalapino, Robert A. and Lee, Chong-sik (1972) *Communism in Korea Part 1: The Movement*. University of California Press: Berkeley, CA.

Schlogel, Karl (2012) *Moscow 1937*. Polity Press: Cambridge.

Seiler, Sydney A. (1994) *Kim Il-song 1941–48: The Creation of a Legend, The Building of a Regime*. University Press of America: Lantham, MD.

Skilling, H. Gordon (1977) Stalinism and Czechoslovak political Culture, in *Stalinism: Essays in Historical Interpretation*, Robert C. Tucker (ed.). W.W. Norton: New York, pp. 257–80.

Starkov, Boris A. (1994) The trial that was not held, *Europe–Asia Studies*, 46(8): 1297–315.

Suh, Dae-Sook (1967) *The Korean Communist Movement 1918–1948*. Princeton University Press: Princeton, NJ.

Suh, Dae-Sook (1970) *Documents of Korean Communism 1918–1948*. Princeton University Press: Princeton, NJ.

Suh, Dae-Sook (1973) The Korean revolutionary movement: A brief evaluation of ideology and leadership, in *Korea Under Japanese Colonial Rule: Studies of the Policy and Techniques of Japanese Colonialism*, Andrew C. Nahm (ed.). The Centre for Korean Studies, Institute of International and Area Studies, Western Michigan University: Michigan, MI, pp. 185–92.

Suh, Dae-Sook (1988) *Kim Il Sung: The North Korean Leader*. New York, Columbia University Press.

Szalontai, Balazs (2005) *Kim Il Sung in the Khrushchev Era: Soviet–Korean Relations and the Roots of North Korean Despotism 1953–1964*. Woodrow Wilson Center Press: Washington, DC.

US Department of State (1961) *North Korea: A Case Study in the Techniques of Takeover*. Department of State Publication 7,118, Far Eastern Series 103, Washington, DC.

van Ree, Erik (1989) *Socialism in One Zone: Stalin's Policy in Korea, 1945–1947*. Berg Publishers: Oxford.

Volkogonov, Dmitri (1991) *Stalin: Triumph and Tragedy*. Weidenfeld & Nicolson, London.

Volkogonov, Dmitri (1999) *The Rise and Fall of the Soviet Empire*. HarperCollins: London.

Weathersby, Kathryn (1990) Soviet policy toward Korea: 1944–46. Ph.D thesis. Indiana University, IN.

Yang, Sung-Chul (1981) *Korea and Two Regimes: Kim Il Sung and Park Chung Hee*. Schenckman Publishing Company: Cambridge, MA.

Yang, Sung-Chul (1990) A leftist antithesis against the rightist thesis on post-liberation Korean politics and a need for its synthesis, *Korea and World Affairs*, 14(2): 371–87.

2 The enemy on all sides: 1950–70

Introduction

Among the more improbable outcomes of the Korean War was that Kim Il Sung emerged from a disaster of his own making with his political position enhanced. Along with Pak Hon-yong, he had been the strongest advocate of the invasion, he had brushed aside the concerns of his more cautious colleagues, and during the war his ability as a military leader had been widely criticised, both within North Korea and among his allies. Nevertheless, defeat made him. In fact, he more than survived: with his talents he thrived, and in a display of relentless energy he revived the shattered ruling Korean Workers' Party (KWP) and instituted the first of a series of attacks against his opponents within the oligarchy, so that by the time the Military Armistice Agreement ended the actual battlefield fighting phase of the war in July 1953, he had laid the essential groundwork for his ultimate supremacy within the Party and for rededication to the conflict. We still know very little about the actual dynamics of power and leadership in this setting of war and survival, but Kim's success suggests the value of being a person of clear determination and vision amid more hesitant co-actors, for this enabled him to exploit opportunities which on first sight might not seem to have existed.

The political landscape in the immediate post-armistice period was challenging. Whereas during 1945–50 Kim had moved within the protective confines of Soviet patronage, and still in fact enjoyed this patronage in the wake of the armistice, he now had to deal with military defeat, huge loss of life, a destroyed army, a demoralised and divided party, a devastated country, a destitute people, and an uncertain diplomatic terrain. The latter especially emerged following the death of the DPRK's avatar, Joseph Stalin, in April 1953, for it initiated a process of ideological thaw in the Soviet Union as Stalin's heirs and successors sought some viable alternative to the personal autocracy and the extreme degree of state violence that his rule had rested upon. This in turn threatened the status of the various leaders in the Soviet orbit who owed their status directly to the Stalinist order and who were wedded to Stalinist ways, and here Kim stood in the forefront.

In this environment the wisdom of state policies pushed by Kim was called into question, especially post-war recovery strategies. Here Kim had pressed for the immediate reconstruction of the pre-war industrial base and the re-creation of the country's war-making potential, much as Stalin had done after the Second World War, whereas other colleagues had advocated less draconian measures, specifically placing a stronger priority on the resurrection of light industry, because common humanity demanded that the North Korean people's fundamental needs for food, clothing and shelter be addressed as a priority. These more moderate policies were also now more in line with post-Stalin Soviet thinking.

Nevertheless, in a situation fraught with uncertainty, Kim faced down his opponents and in the ensuing five years leading up to his final triumph at the First KWP Conference in 1958, he achieved absolute control over the Party. One can detect three stages in the path to his success: first, the achievement of control of the Party power base during 1950–2, then the deployment of this base during 1953–5 in order to destroy the South Korean communist faction and to weaken the rival Yan'an and Soviet–Korean groups, and then finally an end game during 1956–8 which achieved the final purging of these two factions. Throughout this process he displayed tactical acumen and a ruthless, aggressive political style. He also benefited from the continuing support of the Soviet Union for him as the incumbent Party leader, a stance also accepted by the Chinese.

The result was that by 1958 the post-1945 North Korean Communist oligarchy was no more, and Kim had completed his transition from first among equals to dominant leader. The outlines of the extraordinarily durable entity known as the Kimist state now began to emerge as the final remnants of the old domestic Communists, the Soviet–Korean advisers and bureaucrats, and the military cadres of the Yan'an group all left the scene. Accordingly, the story of the years following 1958 relates how Kim used his power to establish an unparalleled degree of personal autocracy and cult of personality, and how his militarist vision came to dominate not just politics, but every facet of life in the DPRK.

For the Kimist ethos went much further than just an expression of Korean nationalism: it was a militarist ethos that echoed Adolf Hitler's 'war is life' dictum, emphasising that violent conflict was the mainspring of history. Kim's world-view was of life as an unremitting struggle in which sheer strength of will assured eventual triumph, while his real-life experience of war was one of near-victory, followed by the bitter humiliation of defeat amid catastrophic material destruction, and in this combination of ideology and direct experience lay the seeds of his rededication to the cause of Korean reunification. Accordingly, in the aftermath of the Korean War the Kimists reconstituted the DPRK as a militarist society whose major objective was to reverse the verdict of the Korean War. The tactics employed to achieve this objective would vary, but the fundamental strategy remained the maximisation of the military potential of the entire country and people, and the resolute prosecution of the reunification cause.

A new Korean Workers' Party

In June 1950 the North's entire battle plan – in actual fact, the Soviet battle plan since it was drawn up by Soviet staff officers (Goncharov *et al.*, 1993: 149) – had consisted of an all-out frontal assault aimed at capturing Seoul in the belief that the Republic of Korea (ROK) government and military would then collapse, leaving Communist-led uprisings to complete the path to victory. Speed was of the essence, for Stalin had approved the enterprise in the belief that the US was sufficiently ambivalent about defending the ROK not to contest a swift DPRK victory. However, within three months of the outbreak of war, events had taken an altogether different turn. Seoul fell, but the ROK did not collapse, its government relocated to Pusan and remained reasonably coherent, the uprisings did not occur, the Korean People's Army could not finish the job, and the 15 September Inch'on landing by United Nations Command (UNC) forces cut the KPA off at the rear, inflicting heavy losses and forcing it into headlong retreat. By October 1950, the US estimated that the DPRK had only 20,000 combat-ready troops left, the remnants of seven pre-war divisions comprising well over 100,000 men, and the DPRK state was faced with oblivion, forcing Chinese forces to enter the conflict in large numbers. As the Chinese People's Volunteers (CPV) began to enter the conflict in early October, the tide again began to turn, and by year's end they had inflicted a major, demoralising defeat on the UNC forces in the far north and pushed them south once more. Eventually, in the first half of 1951 a relatively stable battle line emerged which left the North in control of roughly the same amount of territory as before the war.[1]

As the UNC forces pushed north of the 38th parallel, the Korean Workers' Party had witnessed the fragility of its control of the population, with the widespread collapse of local-level Party structures and organisations and evidence of open collaboration with UNC forces (Scalapino and Lee, 1972a: 411). The Party now faced the need for massive reconstruction, and in a considerable feat of mobilisation, achieved with great energy and resolution amid wartime conditions of widespread destruction, despair and recrimination, Kim Il Sung directed the task of re-establishing the KWP, emerging in the process with close to effective control at the local level. Initially, the Party had reacted to the collapse of its authority by the orthodox move of scapegoating local level cadres, made under the authority with the Soviet–Korean Ho Ka-i, who was the cadre chiefly responsible for Party organisation work, but this was soon countermanded by Kim (Dae-sook Suh, 1988: 124–5). Instead, in late 1951 Kim dismissed Ho, reinstated most of the expelled Party members, thereby gaining the allegiance of many, and during the course of 1952 the Party enrolled a further 450,000 members to bring the total membership to just over one million by December 1952. Radically liberalised criteria for membership resulted in the recruitment of over 600,000 members between 1951 and 1956, by which time it had more than made good its wartime losses, with membership rising from 800,000 in 1949 to 1,164,000 in 1956 (Scalapino and Lee, 1972b: 712).[2]

People of poor peasant and worker background, enrolled for their class background rather than their grasp of ideology, predominated in this new, mass party. Their experience of – even their memory of – the pre-war anti-Japanese Communist struggle was limited, because by 1956 50 per cent of KWP members had joined since 1950, and 90 per cent had had no experience of political participation prior to 1945 (Scalapino and Lee, 1972a: 469ff.). Moreover, they were drawn from a population that had not joined the large-scale exodus south after 1945 and which had remained loyal despite enormous wartime privation and suffering. Like soldiers and civilians in many other wars, the North Korean population had lived through experiences of great intensity and this had bonded them to their leadership in validation of their sacrifice, irrespective of ideological commitment. Such allegiance in turn was reinforced by isolation, and by Kimist ideology with its high level of military-style mobilisation and its constant, dire warnings of external threats, made real, of course, by the intensive bombing campaign to which the North had been subject throughout the war. Almost everyone left in the North was a true believer.

Kim Il Sung consolidates

The terms of the Party reorganisation enhanced Kim's standing, and so we find the first signs of a cult of personality emerging as the Party sought a new focus for loyalty, and as Kim approached his fortieth birthday.[3] Kim's strength was boosted in other, more immediate ways as well, both because most of the reinstated and new Party members owed their status to Kim's work, and because the more intellectually sophisticated, elitist members of the oligarchy had consequently been further distanced from the Party base. Therefore, even with the new Party only in the early stages of reconstitution, Kim seized the moment and made his first serious moves against rival individuals. Ho Ka-i had essentially been the Soviet–Korean faction leader, and after his demotion from high office over the Party membership issue, he began a rapid descent which led to his suicide in July 1953 (Szalontai, 2005: 38). At this stage, however, Kim did not make any moves against the Soviet–Koreans as a group, but nevertheless he achieved a significant tactical victory, for the members of this group who were playing active roles within the Party were weakened and intimidated by Ho's fate, while the Soviets did not intervene in support of their man.[4]

Another early victim of Kim's enhanced authority was Mu Chong, the senior Yan'an group military leader and commander of the KPA Second Corps, who was dismissed from office in December 1950 and died soon afterwards of as yet unrevealed causes. Mu was charged with a series of 'crimes', ranging from failure to defend Pyongyang – a clear military impossibility – to the unlawful execution of subordinates, a duty Kim himself never shrank from. But ostensibly

Mu was called upon to shoulder the chief blame for the reverses suffered after the Inch'on landing, which were the direct consequence of a failed military strategy that Mu himself had not formulated. Kim may also have assessed that Mu's Chinese military connections from the pre-1945 period were a potential threat now that Chinese forces were in Korea in large numbers and doing almost all of the fighting,[5] but again, he chose an issue on which a foreign patron felt that it could not intervene to good purpose. For the Chinese to have done so would have been contrary to Mao Zedong's standing orders not to become embroiled in internal Korean matters,[6] and may have both undermined what was left of the KPA command structure and contributed to uncertainties in their delicate – and at this stage subservient – relationship with the Soviets. Again, Kim had asserted his authority against a leading cadre – *the* leading military cadre in a rival faction – and prevailed.

Demise of the oligarchy

Ho and Mu were purged as prominent individuals, but in December 1952 Kim Il Sung proceeded with his first concerted attack on an entire faction when at the Fifth Plenum of the KWP Central Committee (CC) he targeted the South Korean faction led by Pak Hon-yong. In the months that followed, prominent South Korean faction leaders, including Pak, were dismissed from office and arrested, accompanied by the classic Stalinist purge formula of public denunciation for 'spying' and 'sabotage', then followed by a show trial of twelve selected 'conspirators' in August 1953. This faction was an obvious target, since it had no foreign power backing, its southern operatives had failed to deliver uprisings during the initial invasion, and the present outcome of the war clearly indicated that they had irretrievably lost their southern support base.[7] Moreover, Kim Il Sung had a history of fractious dealings with Pak, for it is hard to think of two more dissimilar types – the 39-year-old ex-guerilla and the 51-year-old urban intellectual. Tactically, the move proved astute, for having an obvious target made it easier for the others to acquiesce in the attack, but in doing so they were also manoeuvred into accepting an outcome that in fact further weakened them by further strengthening Kim's hand: such was the zero-sum game in play.

With a Party power base re-formed largely in his own image, during 1953–5 Kim Il Sung felt secure enough to launch a major struggle within the KWP over the economic direction of the country, which quickly encompassed other major areas of policy. This struggle pitted the extreme mobilisation measures of Kim, who sought immediate and strong levels of investment in heavy industry in a rapid, forced pace of post-war reconstruction, against the more gradualist approach of the Soviet–Korean camp and most of the Yan'an camp, both of whom sought a rehabilitation phase marked by a greater concentration of investment in light industry and agriculture.[8] To put this debate into context, in the war itself the DPRK had experienced human and material losses on a scale hitherto suffered only by the major protagonists of the Second

World War. It had suffered huge military and civilian casualties, while approximately three million of its citizens had fled to the South. Intensive bombing by the UNC forces – i.e. the US Air Force – had severely damaged every major centre of population and production in the North, the basis of agricultural production had been severely degraded, and the threat of widespread famine was averted only by substantial food aid from the Soviet Bloc and China. Recrimination following defeat had exacerbated bitter internal Party fighting, and the Party harboured serious doubts about the loyalty of the remaining population. This was why Kim's economic strategy was widely viewed as inappropriate, but nevertheless, this policy conflict ended in the complete triumph of Kim's option of early and rapid investment in the means of production, and in the entrenchment of a high degree of commandism, autarky and repression within the system.[9]

The collectivisation of agriculture provides a significant illustration of the emerging Kimist economic policy matrix. The DPRK was no different from many other developing economies in seeking to generate capital for industrialisation from the agricultural sector, and Stalinist precedent mandated the strategy of agricultural collectivisation. The point of interest is therefore not so much that Kim also opted for collectivisation but that he carried it out with exceptional speed and intensity, and in close emulation of Soviet policy.[10] In actual fact, he was emulating a policy that had no roots in either Marxist–Leninist ideology or Bolshevik practice, for Lenin had not sought collectivisation, viewing peasants somewhat ambivalently as 'reserve proletarians'. Rather, it was a policy that Stalin had implemented beginning in 1928 primarily as a measure of political control in response to widespread peasant resistance to Leninist party rule. As a political move, Stalin's policy may have been effective, but as an economic policy, it was disastrous and it permanently hobbled Soviet agriculture.

The same policies produced the same outcomes in the DPRK. Twenty-five years after its adoption in the Soviet Union, DPRK cadres and technocrats would have been well aware of the shortcomings of collectivisation, but of course it was not viewed as an economic policy per se. It was in the Stalin canon, and, like Stalin, Kim would have viewed the option of collectivisation as an efficient means of gaining both economic control over the country's food supply and ideological control over the rural population. Thus, agricultural workers were subjected to a ferocious campaign of intimidation led by the zealots of the new Party as the government sought to maintain the level of its compulsory grain levies in the face of poor harvests. By spring 1955, famine conditions prevailed in many areas as a result of these seizures, before Soviet Bloc food aid and a slowdown in the pace of collectivisation prevented outright disaster.[11]

Behind this move lay not just dogmatism but antipathy, for Kim had little reason to feel well disposed towards the peasantry, a rather signal defect in the leader of such a highly ruralised country. In the 1930s he had had an essentially exploitive relationship with farmers, which was typical of the guerilla movement, extracting produce from the farms in his theatre of operations by a variety of means, mostly coercive. Subsequently, after coming to power, he viewed the agricultural sector as a source of manpower and food for the industrial sector, and as the home of ideologically suspect elements.[12] Wherever possible, agricultural workers were to be proletarianised and agriculture itself routinised to the level of factory work. Retreats from this ideal, such as the introduction of the subteam system in the 1960s, were effected grudgingly as a result of production failures and loss of food self-sufficiency,[13] but from the 1960s on, Kim remained resolutely uninterested in anything that smacked of decollectivisation. Therein lay the roots of future tragedy in the 1990s, for to anticipate one strand of our narrative, in an environmentally fragile country which by climate and availability of arable land required especially judicious agricultural inputs, a pattern of neglect, disincentive, lack of investment, technological backwardness and the application of dogmatic ideology delivered an inefficient, impoverished rural sector which was especially vulnerable to abrupt political change as well as to the forces of nature.

Behind these policies lay a drive to secure economic autarky, and in turn behind this drive lay the emerging strategic and ideological divergence of DPRK and Soviet interests, which was to lead to a significant rift in the early 1960s. Strategically, the DPRK had secured Soviet support for the June 1950 invasion because Kim and Pak Hon-yong, backed up by the judgement of Soviet military advisers in Pyongyang, had persuaded Stalin that they could achieve a swift victory (Goncharov et al., 1993: 143). When this did not happen, the Soviets gradually accepted a battlefield stalemate and a negotiated settlement that would still leave them with their desired buffer state against Japan, but which would also leave Korea divided. They were also prepared to use their considerable powers of persuasion to force acceptance of this fundamentally unpalatable outcome on the North. While the DPRK never engaged in open criticism of the Soviet role in the Korean War, Kim Il Sung's drive to control his own destiny intensified as Soviet strategic interests came to override his own interests and to determine the outcome of the Korean War.

Ideologically, the death of Stalin in April 1953 accelerated this divergence. In addition to a mild political and cultural thaw in the wake of Stalin's death, Soviet economic policy veered away from the harsh commandism enforced under Stalin and acquired an emphasis on light industry aimed at raising people's standard of living. This was a new policy framework that was unwelcome, if not threatening, to Kim, for in every conceivable way Kim did not share the Soviet need for a revision of Stalinism. Accordingly, beginning with Party purges, he began a steady process of dissociation from the objectives of the thaw. Thus, when Soviet–Korean advisers and colleagues such as Pak Ch'ang-ok, joined by Yan'an group cadres such as Ch'oe Ch'ang-ik, recommended a more light industry-oriented approach to economic recovery, Kim attacked them as 'dogmatists' and 'formalists' who were uncritically advocating the new Soviet-style policies.[14] Against this, he contrasted his own determination to apply the principles of Marxism–Leninism to his own version of Korean realities and so, in a landmark speech on 28 December 1955, the ideological framework that was gradually to be systematised under the slogan of Juche began to emerge.[15] The emergence of a distinctive Kimist ideology was then accelerated with Khrushchev's denunciation of Stalin at a closed session of the 20th Congress of the Communist Party of the Soviet Union two months later in February 1956.

The result of Kim's on-going attacks on his oligarchy colleagues was that the Korean Workers' Party, which assembled in Pyongyang for the Third KWP Congress during 23–9 April 1956, was very different from the KWP of the Second Congress in 1948. The Third Congress confirmed that Kim had achieved overall control over the Party, but he had not yet achieved total domination. His ex-Manchurian guerilla group provided seven members of the eleven-man Political Committee, or Politburo, elected at the Congress,[16] while many of the key members of the pre-1950 oligarchy, including almost all the Party's intellectual assets had disappeared. The KWP was no longer a self-described vanguard revolutionary party, but was a mass party which had been formed under the influence of Kim's organisational skills, and which increasingly reflected the personality of its chief architect – rural, patchily educated, ideologically unsophisticated, xenophobic, rigidly disciplined and inured to hardship. This achievement was durable, for while the Party was to undergo further upheaval in the late 1960s, it never lost this essential character.

The April 1956 Congress also took place against a background of unrest in the Soviet Bloc, for Khrushchev's moves had forced many Stalinist Eastern European states to adopt liberalised policies, and this had led to major social unrest in Poland in June, and most notably in Hungary in October 1956, where Soviet military intervention was required to restore Party rule. In the DPRK, the effects of Khrushchev's denunciation of Stalin were not evident at the Third KWP Congress, but soon after the Congress concluded, Kim Il Sung's opponents decided to openly challenge Kim's policies and leadership style.[17] The Yan'an group led this move, and as leading cadre after leading cadre briefed rather non-committal Soviet Embassy officials on their intentions during the summer of 1956, we see in their criticisms reflections of the emerging Kimist style. Chief among these criticisms were his promotion of his cult of personality, his 'distortions of socialist legality' – that is, his use of coercion and terror – and his promotion of cadres on the basis of personal loyalty, not ability.[18] Their dominant alternative policy advocacy was the need to moderate the heavy industry drive and to improve people's standard of living.

Kim's critics planned to confront Kim at the forthcoming First Plenum of the new Central Committee in early August. However, Kim was their tactical master, and upon learning of the likelihood of such moves against him, he contrived to delay the Plenum until the end of August, using the intervening time to consolidate his hold on CC members. He was, of course, in a position of strength after the Third Party Congress, and this causes one to wonder at the tactical acumen of Kim's opponents in seeking to attack him in such a forum. In the event, the Plenum proved to be a debacle for Kim's challengers, and their leaders were dismissed from the Party. Joint Soviet and Chinese intervention secured their formal reinstatement in September 1956,[19] but with Kimists in effective command of the Party base, an intra-Party campaign against them began almost immediately, leading to their final ouster at the First KWP Conference in March 1958. In this manner Kim and his followers removed the last obstacles to policies of radical mobilisation and militarisation. Kim Il Sung had not yet established his personal autocracy, nor had his cult of personality achieved its later level of intensity, but during 1956–8 he achieved dominant leadership of the Korean Workers' Party.[20]

Stalinism in the emerging Kimist state

The destruction of the Communist oligarchy was a decisive moment in the history of the DPRK, for by eliminating all leading figures in the Party outside his own group, Kim also radically narrowed the intellectual base of the Party. The many and varied strains of the pre-war Korean Communist tradition, especially its urbanised intelligentsia wing, fell by the wayside as Kim established a leadership group almost totally dominated by former Manchurian guerillas who in turn were under his sway. How, then, would such a group rule? As previous constraints were removed, many ideological tendencies already foreshadowed emerged into the open, and we see two major themes emerging: overwhelming reliance on Stalinist practice for concrete ideological guidance reified in a distinctive set of state institutions, and appeals to the mystical catch-cry of Juche as a slogan – it could not be called an ideology – as a means of deploying the obfuscating, abstract rhetoric of Korean nationalism in almost every sphere of government, politics and society.

The generic influence of Stalinism on the DPRK has been profound, and despite significant modifications to traditional economic policy this influence continues to this day. As memories of Stalin and Stalinism fade, and especially as Soviet scholarship turns to other themes, it becomes harder to fully comprehend his impact, not just on the Soviet Union but on the international Communist movement. Thus, much of what otherwise appears obscure or difficult to comprehend in the DPRK only becomes clearer when we factor in the enormous debt that Kim Il Sung owed to this canonic policy framework. It is also important to reiterate that there were other shaping influences on the DPRK, including the Japanese colonial legacy, the backgrounds of the North Korean Party leaders and the level of their ideological sophistication and managerial ability, the underdeveloped, highly agrarian nature of the North Korean economy in 1945, its cultural heritage, its modes of societal organisation, and the policy priorities of its leadership, beginning with reunification. However, one should not conflate these influences, for while they contributed to the distinctive character of North Korean Stalinism, they did not succeed in modifying the wholesale adopting of Stalinist norms to any significant degree.[21]

Various commentators place different emphases on aspects of Stalinism, but they all agree on the interrelated political phenomena of extreme centralisation, high levels of social mobilisation and personal autocracy reinforced by pervasive state terror and cult of personality. In its mature stage from the mid-1930s on, Stalinism employed these features in order to seek the economic transformation of the Soviet Union by means of rapid, heavy industrialisation, collectivisation of agriculture, the mass mobilisation of labour, high levels of reinvestment and the almost complete suppression of social forces. The result was, in Robert Conquest's words, 'a command economy and a command society' (Conquest, 1973: 180).[22] Directing this process was a genius-leader, employing an engineered charismatic form of political leadership, or cult of personality, as a fundamental organising principle of politics. The genius-leader's authority issued in the first place from his absolute domination of the Party, and in turn of state and social institutions, while the media took as its first order of business the projection of his infallibility and the popular devotion this inspired.

This description, of course, applies equally well to the DPRK, whose Party organisations, ideology, styles of leadership, social organisation, state terror bureaucracies and economic policies mirrored the Soviet Union under mature Stalinism. Politically, both systems featured a mass party headed by a Central Committee and an inner sanctum Politburo. The practice of maintaining a high turnover of Central Committee members between Party Congresses, the holding of Party congresses at irregular intervals, the disregarding of the Party constitution and the general violation of socialist legality were also common to both. In ideology, the DPRK adopted Stalin's view on the need to intensify class struggle as socialist transformation proceeded, and emphasised the remoulding of human nature and the creating of 'a new type of man', with the hallmarks of the 'Juche-type man' in the DPRK virtually indistinguishable from those of the 'New Soviet Man', and both deriving from the strongly voluntaristic 'man is the master' ideological position. In the actual language of politics, we also see resonances in the permeating influence of military imagery – a Trotsky innovation, the wholesale incorporation of grossly abusive language into public political debate, the exaltation of violence and the encouragement of feelings of profound hatred towards designated enemies.[23]

Meanwhile, the demands of the personality cult went further than appeals to the intellect and to the mind, and central to both the Stalin and Kim cults were efforts to eliminate family and kinship loyalties and replace them with transcendent political and state loyalties centred on the person of the leader. Major propaganda themes in support of this focus included stress on the leader's nonpareil genius, his role as the initiator and creator of a new way of life, and indeed the source of life through identification with the sun.[24] Both cults reinforced this concept by the pervasive use of kinship images of Stalin/Kim as the all-wise, benevolent parent caring for the extended family of Russia/Korea.[25] Thematically, the heavy use of kinship metaphors (e.g. 'the Fatherly Leader') to reinforce political hierarchical relationships is a feature that often draws comment as a distinctly North Korean trait derived from

Confucian heritage, whereas in fact it is quite alien to this tradition, but it does rest on strong Stalinist precedent, as is the practice of attributing the basis for all policies and actions of the Party and government to the genius of the Great Leader.[26] We also find the same projection of intense, extrovert feelings of love and loyalty through public events and media reports, where Kim's personal appearances were ritually accompanied by prolonged stormy applause, calls of praise and manufactured manifestations of emotional frenzy. Again, these displays are often assumed to be peculiarly Korean, but in fact they find close parallels in the highly orchestrated public receptions accorded Stalin.

After all this, it is not surprising to see that in protocol and style Kim emulated Stalin in such features as the title of Leader (to which he added 'Great'), and the standard formula 'Under the wise direction of our great genius teacher and leader . . .' which began virtually every significant publication in the Soviet Union from 1929 on; in the expropriating of the revolutionary past to diminish or delete altogether the contribution of people and groups other than the Leader;[27] in the ceremonial bold type-setting of the leader's name in the print media, and its accompaniment with a string of laudatory descriptive phrases (in Kim's case, for example, 'ever-victorious, iron-willed brilliant commander'); in the canonical pronouncements over a broad range of subjects, including economics, history, philosophy, literature, and the social sciences;[28] in the characteristic way of communicating with the outside world through interviews, sometimes in person, but mainly in the form of extended responses to questions ostensibly submitted by the representative of a friendly foreign news agency;[29] in a highly interventionist working style, and even in the construction of a museum of gifts from foreign personages, with Kim Il Sung's Myohyang-san edifices paralleling Stalin's in his birthplace of Gori, Georgia.

Internal security and punishment structures have remained closely modelled on Stalinist practice to this day, reflecting a shared foundation in the prosecution of class warfare. These structures include the operation of multiple, overlapping security bureaucracies, the institution of an extensive network of especially rigorous labour and re-education *gulag* camps, and systematic discrimination against segments of the population on the basis of their 'class' background, including punishment extending beyond the individual to take in the entire family. The North Korean *songbun* system is often assumed to be an example of the North's 'neo-traditionalism' as the Choson dynasty also applied a system of ascriptive status,[30] but again, one does not need to return to the Korean past with all the attendant problems of historical context in order to find the genesis of this system, for it was an integral part of the Soviet system, where after 1917 millions of families, usually called 'disenfranchised', were designated as 'capitalist elements' and were subject to systematic, legal discrimination, including loss of access to state-provided services such as housing, work, education, food rations, pensions and medical care.[31]

In the economic sphere, before the DPRK's economic collapse in the 1990s, Stalin era economic principles and practice constituted the fundamental means by which the DPRK ordered its economy and society. In fact, despite the sustained focus on market activities and putative reform moves afforded by external commentary in recent years, fundamental residues of these principles remain in place, and constitute a major reason why the DPRK has not moved beyond heavily circumscribed tolerance of private market activity. The principles began with a growth strategy aimed at achieving rapid economic and social transformation and the establishment of a heavy military–industrial base, with little priority accorded to light industry, consumer goods production and the service sector. This in turn mandated a highly centralised, planned economy, featuring state ownership of industrial enterprises, collectivised agriculture,[32] close Party and bureaucratic involvement in all aspects of economic planning, including the setting of national and sectoral economic targets, output and supply quotas, and prices and wages.[33] In the planning process, both systems shared overt suspicion and outright rejection of mathematical, scientific and technical planning aids,[34] for which they substituted heavy, sustained reliance on ideological motivation and 'speed' campaigns. In the external sphere, both of them constructed autarchic economies closed off as far as possible from the international capitalist economy, featuring government foreign trade monopolies, the widespread practice of barter trade and little or no foreign investment. Finally, both indulged in grandiose projects of transformation – canals, dams, remaking nature in general and 'transforming the face of the capital' via skyscrapers and monuments.[35]

However, we still need to go beyond what was borrowed to consider how and why these practices were borrowed, and this raises considerations of time and place. Of course, to be a good communist in the 1940s *was* to be a Stalinist and one did not get to pick or choose which aspects of the Stalin system one might adopt. Cadres had to accept it whole, as it was an ideology that demanded total and unconditional obedience, not debate, and the scale of the Great Terror liquidations during the 1930s had driven that point home forcefully. Moreover, when it came to actual practice, for at least a decade after 1945 the entire senior bureaucracy in the North was directed by CPSU members who were products of this system, further narrowing options. Meanwhile in Kim Il Sung's specific case, there were further factors in his life experience that led to a more intense embrace of Stalinism than his colleagues, including his pronounced alienation from established Korean cultural and social norms, his overriding commitment to reunification by military means under his leadership, his direct observation of Soviet wartime mobilisation during 1941–5, and the lack of exposure to, let alone reflection on, alternative models, including alternative Marxist models.[36]

We are therefore left with a list of borrowings that were both systematic and systemic. They range over virtually every significant area of state activity – politics, leadership, ideology, economics and social mobilisation, such that one cannot imagine the DPRK as we know it without a Stalinist blueprint. In a state that underwent such extensive tutelage that basic documents such as Kim's initial public speeches, the 1948 DPRK constitution and the order of battle for the 1950 invasion of the South were written in Russian by Soviet personnel, the chief impression is that for Kim the Stalinist model was canonic: he did not want to leave anything out, he did not know what to leave out, nor did he know how to leave it out.[37]

Finally, it remains for us to stress that this ingestion of Stalinist institutional practice was highly influential then and is still highly influential now. Institutions are not extrinsic to the core ideology of the state. On the contrary, they are important, for not only are they expressions of regime ideology, but in their total effect they constitute powerful levers of control over the population. Thus, at every stage of life and in every walk of life in the North, social institutions exist to channel people into constant ideological training environments within all facets of education, working and social life, where in many fundamental ways the ideology reflects Stalinist values. It is therefore an exaggeration to proclaim the death of Stalinism in the DPRK since the 1990s famine on the grounds that the country now has a market economy sector or because many people no longer believe government propaganda, for that matters less than one might imagine. From Party elite to junior cadre to average citizen to school students of all ages to soldiers engaged in extended military service, powerful drive reins continue to exist, and with them policy guidelines and habits of mind continue to be given daily reinforcement. In no small measure the intense socialisation that these practices impart is a major factor in reinforcing the allegiance of DPRK citizens to the DPRK state.

The origins and development of Juche

Stalinism had been embedded in the DPRK system for more than a decade before the post-Korean War ideological and policy framework and the onset of de-Stalinisation induced the emergence of the ultra-nationalist catchcry of Juche, which is at once both fundamental to the DPRK's ideological self-definition and highly derived from Soviet ideology.[38] For the better part of sixty years, scholars and observers have examined Juche and found themselves unable to detect, much less grasp, any explanatory power,[39] with Cumings probably coming closest when he states that 'The closer one gets to its meaning the more its meaning recedes. It is the opaque core of Korean national solipsism . . . a term defining an emotion that puts the nation first, or the Leader's wishes first, in everything' (Cumings, 1982–83: 289). Scalapino and Lee put a finer point on it in commenting that

> Juche as preached and practised in North Korea could easily be regarded as the antithesis of Marxism; and in any case, it is scarcely a theoretical innovation. Rather, it is a straightforward, orthodox form of nationalism, wholly unoriginal, albeit very powerful.
>
> (Scalapino and Lee, 1972b: 868)

It is therefore significant chiefly in a specific historical and political context, rather than an ideological context.

After first emerging as a term used in public ideological discourse in December 1955, the phasing out of fulsome praise for Stalin and the Soviet Union as major propaganda themes as the 1950s wore on brought Juche more and more to the fore.[40] It was given strong emphasis from the early 1960s on, and formal status as the guiding ideology of the state in the 1972 DPRK Constitution. Thus, Juche initially began to take shape during the final period of struggle against the remnants of Kim's oligarchy colleagues as little more than a nationalist catch-phrase based on an obscure philosophical term of Japanese derivation (Myers, 2015: 11), to be deployed against Kim's factional rivals who, of course, had important Chinese and Soviet linkages – especially the Soviet-Korean technocrats who were, of course, still Soviet citizens and mostly members of the CPSU. It enabled Kim to accuse such colleagues in clear, simple terms of ignorance and neglect of Korean history and traditions and of mechanical borrowing from other socialist countries' experiences. The somewhat less than sublime irony here was that from his twenty-year sojourn in Manchuria and the Soviet Union to his ten years in the Chinese Communist Party to his leading role in domesticating Soviet norms post- 1945, Kim's claims to be able to formulate and practise an authentic Korean nationalism were ambiguous at best.

As a means of understanding DPRK state policy and political behaviour, then, the explanatory power of Juche is weak. Its only sanctioned ideologues so far have been Kim Il Sung and Kim Jong Il, and as a substitute for thought North Koreans are required to repeat their formulations word for word, and are specifically ordered to display enthusiasm for them when in company, and especially when in the company of foreigners. Juche does not intersect with other major thought systems, nor does it take the expression of a distinctively DPRK world view past the level of a few simplistic nationalist maxims. The main point to make about Juche is that it did not in any way supersede Stalinism because it was not competing in the same space, simply because it is a slogan, not a blueprint.

Kim triumphant

The March 1958 Party Conference set the seal on Kim Il Sung's domination of the KWP, and the last vestiges of open public ideological debate ceased. The prime functions of the Party now became increasingly organisational and devotional – to organise the people in pursuit of policies of industrialisation, modernisation and reunification, and to reinforce Kim Il Sung's growing personal dictatorship and cult of personality.[41] In the first few years after 1958, the pursuit of these two tasks involved little contradiction, since there was now little, if any, disagreement on the wholesale adoption of political and economic development strategies modelled closely on Soviet practices of the 1930s, and since the expulsion of gradualists, doubters, and other independently minded cadres had gradually left a Party elite bound by long-standing personal ties with Kim, long accustomed to living with and responding to his requirements, and accepting of the firm Stalinist precedent for cult of personality leadership. In the years immediately after 1958, the country mobilised on this basis.

At the top, the DPRK state was now directed by a new elite that was effecting a profound material and ideological transformation of the country. Economically, completing the extension of state ownership had presented little challenge in the DPRK after 1953, for this was a process that began with the propagation of class warfare in the North during 1945–50, and which was consolidated by the flight southward of business owners, the destruction wrought by the Korean War and Kim's radical post-war policies, all of which had effectively destroyed the basis for private ownership. By 1959 the government was able to claim that the industrial sector had been fully socialised.

The effects of intense economic and social mobilisation were felt throughout the country. Rapid urbanisation, mainly in the industrial north-east and around Pyongyang, had brought many rural dwellers into contact with broader horizons. The creation of a large standing army had introduced numerous young men to new technologies, methods of organisation and work, while marked progress in public health, literacy and, at least initially, the diffusion of technology likewise contributed to a pattern of growing urbanisation, industrialisation and unprecedented social mobility. While individual movement and communication were restricted, the country was tightly linked as never before by new networks, by a pervasive print and electronic media, by a universal education system and by a web of Party-controlled mass organisations that drew agricultural and industrial workers, women, youth, professionals, the military, artists, writers and intellectuals into the direct orbit of the political centre.

However, this on-going process of transformation differed from similar processes in other developing countries during the course of the twentieth century. In short, it was form without substance, for it assigned no role to the development of an autonomous civil society, and it remained rigorously and coercively controlled from the top through Party and government institutions. It also took place in enforced isolation from international contact beyond the Soviet Bloc, and its essence, first and last, was primarily military and only secondarily developmental. As a result, the commitment to modernisation was not open-ended, but was firmly circumscribed by the aims and objectives of a leader whose rhetoric looked to the future but whose vision of the ultimate purpose of life for his countrymen lay in the ever-receding past of his guerilla days. It was therefore rife with contradictions and anti-modern features, including rigorous denial of freedom of information, education indistinguishable from indoctrination, pervasive militarism, the application of the Soviet-derived *songbun* regime loyalty classification system, and of a *gulag* system of extra-judicial seizure, torture, imprisonment and execution as punishment for infractions of 'socialist discipline'.

Many of these anti-modern features were summed up in the first of Kim's major mobilisation campaigns, the Chollima Movement,[42] an ideological mobilisation campaign designed to increase production across all major sectors of the economy launched in August 1958. The major organisational feature of Chollima was the formation of work teams, which in their ideological fervour were to perform Stakhanovite feats in prodigiously increasing production without increased inputs. Sharing generic features with China's Great Leap Forward,[43] which had just been launched the previous May, and with Soviet campaigns in the 1930s, Chollima-style campaigns aimed at achieving quantitative increases in production – 'dramatic upsurges' in agitprop parlance – but they also had a number of drawbacks. Saddled with unreasonable quotas and facing punishment for non-performance, managers and workers resorted to various strategems, such as boosting grain production figures by adulterating grain with chaff, mining more plentiful and accessible but inferior grades of ore, meeting quotas for products, components and services with no recourse to time-consuming quality-control procedures, and generally cutting corners, but these had a significant knock-on effect in the form of uneven supply patterns, shoddy product quality, sectoral imbalances and a general loss of production discipline. Thus, over the ensuing five years or so the Chollima-speed production periodically required 'adjustment periods', which of course gave back a good deal of the quantitative upsurge in production initially achieved.[44] Despite such drawbacks, however, it was noteworthy that unlike the Great Leap Forward, the Chollima Movement has never been abandoned by the leadership, and today the regime continues to cite the 'spirit of Chollima' in major speeches and slogans, and to apply its central technique of intense, mass ideological mobilisation on a regular basis. The continuation of this quantitative approach was still in evidence in February 2016 with the KWP Politburo declaring a 'seventy-day speed battle' in the lead-up to the Seventh KWP Party Congress in May.[45]

The Chollima Movement expressed the very essence of Kim Il Sung's fundamental 'politics-first' line – that increased production was foremost a function of ideological, not material incentive. He then intensified this line through two further ideological campaigns, the Chongsanri Method in February 1960 and the Taean Work System the following December. The Chongsanri Method was an approach to fulfilling assigned production tasks, especially in the agriculture sector, which mandated close ideological supervision of production practices by the Party.[46] What began as an agricultural guidance technique spread to other sectors, including the Party and the bureaucracy, and, like Juche, achieved canonic status in the revised DPRK Constitution of 1972.[47] Similarly, the Taean Work System took management of factories and other industrial economic units away from a single technician-manager and vested it in the unit's Party political committee, and again this rapidly became the norm for the operation of all industrial enterprises.[48] Such hallmarks of a politics-first economic mobilisation system were given the stamp of Kim Il Sung's personal approval, and as such have remained in place as integral features of the Kimist system under his successors.

However, although these methods were central to Kim's vision, their cumulative effect was counterproductive. Post-war recovery required planning, skilled human resources, and above all the steady disciplines and routines of production. Instead, Kim unleashed and sustained ideological attacks in which established socialist managerial structures were uprooted and replaced by committees whose members owed their position not to their workplace skills but first and foremost to the ardour with which they expressed their political loyalty, and who were furthermore backed by the full coercive powers of the state. Far from being cooperative, workplace relationships were now adversarial, split between 'red' and 'expert' perspectives, garnished with the fear of further arbitrary Party interventions, and with safety lying as intended in the outward appearance of unquestioning acceptance of the Great Leader's eccentric vision of the industrial process as foremost the pursuit of quantitative output as an end in itself. These years are often referred to as golden years, in which the DPRK was building a 'solid foundation' for modernisation (Joseph Chung, 1974: 98), but the worm was already in the apple. It is little wonder that the characteristic North Korean management and workforce that emerged from these depredations were neither skilled enough, organised enough, nor even disciplined enough within the industrial process to graduate to more advanced levels of industrialisation.

The Fourth KWP Congress

The Fourth KWP Congress convened in Pyongyang during 11–18 September 1961 and strongly reflected the trends noted above. It also served as a suitable occasion for Kim to give an authoritative version of the Party's ideology, to rally the country to achieve the goals of the 1961–67 Seven-Year Plan, and to fill the many Central Committee places left vacant by the post-April 1956 purges. The reports and speeches at this 'Congress of Victors'[49] affirmed key Kimist beliefs concerning the efficacy of mass campaigns and the necessity for close, direct Party guidance in the economic development process. They therefore endorsed the politics-first line embodied in the Chollima, Chongsanri and Taean campaigns, pronounced them successful and presaged more of the same in the years ahead.

In particular, the effects of the political battles of the previous five years became clear when the Congress elected the new 135-member Central Committee (85 full and 50 alternate). Of the 85 full members, only 28 had survived from the 1956 Third Party Congress, while a further 12 were promoted from alternate membership. Over half of the 1956 Party elite had vanished, and similarly, 32 of the 50 alternate members were also new. This meant that of the 116 (71 full and 45 alternate) elected at the Third Congress in 1956, 75 (64.6 per cent) had disappeared, to be replaced by cadres with strong links to the pre-war Manchurian guerilla movement, or else those from other backgrounds who had become long-time Kim loyalists, such as Ch'oe Yong-gon.[50] The outlook of the small number who had reached the pinnacle after post-1945 careers in the Party apparatus had obviously been shaped by the profound experience of the Korean War and the intense ideological struggles and mobilisation campaigns of the 1950s, while cadres with a technical or managerial background – indeed, 'specialists' or 'experts' of any description – were conspicuous by their absence. Not only had all groups of the former Communist oligarchy other than the Manchurian guerillas and their allies effectively disappeared, but Kim, now 49 years old, was already beginning to show signs of an inability to appoint men from the post-guerilla period to senior positions. Few post-1945 recruits achieved Central Committee status, and during the 1960s the average age of Politburo members increased substantially, from 51.7 to 58.2 by the end of the decade.

Equal Emphasis and DPRK militarism

The securing of domination over the KWP in 1958 had left Kim free to adopt military norms in economic and social development, and as the state began to acquire some of the basic means of production, the direction of a substantial proportion of these means to military production was, from Kim's perspective, a logical next step. Accordingly, in December 1962 Pyongyang initiated a military build-up which, in relation to the scale of the human and material resources of the country, can only be described as staggering. Under the slogan 'Arms in the one hand and a hammer and sickle in the other!' the Fifth Plenum of the Fourth KWP Central Committee adopted the policy of Equal Emphasis, signifying that the country would place equal emphasis on military preparedness and economic development, but of course privilege the former. In doing so, Kim countermanded the original basic economic strategy set forth under the First Seven-Year Plan (1961–7) – namely, recovery from the excesses of the Chollima Movement and moderation of the on-going drive for rapid, heavy industrialisation – and re-emphasised the Chollima policies of far-reaching economic and political mobilisation.[51]

Equal Emphasis emerged two months after the resolution of the October 1962 Cuban missile crisis, in which the Soviet Union had retreated from outright confrontation with the United States and removed its missiles from the island. This appears to have been alarming to Kim, because as a small, weak state, the DPRK's underlying reunification strategy had been to rely on the Socialist Bloc for security, and to anticipate that global Soviet pressure on the US might one day secure a US retreat from Northeast Asia. However, the Cuban outcome clarified that the Soviet commitment to peaceful coexistence with the US was core policy and that the Soviet interest would support the continuing division of Korea. This was hardly news to Kim, but judging from his response, he now appeared to take this revelation to heart, and with the increasing means of military production and organisation becoming available to him, he determined to press ahead to achieve reunification relying on his own resources.

The December 1962 Plenum shaped Equal Emphasis by establishing four basic military policies: arming the entire population, providing extensive additional training for existing soldiers, converting the entire country into a fortress and modernising the armed forces.[52] Arming the entire population went further than the norms of universal conscription by establishing a military basis for the daily life of the entire population with weapons training, military drill and instruction. Maximum use was also made of existing regular soldiers by training them to perform the duties of their immediate superior in the chain of command, thus enabling both rapid expansion of the armed forces in times of emergency and speedy replacement of command losses in battle. Fortification of the entire country meant the establishment of substantial strategic stockpiles and the construction of vast complexes of shelters, bunkers and underground facilities, including whole armament factories. The modernisation process meant that the proportion of total state investment devoted to military production rose from about 6 per cent to 30 per cent during the period 1964 to 1967 as the military-industrial sector expanded to roughly four times the size of its Soviet model in proportional terms.[53]

Why did the DPRK adopt and then sustain measures equivalent to wartime mobilisation at this time? The question is a crucial one for our understanding of subsequent DPRK state policies, for it set in place a strategic and policy framework that Kim pursued for the rest of his life and one that his successors have pursued to this day.[54] When Kim explained the rationale for these measures, he characteristically painted a picture of extreme threat to the DPRK, but this does not reflect the objective situation facing the DPRK in 1962, for no recent new sources of threat had entered the security equation.[55] Rather, efforts to understand the logic behind a policy that had such devastating consequences for the country and its people again draw us into the Kimist mind-set and in particular to its pervasive militarist perspective.

DPRK militarism was a broad confluence with many tributaries – historical, situational, ideological and psychological. To begin with, it was historical, since militarism was deeply embedded in the state ideologies of all major powers in the first half of the twentieth century, and the North Koreans had been exposed to both Japanese militarism during the 1920s and 1930s, and Stalinism in the 1940s and 1950s. It was also situational, arising from geopolitical factors, including the size and nature of the country's human and natural resources, fears of encirclement, uncertain alliances, the experience of the Korean War, and the post-1945 regional military hegemony of the United States – though, of course, as the very different reaction of the ROK to this same set of circumstances shows, choices, not imperatives, were at work. It was also ideological, for while Kim did not need to look further than the recent history of Korea and the experience of armed resistance to Japanese imperialism to validate his cause, he also habitually conflated it by identifying his struggle with the global anti-imperialist struggle. And, of course, the Leninist–Stalinist world-view, with its ethos of struggle and its fundamental scepticism regarding the outcome of continuing peaceful coexistence with capitalism, further buttressed this view. Finally, it was pathological, deriving from Kim's life-long unwavering commitment to war making. All these layers of perception and experience refracted through his mind, where they approached the level of obsession, and their net effect was that by 1962 militarism exercised a dominant influence on DPRK state policy.[56]

Kim's personal experience of armed conflict had been profound and seemed to grow even more profound as the years passed, but in this he was not eccentric. Rather, his reaction to combat accorded with a common enough tendency of men under arms to see the experience of regimentation, fear, bravery, sacrifice, bloodshed and bloodlust as among the most profound of their lives. The DPRK leadership now consisted almost entirely of men who in their youth had been socialised primarily within the military brotherhood of the anti-Japanese guerilla movement and who had followed no other calling in their lives other than preparation for war and engagement in war. Since Marxist–Leninist ideology had played a weak role in the intellectual development of the Korean Communist movement as a whole, and especially the Manchurian guerilla movement, the instinctive ethos of the military brotherhood provided a compensating framework which possessed many points of affinity with Marxism–Leninism theory and Stalinist practice, but which drew decisively upon the defining life-experiences of the DPRK leader and his men for its innermost guiding principles. The characteristics of such brotherhoods have been described by various social anthropologists,[57] and they revolve around the inculcation of discipline based upon the exact, unconditional and immediate execution of orders from superiors; the consecration to violence, acceptance of the legitimacy of violence in pursuit of given ends, and willingness to engage in violence; emphasis on qualities necessary for effective aggression, such as physical strength, endurance and adaptability; release from accountability to the authority of the broader community, and especially from the ethical, religious and moral norms of that community; and the acceptance of centralised authority.[58]

The country felt the consequences of the December 1962 Plenum decisions with its massive diversion of resources away from a still-fragile economy into military production almost immediately. Agriculture and light industry had enjoyed a brief respite in the period 1960–2 as some of the imbalances of the Chollima campaigns were ironed out, but now rates of investment in the non-military economy again fell sharply since the cutting edge for achieving independence in military production was the heavy industry sector, where rates of investment now soared past the already-high allocations made during the 1950s.[59] The economy as a whole proved unable to bear the weight of imbalanced, preponderant heavy industry investment, which starved practically all other sectors of investment input. Nor could it meet the associated demands for sophisticated logistics, manpower, technical training, transport and power infrastructure demands, and so severe bottlenecks and shortages began to appear. In 1963, all major sectors fell below Plan targets, steel and textiles production dropped below 1962 levels, and figures for agricultural production were too discouraging to be released. The statistical blackout then spread to the entire economy in 1964, and at the beginning of 1965 Kim Il Sung acknowledged that the country would be unable to meet the targets of the Seven-Year Plan.[60] As defence-related expenditure continued to rise in proportional terms, the economic situation steadily worsened to crisis point. Total industrial production, which rose by an estimated 17 per cent in 1964 and by 14 per cent in 1965, actually contracted by an estimated 3 per cent in 1966,[61] and the 1961–67 Seven Year Plan eventually became a Ten Year Plan, announced as completed in 1970.

Militancy toward the South

The objective of Equal Emphasis was to maximise the chances of a successful push for reunification, and accordingly, a revised economic plan meant a reformulated reunification plan. Whereas in 1950 Kim Il Sung and his colleagues had overwhelmingly seen the situation in terms of military action with the Soviets holding a veto over such action, in the early 1960s Kim began to talk more in terms of the need to combine an independent military struggle with political and diplomatic campaigns. In 1964 he articulated this strategy of combined struggle in his Three Fronts strategy, a strategy which defined the Korean reunification as a task requiring revolutions within the DPRK, within the ROK, and internationally. Within the DPRK, the task of the KWP was to bring about a far-ranging political, military and economic transformation that would provide a strong material base for future reunification. Within the ROK the task was to establish a Marxist–Leninist party to support anti-government forces, and to instil in them Kimist-style revolutionary consciousness. Internationally, the major task was to encourage revolutionary forces with the object of bringing maximum pressure to bear on the United States to withdraw its armed forces from ROK territory.[62] At different times Pyongyang emphasised one aspect over another, depending on Kim's assessment of the situation, but the overall framework of the Three Fronts remained consistent until aggressive pursuit of reunification gradually gave way to survivalism during the 1980s.

During the early 1960s, the South Korean front had remained especially problematic, for the ROK refused to conform to Kim's analysis of a society which, under 'correct' leadership, would manifest its full revolutionary potential. Kim would have taken heart from the overthrow of Syngman Rhee in April 1960, for it replaced a virulently anti-communist strongman with the weak, civilian government of the Second Republic (1960–61), in which leftist, pro-reunification activities were given freer rein. However, the seizure and consolidation of power by Park Chung-hee beginning in May 1961 was a decided negative. More competent and pragmatic than Rhee, Park also quickly placed strong restraints on domestic political debate relating to reunification, and as he began to exercise effective leadership in the economic sphere, he induced increasing levels of economic and diplomatic support from major allies. Park effected the normalisation of relations with Tokyo via a Treaty on Basic Relations in June 1965, and concluded a comprehensive Status of Forces Agreement with the US in July 1966, while the ROK also became increasingly active in regional anti-communist diplomacy, most notably in its dispatch of troops to fight in the Vietnam War during 1964–73, where a total of 300,000 ROK army troops ultimately fought.

Kim's response to these developments was to raise the level of confrontation along the DMZ in December 1962, and as the Vietnam conflict developed he applied further pressure beginning in late 1966, which led to an elevenfold increase in significant DMZ incidents in 1967,[63] especially in the run-up to the June 1967 ROK presidential election. When Park was elected for a further four-year term, plans began immediately for an assassination mission, which culminated in the abortive Blue House raid by a commando team on 21 January 1968.[64] Two days later, the DPRK navy seized the US surveillance vessel *Pueblo* in international waters off its east coast, and in October 1968 teams of guerillas landed on a sparsely populated section of the east coast of the ROK near Samch'ok, apparently in an unsuccessful effort to establish a base for guerilla warfare in the mountainous hinterland.[65]

It is always difficult to account fully for the actions of leaders who are driven by dogmatic convictions and who often pursue high-risk scenarios involving violence. In accounting for Kim's willingness to confront the ROK and the US and to invite retaliation, we should note first of all that military confrontation was consistent with the DPRK's broader strategies and past behaviour. We should also factor in Kim's dogmatic conviction that under the right circumstances the populace of the South would rise up against the ROK government. Shows of strength and various forms of intimidation constituted the basic DPRK approach to dealing with its own people, and Kim appears to have projected this mind-set on to the South, concluding that such pressure would demoralise the ROK government and embolden groups sympathetic to the DPRK. This in turn might open up new possibilities in the inter-Korean conflict, for which the DPRK was well prepared militarily. Kim may also have assessed that with the war in Vietnam not going well for the US by 1967, creating a diversion might increase the possibility of defeat in Vietnam, which would undermine the US position in the entire region. Whatever his calculations, though, these operations achieved little. The *Pueblo* incident delivered a substantial propaganda victory to Pyongyang, but the Soviets disapproved of such adventurism, causing new strains to appear in the DPRK–Soviet relationship, and if anything, the affair strengthened the resolve of the US to remain in Korea. The DMZ incidents did not have any noticeable effect on morale in the South, and the east coast landings failed, and so by 1969 the DPRK had reassessed strategy and the number and scale of DMZ incidents began to fall as this phase of direct military pressure was abandoned.[66]

The Party in crisis

Meanwhile, by 1966 the practical effects of Kim's Equal Emphasis policy had gone past economic debilitation and had reached political crisis point. Within the Party the genesis of this crisis was the on-going debate on economic priorities, and it pitted Kim and supporters of Equal Emphasis against less militant, more technocratically minded cadres who sought to modify the commitment to military production and pursue lower but more sustainable rates of growth (Scalapino and Lee, 1972b: 611). Many of the details of this dispute are still unknown, but the outcome is clear: on-going tension triggered a Second Party Conference in October 1966 to debate and resolve these issues, and when a revised leadership line-up was announced at the conclusion of the Conference, it was clear that Kim had prevailed.[67] Within six months, nine of the sixteen full and alternate members of the Politburo elected as Kim loyalists at the Congress of Victors in 1961 had been replaced, and the Conference had resolved the economic debate by reaffirming Equal Emphasis.[68] The ructions were not confined to the Politburo level, for an estimated one-fifth of Central Committee members were also replaced at the Conference (Dae-sook Suh, 1988: 220).[69]

The issue of actual policy differences remains murky, for this was a time of turbulence on multiple fronts – unprecedented military pressure directed against the South, serious economic setbacks, and the promotion of Kim Jong Il and the hereditary succession. It was clear, however, that the victims were not from different streams of the Korean Communist movement with different policy perspectives, for these no longer existed. Rather, they were Kim loyalists with records of association and support dating back to pre-1945 days, and they included economic managers, military leaders, Party functionaries, and the President of Kimilsung University.[70] This wholesale purging of loyalists across a range of portfolios and areas of expertise, coupled with a new campaign glorifying Kim's family as a model revolutionary family and later revelations that Kim Il Sung's son Kim Jong Il began to play an active behind-the-scenes role in the Party Secretariat beginning about 1965, indicated that the Party itself was undergoing a further major transformation.[71] It was now unimpeachably an instrument of Kimist rule, peopled at the senior level exclusively by cadres who were willing to give Kim the degree of unquestioning personal loyalty that he demanded, above and beyond what might be sanctioned by Party rules, procedures and practices. The final transition to personal autocracy was relatively swift, and by 1970 those who remained as members of the Party elite were those who had accepted a system in which policy decisions no longer issued from Party deliberations but from Kim's personal conviction.

Kim's victory was therefore more than just a victory in an economic policy debate. This was in essence the final act in the struggle for the soul of the

KWP, and hence for the DPRK state, for the Conference outcome marked the culmination of a long struggle to establish his personal autocracy, and with it the Party now completed its final major reconstitution. The remaining scope for meaningful ideological and policy debate, already confined to the margins and conducted solely within the Kimist ranks, effectively disappeared under the influence of Kim's self-proclaimed 'monolithic ideology' and personality cult with its associated claims of infallibility. The Politburo purges during 1966–9 were the last of their kind and with practically only ex-guerillas now remaining, a notable stability in Politburo membership ensued.[72]

Foreign relations

The broader international background to Kim's policies during the 1960s contained a number of elements, and alongside the Vietnam War, the most salient of these was the Sino–Soviet split. The split began in earnest in 1959 with a series of disputes over the terms and conditions of Soviet aid to China, but was essentially the product of broader disagreements involving national interests, competing security concepts, ideological positions and personality clashes. During 1959–61, the Chinese steadily ceased to recognise the Soviet Union's traditional position of leadership of the international Communist movement, also rejecting the Soviet doctrine of peaceful coexistence. Instead, it insisted on its right to maintain a strong commitment to the anti-imperialist, anti-US struggle, and insisted on the right of each fraternal party to pursue its own path to socialist economic construction.

The historical experience and hence the ideology of the DPRK, China, Vietnam, Indonesia and other major Asian communist parties was based foremost on anti-colonialist, anti-imperialist struggle, and this was now a far cry from the Soviet Union's own eurocentric historical experience. The DPRK therefore found much to agree with in the Chinese position, because maintenance of a strong anti-US stance was the very essence of Kim Il Sung's ideological stance and because independence meant independence to pursue its armed struggle against the South in ways other than those compatible with Soviet interests. Accordingly, as Beijing drifted more and more towards open hostility with Moscow in the early 1960s, Pyongyang drifted with it. As late as September 1961, a semblance of even-handedness was maintained when the DPRK signed matching defence treaties in quick succession with the Soviet Union and China, but the deeply disappointing outcome of the Cuban missile crisis then spilled over into DPRK foreign policy, and attacks on Soviet revisionism became more and more overt during 1963 (Scalapino and Lee, 1972b: 624–37).

DPRK-Soviet relations then reached their nadir during 1963–4, before Khrushchev's ouster in October 1964 and the advent of a new, cautious and conservative leadership in Moscow led to a significant improvement in bilateral relations. Soviet Premier Alexei Kosygin visited Pyongyang in 1965, and the Soviet Union resumed substantial economic and military relations. However, although the Kosygin visit did much to remove immediate sources of irritation, the steady divergence of national interests meant that relations never returned to their former closeness. The Soviet Union's interests lay in institutionalising its political system at home and consolidating its international position as a super-power. It had publicly denounced what it termed the 'excesses' of the Stalin era and had substantially modified many hallmark Stalinist policies. It had accepted coexistence and business-like relations with the capitalist world, and its economic plans focused increasingly on the need to raise the average citizen's standard of living. The DPRK, on the other hand, reflected the Soviet Union's past. It preserved the personality cult leadership, mass mobilisation techniques and militant political rhetoric of the Stalin era, and it actively promoted confrontation with the capitalist world. Under these circumstances only limited rapprochement was possible.[73]

Improvement in DPRK–Soviet relations occurred just as DPRK–China relations underwent a marked deterioration with the outbreak of the Great Proletarian Cultural Revolution in China in late 1965. Although the respective interests of Pyongyang and Beijing had earlier coincided, within a year of the launching of the first attacks of the Cultural Revolution the Chinese began to pressure Pyongyang to match Beijing's criticism of Moscow. The DPRK resisted these calls, and although it continued to criticise the Soviets periodically during this period, most notably for pursuing an 'exploitative' foreign trade policy (Joseph Chung, 1974: 117), the major development in DPRK foreign policy at this time was the clear articulation of DPRK claims for complete independence within the international Communist movement (Paige, 1967: 28; Dae-Sook Suh, 1988: 205–6). This development did not please Beijing, and in January 1967 Red Guard wall posters criticising the DPRK, as well as Kim Il Sung personally, began to appear.

These attacks continued throughout 1967–8, reaching a crescendo in February 1968 (Ho-Min Yang, 1988: 60; Dae-Sook Suh, 1988: 191–2). The posters reflected official Chinese criticism at the time that the DPRK had been 'sitting on the fence' in the Sino-Soviet dispute (Scalapino and Lee, 1972a: 641). On a more serious note, unofficial reports of military clashes between Chinese and DPRK troops along their common border in the vicinity of Paektu-san began to circulate.[74] However, as government in China began to regain coherency after the Cultural Revolution, tension with the DPRK abated. In October 1969 China and the DPRK resumed the exchange of delegations, broken off in 1965, and the rapprochement process was consolidated with a visit to Pyongyang by Zhou Enlai in April 1970, the first leadership visit between the two countries in six years (Simmons, 1971: 105).

In summing up the DPRK's relations with the Soviet Union and China, we may begin by noting that while relations between fraternal parties were conducted with all the murky passion one would expect of people holding a fundamentally ideological view of the world, this should not be confused with stronger, abiding geopolitical interests. In this category we find that the centuries-old 'guardian state of our eastern border' Chinese formula for ordering its relations with Korea has been remarkably resilient in its modern 'lips-and-teeth' guise, while for forty years until the Gorbachev accession the Soviets clung tenaciously to a contain-Japan strategy. In a nutshell, then, both China and the Soviet Union had non-competing reasons for maintaining good relations with the DPRK, though these could always fracture in times of ideological stress.

In the meantime, as a small weak state, Pyongyang did not have much purchase on events, and although one finds the imputation of skill or finesse to Kim in his so-called 'balancing act' between China and the Soviet Union, this involves considerable exaggeration.[75] As in domestic policy, it defies credibility to imagine Kim Il Sung, so astray in so many areas of state policy, making informed, nuanced calculations in foreign policy, much less allowing others around him to make them for him. By the 1960s the entire residual DPRK academic and intellectual community had been cowed, and Kim's chosen foreign ministers were not specialists or men of international experience but inner circle loyalists who were there primarily because of their ability to reflexively cast the Kimist ideological net over all matters of state. The result was a blunt, unsophisticated foreign policy, characterised by a set of alienating behaviours, driven by expediency and incapable of responding flexibly to challenges. We will see more of this later in such matters as Kim's Non-Aligned Movement diplomacy in the 1970s, his reaction to the ROK's expanding diplomatic reach in the late 1980s, and of course his response to the fall of the Soviet Union, but even at this stage in the 1960s Kim was presiding over the DPRK's steady loss of influence in both Moscow and Beijing where it was always paid attention for strategic reasons, chiefly in recognition of its disruptive capacities.

Concluding remarks

What lessons did Kim learn from the Korean War? There is obviously no clear answer to this, other than he learned what he chose to learn and what he was capable of learning, and Kim was a person of very fixed ideas. So perhaps we should rather ask what was available for him to learn. To begin with the dark side, the day-to-day business of war induces extreme moral relativism, and only afterwards in peacetime do soldiers truly reflect on the things they have seen and done. Abhorrence and mental scarring are usually strong legacies, but a minority opt for glorification, and Kim was one of these, for it was his special talent to ensure that war remained publicly glorified in the North so that gentler passions would never poison peacetime morale. In this lay the roots of the remorseless, militarist underpinnings of the Kimist vision.

More fundamentally, from the standpoint of a person who had spent his entire adult life constantly and directly involved in either military struggle or preparation for military struggle to regain Korea, the Korean War left Kim with the searing experience of having victory seemingly within his grasp before suffering humiliating defeat, followed by the deeply unsatisfactory outcome of an armistice agreement which gave him control of roughly one-third of the Korean population. Thus, it is also not surprising that he should have viewed the process of post-war reconstruction as inseparable from the process of rearmament and rededication to fighting the same war again. Nor is it surprising that his concept of the modern state should have been that of a righteous warmaking state whose central purpose was to conduct effective warfare against a very broad range of enemies. It is this perspective that helps us to understand DPRK policies in the 1960s. Both the nature of his idiosyncratic interventions in policy-making such as Chollima, Chongsanri and Taean, undertaken in the face of overwhelming evidence that these were counter-productive strategies, and the 1962 proclamation of Equal Emphasis confirmed that he was not in any sense a nation builder, for he had little grasp of the fundamentals of economic planning and development, and next to no concept of the raising of people's standards of living as an end in itself.

If Kim reflected on the Chinese experience of the Korean War, then he may have seen that this was China's coming of age in modern warfare – China's equivalent of the Russo–Japanese War, where it put the humiliations of the previous century behind, challenged the world's strongest army and fought it to a draw. By intervening in strength, Mao Zedong took a characteristically audacious gamble for which China could have paid dearly, for sections of the US military leadership were seriously attracted to the option of deploying tactical nuclear weapons and pursuing a wider war against China, a course of action in which they were chiefly constrained by the strong possibility that this might mean war with the Soviet Union. In the end, though, the CPV fought against a politically constrained enemy which initially was grossly under-prepared and ill-motivated to fight on difficult terrain in the appalling climatic conditions of a severe Korean winter, and this went a long way towards equalizing the gross paper disparity between the two sides. This could not but be inspiring to Kim, and he may well have drawn encouragement for fighting a similar asymmetric war in the future.

Post-war, Kim's characteristic leadership style was strongly in evidence, for such features as cronyism, promotion of his own personality cult, a hectoring, intimidating manner and hostility not just to debate but to any and all differing views, all feature prominently in the criticisms levelled at him by his colleagues in the lead-up to the August 1956 challenge. One pointer to the future in this was that in his 1950–1 campaigns against fellow Communist oligarchs, Kim was decisive in adopting strategies of frontal attack that appeared to involve high elements of risk. He engaged in sustained, unforgiving political combat against many other elements in the Party's leadership while the country was still engaged in a disastrous war, and in the immediate post-Korean War period he tested the allegiance of the population by forcing them into the immediate and rapid pursuit of heavy industrialisation at a time when virtually no one outside the party elite could claim access to anything like adequate food, clothing or shelter. Moreover, Kim pursued these policies against the advice of the Soviet Union and China, and at a time when significant voices within the party leadership were advocating more moderate policies.

In the course of this struggle against factional opponents, for the first time Kim began to temper effusive praise for the Soviet Union with the ultra-nationalist rhetoric of Juche as a means of rallying the population to the enormous sacrifices needed for post-war recovery. Kim's nationalism did not draw inspiration from Korean history, nor did it dwell on past political or cultural achievements, for in the course of his upbringing and early adulthood, Kim had acquired no stake in the norms of Korean society and culture, which had given him neither security nor prospects in life. He did not rise above such circumstances and came to believe that what held for him held for all Koreans, and so he became the final arbiter of what was and what was not 'Korean'. And so his was a harsh nationalist creed that dwelt on past wrongs and promises of retribution for 'national traitors' and their foreign backers, while in the cultural sphere the entire world of traditional Korean cultural achievement, Korean rituals and practices of Korean life, including celebration of *ch'usok* and all Confucian rites of passage were deemed worthless. This world was replaced with a spurious stress on the 'purity' of all things Korean against the 'contamination' of all things foreign, all with the aim of inculcating in people a sense of fear and animosity toward the outside world, and especially toward the emerging capitalist, cosmopolitan Korean world of the ROK as well.

We can scarcely begin to comprehend subsequent political, economic or foreign policy developments without reference to this context. The colossal proportions of the 1962 Equal Emphasis build-up and its enduring nature cannot be explained by any objective analysis of possible threats to the DPRK at the time, but rather as a reflection of the profoundly militarist nature of Kim Il Sung's worldview and his overriding commitment to resuming the Korean War. This vision in itself was not eccentric, and its central theme of unending struggle against imperialist invaders until their oppressed countrymen were liberated and the beloved motherland reunified had its attractions. But even Kim himself was not confident on this point, and as the 1960s wore on, he obviously believed that the bulk of the population would not follow him unless he deployed ever higher levels of regimentation, repression and terror against them.

And so we see a familiar pattern. In theory, rule by a disciplined, authoritarian leader raises the prospect of vigour and consistency in policy, but it also deprives the state of even the tenuous checks and balances of the Leninist party-state, and opens the path to tyranny. We do not know the precise contours of debate within the Party leadership in the years 1958–68, but some restraints on Kim obviously existed because the 1967–8 purges indicate that many loyalists had not yet learnt the later habit of docility and self-censorship and so they brought their challenge to a Party Conference. The cessation of any semblance of meaningful debate among senior cadres after this conference meant that Kim lost a vital remaining source of restraint in all spheres of policy – political, economic, social and cultural.

To date, our discussion on the personality of Kim Il Sung has focused largely on the twin influences of the Manchurian guerilla campaign and wartime Stalinism, but now the corrupting effects of power without accountability also begin to emerge. In 1970 Kim Il Sung was 58 years old and had been the dominant voice in the Party since 1958, and in some policy areas for quite a few years prior to that. When we observe such key features of DPRK state policy in the 1960s as irrational use of economic resources, military adventurism, the promotion of an almost entirely fictitious rewriting of Kim's life and times, the genesis of plans for the eventual succession of Kim Jong Il and the purging of many colleagues who had stood with him since the 1930s, we see signs of a fundamental loss of perspective, precipitated by pathological drives and demonstrated in his extravagant cult of personality, xenophobia, proclamation of infallibility and blind insistence on a manifest destiny. The chief Kimist policy objective remained the reunification of Korea under KWP leadership, but Kim's chosen means were becoming increasingly anachronistic and counter-productive. The point at which Kim arrived at his goal of unobstructed rule was also the very point at which the attainment of his final objective began to recede and the country began a long, slow march into stagnation and decline.

Notes

1 As mentioned in passing above, Kim Il Sung's ability as a military commander had come into question during this process, especially among the Chinese. See, for example, Stueck (1995: 218) citing a contemporary Soviet report that CPV commander Peng Dehuai 'was not ashamed to express his low opinion of [Kim's] . . . military capabilities'. More specifically, from July 1950 onwards, senior Chinese military planners regularly discussed the Korean situation and concluded that a straightforward United Nations Command (UNC) break-out north from the Pusan–Taegu perimeter was unlikely because of the terrain, and that any counter-attack north was also likely to involve an amphibious landing behind North Korea lines in the vicinity of Inch'on, especially in view of the US forces' experience of such operations during the Pacific War. They advised senior North Korean counterparts, who do not appear to have had a military planning group of comparable sophistication, to take appropriate precautions, but to little effect, and Inch'on remained virtually undefended (Zhang, 1995: 71–4). Kim evidently learned nothing from the consequent Inch'on debacle, for the following January, when amid high casualties, daunting winter conditions and general exhaustion, the Chinese opted to halt their offensive and regroup just south of Seoul, he made strenuous representations to seek the early continuation of all-out pursuit (Zhang, 1995: 132). This was a typically compulsive advocacy that was not only impossible given the degraded state of the Chinese forces, but was a potentially disastrous strategy, since it stood to re-create the long, vulnerable supply lines that in August and September 1950 had made the KPA so vulnerable and the Inch'on landing so effective.
2 The KWP was now well on its way to enrolling a higher proportion of the population (c. 12.5 per cent) than any other Leninist Party state. On the Party membership policies of the Korean War years, see Scalapino and Lee (1972a: 456–7) and Koon-Woo Nam (1974: 86ff.).
3 See Scalapino and Lee (1972a: 428) for examples of the praise generated for Kim in the official media to mark his milestone fortieth birthday in April 1952, where

58   *The enemy on all sides: 1950–70*

the *Rodong Shinmun* assessed that Kim had 'totally devoted his energies and genius to the cause of the freedom, independence, happiness, democracy and peace of the fatherland. He has become the torchlight for all the pioneers of our country'. As overblown as this might seem, it is quite self-effacing compared with what was later to become standard rhetoric.

4   Certainly, while the Soviets had always evinced support but not much enthusiasm for Kim, the issue in dispute was one that they had little to quibble with on ideological grounds, since Kim's drive to create a mass Party was modelled very much on Stalinist precedent and he was apparently effective in restoring Party discipline. If Kim had shown signs of losing control it might have been a different matter, as it was in Afghanistan in 1979 when the Soviets judged that Party leader Hafizullah Amin, who had just killed off his predecessor, had lost control of the Party, and so they proceeded to invade the country and assassinate him. For more details on Ho's career, especially at this importance juncture, see Lankov (2002: 147ff.).

5   See Scalapino and Lee (1972a: 406). On Mu's actual role in the lead-up to and early stages of the Korean War, see Myung-Lim Park (1995: 266). Mu had been one of the members of the Yan'an group with close CCP ties and had served as Peng Dehuai's Chief of Staff (Sung-Chul Yang, 1981: 165). Peng was, of course, now the commander of the Chinese forces in Korea.

6   See Zhang (1995: 205) for Mao's injunction to the Chinese People's Volunteers (CPV) that sensitivity to and respect for the North Koreans was good politics: 'Treat Korean problems as ours and care about everything in Korea and never touch Korean people's [property]. Just as we have experienced at home, this is a political safeguard for victory.'

7   Their fate was sealed by mid-1951. Szalontai (2005: 41) quotes the Hungarian chargé d'affaires in Pyongyang, writing in May 1951, as noting 'With the exception of known leaders, South Korean party members are treated here as non-members [of the Party]. They must ask again for their admission as if they were new members. With references, and so on. Even if the person in question was a registered guerilla.'

8   See Chong-sik Lee (1965), Okonogi (1994) and especially Szalontai (2005) for an account of this policy debate and an assessment of its scale and consequences. In particular, Lee notes that in the first decade after 1953, 75 per cent of all foreign aid was allocated to the means of production and only 25 per cent on agriculture and consumer goods. In order to finance its heavy industrialisation, the DPRK enforced a compulsory savings rate of 25 per cent of national income – 'even higher than those enforced in the Soviet Union and Communist China in similar periods of their history' (Chong-sik Lee, 1965: 121).

9   As did the defining Stalin–Bukharin struggle in the Soviet Union of the late 1920s, and the Mao Zedong–Liu Shaoqi struggle in China in the early 1960s, both of which were fought on similar grounds.

10 For example, in his speech to the All-Nation Agricultural Cooperatives Conference on 5 January 1959, Kim asserted: 'As Marxism–Leninism teaches us and the experience of the Soviet Union demonstrates, the farm problem can be ultimately solved only through the [transformation of] individual farm management to socialistic cooperativisation' (Chong-sik Lee, 1962: 12). Notwithstanding occasional tinkering, collectivisation remains in place today.

11 The excesses of the collectivisation process were both a pointer to Kim's preferred methods and a key issue for Kim's opponents at this time. Lankov quotes one prominent Yan'an group cadre in conversation with a Soviet diplomat in conversation with a Soviet diplomat in July 1956 as follows: 'Instead of 25 to 27 per cent tax they took more than 50 per cent from the farmers. That policy continues to this day. It is not necessary to recount the methods used in 1954–5

to gather taxes. Tax-gathering was accompanied by beatings, murders and arrests. The party's activities are based on violence, not persuasion. The co-operative movement is based on violence' (Lankov, 2002: 182). See Szalontai (2005: 62) for more in this vein, including eye-witness accounts from Hungarian diplomatic staff.

12 For example, Alexander Joungwon Kim (1975: 313–14) quotes Kim in the late 1960s as saying 'it is in the countryside where the survivals and leftovers of the old society are found more than anywhere else, and it is again in the countryside where the materials and technical foundations of socialism are weakest'. The Stalinist perspective was, of course, hostile, as might be expected from the architect of agricultural policies that induced the 1932–3 Ukraine Holodomar, or famine, with deaths measured in the millions. This perspective attacked the reluctance of peasants to be collectivised, due to their 'intrinsic indiscipline and incapacity for cooperation in large-scale organisations, trading mentality, and inherent potential for recreating capitalism' (Lewin, 1977: 122).

13 The smaller work unit, the greater the sense of ownership and the more incentive to increase production but, of course, a greater sense of ownership was ideologically undesirable as it weakened the collective. On the subteam system, see Hy-Sang Lee (1994: 190).

14 On the influence of Soviet policies on the DPRK in the immediate aftermath of Stalin's death, see Okonogi (1994: 177ff.).

15 On the significance of the December 1955 speech 'On Eliminating Dogmatism and Formalism and Establishing Juche in Ideological Work', see Okonogi (1994: 196ff.) and Scalapino and Lee (1972a: 500), and especially Myers (2015: 45–55).

16 For sociological analysis of the 914 delegates to the Third KWP Congress, see Scalapino and Lee (1972a: 505ff.). In age, education and occupation, nearly 60 per cent were 40 years old or younger and had limited formal education; 8 per cent were college graduates. Veterans whose experience extended into the pre-1945 period represented a mere 8 per cent of the total.

17 The following account draws chiefly on the detailed account in Lankov (2002: 154–93). Also see the collection of original documents located at: www.wilsoncenter.org/sites/default/files/CWIHPBulletin16_p51.pdf (accessed October 2016).

18 Since original records of conversation with leading DPRK officials are rare, the following details of their representations to the Soviets concerning Kim are of interest, factoring in, of course, their own self-interest. To Yi P'il-gyu, a prominent Yan'an group member, 'Kim Il Sung's personality cult has become quite intolerable. He will not brook any criticism or self-criticism. Kim Il Sung's word is law. He has gathered sycophants and lackeys all around him in the central Committee and Cabinet (Lankov, 2002: 159).' In a similar vein, Ch'oe Ch'ang-ik is quoted as saying, 'I am becoming more and more convinced that Kim Il Sung does not understand how harmful his behaviour is. He paralyses the initiative of members of the Standing Committee and other executives of the Party and State. He intimidates everyone. Nobody can voice an opinion on any question (Lankov, 2002: 160).'

19 The leaders were then given low-level administrative work, Pak Ch'ang-ok, for example, becoming a factory manager. Thus, the intervention did not alter the fact that their careers were effectively over. The Soviet and Chinese intervention was bitterly resented by Kim and the phrase 'the events of 1956' recurred for many years afterwards in the media in thinly-veiled criticism of Soviet 'dominationism'.

20 The following extract from a record of conversation between a Polish diplomat Henrik Brzezinski and a senior DPRK bureaucrat dated 5 January 1958 helps explain what dominant leadership amounted to. 'The director stated that both at a course in the Central Committee and in individual conversations among Korean comrades, language and formulations from Kim Il Sung's speeches or articles in

the newspapers are used most of all. At the course in the Central Committee one must strongly follow the official formulations and in no case may one use one's own words even while maintaining the official contents, if one does not want to be exposed to harsh criticism. From the top, the director asserted, great stress is placed on using the very political language that is included in official speeches or in the press. An independent way of thinking and one's own interpretation of particular political theses is sharply criticised and viewed badly' (Person, 2009), Document 13, available at: www.wilsoncenter.org/sites/default/files/Chollima_ DocReader_WebFinal.pdf

21 See Szalontai (2005: 34) for more in this vein.
22 This brief description cannot, of course, do full justice to a multifaceted and dynamic phenomenon. For a more detailed description of the core features of Stalinism in particular, see Tucker (1977) and Gill (1990: 1–20). Of particular interest is Schlogel (2012), with his panorama of life in Moscow at the height of the 1937 Great Terror.
23 For details of these and the following traits, see Buzo (1999: 40–9).
24 Gill (1990: 292): 'the creator of the new life', 'the golden sun', 'the sun of a new life, enlightening the whole world', 'the creator of happiness for the Soviet people', 'Due to the genius of Stalin, in the epoch of Stalin, socialism has been victorious.'
25 Clark (1977: 180–98), for example, gives a detailed account of how this process took hold in the Soviet Union in the 1930s. Perhaps the point most relevant to the DPRK is that 'Stalinist society expected of its citizens extraordinarily far-reaching allegiance to the state. The rationalisation for this attachment was found in the analogy between the entire Soviet state and a "family" or "tribe". Soviet Russians were urged to jettison their sense of family based on real blood relationships and to replace it with a higher one based on political kinship.' (Clark 1977: 181) In the DPRK, of course, Kimism made a similar analogy.
26 Gill (1980: 170) notes: 'As a consequence of the claimed infallibility of Stalin's words, the population was continually exhorted to pay the closest attention to his instructions and to be guided in all their activities by them. The people were portrayed as accepting without question what Stalin said, not because of any objectively established criteria of truth and falsehood, but simply because Stalin had said it; if Stalin said something, by definition it must be so'. Again, one needs to emphasise how alien this is to the Korean tradition, especially in view of the ahistorical assertion of Cumings (1993: 210) that 'Koreans have assumed, implicitly and often explicitly that the fount of wisdom, the spark of philosophy, occurs in the mind of the leader – that it resides in an exceptional person. One genius is at the core, one philosopher-king, and he tutors everyone else.' Quite the contrary, the philosopher-king figure simply does not exist in the Korean Confucian tradition: Confucius is the philosopher, the neo-Confucian canon is the text, and the king is the student.
27 Kim's obliteration of all streams of pre-1945 anti-Japanese resistance other than his own has a parallel in a similar process in the Soviet Union, by which reference to practically all Bolshevik heroes other than Stalin ceased in the 1930s and was replaced by the essentially spurious narrative of Stalin's central role in the 1917 October Revolution (Ulam, 1974: 390).
28 Anyone who has casually picked up a DPRK publication on almost any topic will be aware of the mandatory first words of the Foreword: 'The Great Leader Comrade Kim Il Sung taught as follows:. . .'
29 See Ulam (1974: 638) for Stalin's practice.
30 From 1945 onwards, the North began to determine ascriptively what degree of loyalty – defined in a threefold system of core, wavering, or hostile – could be expected from citizens based on their class background, and this practice steadily gained in intensity during the 1950s until it determined access to education and

training, employment, housing and locality, and therefore shaped entire lives. For details on the *songbun* system, especially its formative years, see Collins (2012).
31 They did, of course, still manage to exist in an underground world. See Schlogel (2012: 341–2) for a portrait of the lives of this class in Moscow in the 1930s and Alexopoulos (2003), who estimates that at its peak roughly four million people in the Russian Soviet Federative Socialist Republic were disenfranchised.
32 Collectivisation was not part of the original Bolshevik programme. It first became CPSU policy ten years after the Revolution under Stalin's advocacy at the Fifteenth CPSU Party Congress in 1927.
33 The vision of a centrally planned economy derives partly from the Marxian vision of a unified economy that could impose itself over the vagaries of the capitalist system, but its implementation derives from a series of measures taken by Stalin in the period 1928–30 with the objective of destroying the economic power of all groups outside the direct control of the CPSU and redirecting resources into heavy industry.
34 de Jonge (1986: 262) notes Stalin's tendency to be dismissive of the whole field of mathematical economics on the ground that it was 'idealist' and not Marxist. In a similar vein, Ulam (1974: 444) records a toast to science proposed by Stalin in 1938: 'To the flourishing of science, of that science whose exponents, though they understand and exploit the strength and meaning of scientific tradition, refuse to be slaves of those traditions. To the science which has the courage to break with old traditions, norms, directions if they have outlived their usefulness, if they have become a brake on progress.' In Kim Il Sung's case, this trait took various forms, chiefly the levelling of the accusation of 'empiricism' against his opponents, a charge characteristically brought against technicians and economic planners seeking to apply rational calculations to industrial output. See, for example, Scalapino and Lee (1972a: 510), and especially the report of Kim Il, at that stage the No. 3-ranked Party Presidium member, to the April 1968 Party plenum, in which he castigated 'the passive elements and conservatives [who] clung to the outdated notions of an official capacity and norm, mythicised science and technology, restricted the initiatives of the masses, stopped working people from working more, kneeled before difficulties, feared mass innovation, and attempted to block the grand onward movement' (Scalapino and Lee, 1972a: 611).
35 The pharaonic excesses of the Pyongyang skyline have no parallel in China or the ROK. One has to go further afield to the Soviet Union where, as Tucker (1963) has pointed out in the context of post-war Stalinism, 'transformism' was not just a particular form of ambitious economic planning, but had a strong philosophical basis in the pseudo-scientific doctrines of Michurin and Lysenko.
36 It is doubtful that Kim ever consciously sought to emulate Stalin the man, but we nevertheless keep encountering strange psychological resonances that help us grasp the depth of Kim's attachment to Stalin's example. At least part of the key to this lies in the following comment of Trotsky on Stalin: 'I was repelled by the very qualities that would strengthen him ... namely, the narrowness of his interests, his pragmatism, his psychological coarseness and the special cynicism of the provincial who had been liberated from his prejudices by Marxism but who has not replaced them with a philosophical outlook that has been thoroughly thought out and mentally absorbed.' Quoted in Volkogonov (1991: 57).
37 Discussion of the merits and demerits of the various alternative labels applied to the DPRK, ranging from Cumings's 'corporatism' (Cumings, 1982, 1993), to Wada Haruki's 'partisan-family state', to McEachern's 'institutional pluralism' (McEachern, 2010), to Myers's ultra-rightist racial state (Myers, 2011), to Armstrong's straightforward tyranny (Armstrong, 2013), and onwards to a variety of hybrids, ranging from 'national Stalinism' to 'market Stalinism' is beyond the scope of this present discussion. Despite such taxonomical energy, surprisingly few serious studies

discussing in detail the affinities of Stalinism and Kimism have been written. Cheong (2000) is a noteworthy exception.

There is a further dimension to the issue of Kim Il Sung's political bloodline, and that is the resonances that some people have found between Kimism and the pre-modern Korean political tradition, specifically the practices of the Choson court. See, for example, Scalapino and Lee (1972b: 753), Henderson (1968: 102), Brandt (1983: 627–8), and Cumings (1993: 209–12). Such resonances are characteristically cited in the context of surmising the 'Koreanness' of Kimism and encounter obvious problems of historical and political context, but mainly for reasons of space this issue will not be argued out here. Interested readers are referred to Buzo (1999: 45–52).

38 Scalapino and Lee (1972b: 868) note that ex-North Koreans are almost unanimous in their opinion that Kimism (i.e. Juche) 'has taken its ideological–philosophical foundations (as apart from certain concrete policies) wholly from Soviet sources. They regard Chinese (Maoist) ideological influence as negligible.'

39 Myers's treatment of the philosophical underpinnings of Juche (Myers, 2015) is likely to remain a standard reference work, although at times it becomes difficult to maintain a sense of the obvious difference between Juche's elusive meaning as a philosophical term and the all-too-clear manner in which it is used in practical politics as a call to obedience to the vision of Kim Il Sung.

40 From an examination of the contents of the KWP's theoretical organ *Kulloja*, Chong-sik Lee (1965: 123) notes that Juche first began to develop into a consistent ideological stance about 1957. Dae-Sook Suh (1988: 147) also notes how within two to three years after the 1956 Congress, 'many historical studies blending grossly exaggerated accounts of [Kim's] partisan exploits with traditional Korean history began to appear,' while Scalapino and Lee (1972a: 565) similarly remark on the major DPRK rewriting of the history of the Communist movement that occurred in the late 1950s.

41 The Kimist triumph also caused a rewriting of Party history which proceeded to achieve astounding degrees of mendacity. The new, authorised version portrayed Kim as the leader of the Communist movement from 1931 on, the year he turned 19, the eliminator of sectarianism within the Party, the advocate of armed struggle as the only way forward, and the inspiration for Korean Communist activities in China and within Korea during the 1930s. See *Democratic People's Republic of Korea* (1958: 63–76). One can trace the progress of this cult through successive editions of this basic government-compiled handbook.

42 Chollima literally means a 'thousand-li horse', evoking the image of a winged horse capable of covering vast areas at high speed. On the Chollima Movement, see Alexander Joungwon Kim (1965: 260–1), Ho-Min Yang (1988) and Jae-Jean Suh (1994: 21–2).

43 Ho-Min Yang (1988: 52) points to the similarities with the Great Leap Forward, which began in May 1958, in terms of its coverage of sectors, its collective mass competitiveness, its ideological purpose and its propaganda themes.

44 For details of the implementation of Chollima, see Joseph Chung (1974: 96–97).

45 See '70 Day Speed Battle Declared by WPK Political Bureau', available at: https://nkleadershipwatch.wordpress.com/2016/02/24/70-day-speed-battle-declared-by-wpk-political-bureau/ (accessed November 2016).

46 This method takes its name from a village near Pyongyang. In February 1960 Kim Il Sung spent several days in the village, during which he closely scrutinised existing work practices and put forth a series of definitive guidelines, known collectively as the Chongsanri Method, for improving production and raising ideological consciousness. On the origins and development of the Chongsanri Method, see Scalapino and Lee (1972a: 562–3) and Ki-Hyuk Pak (1983: 224).

47 For further details of these movements, see Joseph Chung (1974: 63–4).

48 This system did not spring from a void. As far back as early 1950, the DPRK was employing a politics-first line in the workplace. See Szalontai (2005: 22) for an interesting anecdote in which a Hungarian visitor to a factory in the North was told that 'the old specialists had been expelled from the factory because of their pernicious activity, and thus they [the managers] had to train new technical experts'.
49 Kim's official biographer Baik Bong (1969, vol. 3, p. 225) uses the same term for the Fourth KWP Congress as the Soviet leadership used for the Seventeenth CPSU Congress in February 1934, which confirmed the personal dictatorship of Stalin, who convened only two more congresses in the remaining nineteen years of his life. Likewise, Kim convened only two more Congresses in the remaining thirty-three years of his life.
50 Koon-Woo Nam (1974: 121–2) offers the following affiliations for the 85 full Central Committee members: pre-war Manchurian guerillas, 57; post-1945 cadres, 13; pre-war domestic Communists, 8; Yan'an group, 3; Soviet–Korean, 1; unknown background, 3. For a detailed analysis of the Fourth KWP Congress Central Committee, see Scalapino and Lee (1972a: 566–71, 732–52).
51 For details of the Plan and the tension between Plan output goals and Chollima-style methods, see Joseph Chung (1974: 90–9).
52 The official version of Kim's concluding speech at the Fifth Plenum made no direct mention of military matters, which is hardly surprising since this was not the type of policy one trumpets to the world. However, a notable theme was the extended attention he paid to shortcomings in economic planning and execution, and his attribution of these shortcomings not to any defects in the Chollima concept, but to the failure to implement Chollima more fully. Thus, he foreshadowed a return to intensive mobilisation methods. See Kim Il Sung (1984), vol. 16, pp. 464–75. For commentary on the decisions of the Fifth Plenum, see Chong-sik Lee (1964: 663) and Dae-Sook Suh (1988: 213–20).
53 Dae-Sook Suh (1988: 219–20) charts the rise in military expenditures as a proportion of the total state budget as follows: 1961 – 2.6 per cent; 1964 – 5.8 per cent; 1966 – 10 per cent; 1967 – 30.4 per cent. Similarly, Joseph Chung (1972: 94) calculates that defence expenditure rose from an average of 4.3 per cent for the period 1956–66 to 31.2 per cent for the period 1967–70. By comparison with the Soviet military–industrial complex, Trigubenko (1991: 106) maintains that in the 1980s the military economy in the DPRK accounted for 30 per cent of aggregate social product compared with 8 per cent in the USSR at its height.
54 Should we grow to doubt the durability of Equal Emphasis, in announcing his hallmark *byungjin* policy framework in March 2013, Kim Jong Un reached back over fifty years to specifically and uniquely cite Equal Emphasis as his precedent in the following terms: 'At the fifth plenary meeting of the fourth party CC in December 1962, the great leader set forth the line on simultaneously carrying out the economic construction and national defense building, the first of its kind in history, and presented the revolutionary slogan called, A gun in one hand, and a sickle and hammer in the other! It is because the leader clarified the simultaneous line and provided national defense capabilities for self-defense, along with the self-supporting national economy, that we were able to firmly defend the gains of the revolution without wavering in the face of the great upheaval of socialism collapsing in various countries.' See: www.ncnk.org/resources/news-items/kim-jong-uns-speeches-and-public-statements-1/KJU_CentralCommittee_KWP.pdf (accessed September 2016).
55 Many and varied factors are cited, from Park Chung-hee's May 1961 coup, to growing US involvement in Vietnam (although we are still nearly two years away from the pivotal Gulf of Tonkin Resolution), to the general effects of the Sino–Soviet split, but these are unconvincing when measured against the enormity of the policy measures taken by Kim.

64 *The enemy on all sides: 1950–70*

56 As already noted in passing, the one thing Kimist militarism was not was cultural, for one finds no sanction for militarism or political authoritarianism in the deeply civilianised culture and polity of pre-modern Korea. Further discussion on this point is beyond our present scope, so the reader is directed in the first instance to Palais (1975).
57 The following description is drawn chiefly from Nisbet (1976). While it obviously closely resembles the characteristics of Kim's Manchurian guerilla community, Nisbet is, of course, approaching the issue from a theoretical perspective and makes no reference to the DPRK.
58 'The authority of the warrior chief was prescriptive, centralised in him and his lieutenants, and applied directly, without qualification, to each and every individual in the war band' (Nisbet, 1976: 29).
59 For a comparison of rates of investment in the heavy and light industry sectors, see Joseph Chung (1974: 73).
60 In his 1965 New Year speech, Kim Il Sung acknowledged the slowdown: 'It is true that the economic development of our country has been delayed somewhat compared with what was expected, because we had to direct great strength to further increase the defence capacity in the last two or three years to meet the changing turn of events.' (quoted in Joseph Chung, 1974: 93)
61 On the calculation of these rates in conditions of statistical black-out, see Scalapino and Lee (1972b: 1258–60).
62 Kim first elaborated on the 'strategy of the triple revolutions' at the Eighth Plenum of the Fourth KWP Central Committee in February 1964. For the open sections of Kim's speech, see Kim Il Sung (1984), vol. 18, pp. 213–31. For analysis, see Byung-Chul Koh (1984: 123ff.).
63 For details, see Koh (1984: 133). Significant DMZ incidents increased exponentially between 1965 and 1968 (1965 – 59; 1966 – 50; 1967 – 566, 1968 – 629), and declined from 1969 (1969 – 111; 1970 – 113; 1971 – 47; 1972 – none). At the same time, during 1967 the characteristic form of infiltration across the DMZ underwent a qualitative change from individuals or two-man teams on surveillance missions to larger, well-armed groups evidently seeking to penetrate southward and establish bases for guerilla warfare, as the DPRK had done in the period immediately prior to the Korean War.
64 This tendency in DPRK strategy was evidently easy to detect. In July 1967, the GDR embassy in Pyongyang reported in detail on the July 1967 KWP CC Plenum and associated media commentary, detecting 'a dangerous nationalistic course which does not exclude the option of adventurist activities'. See: *Information about the Central Committee Plenum of the Korean Workers' Party between 28 June and 3 July 1967*, 4 August 1967, available at: www.wilsoncenter.org/publication/the-1967-purge-the-gapsan-faction-and-establishment-the-monolithic-ideological-system#sthash.RRFVv3Ir.dpuf (accessed December 2016).
65 For further information on these incidents, see Byung-Chul Koh (1969) and Zagoria and Zagoria (1981).
66 This outline of events cannot do full justice to a complicated issue. For a more detailed analysis of DPRK strategy during this period, see Szalontai (2012).
67 A further plenum, at the time held in secret, was held on 25 May 1967 to provide final ratification the new order (Tertitskiy, 2017).
68 Key Politburo figures involved in economic management dismissed at this stage include Chong Il-yong, Nam Il, Yi Chong-ok, Yi Chu-yon, Hyon Mu-gwang, and Han Sang-du. Their shortcomings appear to have been purely performance-related, rather than involving challenging Kim's authority, as none of them were actually purged, with Yi Chong-ok and Hyon Mu-gwang in particular re-emerging to later occupy the office of Premier. The three cadres not directly involved in economic administration who were purged at this point were Kim Ch'ang-man

(military education), Ha Ang-ch'on (President of Kimilsung University) and Pak Chong-ae (party functionary). They were joined by two further high-level casualties in the first half of 1967 – Pak Kum-ch'ol (career military man) and Yi Hyo-sun (civilian Party functionary), ranked at no. 4 and no. 5 in the Party respectively.

69 If ever there was a period where Kim Il Sung achieved a level of terror and paranoia that approached that of Stalin, it was during this period. Something of the atmosphere into which the country descended at this time may be gained from the account of Ali Lameda, a Venezuelan Communist working for the Department of Foreign Publications under the Ministry of Foreign Affairs at the time. See: www.amnesty.org/download/Documents/204000/asa240021979en.pdf (accessed December 2016).

70 Although the vestige of a factional battle was still present. Pak Kum-ch'ol and Yi Hyo-sun were leading members of the Kapsan Group, a group that had functioned as a rear area support network for Kim Il Sung and the frontline guerillas and that had helped Kim carry out the 1937 Bochonbo raid. During the 1950s, Pak and Yi were seen as part of the Manchurian group, with whom they obviously had the most in common. However, now that the other groups had all been purged, the distinction between the Kapsan group and the Manchurian guerilla group probably appeared more and more salient.

71 See Chong-sik Lee (1982: 441), who also quotes Rinn-Sup Shinn as having been told by DPRK interlocutors that the process began in 1966. This, of course, presaged the emergence of Kim Jong Il, who had begun working within the Party in 1964, as heir and successor.

72 New ex-guerrilla appointees included Kim Ch'ang-bong, Ho Pong-hak, Ch'oe Kwang, Ch'oe Hyon and O Chin-u. Kim and Ho were purged the following year, Ch'oe Kwang was also purged but rehabilitated in the 1970s, and Ch'oe Hyon and O remained at the very pinnacle of the military establishment until the end of their careers. By contrast, while Kim lived, the economic cadres never again approached their pre-1967 level of Politburo representation.

73 For the Soviet perspective on this era, see Boulychev (1994: 90): 'The post-1965 Kosygin visit thaw never managed to restore relations to their former closeness. Soviet ideology, internal and external policy was viewed with suspicion in Pyongyang and the Soviet people in North Korea were virtually isolated.'

74 After signing the 1961 mutual defence treaty, China and the DPRK settled a long-standing territorial dispute in 1963, with the Chinese negotiators under instructions from Premier Zhou Enlai to accommodate DPRK demands as far as possible in order to retain DPRK goodwill in the ongoing Sino-Soviet rivalry (Chae-Jin Lee, 1996: 99). It was this settlement, and especially the agreement to share sovereignty over Ch'onji, the crater-lake in Paekdu-san that appears to have temporarily unravelled in the late 1960s. Also see Hunter (1983: 198).

75 Among many, see, for example, Sung-Chul Yang (1994: 183): 'Kim's consummate balancing act throughout the years of the slowly changing Sino–Soviet rivalry has, in fact, been one of his political trademarks.' Similarly, Joseph M. Ha (1983: 226): 'North Korea, fearful of becoming overly dependent upon the Soviet Union for economic or military assistance, has played a skilful game of maneuvering between the USSR and China.'

References

Alexopoulos, Golfo (2008) Stalin and the politics of kinship: Practices of collective punishment, 1920s–1940s, in *Comparative Studies in Society and History*, 50(1): 91–117.

Armstrong, Charles (2013) *Tyranny of the Weak: North Korea and the World 1950–1992* Cornell University Press: Ithaca, NY.

Baik, Bong (1969) *Kim Il Sung: Biography*. 3 volumes. Miraisha: Tokyo.
Boulychev, Georgi D. (1994) Moscow and North Korea: The 1961 treaty and after, in *Russia in the Far East and Pacific Region*, Il-Yung Chung and Eunsook Chung (eds), The Sejong Institute, Seoul, pp. 81–118.
Brandt, Vincent S.R. (1983) North Korea: Anthropological speculation, *Korea and World Affairs*, 7(4): 617–29.
Buzo, Adrian (1999) *The Guerilla Dynasty: Politics and Leadership in North Korea*. I.B. Tauris: London.
Cheong, Seong-Chang (2000) Stalinism and Kimilsungism: A comparative analysis of ideology and power, *Asian Perspective*, 2(91): 133–61.
Chung, Joseph S. (1974) *The North Korean Economy: Structure and Development*. Hoover Institution Press: Stanford, CA.
Clark, Katerina (1977) Utopian anthropology as a context for Stalinist literature, in *Stalinism: Essays in Historical Interpretation*, Robert C. Tucker (ed.). W.W. Norton: New York, pp. 180–98.
Collins, Robert (2012) *Marked for Life: Songbun, North Korea's Social Classification System*. The Committee for Human Rights in North Korea: Washington, DC.
Conquest, Robert (1973) *The Great Terror*. Collier: New York.
Cumings, Bruce (1982–83) Corporatism in North Korea, *Journal of Korean Studies*, 4, pp. 269–94.
Cumings, Bruce (1993) The corporate state in North Korea, in *State and Society in Contemporary Korea*, Hagen Koo (ed.), Cornell University Press: Ithaca, NY, pp. 197–230.
de Jonge, Alex (1986) *Stalin and the Shaping of the Soviet Union*. Collins: Glasgow.
Democratic People's Republic of Korea, 1958, Foreign Languages Publishing House, Pyongyang.
Gill, Graeme (1990) *The Origins of the Stalinist Political System*. Cambridge University Press: Cambridge.
Goncharov, Sergei N., Lewis, John W. and Xue, Litai (1993) *Uncertain Partners: Stalin, Mao, and the Korean War*. Stanford University Press: Stanford, CA.
Ha, Joseph M. (1983) The impact of the Sino–Soviet conflict on the Korean Peninsula, in *The Two Koreas in World Politics*, Tae-Hwan Kwak (eds). Wayne Patterson and Edward A. Olsen, The Institute for Far Eastern Studies, Kyungnam University, Seoul, pp. 211–30.
Henderson, Gregory (1968) *The Politics of the Vortex*. Harvard University Press: Cambridge, MA.
Hunter, Helen-Louise (1983) North Korea and the myth of equidistance, in *The Two Koreas in World Politics*, Tae-Hwan Kwak, Wayne Patterson and Edward A. Olsen (eds), The Institute for Far Eastern Studies, Kyungnam University, Seoul, pp. 195–210.
Kim, Alexander Joungwon (1975) *Divided Korea: The Politics of Development 1945–1972*, East Asian Research Center, Harvard University Press: Cambridge, MA.
Kim, Il Sung (1984) *Works Vols 1–39*, Foreign Languages Publishing House, Pyongyang.
Koh, Byung-Chul (1969) The *Pueblo* incident in perspective, *Asian Survey*, IX(4): 264–80.
Koh, Byung-Chul (1984) *The Foreign Policy Systems of North and South Korea*. University of California Press: Berkeley, CA.

Lankov, Andrei (2002) *From Stalin to Kim Il Sung: The Formation of North Korea 1945–1960*. Rutgers University Press: New Brunswick, NJ.

Lee, Chae-Jin (1996) *China and Korea: Dynamic Relations*. The Hoover Press: Stanford, CA.

Lee, Chong-sok (1962) The 'Socialiast Revolution' in the North Korean countryside, *Asian Survey*, II(8): 1–22.

Lee, Chong-sik (1964) Korea: In search of stability, *Asian Survey*, 4(1): 656–65.

Lee, Chong-sik (1965) Stalinism in the East, in *The Communist Revolution in Asia: Tactics, Goals and Achievements*, Robert A. Scalapino (ed.). University of California: Berkeley, CA, pp. 114–39.

Lee, Chong-sik (1982) Evolution of the Korean Workers' Party and the rise of Kim Chong-il, *Asian Survey*, XXII(5): 434–448.

Lee, Hy-Sang (1994) Economic factors in Korean reunification, in *Korea and the World: Beyond the Cold War*, Young-Whan Kihl (ed.). Westview Press: Boulder, CO, pp. 189–216.

Lewin, Moshe (1977) The social background of Stalinism, in *Stalinism: Essays in Historical Interpretation*, Robert C. Tucker (ed.). W.W. Norton: New York.

McEachern, Patrick (2010), *Inside the Red Box: North Korea's Post-Totalitarian Politics*. Coumbia University Press: New York.

Myers, B.R. (2011) *The Cleanest Race*. Melville House: New York.

Myers, B.R. (2015) *North Korea's Juche Myth*. Stehle Press: Busan.

Nam, Koon-Woo (1974) *The North Korean Communist Leadership, 1945–1965: A Study of Factionalism and Political Consolidation*. The University of Alabama Press: Tuscaloosa, AL.

Nisbet, Robert (1976) *The Social Philosophers*. Paladin: St Albans.

Okonogi, Masao (1994) North Korean communism: In search of its prototype, in *Korean Studies: New Pacific Currents*, Dae-Sook Suh (ed.). Center for Korean Studies, University of Hawaii Press: Honolulu, Hawaii, pp. 177–206.

Paige, Glenn D. (1967) Korea, *Asian Survey*, 7(1): 25–9.

Pak, Ki-Hyuk (1983) Agricultural policy and development in North Korea, in *North Korea Today: Strategic and Domestic Issues*, Robert A. Scalapino and Jun-Yop Kim (eds), Institute of East Asian Studies, University of California Press: Berkeley, CA, pp. 214–29.

Palais, James B. (1975) *Politics and Policy in Traditional Korea*. Harvard University Press: Cambridge, MA.

Park, Myung-Lim (1995) North Korea's inner leadership and the decision to launch the Korean war, *Korea and World Affairs*, 19(2): 240–68.

Person, James (ed.) (2009) New evidence on North Korea's chollima movement and first Five Year Plan *1957–61*, available at: www.wilsoncenter.org/sites/default/files/Chollima_DocReader_WebFinal.pdf (accessed September 2016).

Scalapino, Robert A. and Lee, Chong-sik (1972a) *Communism in Korea Part 1: The Movement*. The University of California Press: Berkeley, CA.

Scalapino, Robert A. and Lee, Chong-sik (1972b) *Communism in Korea Part 2: The Society*, The University of California Press: Berkeley, CA.

Schlogel, Karl (2012) *Moscow 1937*. Polity Press: Cambridge.

Simmons, Robert (1971) North Korea: Silver Anniversary, *Asian Survey*, XI(1): 104–10.

Stueck, William (1995) *The Korean War: An International History*. Princeton University Press: Princeton, NJ.

Suh, Dae-Sook (1988) *Kim Il Sung: The North Korean Leader*. Columbia University Press: New York.

Suh, Jae-Jean (1994) Ideology, in *Prospects for Change in North Korea*, Tae-Hwan Ok and Hong-Yung Lee (eds). Institute of East Asian Studies, University of California Press: Berkeley, CA.

Szalontai, Balazs (2005) *Kim Il Sung in the Khrushchev Era: Soviet–Korean Relations and the Roots of North Korean Despotism 1953–1964*. Woodrow Wilson Center Press: Washington, DC.

Szalontai, Balazs (2012) In the shadow of Vietnam: A new look at North Korea's militant strategy,1962–1970, *Journal of Cold War Studies*, 14(4): 122–66.

Tertitskiy, Fyodor (2017) 1967: Transition to absolute autocracy in North Korea, *Change and Continuity in North Korean Politics*, Adam Cathcart, Robert Winstanley-Chesters and Christopher Green (eds). Routledge: London.

Trigubenko, Marina (1991) Industry of the DPRK: Specific features of the industrial policy, sectoral structure and prospects, in *Pukhan kyongje ui hyonhwang gwa chonmang (Current Situation and Outlook for the North Korean Economy)*. Korea Development Institute: Seoul, pp. 101–35.

Tucker, Robert C. (1963) *The Soviet Political Mind: Studies in Stalinism and Post-Stalin Change*. Praeger: New York.

Tucker, Robert C. (1977) Stalinism as revolution from above, in *Stalinism: Essays in Historical Interpretation*, Robert C. Tucker (ed.), W.W. Norton: New York, pp. 77–110.

Ulam, Adam B. (1974) *Stalin: The Man and His Era*. Allen Lane: London.

UN Office of the High Commissioner for Human Rights, Report of the Commission of Inquiry on human rights in the Democratic People's Republic of Korea – A/HRC/25/63.

Volkogonov, Dmitri (1991) *Stalin: Triumph and Tragedy*. Weidenfeld & Nicolson: London.

Yang, Ho-Min (1988) Mao Zedong's Ideological Influence on Pyongyang and Hanoi: Some Historical Roots Reconsidered, in *Asian Communism Continuity and Transition*, Robert A. Scalapino and Dalchoong Kim (eds), Institute of East Asian Studies, University of California: Berkeley, CA, pp. 37–75.

Yang, Sung-Chul (1981) *Korea and two regimes: Kim Il Sung and Park Chung Hee*. Schenckman Publishing Company: Cambridge, MA.

Yang, Sung-Chul (1994) *The North and South Korean Political Systems: A Comparative Analysis*. Westview Press/Seoul Press: Seoul.

Zagoria, Donald S. and Zagoria, Janet D. (1981) Crisis on the Korean Peninsula, in *The Diplomacy of Power: Soviet Armed Forces as a Political Instrument*, Stephen Kaplan et al. (eds). The Brookings Institute: Washington, DC, pp. 357–411.

Zagoria, Donald S. (1983) North Korea: Between Moscow and Beijing, in *North Korea Today: Strategic and Domestic Issues*, Robert A. Scalapino and Jun-Yop Kim (eds), Institute of East Asian Studies, University of California Press: Berkeley, CA, pp. 351–71.

Zhang, Shu Guang (1995) *Mao's Military Romanticism: China and the Korean War, 1950–1953*. University of Kansas Press: Lawrence, KS.

3 The tide turns: 1970–80

Introduction

In 1964 Kim Il Sung had defined three revolutionary fronts in the struggle for Korean reunification – within the DPRK, within the ROK and internationally – and in 1970 a survey of these fronts may well have given him some cause for encouragement. Within the DPRK, he would have noted with approval that the political system of the DPRK had graduated through the collectivist, Leninist party stage to exclusive dependence on his personal authority and judgement. He had defined his country's mission, he was far beyond challenge, he had a group of unquestioning loyal lieutenants and he believed that the succession of his son would perpetuate his system. In the economic sphere, fifteen years of intensive mobilisation had produced a military–industrial sector capable of supplying most of the armed forces' basic needs. Serious shortcomings in the economic planning system had emerged during the First Seven-Year Plan period (1961–7), but he was incapable of evaluating the ominous implications of this since the role in cannibalising the economy played by excessive concentration on military–industrial capacity and production was not clear to him. Meanwhile, the country was still well on its way to becoming, as he frequently and ritually described it, an 'impregnable fortress of socialism'.

Kim would have also found grounds for encouragement in developments within the ROK, though not without considerable assistance from ideologically driven faith. The KWP's efforts to conduct effective espionage activities and to build a Marxist–Leninist Party within the ROK had failed, as had the direct military pressure of the 1966–9 period, but Kim was able to convince himself that this was not the result of any strategic miscalculation. Rather, he assessed that the relevant cadres in charge of southern operations had clearly failed to carry out his instructions and he punished them accordingly. Meanwhile, Kim's belief in the revolutionary potential of the South was unshakeable, and since dogma compensated for more sober judgement, he believed that success was only a matter of time. In his analysis, the ROK political system was inherently unstable and he did not see any particular threat in the on-going pattern of rapid economic growth that had begun to take hold, as publicly (and probably privately) he judged it to be the achievement of a 'bubble economy', destined to collapse under the weight of its own contradictions.

The international front was still turbulent and also offered some hope. United States military support for the ROK remained the crucial factor blocking reunification on the North's terms, but in 1970 the US was in a substantially weakened position when compared with even five years previously. In 1968 Lyndon Johnson had been forced to abandon any hope of a further term of office by the depth of anti-Vietnam War feeling in the US, and by 1970 there was evidence of widespread demoralisation in the US military in Vietnam. Also, by 1970 the US was beginning to waver in its twenty-year-old policy of containing China. The 1969 Nixon Doctrine had essentially told Asian allies that they would have to take major responsibility for their own security in future, with the US only providing *matériel* assistance and the backstop of a nuclear umbrella. Related US plans to sharply reduce troop levels in the ROK thus gave the ever-wishful Kim substantial grounds for confidence that the US commitment to defend the ROK might not last.

In contrast to the ROK's uncertainties with the US, the DPRK had the benefit of a pair of stable alliances that guaranteed its security. Neither the Soviet Union nor China would support another war in Korea, but the DPRK's policies of Equal Emphasis and self-reliance meant that its partners could no longer veto the war either. This gave Kim some room to manoeuvre, for if he did resume the Korean conflict and the tide turned against him, the Soviets and the Chinese would probably have to intervene diplomatically, if not militarily, to ensure that the DPRK did not disappear from the map. The alternative would be to forfeit a significant buffer state on their respective eastern borders. This meant that the DPRK could survive military defeat while the ROK could not – perhaps a dire calculation, but it was also a logical one that Kim had already seen borne out during 1950–3.

However, by 1980 much of the sense of satisfaction Kim could derive from these circumstances would have evaporated, for the 1970s laid bare important gaps in Kim's analysis, revealing much that was screened out by ideology, was too hallowed by past experience to invite close scrutiny, or was too abstract for him to grasp. These gaps caused him to not only grossly overestimate the strength of his own system but also to underestimate the growing challenges to the DPRK on all three revolutionary fronts. In the process, they emphasised the primitiveness of the DPRK's adaptive capacities, and so during the 1970s Kim continued to enforce the same policies he had established in the 1960s. Within the North, the terror of the late 1960s subsided, and the composition of the Party elite had at last become relatively stable. However, it was a stability based on overwhelming reliance on the Manchurian guerilla generation, a cadre that may have oiled the machinery of the Kimist system, but which was incapable of contributing anything much beyond continuing unconditional loyalty to the leader. Its members were all to grow old in office together, and thus little new blood appeared, other than Kim Jong Il, a younger man but groomed to rule in the interests of the older generation. Meanwhile, the economy slowly subsided into a period of stagnation from which it would never re-emerge.

In dealing with the ROK, the DPRK had no more success during the 1970s than during the 1960s. Pyongyang discontinued direct military confrontation with the South, partly because of pressure from China and Moscow to reduce tension on the Korean Peninsula, and perhaps partly because Kim no longer believed that small-scale special operations were effective under prevailing circumstances. Instead, the DPRK intensified its on-going build-up of the KPA in anticipation of opportunities for full-scale warfare emerging from the fluid international situation. Meanwhile, in July 1972 the two sides at last met face to face in high-level negotiations on reunification, but within eighteen months the dialogue was stalemated. The years that followed were then marked by the continuing refusal of the DPRK to recognise the existence of the ROK Government, by a continuing, massive DPRK military build-up and by strong evidence of the DPRK's continuing aggressive intent. But despite significant political unrest in the ROK during the period of Park Chung-hee's restrictive Yushin Constitution (1972–9), popular opinion in the South remained strongly anti-communist, while the ROK economy maintained a rapid growth trajectory, such that by 1980 the size of its economy was nearly four times that of the DPRK.

In the international arena the principal challenge to the DPRK came from the US. After 1968, the Nixon administration adjusted rapidly and effectively to the looming reality of defeat in Vietnam, and in 1970 it initiated a substantial rapprochement with China. Soon after, it also initiated a compensatory process of détente with the Soviet Union. The overall effect of these two moves was to greatly enhance the commitment of the DPRK's major allies to maintaining stability on the Korean Peninsula, and perforce this meant tacit recognition of the status quo. Moreover, the DPRK was forced to confront the continuing re-emergence of Japan as a major regional economic and diplomatic power, a development that worked sharply against DPRK interests, for the revived Japanese state was influential as a strong US ally, was achieving rapprochement with China and was playing an ever-expanding role in support of the ROK's economic growth.

In the 1960s, Kim Il Sung had erected the Kimist system on the pillars of personal autocracy, a militarised economy and society, and independence within the international communist movement. However, as the 1970s progressed, the system he had created proved to be rigid and ineffective in identifying and responding to an array of significant challenges. The major questions for an understanding of the DPRK during the 1970s therefore revolve around the nature of these challenges and the reasons why the DPRK advanced such a minimal response to mounting evidence of unsuccessful state policies.

Changes in the Party: the rise of Kim Jong Il

The full extent of the 1967–8 purges became clear when the Fifth Party Congress convened in Pyongyang during 2–13 November 1970. After the events of the 1960s, it was not surprising to note a heavy turnover of cadres in the new Politburo, comprising eleven full members and four alternate members.[1] Some idea of this turnover emerges from a comparison with the Politburo elected by the Fourth Congress. Of the sixteen full and alternate members of the Politburo who were elected in 1961, only four had survived the ensuing decade of intra-Party warfare (see Table 3.1). For their replacements, Kim turned again to the ranks of his former Manchurian colleagues and this time found a group willing to accept his personal autocracy. All the new members except Kim Chung-nin, Yang Hyong-sop and Chong Chun-t'aek are believed to have fought in Manchuria with Kim Il Sung, while Kim Yong-ju was Kim's younger brother.[2] The Central Committee as a whole also continued to experience rapid turnover. Eighteen of the top thirty were new appointees, as were 72 per cent of the 117 full members and 87 per cent of the alternate members. Only 31 of the 85 full members elected at the 1961 Congress of Victors were among the 117 full members elected to Fifth KWP Central Committee, a survival rate of 26.5 per cent.

With the election of the Fifth KWP Congress Politburo, the practice of rapid turnover in its ranks ceased. All but three of the fifteen Politburo members elected in 1970 either died with their ranking intact or else were still Politburo members at the time of Kim Il Sung's death in 1994. This onset

Table 3.1 Comparison of Fourth and Fifth KWP Congress Politburos

The Fourth KWP Congress (1961) Politburo	The Fifth KWP Congress (1970) Politburo
1 – Kim Il Sung	1 – Kim Il Sung
2 – Ch'oe Yong-gon	2 – Ch'oe Yong-gon#
3 – Kim Il	3 – Kim Il#
4 – Pak Kum-ch'ol*	4 – Park Song-ch'ol##
5 – Kim Ch'ang-man*	5 – Ch'oe Hyon##
6 – Yi Hyo-sun*	6 – Kim Yong-ju##
7 – Pak Chong-ae*	7 – O Jin-u##
8 – Kim Kwang-hyop*	8 – Kim Tong-gyu**
9 – Chong Il-yong*	9 – So Ch'ol#
10 – Nam Il*	10 – Kim Chung-nin##
11 – Yi Chong-ok*#	11 – Han Ik-su**
12 – Kim Ik-son*	12 – Hyon Mu-gwang ##
13 – Yi Chu-yon*	13 – Chong Chun-t'aek #
14 – Ha Ang-ch'on*	14 – Yang Hyong-sop##
15 – Han Sang-du*	15 – Kim Man-gum**
16 – Hyon Mu-gwang	

Notes: * purged during the 1960s; *# purged during the 1960s, rehabilitated during the 1970s; ** purged during the 1970s; # died in office with state funeral; ## outlived Kim Il Sung.

Source: DPRK media

of stability closely coincided with the final establishment of Kim's personal autocracy and indicated that Kim had at last succeeded in assembling a group of cadres who unconditionally supported this autocracy or else had put aside any vestige of independent thinking. Moreover, in a manner strongly reminiscent of Mao and Stalin, Kim Il had a fraught relationship with technocrats, or 'experts', regarding them with suspicion and always subordinating them to cadres in the Party organization–military generalist mould. And so like the intellectuals, many technocrats fell steadily by the wayside during the 1950s, leaving behind a new generation of economic managers who were not experts in economic management per se, but were technologically minded loyalist cadres capable of applying Chollima-type mass mobilisation techniques to the operation of the economy. Some of these cadres eventually advanced to the status of alternate Politburo member in the 1980s, but a solid phalanx of ex-Manchurian guerilla Party organisation and military men always remained above them in the rankings.[3] At all times, the Party controlled not only the gun, but also the library, the science laboratory, the lecture hall, and especially the factory floor and the factory manager's office.

The slow, measured emergence of Kim Jong Il as a force within the KWP constituted the major development in DPRK domestic politics during the 1970s, and it had far-reaching consequences. Kim was born in the Soviet Union on 16 February 1942 to Kim Chong-suk, Kim Il Sung's first wife who died in 1949.[4] He could not have had a more different upbringing from his father, for in contrast to the latter's story of privation, exile, early orphanhood and immersion in guerilla violence, the son was a princeling, raised in comparative comfort, though he lost a brother to a pool drowning accident in 1948 and his mother to illness the following year when he was seven years old. During the Korean War, Kim Il Sung's immediate family members were evacuated to the far north, then to Jilin in Manchuria, and after the war comfort became egregious privilege, though it also led to social isolation, first within the world of the Party elite and further within the world of the other children of ex-guerillas. Hagiography has, of course, portrayed Kim Jong Il as revealing the outstanding attributes of a future leader from an early age, but from the more mundane reports of those who knew him at the time we can conclude that he was a well-socialised, intellectually bright adolescent.[5]

After four years at Kimilsung University (1960–4), during which his training for a future leading role in the Party became more and more overt, Kim Jong Il entered the KWP Organisation and Guidance Department, where he began to acquire the type of situational awareness necessary for future leadership with an initial focus on the world of culture and the arts, and where he oversaw the creation of a canon of appalling militarist stage spectacles whose deeply disturbing characteristics often seem to evade the sensibilities of outside observers who simply regard them as bizarre, exotic kitsch. That aside, the timing of his entry into formal Party work meant that he never experienced the KWP as an even vaguely collectivist Marxist–Leninist Party, for it had now entered the final stages of accepting Kim Il Sung's monolithic ideology and leadership.[6] To him, the task was to secure his father's personal autocracy as a necessary condition for his own advancement, and in this process the Party was an adversary, not an ally, for prior to the 1967–68 purges significant elements in the Party leadership had opposed Kim Il Sung's emerging plans for hereditary succession.[7]

We do not know how or when Kim Il Sung settled on the idea of a dynastic succession. He may have always harboured it, for we see no sign of any mentoring or the designating of any other successor within the Party. Somewhere along the line, though, his ambitions changed from playing a paramount role in the shaping of the future of the DPRK while he lived to ruling the DPRK from beyond the grave, with evidence pointing to the period 1967–68 as crucial (Chong-sik Lee, 1982: 441), for this was the period when selected members of his family, especially his parents, also began to be portrayed in the media as revolutionary heroes, suggesting that by this time Kim had already decided on Kim Jong Il as the inheritor of such virtues and a worthy guardian of the country's fortunes.

Following his milestone thirtieth birthday in February 1972, the younger Kim's process of emergence gathered pace. In terms of his institutional power within the KWP, from his base in culture and the arts he began to expand his activities to cover agitprop and ideology, and in order to carry out an ever-expanding number of tasks Kim began to put together a major personal secretariat, widely assumed to have been founded on the now-purified KWP Organisation and Guidance Department (OGD), the direction of which he took over from his uncle in 1973. As its name suggests, the OGD had wide powers in organising the fundamental structure of Party and government and in determining the career paths of key personnel, and it was therefore able to intervene at will in many specialist areas of policy.

All the while, Kim Jong Il made no official public appearances, gave no official speeches and the media did not mention him by name, an item of protocol that continued until the Sixth KWP Congress in 1980. Thus, his elevation to the KWP Politburo at the Eighth Plenum of the Fifth KWP Central Committee in February 1974 was not announced publicly. Nevertheless, beginning around April 1974 people became aware of his activities chiefly through the activities of an entity called the Party Centre (*Tang chung'ang*), whereby references to the Party Centre or else to specific code words and phrases in Party literature and the public media indicated ideological pronouncements whose authority emanated from Kim Jong Il. Simultaneously, a cult of personality began to form around him, featuring songs of loyalty and study sessions on his writings. By 1975 his portrait hung in schools, uncaptioned magazine photos showed him in the company of top military leaders such as O Chin-u, and Party cadres and government workers were well aware which senior Party figures were close to Kim Jong Il.[8]

Why did Kim Jong Il remain behind the scenes for such an extended period of time? This seeming coyness on the part of an absolute ruler who could have simply forced this issue might seem strange, but there were basic sensitivities involved, probably best illustrated by the fact that the 1970 edition of the DPRK Academy of Social Science's own *Dictionary of Political Terminologies* carried the general Marxist definition of hereditary succession as 'a reactionary custom practised in exploitive societies'.[9] Internationally, the marriage of Marxist–Leninist ideology with hereditary succession also carried a price, for it gave the DPRK considerable presentational problems in dealing with fraternal parties and with the more politically sophisticated members of the Non-Aligned Movement. Within the DPRK, Kim Il Sung might well have viewed the hereditary succession as essential for the preservation and continuation of his life's work, but the careful preparation he devoted to building up his son's claims to political leadership shows that he was not sure whether either senior cadres or the general populace would as yet willingly and spontaneously accept his son as leader. In these circumstances, Kim appears to have decided to take a longer way around, clearing the way for his son at the top level and then disingenuously portraying his rise as an irresistible tide issuing from within the Party.

After 1974, Kim Jong Il became associated with the specific policy areas of literature and the arts, economic production 'speed battles', the glorification of Kim Il Sung and especially Kim's anti-Japanese guerilla activities, the strengthening of cadre study practices,[10] and especially the direction of the Red Guard-like 'Three Revolutions Teams'.[11] These teams comprised groups of young Party zealots who were dispatched to various economic and administrative organs of the state with the mission of uncovering and correcting ideologically unhealthy practices. The nature of such practices can only be guessed at, but given the ideological rigours of the previous fifteen years or so, TRT's activities could hardly have been practical. More plausibly, they would probably have been directed towards testing out the loyalty of local cadres and their responsiveness to the succession, identifying true believers and empowering them to deal with recalcitrants. In this manner, Kim Jong Il was able to refocus the Party on his agenda, based on even more rigorous definitions of ideological correctness than had previously been tolerated.

However, even such careful preparation plans did not guarantee success, and in fact the hitherto smooth pattern of references to the Party Centre in the KWP theoretical journal *Kulloja* was broken and references ceased almost entirely between April 1977 and February 1979, indicating a marked decline in the significance being attributed to the younger Kim's activities.[12] This was reportedly because some senior cadres were uneasy with Kim Jong Il's activities, but again Kim Il Sung forced the issue, and in 1977 purged Politburo members Kim Tong-gyu, Yu Chang-sik and Yi Yong-mu, and demoted Politburo members Yang Hyong-sop and Kim Chung-nin (Mansourov, 2006: 57–58). Kim Tong-gyu and Yi Yong-mu made their last public appearances in September and October 1977 respectively, Yang Hyong-sop and Kim Chung-nin were dropped from the Politburo in May and September 1977 respectively (Dae-Sook Suh, 1988: 281), and by 1980 Kim Il Sung had surmounted these difficulties so that his son could publicly assume his place at the apex of the Party at the Sixth KWP Congress in October 1980.[13]

The Kim Jong Il succession was a reactionary move, centred on the need for a 'model revolutionary' to consolidate Kim's ideological system. This was duly accomplished, but in the economic sphere the younger Kim's name was associated with policies and activities that were the antithesis of reform, including prestige and monumental constructions, Stakhanovite 'speed battles' and a further tightening of Party control over economic activity. In the ideological sphere, his consolidation of a power base within the Party through direction of the activities of the Three Revolutions Teams helped to maintain the rigidity of the system. This meant that at a time when some expected the DPRK, as an industrialising society, to begin manifesting increasing technological sophistication and specialisation, and also to begin moving in the direction of political pragmatism, the younger Kim emerged not as an embodiment of a new generation reflecting this trend, but as an agent of the old revolutionary generation of his father. From the beginning, the role of Kim Jong Il aimed at perpetuating the ideology of the 1950s and forestalling any attempts at reform by subsequent generations.

Economic decline

The effects of this new ideological orientation on the economy were severe. At the Fifth KWP Congress in 1970, Kim Il Sung had endorsed much of the country's economic performance during the 1960s by proclaiming the successful completion of the First Seven-Year Plan (1961–7) after a three-year extension (1967–70), and by promulgating the new Six-Year Plan (1971–6), which projected rates of state investment comparable to rates during the 1960s and which unambiguously continued the emphasis on heavy industry. However, Kim's euphoria over the results of the First Seven-Year Plan was not justified by actual economic performance. Even from the sparse and selective statistics available, there are clear indications that in many sectors the First Seven-Year Plan did not meet its stated targets or, where it did, it needed three extra years of production to do so. Nevertheless, the outcomes were clearly acceptable to Kim, because they were placing at his disposal substantial military assets that might be crucial in the years ahead.

The full extent of the DPRK's economic backwardness and mismanagement began to become clear during 1972–4 when the DPRK carried out a shortlived programme of massive purchases of Western plant and machinery on credit. The purchases included a complete French petrochemical plant, one of the world's largest cement plants, a large fertiliser plant, Japanese textile factories and steel-making equipment, a Swiss watch factory, a Finnish pulp and paper mill, and substantial amounts of Swedish mining and smelting equipment.[14] As a result, trade with the West as a proportion of total foreign trade rose from 11.1 per cent in 1965 to 40.6 per cent in 1975 (Namkoong and Yoo, 1994: 132). Evidently, the DPRK planned to pay for these purchases with the export income they were expected to generate, but in a re-run of its economic planning in the reconstruction period immediately after the Korean War, its economic planning skills proved grossly deficient.[15] In many cases, economic sectors and units did not possess the planning capacities, building technology skills, infrastructure sophistication or managerial skills to absorb the purchases, while workmen were deficient in basic tradesman skills and not able to adapt to the precision construction and operating demands of plants using advanced Western technology.[16] Many plants remained inoperable or else made only a marginal contribution to the national economy, and in these circumstances, other setbacks such as the first oil crisis in 1973 and the depressed state of the international commodity market for the DPRK's non-ferrous metals had a considerable effect. By 1974, these large-scale foreign purchases had almost ceased, though not before the DPRK had acquired a sizeable foreign debt.[17]

These efforts to address the major problem of declining productivity by introducing advanced Western technology into the economy reflected a leadership that was now clearly out of touch with the realities and capacities of the DPRK economy. The government carried out the purchasing program in an ad hoc manner, so much so that at no time did it link this program to any facet of the on-going Six-Year Plan. In essence, it attempted to graft a series of major industrial projects on to the existing primitive economic structure, seemingly unaware of their economic planning and technological implications. More tellingly, this initiative did not signal any modification of ideological parameters, and in fact was contradicted by the further entrenching of mass mobilisation campaigns through the Three Revolutions Teams movement.

The failure to achieve any significant economic result from these purchases other than a sizeable foreign debt did not seem to make any particular impression on Kim. In the area of economic administration, one would naturally have expected the government ministers and Party officials responsible for what can only be described as a debacle to suffer demotion or dismissal, yet this did not occur. The Minister for External Economic Affairs during this period (1972–5), Kong Chin-t'ae, was in fact promoted to a Vice Premiership in 1975, and both Kong and the nominal Minister for Foreign Trade during this period, Kye Ung-t'ae, both Politburo members, continued to play a major role in foreign trade and to enjoy high Party ranking for many years afterwards, signalling that Kim did not regard their actions as in any way blameworthy. Nor did comprehension come with the passage of time, for in an interview on 20 June 1977 with a *Le Monde* correspondent, we find him dismissing the trade deficit as 'a passing phenomenon' and 'a temporary difficulty'. Characteristically, fault lay elsewhere, in this case with 'the economic difficulty of the advanced capitalist countries of the West caused by the [oil shocks] ... they are unable to purchase our goods' (Byung-Chul Koh, 1978: 39).

The significance of this failure was considerable, however. It reflected the extent to which the leadership had become endemically removed from competent economic advice and management through its purges of the technocrats in the mid-1960s. It also provided clear evidence that the economy had become technologically backward and inefficient, and this had clear long-term implications for the war-making potential of the state, not to mention people's standard of living, which now went into a steady, unbroken decline.[18] Internationally, the erratic fashion in which the DPRK had gone about these purchases and then the way it dealt with the aftermath – frequent defaulting and then outright reneging on repayment schedules – effectively cut the country off from further access to foreign investment and advanced technology with serious long-term consequences. While ignorance of what constituted acceptable international commercial practice is the most frequently offered explanation for the DPRK's actions in this sphere, this is too simple an explanation for such repeat offences. The DPRK's attitude was more calculated than this, demonstrating a fixed, cynical view of the international economy as a predatory environment in which flouting the conventions of normal international commercial behaviour was justified.

Changes on the international front

The intellectual limitations of Kimist ideology were especially in evidence through Pyongyang's responses to the important shifts that were taking place in the strategic thinking of both Korea's major big power allies during this period. In June 1971, US National Security Advisor Henry Kissinger visited Beijing, formally inaugurating the process of Sino–US rapprochement that led to US President Richard M. Nixon's visit to Beijing in February 1972, and eventually to full normalisation of relations in 1979. Sino–US rapprochement had a substantial impact on the Korean Peninsula because as part of this rapprochement, both the US and China sought to stabilise the situation there, and so they encouraged their respective Korean allies to engage in dialogue.

To the two Koreas, these moves emphasised the speed at which the regional balance of power could change and also emphasised their vulnerability to changes in the national interests of their respective patrons. The DPRK had already sought to eliminate this vulnerability with a policy of extreme self-reliance, and now the ROK leadership also began to question the extent of its military dependence on the US. In the space of five years, Park Chung-hee had seen the US position in the region change from resolute prosecution of the Vietnam War to demoralisation and defeat. By 1970, the US security role in Korea seemed especially fragile, and so when in March 1970 the US advised the ROK government that it was withdrawing 20,000 troops – one-third of its total force in Korea – the ROK made no attempt to conceal its distress and anger at this development, and the acrimonious exchanges that followed precipitated some very deep and fundamental rethinking in Seoul about the shape of a future without firm US security guarantees.[19] Motivation to seek some sort of political accommodation with the DPRK strengthened accordingly.

The situation had also changed for the DPRK, though not nearly to the same extent because the underlying Chinese commitment to the security of the DPRK remained far less in doubt. However, in less than three years Kim Il Sung had seen Chinese foreign policy change from energetic confrontation with US imperialism to the advocacy of dialogue. Kim interpreted the July 1971 announcement of the Nixon visit as 'a trip of the defeated that fully reflects the declining fate of US imperialism'[20] and this comment, along with many similar comments, reflects a characteristic, profound misjudgement. In addition, Sino–US rapprochement came at a time when Kim was regrouping after the failure of his 1966–69 campaign of confrontation against the South and reassessing tactics, though not strategy. He therefore had nothing to lose and everything to gain from entering into dialogue.

Both Koreas therefore had reason to begin talks, and so when in August 1971 the ROK Red Cross Committee proposed talks on humanitarian issues such as the reuniting of separated families, their northern counterparts accepted this proposal. A year-long process of liaison committee and preparatory committee talks followed, leading to full-scale talks in Pyongyang in August 1972 and in Seoul in September. On the political level, in May 1972 the two sides exchanged top-level secret envoys and on 4 July signed an agreement to hold full political talks. Thus began what has become a long, drawn-out process of sporadic contact and negotiation between the two Koreas.

This process has not been continuous, with almost all significant negotiation concentrated into four short passages of negotiation, each lasting less than two years: 1972–3, 1984–6, 1990–1 and 2000–2. The intervening periods have seen a resumption of traditional DPRK policies of military confrontation and in the 1980s outright terrorism against the ROK. Moreover, the actual achievements of these negotiations have been meagre. Despite summit talks in 2000 and 2007 and the convening of a variety of official, unofficial, open and secret meetings to discuss political, economic, military, humanitarian, cultural and sporting issues, the two Koreas have rarely moved past procedural matters. Where they have signed communiqués or agreements, sufficient commonality of purpose to achieve meaningful implementation has not been present. Typically, such agreements were hailed in the international media as breakthroughs heralding change, but this was not so: they were, in fact, agreements on the ground rules for the beginning of negotiation. However, in each case the next development was not substantive negotiation based on the framework of the agreements, but insistence by the North that the South accept unilateral Pyongyang interpretations of the statements as preconditions to further talks. In each case the interpretations defined either the continued presence of US forces in the ROK or ROK internal security laws, or both, as incompatible with further negotiation. Stalemate then ensued, with the DPRK bringing a unilateral halt to negotiations at a time of its own choosing amid charges of bad faith against the South.

The 1972–73 phase of talks proceeded in accordance with this pattern. It began with a pair of far-reaching umbrella agreements in both the humanitarian and political fields. In June 1972 Red Cross committees exchanged documents of agreement on an agenda for full-dress talks that included locating dispersed families, home visits, facilitating the reunion of dispersed families and the free exchange of mail. Shortly after, discussions between senior political figures produced the 4 July 1972 joint communiqué, which enunciated three fundamental principles for the achievement of unification: that it be pursued independently without outside interference, that it be pursued peacefully and that 'a great national unity, as a homogeneous people, shall be sought first, transcending differences in ideas, ideologies and systems'.[21] However, in October Pyongyang indicated that Red Cross talks could not proceed while ROK national security laws remained in force. Evidently, the North's far more draconian set of security laws was not a barrier, but this aside, Pyongyang's stance effectively deadlocked the Red Cross talks.

In March 1973, the deadlock spread to the high-level political talks, when the DPRK drew up this stance into a five-point proposal that included withdrawal of US troops, mutual troop reductions and weapons controls, all to be guaranteed by a peace treaty. The proposed first order of business was to negotiate a military withdrawal and peace treaty to replace the Military Armistice Agreement with the US since it viewed the latter as the real belligerent on the southern side. Upon the removal of what among other things was the cornerstone of the ROK's national defence structure without corresponding concessions of its own, the DPRK's second order of business was then to negotiate a political settlement with the ROK government. After a fruitless exchange of positions at the second plenary meeting of the South–North Coordinating Committee (SNCC) in Pyongyang in March 1973, the DPRK resumed low-level military violence on the DMZ, and in August 1973 the talks effectively ceased altogether. The two Koreas held a series of brief and insubstantial meetings in early 1980 after the assassination of Park Chung-hee in October 1979, but no further substantive negotiations took place until 1984.

To the North, the 1972–73 talks revealed no evidence of exploitable disorganisation or demoralisation in the South, and this encouraged a continuation of its traditional policy of maintaining strong military pressure on the ROK. In breaking off dialogue, Kim Il Sung demonstrated tactical rigidity, but also a continuing conviction that he was dealing from a position of strength and could afford to wait. Here he was encouraged by the restored DPRK–Chinese alliance under which China had become Pyongyang's leading arms supplier by 1973, by a belief that the tide of international events, as measured by events in Indochina, the Middle East and in the Third World, was flowing against the imperialist camp, and by the capacity of his own on-going military build-up to force the issue more effectively than negotiation in the foreseeable future.[22]

The military option

The evidence for DPRK preparedness to pursue a military option for reunification during the 1970s is substantial. First, there was a considerable build-up of offensive weapons such as tanks (750 in 1971 to 2,650 in 1980), field artillery pieces (2,300 to 4,000) and armoured personnel carriers (192 to 1,000). Second, this build-up was matched by the continued forward deployment of the bulk of the DPRK's combat divisions.[23] Third, analysis of DPRK population figures from the 1970s suggest that the size of the DPRK's armed forces also rose substantially during this period, from about 400,000 in 1970 to 700,000 in 1975 to nearly 1 million in the late 1970s, in a process that fixed the period of national service at ten years.[24] Fourth, beginning in November 1974, the South detected three elaborate infiltration tunnels entering the DMZ from the North, whose construction is believed to date from 1972. Fifth, and most important, at no stage had the DPRK forsworn the policies of the 1960s. The same leader was in charge, surrounded by the same men who had fully backed his militancy, the rhetoric was the same, and there had been neither public redefinition of Pyongyang's strategy nor evidence of private redefinition.

However, the North could not act unilaterally without facing oblivion. Hence, it continued to look to the re-creation of the same kind of international situation that had enabled it to go to war in 1950: a strong, international anti-imperialist coalition that would provide backing for its reunification strategy and enable effective military action against the ROK without the threat of US intervention. However, with the Sino–Soviet split and the growing Soviet commitment to peaceful coexistence with the US during the 1960s, the DPRK had seen hopes of that coalition ever re-emerging fade, and by the early 1970s US–Soviet détente had become a further alarming trend for the DPRK. Within the limits imposed by rivalry with China in the region, Moscow now actively sought to persuade the DPRK to acknowledge the larger web of national interests that made up the balance of power in Northeast Asia and especially to acknowledge the desire of the USSR to avoid military confrontation with the US. This was not a message that was well received in Pyongyang, and so relations with the Soviets remained cool, correct and low key for much of the 1970s, with routine, non-political exchanges continuing, but without high-level political exchanges or visits. In 1972–3, Moscow's reservations were reflected in a series of low-key but significant gestures towards the ROK, which signalled Soviet readiness to have dealings with the Park regime in the course of ordinary international sporting and commercial transactions,[25] and the same thinking was evident in the withholding of advanced weaponry from the DPRK while at the same time supplying this weaponry to Egypt and Syria.

Relations became especially strained in the mid-1970s, first when the DPRK implicitly began to endorse Chinese criticism of Soviet 'dominationism', which referred to residual Soviet claims to a position of international leadership of the communist movement, and then in the aftermath of the August 1976 axe killings incident at Panmunjom.[26] This incident seemed to confirm the Soviets' worst fears about DPRK adventurism and, as a mark of displeasure, they refused DPRK requests for assistance in meeting initial payments on their recently acquired hard currency debts, precipitating both a rescheduling of the debt and a significant downturn in DPRK trade with the Soviet Bloc.[27] At the very end of the 1970s, however, relations again improved as the DPRK expressed support for the December 1979 Soviet intervention in Afghanistan, accepting the Soviet assertion so widely rejected elsewhere that an intra-party putsch in Kabul had necessitated intervention.

In contrast to the tensions in the Soviet relationship, the DPRK maintained warm, steady relations with China, where policies remained essentially driven by Maoism until the late 1970s. There had always been a more solid basis for a friendly, pragmatic China–DPRK relationship than was the case with the Soviet Union, although this never translated into more Chinese leverage in Pyongyang, and certainly not into any Chinese role as a 'restraining hand'. The main drivers of the relationship were the DPRK's greater strategic interdependence with China, its closer ideological affinity with a China untainted by revisionism and the strength of China's support for the DPRK position on reunification, which in no small part issued out of Beijing's need for consistency with its own policy on Taiwan. Following Zhou Enlai's 1970 visit to Pyongyang, there were continual exchanges at the highest level, and as the Soviets grew increasingly reluctant to supply the DPRK with up-to-date military hardware, China stepped in and became Pyongyang's leading supplier. This phase of relations culminated in Kim Il Sung's April 1975 visit to China, his first official overseas visit in thirteen years, where he reportedly asked the Chinese bluntly if they would support a military strike against the South, an option under more than usually active consideration in Pyongyang at the time, immensely encouraged as Kim was by the fall of Saigon only a few days previously.

However, at the close of the 1970s, relations with China again grew more distant following the signing of the Sino–Japanese peace treaty in September 1978, the full normalisation of US–China relations on 1 January 1979 and the China–Vietnam border conflict in February 1979, the latter alarming to the DPRK, also a border state with China pursuing policies not always in China's interest. While to some extent the DPRK had been able to rationalise away the first Chinese moves towards the US and Japan in the early 1970s, these subsequent events provided clear evidence that good relations with these two bitter enemies of the DPRK were now a central feature of Chinese foreign policy.[28]

The other major feature of the DPRK's international relations in the 1970s was its participation in the Non-Aligned Movement (NAM). After energetic lobbying, the DPRK was admitted to the NAM as a full member at the Lima Conference of August 1975. In joining the NAM, Kim seems to have genuinely believed that this movement would become a powerful force in international politics, and despite an obvious array of weaknesses and limiting factors, many other people also thought this way at the time. In the avowed principles and especially in the rhetoric of the NAM, Kim thought he detected a valuable forum in which to promote an anti-imperialist agenda, to promote the DPRK's reunification policies and, of course, to promote his own image as a significant international figure.

At the NAM Summit Conference in Colombo in August 1976, the DPRK made a massive lobbying effort to have this meeting endorse its stance on Korean reunification, but while it achieved its objective, its aggressive methods of diplomacy proved counter-productive. An unprecedented number of countries recorded written reservations on the relevant resolution, while still more were reportedly offended by the DPRK's resort to bribery and physical threats to secure votes.[29] Thereafter, diplomatic support for the DPRK within the NAM also began to dwindle. To many influential NAM members such as Josip Broz Tito of Yugoslavia, the DPRK had initially seemed a hopeful sign of the future – a former close Soviet ally which now embraced non-alignment. However, once admitted to the NAM, the DPRK pursued a highly political agenda based on anti-imperialist ideology. It failed to perceive the diversity, disunity and multiple agendas operating within the NAM, and was especially out of touch with the views of the more moderate and diplomatically sophisticated members who had no interest in the adoption of a highly political, confrontationist agenda. Moreover, in the wake of the Panmunjom axe killings and as the extent of the DPRK's foreign debt and its erratic way of dealing with this debt became clear in 1975–6, the DPRK lost credibility as a responsible NAM member-state. The NAM did not, of course, become anything like the powerful anti-imperialist force envisioned by Pyongyang, but even in dealing with the movement as it was, the DPRK reinforced the general international perception that it was out of touch with international political and economic realities to an often staggering degree.[30]

Concluding remarks

By 1980, the situation on all three fronts of Kim Il Sung's revolution had begun to deteriorate markedly. Within the DPRK his personal autocracy remained unchallenged and unchallengeable, and after some vicissitudes he had managed to have his son accepted as his heir and successor, thus guaranteeing that, should he die before his time, the country would continue to follow his policies. Furthermore, he continued a substantial military build-up and maintained a credible military threat despite ever-diminishing economic resources, but perversely, these apparent sources of strength were in fact further weakening the state. The economy had stagnated and had no means of accessing new inputs other than human labour, especially since Pyongyang's unwillingness to take responsibility for its sizeable foreign debt had cut it off from further external credit. Moreover, a simple extrapolation of the respective growth rates achieved by the two Koreas in the 1970s suggested that whether or not the South eventually collapsed under the weight of its own economic contradictions as Kim believed it would, in the meantime the ROK would enjoy an alarming economic superiority over the DPRK with obvious diplomatic and military consequences.

Developments in the ROK were likewise unfavourable for the DPRK cause. Pyongyang remained optimistic of political and economic collapse in the South and had some grounds for optimism. The domestic political unrest that had continued for much of the decade culminated indirectly in the assassination of Park Chung-hee on 26 October 1979, and the country faced an uncertain political future in the immediate aftermath. On the economic front as well, the ROK economy entered into a deep recession in the wake of the 1979 oil shocks, and this probably again raised DPRK hopes that its bubble economy prediction was well founded, despite a subsequent swift rebound. However, wishful thinking and ideological dogma obscured the underlying reality that the ROK economy was immeasurably stronger in 1980 than in 1970. While industrial development had been uneven, the ROK had become a growing regional economic power. It possessed a substantial industrial infrastructure, with an international standard integrated steel mill in POSCO, massive shipyards, vast and sophisticated metal processing, chemical, machine tool and electronics sectors, and an automobile industry that had just launched the first Korea-designed and built automobile, the Hyundai Pony, on the international market.

However, it was on the international front that the DPRK suffered its most serious reverses during the 1970s. The US recovered from its post-Vietnam War malaise and again became a stable regional presence, its commitment to the defence of the ROK acquiring a new firmness by the end of the decade. During the 1970s, the US also entered into a process of détente with the Soviet Union and effected diplomatic normalisation with China, thus extinguishing any lingering hopes the DPRK might have held for support from such quarters if it were to invade the South. Finally, the hopes that Kim Il Sung had pinned on DPRK participation in the Non-Aligned Movement proved to be illusory. The movement itself displayed little interest in the DPRK cause, and individual members were interested strictly in proportion to the provision of foreign aid or other material benefits on offer. In sum, in dealing with a rapidly changing situation, DPRK foreign policy remained ideologically driven and ineffective.

Why, then, did the DPRK display such an almost total lack of interest in change or even marginal adjustment throughout this decade despite the clear development of adverse economic and diplomatic trends? Here there were several factors at work. First, there was the nature of the changes themselves. Whereas the major challenges to Kim Il Sung during the 1960s had been relatively straightforward, quantifiable and, to the military mind, susceptible to clear, albeit extreme, countermeasures, the economic and diplomatic challenges of the 1970s were of a different nature – more abstract, subtle and increasingly impossible to counter from within the corrosive simplicity of Kimist ideology. It is therefore not surprising that Kim had limited success in analysing these challenges and taking effective countermeasures. Second, Kim turned 60 in 1972 and, as he aged, his own lifetime experiences increasingly dominated his thinking. The cumulative weight of past decisions and practices lay heavily over his mind, exerting an ever-stronger influence on state policy. Any reassessment of strategy would entail a reassessment of his life's work, and Kim gives no sign of ever having possessed the type of self-reflecting nature that might have permitted this.

Third, as his lack of military strategic acumen had demonstrated during the Korean War, Kim was a short-term thinker, thinking only forward to the next skirmish and possibly the next battle but no further, and, as his disastrous role in post-war reconstruction showed, he was no planner. The ability to assess broader strategic implications was not in his make-up. Finally, his own intellectual insularity was reinforced by an inner circle consisting of ageing, poorly educated politico–military generalists, strangers in the modern world, either blindly loyal by instinct or brow-beaten into the semblance of absolute and unconditional loyalty. Whatever the contradicting information that penetrated these layers of insularity, it could not linger in Kim's mind for long, for he had cut himself off from expert, effective counselling in matters beyond his own concrete experience and therefore had no means of approaching the international community other than by projecting the 'realities' he had fashioned at home on to the outside world. Dogmatic belief that he had correctly read the tide of history induced a string of failures abroad, but these made little impression alongside the daily evidence he saw of his power within his own domain.

The major challenges in Kim Il Sung's pursuit of his objectives were a changing strategic environment and a failing economic base. In fact, the two were in some ways connected, for the deeply ingrained ignorance and hostility that characterised his attitude towards the capitalist systems of the US, Japan, the ROK and Western Europe led him to underestimate their power and resilience, and thus to dismiss their threat potential. Instead, the only economic models that Kim even marginally understood derived from the war-making states of Japan in the 1930s and the Soviet Union in the early 1940s, and so he saw little value in economic activity that did not boost the war-making potential of the DPRK state. Thus, he could not clearly perceive the extent to which the DPRK economy was being cannibalised by a military–industrial sector that now operated as an almost separate economy, accounting for a huge proportion of the country's total industrial output.

And so Kim remained committed to the fundamental proposition that his personal autocracy would lead the people to victory. As a deep article of faith, he believed that unleashing the revolutionary potential of the Korean people – both North and South – was simply a matter of leadership and ideology, but while he was capable of making the DPRK polity fit this formula by the pervasive application of state violence and terror, it was useless as a revolutionary stratagem when applied to South Korean society, let alone the international community. In fact, ROK society was developing in a direction vastly different from anything Kim had ever experienced. The traditional DPRK image of the ROK as a US puppet, mired in mid-1950s poverty and degradation, remained a staple feature not just of propaganda, but was also mandated by Kim to be part of otherwise sober diplomatic representations, and it engendered unrealistic, dismissive assessments of ROK economic and military power. Kim's analysis could not comprehend either the vigour of the strong civil society taking shape in the South or the widespread rejection by the South Korean masses of communist ideology, and he therefore continued to base his reunification policy on the conviction that the overwhelming majority of South Korean people harboured a deep dislike for their government and were innately well disposed to reunification under the banner of the North – and to his personal leadership. In fact, while many South Koreans were dissatisfied with their government on any number of grounds, reunification policy was not one of these, for any appeal the model of the North may have once exerted in the South had almost entirely disappeared by 1980.

Thus, Kim ended the decade of the 1970s with the same set of core ideological positions with which he had started. He remained a virulent opponent of peaceful coexistence, a firm believer in the unchanging, malevolent nature of capitalism, a resolute advocate of an unending anti-imperialist, anti-US struggle, and a critic of modern revisionism. In both rhetoric and actual policy measures, he was as firmly committed as ever to the reunification of Korea under the KWP and was just as firmly convinced that the North would prevail. He also remained committed to Equal Emphasis and to the efficacy of mobilisation policies such as Chollima that had long outlived whatever utility they had once possessed, and in consequence he presided over an increasingly exhausted and demoralised population that had little prospect of ever seeing its living standards rise. His perception remained that no change in strategy was called for, but meanwhile beyond the country's borders a vast process of modernisation continued to transform the Asia–Pacific region, further condemning the DPRK to political and economic backwardness and sterility.

Notes

1 See Simmons (1971: 108–9), Byung-Chul Koh (1971:22–36) and Scalapino and Lee (1972: 653–68) for coverage of the Fifth KWP Congress.
2 Kim Yong-ju, who was ranked 41 in the Fourth KWP Congress Central Committee, was the first but by no means the last member of Kim's extended family to gain high rank. In the 1970s and 1980s, he was joined by other family members and relatives by blood and by marriage, including, of course, Kim Jong Il. While observers speculated that Kim Il Sung wished his younger brother to succeed him (e.g. Chong-sik Lee, 1982: 442) this is doubtful. Kim Il Sung would not have accomplished much by the succession of someone only nine years younger and by all accounts not possessed of any special ability. Moreover, by the time that Kim Yong-ju appeared in the Politburo rankings, plans for the succession of his nephew were already well advanced. Before his recall to the Politburo in 1993, Kim Yong-ju had spent only the period 1966–73 in high office. These were precisely the early years of the Kim Jong Il ascendancy, and it seems probable that

his prominence at this time was in support of his nephew, most notably as head of the Party's nerve-centre, the Organisation and Guidance Department, before Kim Jong Il succeeded him in 1973, whereupon he retired to obscurity for the ensuing twenty years or so.

3 The sole 'technocrat' to rise higher was Yi Chong-ok (1916–99), who after being dismissed from office in 1967 was rehabilitated in the 1970s and served as Premier (1977–84) before being appointed as Vice President.

4 Most commentators accept that Kim Jong Il was born in the Siberian village of Vyatsuk. His official biography describes his birthplace as 'a secret camp of anti-Japanese guerillas on Mt Paekdu' (Tak *et al.*, 1985: 9). Apparently, his birth did not go unnoticed: 'At that time, a number of impressive stories about the birth of Comrade Kim Jong Il began to circulate, instant legends among the public. Some of the myths were: the Sobaeksu Valley, where the birthplace of Comrade Kim Jong Il is situated, was mistified [*sic*] as a holy place for a saint from the heavens; a new general star rose in the sky over Mt Paektu, predicting the birth of a new general; and a swift horse appeared on Mt Paektu and a young general trained military arts and cultivated his strength, riding the horse' (see 'Secret Camp on Mt. Paektu', *DPRK* no. 478, February 1996). Kim Jong Il was the eldest of three children born to Kim Il Sung and Kim Chong-suk. After Kim Chong-suk's death in 1949, Kim Il Sung remarried and had four children by his second wife, Kim Song-ae (Dae-Sook Suh, 1988: 282, 395). Apart from Kim Jong Il and his younger sister Kim Kyong-hui, none of Kim Il Sung's children have ever played a significant political role.

5 Brief, sober accounts of what is reliably known of Kim Jong Il's early years include Jae-Cheon Lim (2009: 25ff.) and Dae-Sook Suh (1998: 15–24).

6 Nor did he undertake any term of military service, which was highly unusual in such a militarised country, but there may well be some explanation for this. Perhaps his already exalted status made descent to the common level of military discipline awkward. Who would give him orders?

7 For the regime account of Kim's activities during these early years in the Party, see his biographers Tak *et al.* (1985: 108–27). They appear to be entirely straight-faced in listing combatting nepotism among his early major activities. For more objective accounts of this phase of Kim's career, see Clippinger (1981: 290) and Suh (1998: 17–24).

8 These manifestations are the author's personal observations at the time.

9 Cited by Dong-Bok Lee (1981a: 415), who also noted that this reference was omitted from the 1973 edition.

10 And in particular the transformation into canonic status of the Ten Principles on the Establishing of the Monolithic Ideology of the Party, first codified by Kim Jong Il in 1974. They comprise principles and an accompanying exegesis that remain the cornerstone of mandatory daily ideological study session in the DPRK to this day, subject only to some slight updating amendments inserted to accommodate Kim Jong Un in 2012 (Tertitskiy, 2014). A translation of the Principles themselves may be found at: http://eng.nkhumanrights.or.kr/board/download.php?fileno=1101&no=3&board_table=bbs_literature (accessed November 2016).

11 As usual, the DPRK portrays this movement as beginning from below, when in December 1975 the Komdok Mine in the industrial domain and the showpiece Chongsan-ri Cooperative Farm in the agricultural domain 'raised first the torch of this movement and called upon the whole country to launch this movement' (*PT* 9, January 1982). See Clippinger (1981: 294–8) for further details.

12 See Clippinger (1981: 292) for a table listing the frequency of the use of the term 'Party Centre' in *Kulloja* from 1973 to 1980. The significance of this table, of course, is that it reflects the extent to which coded reference was being made to the activities of Kim Jong Il during this period. Clippinger's table lists 378 references

in 1976, falling to 163 in 1977, all of which occurred in the period January–March, then falling to just four references in 1978.
13 Kim Chung-nin was reinstated in 1980 and Yang in 1993.
14 For more details on these purchases, see Zagoria and Kim (1976: 37).
15 Szalontai (2005) offers an extended number of examples of poor planning and management during this period, drawn from 1953–6 archival sources.
16 These observations are chiefly the outcome of conversations between the author and trade and business representatives from a number of European countries in Pyongyang in 1975. Many had come to the DPRK to oversee the installation of machinery or carry out construction work, and anecdotes of machinery abuse, lack of basic tradesman's skills, lack of basic infrastructure and shoddy construction work on a scale that surprised experienced international traders and construction workers figured prominently in their conversation, as it continues to do in the case of their counterparts to this day.
17 In 1977, debts accumulated in the early 1970s were consolidated into a loan agreement with a consortium of European banks with an aggregate principal debt of approximately US$700 million. The loan arrangements were rescheduled in March 1980 and May 1984. The DPRK did not repay any of the principal and ceased interest repayments in 1984. For details of Japanese efforts to recover money owed by the DPRK to Japanese companies, see Hong-Nack Kim (1983: 322–3).
18 A Hungarian embassy report from June 1977 provides a useful picture of the social implications of this decline: '"Leisure time" has been completely eliminated. On Sunday they do agricultural work. People have no strength, or opportunity, to meet freely and have informal conversations. Their only desire is to sleep . . . True, they are not discontented, do not grumble, do not want to "rise up". But . . . an inner mental and emotional crisis has started. They are fed up with making sacrifices. Their weariness and indifference are growing. They complain that they cannot get regular rest or take care of their children. They want to live, eat and dress better . . . The shortfalls and reductions in food rations have left [people] demoralised. Shops are empty. People are hungry. In the winter only dried fish was available. There is no meat at all. Now they get sugar only once per quarter.' (Translation by Szalontai in Springer, 2010: xxv) While obviously this did not apply to all DPRK citizens, the description of tension and loss of morale among ordinary people is generally consistent with this writer's personal observations in 1975.
19 Byung-Chul Koh (1984) and others stress the force of domestic political considerations in Park Chung-hee's turn towards autocracy in the early 1970s, but while Park's calculations would, of course, begin with domestic considerations strongly on his mind, we should not lose sight of the broader security context for his policies. The detailed account by Mark Clifford (1994: 78) of the 26 March 1970 ROK–US discussions, for example, leaves little doubt of their profound effect on the ROK leadership at the time.
20 *PT* 14 August 1971, quoted by Byung-Chul Koh (1984: 87).
21 National Unification Board, Republic of Korea, 1988: 55.
22 See Young C. Kim (1976: 90): 'My conversations with North Koreans [in Pyongyang in August 1975] led me to believe that 1) North Korean leaders feel that the international situation is developing in their favour. The international isolation of South Korea is becoming more pronounced while the international standing of North Korea is improving; 2) There is a tremendous degree of genuine confidence and arrogance North Koreans exude in this regard; 3) There is a North Korean perception, consistent with their ideology, that revolutionary forces in South Korea are gaining strength, political instability is growing ever more acute, and that South Korea is in the process of disintegration.' This author received similar presentations from senior DPRK officials in Pyongyang at precisely the same time as Kim.

23 For details, see Niksch (1981) and Young-ho Lee (1981). For an extended discussion of the factors influencing DPRK strategy during the 1970s, see Sung-Joo Han (1983).
24 In 1989 the DPRK released relatively detailed population statistics to UN representatives for the first time. These statistics revealed that the armed forces had been excluded from the census from the early 1970s on. Calculations based on the otherwise unaccountable fall in the sex ratio from 95.1 to 86.9 in the period 1970–5 down to 84.2 in 1987 provided a basis for the estimates of armed forces manpower given above. Eberstadt (1995: 22) concludes that these statistics 'raise some questions which must still go unanswered and point to discrepancies as yet unresolved. Nevertheless, they seem inadvertently to confirm the proposition that a steady and enormous increase in the country's military population took place between the mid-1970s and the late 1980s.'
25 Dealing with the ROK was a very peripheral issue to the Soviets at this stage and it faded from the agenda as domestic political repression in the ROK grew in 1974, raising questions about the long-term stability of the Park regime. For further details on Soviet–ROK contacts during this period, see Boulychev (1994: 93).
26 On 18 August 1976, Korean People's Army (KPA) guards in the Panmunjom Joint Security Area (JSA) attacked a group of South Korean civilian labourers and their ROK and US military escort while the labourers were trimming a poplar tree that was obscuring the view of a UN observation post. Two American officers were killed with axes seized from the working party, and other injuries were inflicted. The assault appeared to be premeditated and there was some question both as to what level of KPA command had ordered it and whether or not it signalled the start of a wider confrontation. As a result, the US put its forces in Korea on alert, the carrier USS *Midway* moved towards the east coast of Korea and on 21 August the tree was felled by the United Nations Command in a show of force. At a Military Armistice Commission meeting on 21 August, the KPA side conveyed an unprecedented message from Kim Il Sung expressing regret over the incident. On 6 September, the two sides agreed to redivide the JSA to minimise instances of direct contact. On the Soviet reaction, see Zagoria and Zagoria (1981).
27 For further details, see Hunter (1983: 201–2).
28 See Zagoria (1983: 360) and Hunter (1983: 204) for details of the DPRK's unfavourable reaction to the Sino–Japanese treaty and the US–PRC normalisation.
29 For accounts of the DPRK's participation in the Colombo Summit, see Byung-Chul Koh (1977: 65) and Dae-Sook Suh (1988: 265).
30 The perception that the DPRK was reaching out was widespread. Among others, Armstrong sums it up: 'The 1970s were a decade of unprecedented outward expansion for North Korea. Admission to several UN bodies, active lobbying at the UN General Assembly, a successful diplomatic offensive in the Third World, and new economic and political ties to advanced capitalist countries all reflected a new global presence for the DPRK' (Armstrong, 2013: 168). In assessing DPRK diplomacy during this period, however, one should be careful not confuse outreach with a wider search for low-hanging fruit as well as opportunities to gratify Kim Il Sung's vanity. There was, of course, no corresponding adjustment in basic DPRK state policies and by the end of the decade it had little to show for its efforts.

References

Armstrong, Charles (2013) *Tyranny of the Weak: North Korea and the World 1950–1992*. Cornell University Press: Ithaca, NY.
Clifford, Mark (1994) *Troubled Tiger: Businessmen, Bureaucrats, and Generals in South Korea*. M.E. Sharpe: Armonk, NY.

Clippinger, Morgan E. (1981) Kim Jong Il in the North Korean mass media: A study of semi-esoteric communication, *Asian Survey*, XXI(3): 289–309.

Eberstadt, Nicholas (1995) *Korea Approaches Reunification*. M.E. Sharpe: Armonk, NY.

Han, Sung-Joo (1983) North Korea's security policy and military strategy, in *North Korea Today: Strategic and Domestic Issues*, Robert A. Scalapino and Jun-Yop Kim (eds). Institute of East Asian Studies, University of California: Berkeley, CA, pp. 144–63.

Joy, C. Turner (1955) *How Communists Negotiate*. Macmillan: New York.

Kim, Hong-Nack (1983) Japan's policy toward the Korean Peninsula since 1965, in *The Two Koreas in World Politics*, Tae-Hwan Kwak, Wayne Patterson and Edward A. Olsen (eds). The Institute for Far Eastern Studies, Kyungnam University: Seoul, pp. 305–30.

Kim, Young C. (1976) The Democratic People's Republic of Korea in 1975, *Asian Survey*, XVI(1): 82–94.

Koh, Byung-Chul (1971) Anatomy of a revolution: Some implications of the Fifth KWP Congress, *Journal of Korea Studies*, I(3): 22–36.

Koh, Byung-Chul (1977) North Korea 1976: Under stress, *Asian Survey*, XVII(1): 61–70.

Koh, Byung-Chul (1978) North Korea in 1977: Year of 'readjustment', *Asian Survey*, XVIII(1): 36–44.

Koh, Byung-Chul (1984) *The Foreign Policy Systems of North and South Korea*. University of California Press: Berkeley, CA.

Lee, Chong-sik (1982) Evolution of the Korean Workers' Party and the rise of Kim Chong-il, *Asian Survey*, XXII(5): 434–448.

Lee, Dong-Bok (1981) Present and future of inter-Korean relations: The January 12 Proposal and the Sixth Congress of the KWP, *Korea & World Affairs*, 5(1): 36–52.

Lee, Young-Ho 1981, Military balance and peace in the Korean Peninsula, *Asian Survey*, XXI(8): 852–64.

Lim, Jae-Cheon 2009, *Kim Jong Il's Leadership of North Korea*. Routledge: London and New York.

Mansourov, Alexandre (2006) Emergence of the Second Republic: The Kim regime adapts to the challenges of modernity, in *North Korea: The Politics of Regime Survival*, Young Whan Kihl and Hong Nack Kim (eds). M. E. Sharpe: Armonk, NY.

Namkoong, Young and Yoo, Ho-Yeol (1994) North Korea's Economic System, in *Prospects for Change in North Korea*, Tae Hwan Ok and Hong Yung Lee I (eds). Institute of East Asian Studies, University of California: Berkeley, CA.

National Unification Board, Republic of Korea (1988) A white paper on South–North dialogue in Korea, Seoul.

Niksch, Larry A. (1981) US troop withdrawal from South Korea: Past shortcomings and future prospects, *Asian Survey*, XXI(3): 325–41.

Scalapino, Robert A. and Lee, Chong-sik (1972) *Communism in Korea Part 1: The Movement*. The University of California Press: Berkeley, CA.

Simmons, Robert (1971) North Korea: Silver anniversary, *Asian Survey*, XI(1): 104–10.

Snyder, Scott (2000) Negotiating on the edge: Patterns in North Korea's diplomatic style, *World Affairs*, 163(1): 3–17.

Song, Jong-Hwan (1984) How the North Korean communists negotiate: A case study of the South–North Korean dialogue of the early 1970s, *Korea and World Affairs*, 8(3): 610–64.

Springer, Chris (2010) *North Korea, Caught in Time: Images of War and Reconstruction*. Garnet Publishing: Reading.

Suh, Dae-Sook (1988) *Kim Il Sung: The North Korean Leader*. Columbia University Press: New York.

Suh, Dae-Sook (1998) Kim Jong Il and new leadership in North Korea, in *North Korea after Kim Il Sung*, Dae-Sook Suh and Chae-Jin Lee (eds). Lynne Rienner: Boulder, CO, pp. 13–32.

Szalontai, Balazs (2005) *Kim Il Sung in the Khrushchev Era: Soviet–Korean Relations and the Roots of North Korean Despotism 1953–1964*. Woodrow Wilson Center Press: Washington, DC.

Tak, J., Kim, G I. and Pak, H. J. (1985) *Great Leader Kim Jong Il* (2 vols). Sorinsha Publishers: Tokyo.

Tertitskiy, Fydor (2014) Evolution of Party credo shows effort to elevate Kim Jong Il, the Worker's Party, available at: www.nknews.org/2014/12/the-partys-10-principles-then-and-now/(accessed August 2016).

Zagoria, Donald S. and Kim, Young Kun 1976, North Korea and the major powers, in *The Two Koreas in East Asian Affairs*, William J. Barnds (ed.). New York University Press: New York, pp. 19–59.

Zagoria, Donald S. 1983, North Korea: Between Moscow and Beijing, in *North Korea Today: Strategic and Domestic Issues*, Robert A. Scalapino and Jun-Yop Kim (eds). Institute of East Asian Studies, University of California: Berkeley, CA, pp. 351–71.

4   Dwindling options: 1980–6

Introduction

After exercising considerable power for many years behind the scenes, Kim Jong Il became a public figure when he was elected to a series of high Party positions at the Sixth Korean Workers' Party Congress in October 1980. Following this unveiling, Party cadres began to make open reference to the younger Kim's role as his father's successor, and during 1980–2 a further series of moves confirmed his authority. This brought to a successful conclusion a long, drawn-out and at times contested process of embedding hereditary rule into an historically Marxist–Leninist polity, and what it ultimately signalled was that the fundamental pillars of Kimist rule – militarism, a rigid command economy, high levels of state indoctrination and violence, continuing confrontation with the ROK, the US and Japan, and quarantining from almost every aspect of the international economic and political system, would continue as unchanged as the regime could manage.

The DPRK faced these challenges at precisely the time that the KWP party elite was entering old age. Kim Il Sung turned 68 in 1980 and the average age of the Politburo elected at the Sixth KWP Congress was 61.2.[1] Although academic and media commentary during this time speculated that Kim Jong Il heralded the emergence of a younger, more technocratic–pragmatic group within the leadership, no policy or personnel moves emerged to support this. Moreover, it is debatable whether even a younger, more vigorous Party elite could have tackled the country's problems more flexibly and creatively, for it would have had to act as an insurgency movement against the Kimist system itself. And so the decline of the DPRK continued unabated, and it proved unable to respond with any flexibility to a mounting array of economic and strategic challenges.

This decline was thrown into sharper relief by the high economic growth rates of the ROK, and the military implications were especially worrisome, for higher and higher rates of expenditure were now necessary simply in order to maintain a credible conventional military threat. The only countermeasure that offered a long-term prospect of halting a further deterioration in the DPRK's military position was the development of nuclear weapons, so in the early1980s the DPRK began construction of a 5 MWe reactor fuelled with natural uranium and moderated with graphite for the purpose of plutonium production. The nuclear age began to arrive in the DPRK and would have momentous consequences across a whole spectrum of state policies.

Meanwhile, the revolutionary outlook in the South began to look increasingly unfavourable. The assassination of Park Chung-hee in October 1979 had produced a temporary power vacuum, but after a short period of vigorous, open political life, the ROK military again took control when General Chun Doo-hwan seized power on 17 May 1980. An enforced calm descended on ROK politics and, after a severe slump during 1979–80, the South's economy recovered and began to grow rapidly again. This growing economic strength translated into substantial diplomatic gains, best symbolised by the awarding of the 1988 Olympiad to Seoul in November 1981, and as Chun consolidated his hold on power, the North resorted to past patterns of intransigence and violence. Thus, in October 1983 it carried out a terrorist bombing attack in Rangoon on Chun and his entourage during a state visit to Burma, which missed its main target but took the lives of four ROK Cabinet ministers and thirteen other senior ROK officials.

Almost immediately, however, the fight–talk–fight pattern of negotiations was again in evidence in January 1984 with a DPRK proposal for tripartite talks involving the two Koreas and the US. This seemed at the time to herald a departure from the long-standing refusal of the DPRK to recognise the existence of the ROK, but on closer examination the proposal broke no new ground. This was followed by an active round of inter-Korean talks on sporting, economic, parliamentary and humanitarian cooperation, in which the high points were a DPRK shipment of flood relief goods to the South in September 1984 and the first-ever exchange of home visits between the two Koreas in August 1985. However, once again, the essence of Kim Il Sung's démarche was tactical, and by the end of 1986 the talks had fallen into stalemate amid mutual recrimination.

Moreover, the international outlook was also becoming more and more problematic for the DPRK. The new reality in the 1980s was an emerging China–Japan–US triangle of common policy interests in Northeast Asia generally and on the Korean Peninsula in particular, and this profoundly challenged the underlying premises of the Kimist worldview. Ideology dictated a resolute confrontation with US imperialism and Japanese militarism, and Kim maintained this struggle in the 1980s, but its terms were becoming rapidly more unfavourable in the face of rapid economic change in China, consolidation of Japan's superpower economic status, and an increasingly stable, long-term US political and military footprint in Northeast Asia. China's expanding ties with both countries initially led to a period of coolness in Beijing–Pyongyang relations in the early 1980s, but in 1982 the two countries succeeded in establishing a new, pragmatic basis for relations. Meanwhile, the major DPRK strategic countermove to these regional developments and also to its economic decline was rapprochement with the Soviet Union. The Soviets shared DPRK fears about the consequences of an emerging China–US–Japan axis, which essentially represented an anti-Soviet alliance on Moscow's eastern flank, and by 1984 bilateral relations had achieved a level of economic and military cooperation not seen since the death of Stalin.

The Sixth KWP Congress

The Sixth KWP Congress convened in Pyongyang during 10–14 October 1980, and was the final congress to be held in Kim Il Sung's lifetime.[2] Its chief points of interest lay in Kim Il Sung's lengthy report on the work of the Party since the Fifth KWP Congress in 1970, and of course in the election of office bearers, specifically Kim Jong Il. Kim Il Sung's speech was ebullient and self-congratulatory, as, of course, the occasion demanded. It was also ideologically unflinching, re-endorsing the mass-mobilisation techniques of the early stages of the North's economic development, with the Chollima Movement, Chongsanri Method and Taean Work Systems receiving specific re-endorsement. The ruinous Three Revolutions Team movement likewise received praise for its contribution to the success of the DPRK economic model.[3]

Since there was no other discernible reason for holding what had become a rare event – this was the only Congress that Kim Il Sung would call in the last twenty-four years of his life – the chief motive for convening the Congress was clearly the formal, public celebration of the Kim Jong Il succession, two years shy of his fortieth birthday. Accordingly, he now publicly assumed a string of leading Party, government and military positions.[4] In terms of ideology, this ascendancy was presented as the means by which the anti-Japanese guerilla tradition could be passed as intact as human agency could devise to future generations, for long after the demise of the last of the guerilla generation, the Party would now be led by someone who was deeply imbued with its spirit. It was therefore not surprising that the Sixth Congress was not interested in effecting any measures of generational change. At age 38, Kim Jong Il was nine years younger than the second youngest member of the new Politburo, O Kuk-ryol, who was himself the son of a Manchurian guerilla comrade of Kim Il Sung. Kim Il Sung's intention was clearly that the guerilla generation should rule as long as possible in order to instil its traditions, by which he really meant a fictionalised distillation of his personal experience during those years, in the minds of younger generations, for his bedrock belief remained that here lay the key to victory.

While Kim maintained his characteristic practice of maintaining a high turnover in the ranks of the Central Committee, the new Politburo demonstrated a stability that reflected Kim's personal autocracy. In contrast to the high attrition rate among Politburo members between the Fourth and Fifth Congresses, when only four of sixteen were re-elected, eight of the eleven full Politburo members elected at the Fifth Congress in 1970 retained their full membership in 1980 (see Table 4.1). Moreover, seventeen of the nineteen

Table 4.1 Comparison of Fifth and Sixth KWP Congress Politburos

Rank	The Fifth KWP Congress Politburo (1970)	The Sixth KWP Congress Politburo (1980)
1	Kim Il Sung	Kim Il Sung (aged 69)
2	Ch'oe Yong-gon*	Kim Il (69)
3	Kim Il	O Chin-u (71)
4	Pak Song-ch'ol	Kim Jong Il## (40)
5	Ch'oe Hyon	Yi Chong-ok+ (67)
6	Kim Yong-ju**	Pak Song-ch'ol (69)
7	O Chin-u	Ch'oe Hyon (73)
8	Kim Tong-gyu>	Im Ch'un-ch'u+ (66)
9	So Ch'ol	So Ch'ol (74)
10	Kim Chung-nin	O Paek-ryong# (73)
11	Han Ik-su>	Kim Chung-nin (57)
12		Kim Yong-nam# (56)
13		Chon Mun-sop# (64)
14		Kim Hwan## (52)
15		Yon Hyong-muk# (58)
16		O Kuk-ryol# (49)
17		Kye Ung-t'ae# (58)
18		Kang Song-san# (53)
19		Paek Hak-nim# (63)

Sources: DPRK media. Ages as given in Dong-Bok Lee (1981a).

Notes: * died in office with state funeral during the 1970s; ** retired from active Party work after 1974; > purged during the 1970s; # elected to the CC at the Fifth KWP Congress in 1970; ## entered the Central Committee after 1970; + dismissed from the Politburo in the mid-1960s, reappointed in the mid-1970s.

cadres elected to full membership of the new Sixth Congress Politburo had already entered the Central Committee in 1970, with Kim Jong Il and Kim Hwan the only members who had attained Central Committee ranking after 1970. The new Politburo consisted almost entirely of two elements – the surviving core of Kim Il Sung's pre-war Manchurian guerilla group, into whose ranks Kim Jong Il had now been drafted, and a collection of individuals typically ten to fifteen years younger than the former guerillas with no particular links to each other, but bound by ties of either blood, marriage or patronage to the senior group. As senior Party officials in their fifties, members of this second group had typically spent their entire working lives in the DPRK, had endured the Korean War, and had survived earlier purges.

The military–security–intelligence sector was overwhelmingly present, but with the single exception of O Kuk-ryol, what is often termed the second generation of the DPRK military – the generation that was the product of formal training in the first few years after 1945 at the Mangyongdae Military Academy – was not represented. The military men that Kim felt at home with did not come from officer training schools, but were the product of irregular or conspiratorial modes of warfare, and as they grew old and died or else were demoted from the Politburo during the 1980s and early 1990s, Kim did not replace them with younger products of post-war regular military training.

The confirmation of Kim Jong Il

For its own esoteric reasons, the Sixth KWP Congress stopped short of making public reference to Kim Jong Il as his father's successor, but the younger Kim swiftly took the remaining steps to heir-apparent status by establishing both his cult of personality and his paramount ideological credentials. The final stage of Kim Jong Il's public emergence as a person who was endowed with the same personality, leadership and ideological attributes as his father, and who was thus capable of performing the same role as his father, began in August 1981, when he made his first publicly reported on-the-spot guidance tours, replicating the ritualistic cavalcades of his father (*PT*, 22 August 1981; 28 August 1981).

These visits became part of a build-up to a series of major events in 1982, when Kim Jong Il turned 40. By Stalinist precedent, such milestone birthdays were occasions for the further intensification of cult of personality measures, and so on 15 February 1982, the day before Kim Jong Il's fortieth birthday, he was awarded the title Hero of the Democratic People's Republic of Korea along with the Gold Star medal and the Order of National Flag First Class. Shortly afterwards, two Kim Jong Il treatises were published, *On the Juche Idea* in March 1982 and *The Workers' Party of Korea is a Juche-type Revolutionary Party which Inherited the Glorious Tradition of the Down-with-Imperialism Union* (hereafter *The Workers' Party . . .*) in October 1982. When the collected works of Kim Jong Il were published several years later, they contained speeches and articles going back to 1963, but none of these earlier works had received mention in the media at the time. These two 1982 works, the first to receive widespread media acclamation at the time of their publication, thereby definitively established Kim Jong Il's role as the only person capable of fully interpreting Kim Il Sung's Juche ideology and carrying forward the revolutionary cause.

The extended laudatory descriptions of *On the Juche Idea* which began to appear during the course of 1982 and regularly continued in the years that followed,[5] presented it as an authoritative exegesis of Juche ideology. One early description marvelled at how it 'deals with comprehensively the origin of the Juche idea, its philosophical principle, socio-historical principles, guiding principle and historical significance', making 'a total exposition of the origin of the Juche idea and its components'. Its publication was 'an everlasting ideo-theoretical exploit which clarified like a beacon light important philosophical tasks that had not been raised or solved in the history of human thought and the pressing theoretical and practical problems of our age'.[6] Thus, some eighteen months after Kim had emerged at the Sixth KWP Congress, and less than a year after he had begun his on-the-spot tours, the publication of the two works completed the process of associating Kim Jong Il with the key attributes of his father: formal political authority, authority to give definitive guidance in all areas of the national life and the spiritual aura of one who had mastered the ideology that validated that authority. In a system that gave such primacy to such authority, the assumption of this aura all but completed the process of the younger Kim's emergence.[7]

The economy in decline

While the DPRK remained absorbed in these ideological matters, the economic stagnation which had set in during the 1970s worsened considerably. This was especially identifiable through the DPRK's two-way foreign trade, which declined by 38.4 per cent in the period 1980–82, from US$3.6 billion to US$2.9 billion (see Table 4.2), while the balance of trade grew especially unfavourable during this period. The DPRK had always suffered from chronic trade deficits throughout its existence, usually covered by a variety of Soviet subsidy measures, but in the early 1980s these deficits blew out as the cumulative effect of technological obsolescence and declining productivity led to declining volumes of raw and semi-processed materials available for export, and as the 1978–79 Oil Shock brought about recessionary conditions in many economies, lessening demand for such exports. The estimated average deficit of US$355 million for the four-year period 1980–83 was over three times the estimated average deficit for the four-year period 1976–79 of US$106 million.[8] The traditional DPRK economy never could pay its way, but now things began to reach a tipping point.

The leadership's response to this set of circumstances was instructive and presaged its future response to the economic collapse of the 1990s, for characteristically, it involved a trenchant defence of the Party's ideological parameters which left intact the hallmark features of the DPRK economy – extreme centralisation of management, reliance on ideological incentives, reliance on Stakhanovite mobilisation campaigns, and continuing high levels of military expenditure. Despite growing difficulties, Kim Il Sung's re-endorsement of the Chollima Movement, Chongsanri Method and Taean Work System at the Sixth KWP Congress had indicated that the DPRK economy would continue to operate under traditional ideological parameters.

Table 4.2 DPRK foreign trade: 1980–3 (unit = US$ million)

Year	Imports	Exports	Balance	Total	% increase
1980	1,851.1	1,694.5	−156.6	3,545.6	20.6
1981	1,532.0	1.099.7	−432.3	2,631.7	−25.8
1982	1,596.3	1,314.0	−282.3	2,910.3	10.6
1983	1,367.9	816.7	−551.2	2,184.6	−24.9
1984	1.313.0	1,194.4	−118.6	2,507.4	14.8

Source: Japanese External Trade Organization (JETRO).

The accession of Kim Jong Il then served to reinforce these parameters, for his 1982 treatises again stressed ideology-first economic management. Moreover, the younger Kim imposed a further burden on the economy in the form of the diversion of economic resources to massive prestige construction projects, which became sites for his on-the-spot guidance tours beginning in 1981. These projects included the Juche Tower, the Arch of Triumph, a string of sports facilities, including the Moranbong Stadium with a reported capacity of 150,000, and numerous tourist hotels for the practically non-existent tourist industry, culminating in the ultimate self-indulgence, the unusable 105-storey would-be Ryugyong Hotel.

This was the background for the convening of a special session of the Supreme People's Assembly in January 1984, where the DPRK announced a willingness to trade with capitalist countries and to seek investment capital from abroad. Observers speculated that the DPRK was contemplating significant changes to its economy, citing faint DPRK praise (for the first time) for China's Four Modernisations programme, evidence of DPRK interest in the operation of China's Special Economic Zones (SEZs), the enactment of a Joint Venture Law in September 1984 and signs of focus on the light industrial sector, a sector that had always suffered due to the overwhelming priority accorded to the heavy industry sector. Nevertheless, it soon became clear that these themes were rhetorical and did not involve any change to long-established economic policy.

In the first place, the full title of the relevant Supreme People's Assembly (SPA) of the DPRK agenda item, 'On strengthening South–South cooperation and external economic relations and further developing foreign trade', indicated that the DPRK was not seeking a radical departure from previous policy, but rather placed the development of foreign trade with other countries within the context of its traditional trade policy and structure, which emphasised economic ties with the socialist bloc and the Third World. The Party emphasised this point at the Ninth Plenum of the Sixth KWP Central Committee, held during 6–9 July 1984, when its major references to foreign trade policy gave clear emphasis to ties with the Socialist Bloc and did not contain any reference to trading with capitalist countries (*PT*, 14 July 1984). Second, while there is anecdotal evidence that the Administration Council took some minor steps to streamline the administration of foreign trade within individual ministries at this time, there is no evidence in the form of follow-up public announcements, campaigns or commentary of sustained efforts to give effect to any major new policy direction. For example, the lengthy report of the Ninth Party Plenum mentioned above contained no references to recent developments such as the January SPA resolution on further developing foreign trade (*PT*, 14 July 1984).

Moreover, there is no evidence of trade-related diplomatic activity in 1984. A crucial first step clearly had to be serious negotiations on the DPRK's Western European and Japanese debts, since the confidence of the international banking community would have been crucial to future trade financing, but this did not take place. In fact, quite the contrary, all repayments ceased after May 1984, a move that instead presents as a clear cost-cutting measure in the light of the recent setbacks.[9] If this in itself were not enough, there was also no change to the policy of not releasing even basic economic data. Whatever the role envisaged for foreign investors, the DPRK clearly assumed that they would invest without access to even basic economic data such as GDP and sector output figures. Perhaps most tellingly, in any coherent foreign trade strategy, priority would need to be given to the upgrading of the DPRK's primitive economic infrastructure, but the government made no significant reference to it during this period.

Finally, the extent to which the September 1984 Joint Venture Law represented a new departure tended to be magnified by the standard 'Hermit Kingdom' media images which exaggerated the extent to which the DPRK had hitherto isolated itself from the international economy. In fact, in spite of its Juche rhetoric, the DPRK had conducted significant trade with Japan for a number of years before 1984, while trade with capitalist countries had accounted for 20–30 per cent of total DPRK trade during the 1970s, and in 1979 totalled US$970 million (Bon-hak Koo, 1992: 187), usually for mining equipment and other advanced manufactures which it could not source from within the Soviet Bloc. Moreover, on the ideological level, while the leadership held deep convictions on the predatory nature of international trade, it had never advocated complete economic isolation. Already in 1982, Kim Jong Il had noted in his treatise *On the Juche Idea*: 'Building an independent national economy on the principle of self-reliance does not mean building an economy in isolation. An independent economy is opposed to foreign economic domination and subjugation; but it does not rule out international economic cooperation' (Kim Jong Il, 1982: 48).[10] The measures contemplated by the Party in 1984 seem even less significant when considered against this background.[11]

However, the DPRK's fortunes did, in fact, change significantly in 1984, as the effects of a restored economic relationship with the Soviet Union began to flow through. This followed on from Kim Il Sung's May–June 1984 extended visit to the Soviet Union, with the result that in 1985 two-way trade with the Soviet Union nearly doubled over 1984, giving Kim the sense of a real alternative to unwanted, uncertain contacts with capitalist trading partners. The DPRK had founded and developed its industry with extensive Soviet input, and almost all major economic units functioned according to Soviet blueprints, organisational methods, machinery, spare parts and market requirements. Moreover, the lesser technologies on offer from the Soviets were more suitable for the DPRK economy, for as the disastrous efforts to import Western plant and machinery in the early 1970s had demonstrated, absorbing more advanced technologies was beyond the North's capacity. A further factor was that in dealing with the Soviets, Pyongyang did not have to deal with the threats posed by intercourse with open societies, but instead could deal with the more compatible closed political systems within the Socialist Bloc. Finally, and most importantly, the new Soviet relationship led directly to a renewed flow of up-to-date weaponry and military technology.[12]

As the massive scale of Soviet assistance became increasingly clear, the DPRK retreated behind traditional economic policies. By July 1985, thoughts of introducing joint venture capital were far from Kim's mind as he pronounced:

> We shall never bring in foreign capital. An economy which is built on foreign capital is bound to become a dependent economy. The economic independence of a country is as important as its political independence. If a country is subordinated to another country economically, it will also be subjugated politically. Our country will not be like south Korea which is burdened with 50,000 million dollars of debts.
>
> (*PT*, 17 July 1985)

This last sentence fits so neatly into Kim's analysis that one almost overlooks its unintentional irony. Yet in his words, there is also a significant key to Kim's evident oblivious attitude to his own foreign creditors – namely, that he simply did not see defaulting to foreign banks and the resultant reputational damage as economic factors worthy of attention. We may surmise that in the Manchurian guerilla mind-set, international bankers were themselves seen as predators and he felt under no obligation to honour any agreements made with them.

So, by the end of 1986 the most salient aspect of the DPRK economy was the forthright manner in which Kim Il Sung had reaffirmed and reinforced traditional policies of rigid orthodoxy in economic matters. In his speech to the inaugural session of the Eighth SPA on 29 December 1986, there were no references to material incentives, decentralised planning, independent accounting or other aspects of economic liberalisation (*PT*, 3 January 1987). While the process of economic reform was by this time well entrenched in China and cautious debates on the need for reform had begun in the Soviet Union and Vietnam, in the DPRK tendencies towards reform remained under strong attack in a forceful reassertion of the need to pursue fundamental ideological objectives. Later refugee testimony tells us that this was also precisely the time when the central government began to lose control of local level economic activity, leading to the ignoring of central directives and the spread of various forms of private economic activity (Lankov and Kim, 2008).

There is little reason to dispute the analysis later offered by Soviet economists that the DPRK began to enter into a serious and prolonged economic crisis beginning in the early 1980s (Eberstadt, 2015; Trigubenko 1991: 108). Self-enforced scientific, cultural and educational isolation, the glorification of a spurious form of self-sufficiency, and the alienation of world capital markets through debt delinquency had resulted in low levels of technological input and very little capacity to produce value-added exports. Tiny pockets of high-technology excellence continued to exist in defence-related industries, and missile exports mainly to Middle East clients were becoming a significant source of hard currency (Pollack, 2011), but elsewhere quality problems plagued DPRK manufacturing industry to the extent that Chinese officials routinely cited the quality factor as a major impediment to expanding trade. The products themselves were all but unsaleable except in captive Third World markets.[13] Thus, the DPRK faced a formidable array of problems. The country possessed a stagnant economy, high foreign debt, an enormous burden in military expenditure, few value-added exports, little access to foreign technology and capital, a workforce cut off from even basic foreign training or experience, rapidly ageing and inefficient plants, machinery and infrastructure, an obsolete, highly centralised command system of economic management and no economic administrators with a skill-set relevant to reform. It would face the future with these features intact and with an unassailable leadership almost totally oblivious to their significance.

This notwithstanding, beginning in early 1984, it became commonplace for external observers to perceive significant changes taking place in DPRK politics and personnel.[14] The grounds usually cited were a surmised pattern of Party and appointments that was believed to signal the advancement of technocratically minded cadres, the advancement of the tripartite talks formula, the resumption of the inter-Korean dialogue, economic policy statements that placed a new emphasis on the role of foreign trade and the promulgation of the 1984 Joint Venture Law aimed at inducing foreign investment, all of which were routinely cited as examples of departures from past policies. However, not only has the passage of time itself rather comprehensively undercut such analysis, but even at the time it was almost immediately obvious that the tripartite talks démarche was a chimera, that purported moves towards greater economic flexibility were likewise illusory and that even cursory analysis does not bear out the assertion that significant personnel moves occurred among the DPRK political elite at this time, much less moves aimed at advancing a younger generation associated with Kim Jong Il.[15] Policy formulation and execution in all key areas remained in the hands of people who had no interest in reform.

The South–North dialogue rekindled

This background of unyielding defence of orthodoxy was reflected in Inter-Korean relations. In the wake of the assassination of Park Chung-hee in October 1979, the ROK government acknowledged that the harsher features of Park's Yushin system had died with him and proceeded to adopt policies of reconciliation such as the appointment of a liberal, civilian-dominated Cabinet, the wholesale release of political prisoners and the removal of civil rights restrictions on such political leaders as Kim Young Sam and Kim Dae Jung. As a period of open, active politicking ensued, this series of developments presented the DPRK with the prospect of negotiating with an adversary under considerable domestic pressure, and so in January 1980 it proposed a resumption of the talks that had been suspended in 1975.

However, General Chun Doo-hwan re-established military control over the ROK government in May 1980, and by August 1980 the influence of liberal civilians in the ROK Government had again been marginalised, the civil rights of all leading opposition politicians suspended, and Kim Dae Jung was in prison awaiting trial on the capital charge of sedition. From the DPRK's point of view, therefore, the further pursuit of talks with an increasingly well-entrenched ROK leader was counterproductive, for Pyongyang could no longer effectively exploit political divisions within the ROK, while further negotiation would play into Chun's hands by implying DPRK acceptance of Chun as a legitimate negotiating partner. Therefore, almost immediately after Chun's inauguration as interim president in September 1980, the DPRK signalled that it saw further dialogue as futile.[16]

The DPRK commitment to preventing Chun Doo-hwan from becoming as entrenched in power as Park Chung-hee had been became clear in October 1983 when DPRK commandos detonated a bomb that killed seventeen senior ROK officials, including four Cabinet ministers, at the beginning of an official ceremony at the Martyrs Mausoleum in Rangoon, during Chun's first stop on his first major regional tour. Chun escaped injury because the DPRK commando group evidently detonated the bomb prematurely, and after an official investigation, in November the Burmese authorities pronounced themselves satisfied that the DPRK was responsible for the bombing.

There can be little doubt that the Rangoon operation was carefully planned at the highest level in Pyongyang with the intention of creating an atmosphere of fear, confusion and demoralisation in Seoul. In 1983 the DPRK was under the same leadership and was publicly committed to the same set of policies that had led to similar acts against the ROK in the past, such as the commando raid on the Blue House in 1968. More generally, Kim Il Sung had a worldview of deep, permanent and desperate struggle between the Party and its enemies, and far from reassessing things after the violence of the late 1960s, he had continued to glorify the guerilla tradition with its modes of irregular warfare and terrorism. This signalled a leadership committed to the view that removal of the ROK leadership would constitute a major step towards unleashing the revolutionary potential in ROK society, while also going some of the way towards slowing the rate at which the ROK was now outperforming the DPRK economically and diplomatically.

The South–North dialogue then took an unexpected turn in January 1984, when after a confusing period of diplomacy, Chinese Premier Zhao Ziyang hand-delivered a letter from Kim Il Sung to US President Ronald Reagan proposing that the DPRK, the US and the ROK hold tripartite talks on matters relating to the reunification of Korea.[17] Both the ROK and the US found the proposal unacceptable since it conflicted with their joint position that the North should negotiate directly with the South from the outset, but a period of intensive diplomacy nevertheless followed in an attempt to resolve some of the inevitable ambiguities in the North's proposal.[18] It soon emerged that the proposal did not so much break new ground as reformulate some of the many ambiguities latent in the North's long-established two-tier bilateral talks policy, whereby the North proposed to negotiate a peace treaty with the US bilaterally, with the South on hand as a clearly inferior participant. Success in this endeavour would then pave the way for a post-treaty political settlement with the weakened South. Clarification that this was still the DPRK's position removed all momentum from the tripartite proposal, and while the proposal remained on the table, Reagan did not raise it when he visited Beijing in late April 1984, nor did Kim Il Sung make public reference to it during his May 1984 visit to the Soviet Union.[19] In the years that followed, the DPRK made only occasional, passing references to it.

However, although the tripartite talks proposal had faded from the agenda by mid-1984, in its wake the North proceeded with a raft of talks initiatives to which the South, as anxious as ever to proceed with confidence-building measures, responded positively. This resulted in a series of negotiations relating to sport, flood relief, economic exchanges and parliamentary talks during 1984–5, which collectively constituted the most active phase of inter-Korean negotiation since 1972–3. The first negotiations took place over the issue of joint sporting teams, when in March 1984 the North proposed to the South that a unified Korean team be formed for the 1984 Los Angeles Olympiad. The issue soon became moot when Pyongyang withdrew entirely from the Games as part of a Soviet-led boycott and sporting contacts left the talks agenda.

A second avenue for negotiation then opened up in the humanitarian field in early September 1984 after widespread floods caused substantial loss of life and property damage in the South. On 8 September, the DPRK Red Cross offered supplies of rice, textiles, cement and medicine to aid victims, and Seoul, which had previously declined other international offers, deliberated for several days and then accepted the North's offer.[20] While ROK officials had seen nothing to suggest that the shipment was anything but a one-off exercise, the direct Red Cross telephone link, cut off by the North some years previously, was reopened in late September, ostensibly to coordinate the delivery of supplies, and then a routine proposal by Seoul in October to reopen the Red Cross Talks, which had been suspended unilaterally by the North in 1973, received positive public comment from Pyongyang. The two sides soon agreed to a resumption of the talks, thus opening a humanitarian avenue of contact for the first time in nearly twelve years.

Further avenues for talks opened with discussions on trade and economic cooperation opening in November at Panmunjom, and then in April 1985 the North proposed that a joint conference of parliamentarians be held with a view to making a joint declaration of non-aggression.[21] Seoul's response to this proposal, delivered in June, was lukewarm, not the least because at subsequent meetings in July agreement on an agenda for discussion proved elusive. Meanwhile, the resumed Red Cross talks were more productive, and at the eighth round of talks in Seoul during May 1985, the two sides reached unprecedented agreement on an exchange of visits by members of families divided since the Korean War, and also on an exchange of folk-art troupes (*KH*, 28 May 1985; *PT*, 1 June 1985). The exchanges, the first of their kind, duly took place in September.

However, these exchanges marked the high-point of the 1984–5 passage of negotiation, and the tenth round of Red Cross talks, held in Seoul in December, quickly reached an impasse. The North rejected a South proposal for hometown visits over Lunar New Year on the grounds that this was no longer a significant holiday in the North. Then in January 1986, Pyongyang announced what had become its customary unilateral suspension of all talks for the duration of the annual US–ROK Team Spirit military exercises (February to mid-April). Unlike the previous year, however, the completion of the Team Spirit exercises did not lead to a resumption, and instead, Pyongyang laid down a number of wide-ranging preconditions to a resumption of the dialogue. These related chiefly to the cessation of military exercises such as Team Spirit and the abrogation of the South's national security laws, and they effectively brought this period of dialogue to an end.[22]

A high-level, secret round of talks involving Chairman of the DPRK Committee for the Peaceful Reunification of the Fatherland Ho Tam and senior ROK representatives was another casualty of the North's retreat from dialogue at this time. Despite denials from both sides that such an avenue had been opened, persistent and informed reports portrayed these talks as an attempt by the North to encourage the South into the grand gesture of a summit meeting between President Chun Doo-hwan and Kim Il Sung (Tae-hwan Kwak, 1986: 2). Such a meeting had already been on offer from the South for some time, but one must assume that the details of Ho's proposals gave Seoul little or no encouragement that the North had anything meaningful to offer.

The balance sheet for the 1984–5 period of inter-Korean negotiation was meagre. The only tangible achievements were ephemeral ones in the humanitarian fields of flood relief shipments, the exchange of hometown visits and cultural performances. It underlined again that although Seoul attached particular importance to confidence-building measures, the DPRK did not, so these gestures did not lead to wider forms of agreement. In other areas, all negotiations stalled at the preliminary level of discussion on procedure. Moreover, with the exception of Ho Tam's brief involvement, at no stage did the level of representation on the northern side remotely approach the level of the 1972–3 talks. Negotiations were typically handled by DPRK government officials who had little room to manoeuvre, and who routinely and regularly sought instructions from their superiors even when only minor procedural issues were involved. Nor was there any sign of strategic change in DPRK state policy, for throughout this period there were no significant shifts within the DPRK leadership, and it remained intrinsically improbable that an ageing, doctrinaire revolutionary leadership would undertake a significant rethink of reunification strategy so soon after the Rangoon bombing.

The North's commitment during this period therefore remained highly tactical. It sought to tease out any weaknesses in its adversaries' positions and may also have calculated that this image might help to mute memories of Rangoon, thus making it easier for the Soviet Union and China to extend diplomatic support. Given past Soviet misgivings about Kim's tendency to adventurism, a resumed dialogue may have also eased Moscow's abiding fears and facilitated the resuming flow of economic and military assistance. It may also have helped to secure for the North a hearing that it otherwise might not have received from the International Olympic Committee where it sought to press its case for joint Pyongyang hosting of the Seoul Olympiad.

In search of a past that worked: re-enter the Soviets

The major foreign policy development for the DPRK during this period was rapprochement with the Soviet Union. It made sense, of course, for both parties to make common cause since they both had much to fear from the emerging Japan–China–US axis in the region. Moscow faced an emerging anti-Soviet entente on its eastern flank, spearheaded by three major powers with whom it had profound and seemingly intractable disputes.[23] They had long regarded Japan with a mixture of suspicion and antipathy, feelings that probably dated back to Russia's humiliation in the Russo–Japanese War of 1904–5 and which were reinforced during nearly three decades of dispute over the future of the Soviet-occupied Kurile Islands, while their failure to counteract growing Sino–Japanese cooperation was evident in the 1978 Sino–Japanese Treaty, where a clause expressing mutual opposition to 'dominationism', a code word for Soviet influence, had been inserted at China's insistence. Meanwhile, with China the legacy of the Sino–Soviet split was still strong, so after a brief thaw in relations during 1982, relations again became strained in the face of continued disagreement in three areas of foreign policy known as the 'three obstacles' – Afghanistan, Cambodia and troop levels on the Sino–Soviet border (Kelley, 1987: 96; Joseph M. Ha, 1983: 220–1). With the US, after the high point of détente in the early 1970s, US–Soviet relations deteriorated during the Carter administration (1977–81), especially after the Soviet invasion of Afghanistan in 1979. The Reagan administration's deployment of significant new weaponry in the Northeast Asian region, including cruise missiles and F-16 fighters (Zagoria, 1986: 349), and the Soviet shooting down of a ROK civilian airliner, KAL Flight 007, in September 1983 further raised tension.[24]

These developments therefore set the stage for a major revival of the Soviet–DPRK relationship. Despite the DPRK's past behaviour, the Soviets believed that significant military advantages would accrue from closer ties, since Moscow could bring greater pressure to bear on China's east flank and the Japanese islands generally, while Soviet inputs to the DPRK could help redress a growing military imbalance between the two Koreas, promoting an indefinite stand-off that would pin down the US forces in Korea. The Soviet naval presence in the region would also be enhanced by access to ports on the

DPRK's east coast, especially Wonsan. The DPRK was, of course, more than happy with Soviet strategic thinking, which it could utilise to alleviate growing economic and military pressures.

Such underlying common concerns began to take policy shape after the death of Soviet leader Leonid Brezhnev in November 1982. Brezhnev's last years were years of stagnation across wide areas of Soviet policy-making and it fell to his successor Yuri Andropov to take actual concrete measures. Displays of warmth and solidarity with the DPRK accordingly grew during 1983 and continued into early 1984, culminating in Kim Il Sung's 47-day tour of the Soviet Union and Eastern Europe (16 May to 1 July), his first official visit to the Soviet camp in twenty-three years. Something of the significance Kim attached to the visit may be gauged by the size of his entourage (reportedly 250-strong) and the number of key cadres that accompanied him, including those in charge of the economy (Kang Song-san), the military (O Chin-u) and foreign policy (Kim Yong-nam). Kim Il Sung's numerous visits to plants at the cutting edge of Soviet and East European technology in the fields of precision machinery, automobile manufacture, semiconductors and electronics emphasised his interest in expanding economic relations with the Socialist Bloc, and over the next eighteen months it became clear that both sides were seeking their own version of a substantial strengthening of economic ties.

In 1986, the two sides reached the high point of their restored relationship. The year began with a visit to Pyongyang by Soviet Foreign Minister Edvard Shevardnadze, the first-ever such visit by a Soviet Foreign Minister, and during the visit the two countries signed a number of intergovernmental agreements. Yet even as the two sides reached this high point in 1986, there were signs that the relationship was beginning to exhaust its possibilities. The differences between the two political cultures and the manner in which they set about pursuing their policy goals had induced a relationship 'marked by dualism, a lack of openness and an absence of real mutual confidence' (Zhebin, 1995: 733). The Soviets remained uneasy at the DPRK insistence on constant deference to Kim Jong Il, the almost total disappearance of references to Marxism–Leninism in DPRK ideology and the persistent slighting of the Soviet role in the liberation of Korea. And although the Soviets had the evidence of the *Pueblo*, the Panmunjom axe killings and Rangoon before them, they somehow continued to be surprised and dismayed at the extent to which the DPRK continued to engage in brinkmanship with the US and the ROK. Moreover, the Soviets quickly perceived that they could extract little benefit from their investment in the DPRK economy,[25] and while large numbers of Soviet and Eastern European technicians worked side by side with North Korean counterparts, DPRK politics and society remained closed to its socialist neighbour.[26] Mikhail Gorbachev reportedly contemplated a visit to Pyongyang but his advisers persuaded him not to go, and while the Soviets were prepared to receive Kim Jong Il on an official visit, the two sides were unable to agree on an appropriate level of protocol (Zhebin, 1995: 733).

By 1987 the processes of *perestroika* and *glasnost* had begun to undermine the Soviet Union's strategic premises in pursuing a restored relationship with the DPRK, and as the September 1988 Seoul Olympiad approached, Soviet thinking on security matters in Northeast Asia underwent a significant change, stressing improvement of relations with China and the ROK, and economic development in the Soviet Far East. The DPRK, with its fixed policy of maintaining a high degree of military tension on the Korean Peninsula, was a useful ally when it came to confronting the US military presence in Northeast Asia, but it had significantly less to contribute to these two emerging policy objectives. Moreover, while the DPRK adopted a pro-Soviet slant on a number of issues such as arms control and the Soviet proposal for an Asian security conference (Suck-ho Lee, 1986: 22), its utterances on other aspects of Soviet policies in Asia such as Afghanistan continued to display equivocation – doubtless to avoid damage to the vestiges of Pyongyang's Non-Aligned Movement credentials.[27]

China is near

The DPRK's expanded relationship with the Soviet Union during this period did not occur at the expense of relations with China. Relations had deteriorated sharply in the immediate aftermath of the signing of major Sino–Japanese and Sino–American accords in 1978–9 and the Sino–Vietnamese border conflict in February 1979, where the precedent had been set for China dealing harshly with an independently minded small state with a long common border was clear, but in late 1981 both China and the DPRK took steps to place relations on a pragmatic footing. Although Kim may have longed for a return to radical policies in China, there was little point in taking issue with the pragmatic economic policies then emerging under Deng Xiaoping. Therefore, the DPRK accepted rapprochement with Beijing and the material advantages that came with it, with the two sides agreeing to disagree on some rather basic issues in their foreign and domestic policies.[28]

For the Chinese it was desirable to maintain DPRK goodwill and, as far as possible, to bring Kim Il Sung around to their outlook on the international situation and on the type of outward-looking economic policies they felt were appropriate to this outlook. Moreover, there were still important conservative forces with the CCP and the military for whom the historical and military bonds with the DPRK remained meaningful. In pursuit of this, the Chinese made a series of tangible gestures. They increased oil exports to the DPRK at the discounted 'friendship' price, they made Chinese-built MIG-21As available to the Korean People's Air Force, they scaled down their growing indirect trade with the ROK and they adopted tougher rhetoric in support of the DPRK stand on reunification.[29] This level of Chinese support was useful to the DPRK, given its slowly deteriorating geopolitical environment.

However, this was counterbalanced by growing evidence of China's changing attitude towards the ROK, with unprecedented gestures in the sporting and humanitarian field forthcoming in 1984. ROK sporting teams were allowed to enter China to participate in international tournaments and China began to allow ROK citizens to visit relatives in China. A pair of hijacking incidents at this time emphasised their geographic proximity, and outcomes negotiated to China's satisfaction in both cases contributed to the development of mutual trust.[30] The combination of the DPRK's isolationism and China's on-going process of economic reform was weakening the traditional DPRK–Chinese relationship and rendering it disproportionately based on an obsolete ideological bond, and especially in the light of the forthcoming 1986 Asian Games and the 1988 Olympic Games in Seoul, the China–ROK relationship stood on the threshold of major change.

Concluding remarks

While it often seems easy enough to identify turning-points in the affairs of individuals and nations with hindsight, these are usually less obvious at the actual time they occur. The situation confronting the DPRK in the early 1980s is somewhat of an exception to this, for not only were both the economic and military situations objectively turning against the DPRK, but the leadership appeared to have some consciousness of this. Thus, in October 1982 Kim Jong Il departed briefly from the usually extravagant optimism of the DPRK's public rhetoric to describe the state of the nation in the following terms:

> Today our Party has entered a new stage of development. Our revolution is assuming a protracted and arduous nature and generations are changing among our revolutionary ranks. The internal and external situation of our revolution is strained and complicated. Realities raise the establishment of the monolithic ideological system of the Party as a still more important problem.
>
> (*PT*, 19 October 1982)

This was a rare departure from the triumphalist, esoteric language of the leadership, for by use of the phrases 'protracted and arduous' and 'strained and complicated' the younger Kim was acknowledging the severity of recent setbacks and admitting that the Party was no longer likely to lead the country to reunification in the near future. If others had said as much they would have been punished for defeatism. At the same time, however, he reaffirmed that 'the monolithic ideological system of the Party', by which he meant the Kimist personal autocracy, would be the means by which the country would deal with the situation.

This statement illuminates the contradiction facing the DPRK in the 1980s as few others do, for while acknowledging that the tide of events was running against it, the younger Kim advanced a response drawn from the now distant past: the country should rely even more on the man and the ideology that had led them to their current difficulties. The statement thus foreshadowed that the country's growing isolation and deteriorating economic, military and diplomatic situation would be addressed from within existing ideological parameters, and it is therefore not surprising to see in the DPRK after 1980 a chronic, almost pathological inability to make pragmatic adjustments to changing circumstances, whether internal or external.

Such a response was also emphasised by the rise of Kim Jong Il. Far from heralding the rise of a new generation of technocratically minded cadres oriented towards pragmatic policies, the younger Kim himself emphasised that his role was to ensure that the Party safeguarded the revolutionary tradition of the anti-Japanese guerillas, and so the Three Revolutions Teams fought zealously to ensure that 'formalism' and 'bureaucratism' would not quench this tradition. Thus, throughout this period we find that DPRK priorities did not include generational change, but on the contrary displayed a noteworthy consistency with past practice. Political developments did not follow from a conscious process of 'generational change' in the political leadership, nor from significant modifications to traditional policies. Economic 'reforms' were restricted to minor tinkering with budget structures and accounting systems, much as had been carried out since the early 1970s, while the 1984 Joint Venture Law did not provide a framework for the introduction of Western capital and technology, but instead became largely a vehicle for repatriating funds from pro-DPRK Koreans in Japan (Namkoong, 1995: 468). Meanwhile, engagement with the South remained as tactical as ever.

Obsessive pursuit of reunification blinded Kim Il Sung to many things, but it was especially in the international sphere, where the growing international prestige of the ROK and changing priorities in Chinese foreign policy were eroding the DPRK's diplomatic position, that his limitations continued to be exposed. Fixed, doctrinaire assessments of the international situation prevented the DPRK from adjusting to change in the region. The rapprochement with the Soviet Union was a major step, but it was a conservative option that led Pyongyang to attach itself to a system that was about to enter its terminal crisis period. And, on the other side of the coin, when one looks at the Soviet decision to invest massive resources in an economy such as the DPRK's, one must wonder at the paucity of perceived plausible options open to the Soviets, and especially at the judgement of key Soviet decision-makers at the time.[31]

Kim Il Sung always viewed isolation and economic autarky as essential to the preservation of his system, but this in turn meant a profoundly self-centred, self-indulgent view of the world and a primitive, zero-sum approach to diplomacy that equated DPRK advantage with disadvantage inflicted on others, and that increasingly left the DPRK sterile, backward and friendless. As the Soviets discovered — or rather rediscovered — Kim was hard on adversaries and allies alike, and was dedicated foremost to maximising short-term gain while giving as little as possible in return. The cavalier fashion with which the country treated its foreign debt issues similarly reflected a cynical, predatory approach to international dealings, while the repeated involvement of DPRK diplomats in smuggling and other nefarious activities, intermittent support for international terrorism and, of course, the Rangoon bombing itself underlined the primitive expediency that drove DPRK foreign policy.

Why, then, did so many observers perceive economic and political change during this period? As even a cursory review of the literature reveals, expectations of reform in the DPRK always tend to base themselves on pragmatic and generational premises rather than hard evidence, with perhaps the most common theme being that the regime needed to embrace reform in order to arrest its decline. Less common were attempts to turn this argument around the other way and to see the failure of the DPRK to attempt even marginal reform measures as suggestive of a polity ideologically blind to its failures and obviously lacking many key prerequisites for pragmatic reform, including openness to influence from its own civil society and from participation in the international order. In his isolated vantage-point, Kim did not have to factor in such influence, and so he had no perception that he was facing anything other than minor setbacks and irritations. At most, he felt only the need for minor adjustments in order to reduce the country's trade deficit, so his opportunistic behaviour towards the Soviets was not that of a drowning man grateful for a lifeline but rather that of the eternal optimist, convinced of the righteousness of his cause and forever confident that all setbacks were temporary, because whatever the situation, the tide of history was on his side. The challenges of the 1980s underlined a core dilemma for would-be reformers within the DPRK and would-be external perceivers of reform alike: how could change be generated out of an esoteric, dogmatic ideology by isolated, ill-educated elderly cadres working from within an unchanging set of state and party institutions?

Notes

1 Based on the ages given in Dong-Bok Lee (1981a).
2 For detailed coverage of this Congress, see Buzo (1999:108–116).
3 For the English text of Kim Il Sung's report to the Sixth KWP Congress, see *PT*, 11 October 1980.
4 Kim became the fourth-ranking member of the Politburo, fourth-ranking member of a new five-member Politburo Presidium, second-ranking member of the Party Secretariat and third-ranking member of the Party's Military Commission. See *PT*, 15 October 1980 for full details of the membership of these bodies.
5 See, for example, *PT*, 21 August 1982.
6 *PT*, 21 August 1982. See Induk Kang (1982: 91–8) and Byung-Chul Koh (1986: 21–6) for further discussion of *On the Juche Idea*.
7 The one missing component was, of course, the role of military leadership. Here Kim Il Sung clearly did not wish to share the limelight or else saw potential for confusion, for Kim Jong Il did not receive high military office and honours until 1992.
8 Unless otherwise stated, these calculations are based on figures given in Koo (1992).
9 By the late 1980s, the DPRK owed approximately $2.3 billion to a large consortium of Western banks on loans contracted in 1974 and 1977. No principal repayments had ever been made, and interest repayments had ceased in 1984. In August 1987 the banks declared the DPRK to be in formal default. One major syndicate, led

by Morgan Grenfell, lobbied other banks in support of a joint proposal to the DPRK to settle the issue on the basis of a 70 per cent write-off of the loans but was unsuccessful. In 1990 a committee acting on behalf of the banks instituted legal action in a number of jurisdictions. In 1992 the banks obtained an award by the International Chamber of Commerce requiring immediate payment of the debt. The award was enforceable in over seventy countries and, theoretically at least, opened the way for the sequestering of DPRK goods and property (AA Note for File, 22 January 1992, CRS A1838; 3125/10/1). A lasting stand-off ensued: the DPRK made no move to re-establish its bona fides with the banks, while the banks, having made their point, displayed no interest in pursuing the matter further than the ICC judgement.

10 Byung-chul Koh (1984: 46) also makes the point that there was little new in this emphasis of the importance of foreign trade for the DPRK and cites various supportive statements on the subject by Kim Il Sung during the 1970s. Also see Joseph Chung (1987: 123) who quotes a Kim Il Sung speech of 4 March 1975: 'But from now on we must actively trade with emerging independent countries and capitalist nations. Under the circumstances when the economy is developing rapidly and new economic branches are being created, we cannot satisfactorily meet all our needs if we depend only on socialist markets.'

11 We should also note in passing that Soviet specialists on the DPRK economy have rejected the notion that the DPRK was pursuing a path of economic reform during this period. See Mikheev (1991: 446) and Trigubenko (1991: 108).

12 For details of Soviet weaponry supplied to the DPRK during this period, see Pfaltzgraff (1986).

13 See Trigubenko (1991: 119) for comment on the quality of DPRK manufactures.

14 The following comments on changes in the months following December 1983 are representative: 'Drastic changes in government positions took place, perhaps in reaction to economic failures at home and diplomatic setbacks abroad' (Younghwan Kihl, 1985: 67); 'It is evident from the pattern of new assignments that there has been a generational change among DPRK political leaders in favour of Kim Jong Il. Supporters of Kim Jong Il from the Party are rapidly replacing the old revolutionaries and aging technocrats in important positions' (Dae-Sook Suh, 1986: 14); 'At present, another transition appears to be taking place as Kim Jong Il, heir to his father's position, rises. The replacement of the veteran Ho Tam as Foreign Minister by Kim Yong-nam, who appears to be a key element in the new team, is but one indication of the passing of the old guard' (Scalapino and Hongkoo Lee, 1986: x); 'Kim Chong Il is said to have strengthened the function of the 10-member Secretariat, recruiting relatively young technocrats who are generally Kim Chong Il's alumni ... we may tentatively conclude that North Korea's announcement of her economic policy advocating cooperation with foreign "capitalist" countries should be interpreted as a departure from past policies. In other words, North Korea is slowly, within limits, beginning to open her door to the outside world, and is prepared to introduce "pragmatism" in her economy, science and technology' (Hakjoon Kim, 1984: 18, 24–5); 'A generational shift in the political power structure was begun after the 6th Party Congress in 1980 when people of the revolution's second generation started to be recruited in large numbers ... In particular, almost all newly appointed Alternate Politburo members were economic experts who introduced Party policy directions in the economy, science and technology' (Hyun-Joon Chon, 1994: 59); 'We have seen a replacement of young technocrat elites who are particularly close to Kim Jong Il between the 6th party congress in October 1980 and change of the key members of the Administration Council in July 1985' (Jae-Kyu Park, 1987: 8). The extensiveness and persistence of this literature can also be illustrated by some of the titles of articles reviewing annual developments in North Korea published in the journal

Asian Survey during the period: 'North Korea in 1983: Transforming "The Hermit Kingdom?"'; 'North Korea in 1984: "The Hermit Kingdom" Turns Outward'; 'North Korea in 1985: A New Era After Forty Years'.

15 Essentially, change in the DPRK leadership during the period 1983 to 1986 amounted to minor adjustments within the Politburo and largely routine changes in the Party Secretariat and Administrative Council. For more detailed analysis of these movements, see Buzo (1999: 131–8).
16 For details of the 1980 negotiations, see Dong-Bok Lee (1981b: 37–8).
17 For details, see Buzo (1999: 147–8).
18 The US in particular, convinced of Chinese good intentions, sought to extend the tripartite formula to include the Chinese and, despite a preliminary assessment that the proposal 'looked, in large part, to be propaganda', Washington was also particularly concerned not to be dismissive of a proposal that had been actively brokered by Beijing (AA Cable from Washington to Canberra, 20 January 1984: CRS A1838; 3126/1/1).
19 And in the wake of Kim Il Sung's visit, Soviet Deputy Foreign Minister Mikhail Kapitsa in effect supported the DPRK position, stating that the Soviet Union did not endorse the tripartite formula (AA Cable from Moscow to Canberra, 10 July 1984: CRS A1838; 3126/1/1).
20 For the text of the South's acceptance, see *KWA*, 1984, 8(4): 967–8. Significant as the breakthrough was, the act of giving was far from a gracious one, with the DPRK imposing a number of conditions on delivery that were contrary to the International Red Cross rule of respecting the wishes of the recipient country, and at one stage walking out of the delivery negotiations. For the atmospherics surrounding the DPRK offer, see *Newsreview*, 22 September 1984. For the official announcement of the DPRK's offer, see *PT*, 12 September 1984.
21 With roughly half the population of the ROK, the DPRK's SPA had more than double the number of members. For the full text of the proposal, delivered by Ho Tam at the SPA session in his capacity as Chairman of the Committee for the Peaceful Reunification of the Fatherland, see *PT*, 13 April 1985.
22 For a more detailed account of this period of talks, see Buzo (1999: 146–55).
23 On the Soviet view of developments in the Northeast Asian region at the time, particularly as they affected relations with the DPRK, see Zhebin (1995).
24 On 1 September, Soviet jet fighters shot down Korean Air Lines Flight 007 which had strayed into sensitive Soviet air space around the island of Sakhalin while en route from New York to Seoul via Anchorage. Hassan (1984) provides a full description and discussion of this incident, focusing on its legal implications.
25 Not the least because of DPRK industrial planning follies. Actual case studies are rare, but the Soviet diplomat Valentin Moiseyev (1991: 73) describes the case of the Ryonsong Bearing Plant, completed with Soviet assistance in 1985, which was designed for annual production of 10 million bearings. According to Moiseyev, only upon completion did the Soviets learn that there was neither the steel feed to produce the bearings nor was there any demand for the product.
26 Zhebin (1995: 733) notes that while the DPRK media carried the word '*perestroika*', it never commented on its substance: 'Especially taboo were any references to democratisation, condemnation of Stalin's personality cult, and rehabilitation of the victims of Stalinism. Pyongyang feared that such information would draw parallels with the purges that had taken place in the DPRK in the 1950s and 1960s.'
27 Practically the only visible sign of substantial Soviet diplomatic gain out of all this was the distance Kim Il Sung now placed between himself and the anti-Heng Samrin government forces in Cambodia. As Prince Norodom Sihanouk, the figurehead leader of these forces and no friend of Moscow, himself complained at the time, the DPRK media ceased to mention his regular visits to the DPRK, where Kim had provided him with a villa. See *FEER*, 9 April 1987, p. 11.

28 The number of Chinese delegations visiting the DPRK rose from 38 in 1982 to 62 in 1983. Visits at the vice-ministerial level or above rose from 10 to 16. The corresponding figures for DPRK delegations to China were 34 (9 vice-ministerial or above) in 1982 and 54 (18) in 1983 (Chong-Wook Chung, 1986:54). In private, however, Chinese leaders were telling foreign leaders at the time that they found the Kims difficult to deal with and that China's influence on the DPRK was less than many outsiders imagined (DFAT Cable from Tokyo to Canberra, 22 November 1984: CRS A9737; 91/004008–1).
29 On this passage of China–DPRK diplomacy, see Zagoria (1983: 367).
30 These involved the hijacking to Seoul of a Chinese civilian airliner in May 1983 and the arrival in ROK territorial waters in March 1985 of a Chinese torpedo boat, members of whose crew had mutinied. For details, see Chae-Jin Lee (1996:109–110).
31 The vivid portrait of Soviet Politburo decision-making during this period in Volkogonov (1999) leaves little to the imagination regarding the degree of dysfunctionality that gradually overtook the Politburo beginning in the mid Brezhnev years and continuing on into the Andropov and Chernenko eras.

References

Buzo, Adrian (1999) *The Guerilla Dynasty: Politics and Leadership in North Korea*. I.B. Tauris: London.

Chon, Hyun-Joon (1994) Structure of the power elite of North Korea, *The Korean Journal of National Unification*, special edition.

Chung, Chong-wook (1986) China's role in two-Korea relations in the 1980s, *Journal of Northeast Asian Studies*, V(3): 52–66.

Chung, Joseph S. (1987) North Korea's economic development and capabilities, in *The Foreign Relations of North Korea: New Perspectives*, Jae-Kyu Park, Byung-Chul Koh and Tae-Hwan Kwak (eds). Westview Press and Kyungnam University Press: Seoul, pp. 107–38.

Department of Foreign Affairs and Trade (DFAT). Commonwealth Record series A9737, correspondence files, annual single series 1990–; Commonwealth Record series A1838, correspondence files, multiple number series, 1948–89, recorded by the Australian Department of Foreign Affairs from 1970 to 1987 and thereafter by DFAT. All files consulted were made available to the author under the Special Access provisions of Section 56 of the Archives Act, 1983.

Eberstadt, Nicholas (2015) *North Korea's 'Epic Economic Fail' in International Perspective*. The Asian Institute for Policy Studies: Seoul.

Ha, Joseph M. (1983) The impact of the Sino–Soviet conflict on the Korean Peninsula, in *The Two Koreas in World Politics*, Tae-Hwan Kwak, Wayne Patterson and Edward A. Olsen (eds). The Institute for Far Eastern Studies, Kyungnam University: Seoul, pp. 211–230.

Hassan, Farooq (1984) The shooting down of Korean Airlines Flight 007 by the USSR and the future of air safety for passengers, *International and Comparative Law Quarterly*, 33: 712–25.

Kang, Induk (1982) Kim Jong Il's guidance activities as Mirrored in the Recent Korean Press, in *Journal of Northeast Asian Affairs*, I(4): 91–9.

Kelley, Donald R. (1987) *Soviet Politics from Brezhnev to Gorbachev*. Praeger: New York.

Kihl, Young-Whan (1985) North Korea in 1984: 'The hermit kingdom turns outward!', *Asian Survey*, XXV(1): 65–79.

Kim, Hakjoon (1984) Current major trends in North Korea's domestic politics, *Journal of Northeast Asian Studies*, III(3): 16–29.
Kim, Jong Il (1982) *On the Juche Idea*. Foreign Languages Publishing House: Pyongyang.
Koh, Byung-Chul (1984) *The Foreign Policy Systems of North and South Korea*. University of California Press: Berkeley, CA.
Koh, Byung-Chul (1986) Ideology and North Korean foreign policy, in *North Korea in a Regional and Global Context*, Robert A. Scalapino and Hongkoo Lee (eds). Institute of East Asian Studies, University of California: Berkeley, CA, pp. 20–36.
Koo, Bon-Hak (1992) *Political Economy of Self-Reliance: Juche and Economic Development in North Korea 1961–1990*. Research Centre for Peace and Reunification of Korea: Seoul.
Kwak, Tae-Hwan (1986) *In Search of Peace and Unification on the Korean Peninsula*. Seoul Computer Press: Seoul.
Lankov, Andrei and Kim, Seok-hyang (2008) North Korean market vendors: The rise of grassroots capitalists in a post-Stalinist society, *Pacific Affairs*, 81(1): 68–9.
Lee, Chae-Jin (1996) *China and Korea: Dynamic Relations*. The Hoover Press: Stanford, CA.
Lee, Dong-Bok (1981a) North Korea after Sixth KWP Congress, *Korea & World Affairs*, 5,(3): 415–40.
Lee, Dong-Bok (1981b) Present and future of inter-Korean relations: The January 12 Proposal and the Sixth Congress of the KWP, *Korea & World Affairs*, 5(1): 36–52.
Lee, Suck-Ho (1986) Evolution and prospects of Soviet–North Korean relations in the 1980s, *Journal of Northeast Asian Studies*, V(2): 19–34.
Mikheev, Vasily V. (1991) New Soviet approaches to North Korea, *Korea and World Affairs*, 15(3): 442–56.
Moiseyev, Valentin I. (1991) USSR-North Korea Economic Cooperation, in *Pukhan kyongje ui hyonhwang gwa chonmang (Current Situation and Outlook for the North Korean Economy)*. Korea Development Institute: Seoul, pp. 69–93.
Namkoong, Young (1995) An analysis of North Korea's Policy to attract foreign capital: Management and achievement, *Korea and World Affairs*, 19(3): 459–81.
Park, Jae-Kyu (1987) Introduction: A basic framework for understanding North Korea's foreign policy, in *The Foreign Relations of North Korea: New Perspectives*, Jae-Kyu Park, Byung-Chul Koh and Tae-Hwan Kwak (eds). Westview Press and Kyungnam University Press: Seoul, pp. 3–14.
Pfaltzgraff, Robert L. Jr. (1986) Soviet strategy and North Korea, *Korea and World Affairs*, 10(2): 324–45.
Pollack, Joshua (2011) Ballistic trajectory: The evolution of North Korea's ballistic missile market, *Nonproliferation Review*, 18(2): 412–29.
Scalapino, Robert A. and Lee, Hongkoo (eds) (1986) *North Korea in a Regional and Global Context*. Institute of East Asian Studies, University of California: Berkeley, CA.
Suh, Dae-Sook (1986) The organization and administration of North Korean foreign policy, in *North Korea in a Regional and Global Context*, Robert A. Scalapino and Hongkoo Lee (eds). Institute of East Asian Studies, University of California: Berkeley, CA, pp. 1–19.
Trigubenko, Marina (1991) Industry of the DPRK: Specific features of the industrial policy, sectoral structure and prospects, in *Pukhan kyongje ui hyonhwang gwa chonmang (Current Situation and Outlook for the North Korean Economy)*. Korea Development Institute: Seoul, pp. 101–35.

Volkogonov, Dmitri (1999) *The Rise and Fall of the Soviet Empire*. HarperCollins: London.
Zagoria, Donald S. (1983) North Korea: Between Moscow and Beijing, in *North Korea Today: Strategic and Domestic Issues*, Robert A. Scalapino and Jun-Yop Kim (eds). Institute of East Asian Studies, University of California: Berkeley, CA, pp. 351–371.
Zagoria, Donald S. (1986) The Soviet Union's military–political strategy in the Far East, *Korea and World Affairs*, 10(2): 346–69.
Zhebin, Alexander (1995) Russia and North Korea: An emerging, uneasy partnership, *Asian Survey*, XXXV(8): 727–39.

5 Tactical retreat: 1987–94

Introduction

The renewed DPRK commitment to close military and economic relations with the Soviet Union in 1984 proved to be short-lived, for Pyongyang had bound itself to a country and a system that was itself approaching a terminal crisis and whose collapse in 1989 further undermined the DPRK's own system. The upshot, however, was that when the Soviet Union collapsed, the DPRK lost a vital source of economic subsidy, and so in Kim Il Sung's last years the economy lurched towards crisis point. Again characteristically, in the wake of the Soviet collapse the DPRK evinced a minimalist response consisting of four main policy strands – ideological intransigence, system-defending economic initiatives, tactical re-engagement with the ROK and the ROK's allies, but above all, prioritisation of progress towards developing a credible nuclear threat.

In ideological matters, the speed at which ordinary people in Soviet Bloc countries had abandoned the regimes to which so many of them had always passively submitted was an alarming revelation to the DPRK. To Kim this was not, of course, a reflection on the ideology itself, but rather was a reflection on the regimes concerned and their failure to keep their people in line, and so his resolve to maintain the isolation of the populace from capitalist 'contamination' strengthened accordingly. Accordingly, in the wake of the collapse of global communism, the leadership's first and last instinct was to tighten ideological control over the population, and so we find that Kim Jong Il's canonical writings from this era display even more fantastical definitions of Kimist monolithic ideology, this time casting the leadership in the role of a human brain and the people in the role of limbs and organs who are given 'life' and social purpose as they responded to stimuli from this brain.

System-defending economic policy measures were also undertaken, most noticeably through accepting trade with the ROK, whereupon Seoul rapidly engineered a trade gap of $150 million in the DPRK's favour, partly as a bribe to induce better behaviour, and partly due to a felt need to cushion the North against imminent economic collapse. Illegal and predatory transactions involving large-scale smuggling under diplomatic privilege, counterfeiting, and the organised manufacture and sale of hard drugs such as heroin and methamphetamine, were a further source of budgetary relief, as was the ongoing sale of weaponry to Middle East countries, including large numbers of ballistic missile systems. And while the 1991 designation of the Rajin-Sunbong area in the remote northeast of the country as a Free Economic and Trade Zone (FETZ) led nowhere, unofficial cross-border trade with China expanded, providing an ever-growing source of revenue. Overall, these moves enabled a continuing flow of revenue to the military sector, but only at the expense of bleeding other sectors, especially the state economy sector and the Public Distribution System, in a strategy that led directly to catastrophic famine and the deindustrialisation of the DPRK in the mid-1990s.

Yet another strand of the DPRK's response involved tactical diplomatic moves involving the ROK, the US and Japan. In September–October 1988 the ROK successfully staged the Seoul Olympiad and then proceeded to make substantial inroads into Pyongyang's diplomatic support base by establishing closer ties with both the Soviet Union and China. The uncertainties felt by Kim in the wake of these developments appear to have led him to agree to talks with the ROK at the prime ministerial level in July 1990 after almost five years of stalemate, and in December 1991 these talks culminated in the conclusion of an Agreement on Reconciliation, Nonaggression, and Exchanges and Cooperation Between the South and the North. In addition, in May 1991 Pyongyang bowed to the inevitable and, reversing a long-standing policy, accepted the separate entry of the two Koreas into the United Nations. Meanwhile, in other signs of potential adjustment, the DPRK and the US initiated the first of a series of unofficial diplomatic contacts in Beijing in October 1988, and in September 1990 the DPRK also appeared to reach a breakthrough in its relations with Japan with an agreement to hold talks on the normalisation of relations.

However, as the DPRK absorbed manifold external shocks to its system, Kim Il Sung appeared to gain new confidence in his ability to continue the decades-long struggle against the ROK, the US and the forces of imperialism, with a clear tipping point being reached during 1992. This was the point where the DPRK began to retreat from all dialogues and place ultimate faith in the country's on-going nuclear weapons programme to safeguard its national security, for this programme promised to address the country's on-going military enfeeblement and steer the country into a safer haven of indefinite stalemate – and perhaps open up new strategic possibilities. As the international community became more aware of this programme, the DPRK played adroitly for time, signing a safeguards agreement with the International Atomic Energy Agency (IAEA) in 1991, but then embarking on a protracted stand-off over on-site inspections. Ultimately, this induced a serious confrontation with the US in June 1994, until a compromise brokered by former US President Jimmy Carter resolved the immediate crisis and in October 1994 led to the pact known as the Agreed Framework. Under this agreement, the DPRK undertook to return its nuclear programme to an IAEA inspection regime in return for the US-brokered provision of fuel oil and the construction of two light-water nuclear reactors.

Unshakeable ideology

To the end of his life, whenever invited to give his views on international matters, Kim Il Sung unfailingly began with a vivid description of the desperate, Manichean nature of the global struggle between socialism and imperialism, and the importance of the Korean conflict in that struggle. We have no reason to doubt either the depth of his conviction or his effectiveness in ensuring that the Party and the masses acted in support of this vision, for to the ex-guerillas in the DPRK leadership who had grown to maturity amid a protracted fight for survival with the Japanese and had experienced the founding of the DPRK under Stalinist auspices, the Cold War vision of an immutable global struggle between the forces of socialism and imperialism made profound sense – far more so than to the cadres of more educated, cosmopolitan background scattered through the politburos of other socialist states. Consequently, when the end of the Cold War placed the DPRK under enormous diplomatic and military pressure, this was by no means a daunting situation for Kim Il Sung and the men around him. In many ways, his glorification of the guerilla ethos expressed a worldview built to withstand these very pressures – to accept life in an isolated, hostile environment, enforce rigid Party discipline, endure prolonged privation, be improvisatory and seize whatever advantages might arise, prize only what was within one's grasp and, above all, never submit.

Therefore, it is not surprising that the DPRK's response to the setbacks of the late 1980s was to unflinchingly defend Kimist ideology. Within the Politburo, Kim continued to promote ageing members of the guerilla generation, and no members of the post-war Kim Jong Il generation advanced to full membership of the Politburo during 1987–94.[1] By far the most significant move was the dismissal in February 1988 of O Kuk-ryol (then 57) from the Politburo and from his position as Chief of General Staff of the Korean People's Armed Forces, and his replacement by a considerably older man, the ex-guerilla Ch'oe Kwang (then 72), originally dismissed by Kim from the same position some twenty years previously in 1968. As the second-ranking active military cadre in the Party, O appeared to be heir apparent to the top military post of People's Armed Forces Minister, then occupied by the ageing O Chin-u (no relation).[2] O's father had fought with Kim in Manchuria, and O had been the only member in the Politburo from the post-1945 generation of military cadres, who were products of standard military academy training at Mangyongdae Revolutionary School, but in replacing O, Kim did not hesitate to disregard the claims of this younger generation in favour of a substantially older man who was the product of irregular guerilla warfare and not regular military training.[3]

A major ideological treatise by Kim Jong Il in July 1986 titled *On Some Problems of Education in the Juche Idea* further underlined the hardening attitude of the leadership. In it we find Kim chiefly concerned with the elaboration of a pre-existing metaphor of DPRK political society as a 'living political organism', whereby people received their biological life from their parents but could only realise their full human potential when they lived in organic socio-political unity with the Great Leader and the Party. In this work, and in the sustained exegesis in the media that followed its publication, we find the leadership keen to press its categorical denial of any need to look outside the Juche system or indeed to find new, flexible interpretations of Juche in order to meet a changing situation. Rather, more stringent definitions and elaborations on Juche's characteristic themes of unconditional loyalty and obedience became the new staple of party ideology during this period.[4]

As had been the case on the younger Kim's fortieth birthday in 1982, in a surviving item of Stalinist protocol, the Party used the occasion of his approaching milestone fiftieth birthday on 16 February 1992 to award him further high honours and praise. At the Nineteenth Plenum of the Sixth KWP CC, convened on 24 December 1991, the younger Kim was named Supreme Commander of the Korean People's Armed Forces, marking the final preparatory step in the transfer of power from father to son. Subsequently, not only did his fiftieth birthday messages allude to his leading role in a wide range of party, state and military activities, but when the first volumes of Kim Il Sung's autobiography *Reminiscences with the Century* began to appear in early 1992, the older Kim himself alluded to his son's ever-expanding leadership role in the preface, modestly noting:

> Many people, including celebrated foreign statesmen and well-known literary men, urged me to write my reminiscences, saying that my life would serve as a precious lesson for the people. But I was in no hurry to do so. Now that a large part of my work is done by [OGD Secretary] Kim Jong Il, I have been able to find some time (Kim Il Sung 1992).[5]

In this manner, father and son continued to work effectively together throughout the last years of the older Kim's life. His continuing vitality was evident in an energetic round of on-the-spot guidance tours, including a nineteen-day tour of North Hamgyong Province during 16 August to 3 September 1990 at the height of the hot and humid Korean summer, and the younger Kim was regularly portrayed in the media in ever-broadening areas of the national life as working to give effect to the teachings of his father.

System-defending economic policies

Ideological intransigence naturally flowed through to economic policy, where an unchanging framework remained in place during this period. The interplan period 1984–87 finally limped to a conclusion in April 1987 when the Second Session of the Eighth Supreme People's Assembly announced the Third Seven-Year Plan (1987–93).[6] By now, however, it was clear that multi-year economic plans were serving as fantastic ideological rallying points rather than as sober economic planning documents, while other signs likewise suggest that by the late 1980s the broader DPRK economy had drifted into a state of semi-permanent crisis.[7] The replacement of Prime Minister Yi Kun-mo after only two years in charge of the plan, continuing and uncharacteristic minor tinkering with the structure and top personnel in the economic ministries and commissions, public Soviet criticism of the quality of DPRK steel exports (Kongdan Oh, 1990: 79), and public DPRK statements that agricultural production had been significantly affected by weather patterns since 1984 – the last year that a grain production figure had been announced – all indicated a deteriorating economy.[8]

Even under normal circumstances, the cumulative effect of economic decline and ideological rigidity would eventually have had serious repercussions, but the economy now encountered a further, major setback in the collapse of the Soviet Union. At this time the Soviet Union was the source of about half of the DPRK's foreign trade, a substantial proportion of its oil imports, and almost all of its new technology inputs, but now as the relationship with the DPRK became an increasing liability to the Soviets, Soviet–DPRK trade began to decline in 1989. In September 1990 Soviet Foreign Minister Eduard Shevardnadze officially informed the DPRK that future economic relations would be conducted on a strictly commercial basis (Boulychev, 1994: 103–5), and these new conditions for bilateral trade then combined with a sharp decline in the Soviet Union's production and export capacity due to political and economic turmoil. The result was a sharp contraction in DPRK–USSR trade by 1991. In particular, Soviet oil exports to the DPRK were badly affected, with the 1992 figure amounting to only 10 per cent of the 1990 figure of 410,000 tons (Komaki, 1992: 168) out of an estimated total demand of 700,000–800,000 tons.[9]

From their public statements during this period, it is clear that the Kims continued to believe that these setbacks were temporary, that the contradictions of capitalist system were serious and that 'the end of contemporary imperialism was nigh'.[10] Thus, throughout this period the official media continued to reaffirm both the primacy of capital and heavy industrial construction and the relevance of traditional ideological parameters, including the Chollima Movement and speed campaigns (*PT*, 16 February 1989), Kim Il Sung's Rural Theses (*PT*, 25 February 1989), the Taean Work System (*PT*, 17 June 1989), the Three Revolutions (*PT*, 13 January 1990) and the Chongsanri Method (*PT*, 10 February 1990). Accordingly, the most persuasive course of action was to make tactical adjustments to find new economic inputs until the final battle was won, and so the Party made no radical moves to counter the loss of Soviet economic support. Instead, beginning in about 1988, while neither public statements of policy nor personnel movements within the leadership gave any clear indication of change, a distinct economic strategy aimed at defending, not reforming, the economic system began to emerge piecemeal. Collectively, the moves taken ensured that, as Paul Bracken put it, the DPRK remained 'the hole in the doughnut of East Asian economic development' (Bracken, 1998: 415). The hallmarks included:

- the maintenance of the fundamental features of the command economy;
- the maintenance of collectivised agriculture;
- the maintenance of other basic DPRK state policies, including its nuclear weapons programme;
- a continuing prohibition on public or semi-public debate on economic reform;
- a continued reliance on ideological incentives for the workforce;
- the development of trade with the ROK, but the exclusion of major ROK investment;
- the development of arms sales, especially to the Middle East;
- the maintenance and expansion of a broad suite of predatory and illegal international transactions, including insurance fraud, currency and brand name counterfeiting, diplomatic smuggling, and hard drugs manufacture and sale;
- continuing interest in Free Economic and Trade Zone (FETZ) strategies in the north-east region, and
- the substantial relaxation of controls on border trade in the northeast.

In economic terms, the key element here was the rapid increase in trade with the ROK, which as late as 1988 had totalled only $1 million, but which by 1991 had risen to $111.3 million, making the ROK one of the DPRK's major trading partners.

Leading ROK firms evinced little interest in the few products on offer from the North, but nevertheless swung into line behind their government. In many cases, ROK firms entered the northern trade not for immediate profit but as a bridgehead for the future,[11] while in other cases they found themselves under strong and direct government pressure to accept North Korean commodities and products despite quality problems. ROK firms were also limited in their capacity to export to the North because Pyongyang's lack of foreign exchange largely restricted trade to barter arrangements. Thus, the balance of trade ran heavily in the North's favour, as intended.

The same non-economic motives applied to the DPRK's other neighbours, and so one finds that trade with China and Japan also increased substantially during this period. In particular, as imports of Soviet oil fell in 1991, producing widespread dislocations in industry and agriculture, Chinese and, to a lesser

Table 5.1 DPRK trade with the ROK: 1989–92 (unit: US$ million)

	Exports to the ROK	Imports from the ROK	Balance in the DPRK's favour
1989	18.7	0.1	18.6
1990	12.3	1.2	11.1
1991	105.7	5.6	101.1
1992	162.9	10.6	152.3

Source: ROK National Unification Board

extent, Japanese trade filled this gap, although the overall rapid decline in foreign trade continued and the size of the year-to-year fluctuations indicated the instability associated with this period of adjustment.[12]

In the arms market, specifically ballistic missile systems, the DPRK stumbled on a veritable explosion of demand precisely at this time of great economic need. Beginning about 1987, and continuing for a period of six years encompassing the latter stages of the Iran–Iraq War and Operation Desert Storm, demand for such systems increased exponentially in the Middle East. Thereafter, demand tailed off, but overall between 1987 and 2009, the DPRK is estimated to have sold nearly five hundred such systems, as well as tapping into burgeoning markets in other fields of supply, including system components and updates, tanks, air-defence systems, rocket-propelled grenades and rocket-artillery systems. Sales in uranium conversion and enrichment equipment to Syria and Iran also took place. It is not possible to gauge accurately either the full extent of these sales or their value to the North Korean economy, but they were obviously substantial.[13]

Various forms of illicit trade also flourished, evidently coordinated through a specialised unit known as Central Committee Bureau 39, which dealt with a suite of products and whose revenue went directly towards meeting the expenses of the court economy.[14] In the early 1990s, the leadership evidently made a decision to enter the heroin and methamphetamine markets, and until they opted to substantially withdraw from this trade beginning in about 2005, the DPRK had continuing relationships with established trafficking syndicates (Hastings, 2014: 15). High-quality counterfeiting of US $100 bills, so-called 'supernotes', also began about this time, as did various other kinds of fraudulent production and patent/copyright violation, including US-origin cigarettes and front-shelf pharmaceuticals such as Viagra. These activities had already been around for some time in one form or another since such criminality, often arising from disdain for capitalist norms, had always been a deeply ingrained feature of the Kimist state's external transactions, but they now grew in sophistication, and by the 2000s some specialists were assessing their annual value at several hundred million dollars.[15]

With the ostensible aim of raising foreign capital, the DPRK also announced its version of a Free Economic and Trade Zone (FETZ) in Rajin-Sunbong, in the far northeast of the country in December 1991.[16] Previous attempts to induce foreign capital by means of the Joint Venture Law of September 1984 had been tailored towards accommodating fully vetted investments from pro-DPRK sources in Japan and had rapidly receded into the background as the Soviet relationship grew.[17] As late as August 1989, government spokesmen still routinely dismissed the need to establish a FETZ, but the DPRK then reassessed its attitude, especially in the light of growing regional interest in establishing a multinational Special Economic Zone in the Tumen River estuary region.[18]

Notwithstanding such activity, most observers soon concluded that the government lacked the commitment and the expertise to emulate the growth pattern of the Chinese Special Economic Zones. While many foreign companies surveyed the zone, actual foreign investment remained almost entirely confined to small-scale low-tech ventures by pro-Pyongyang Korean residents of Japan, later joined by Chinese business world fringe-dwellers, which is more or less where the matter has continued to rest. Foreign investor interest in the FETZ remained inhibited by a formidable array of obstacles, including perception of the sizeable political risks involved in investing in a DPRK which was widely believed to have an active nuclear weapons programme, was subject to various types of international sanctions, was still strongly hostile to Japan, the US and the ROK, was ranked at the bottom of international league tables for corruption and lack of transparency, was not interested in extending any semblance of legal protections for foreign companies, and which possessed poor commercial and industrial infrastructure, including the lack of reliable maintenance services, basic tradesmen and business support skills, and power, transport and telecommunications connections.[19]

The DPRK also sought to raise more revenue through a significant relaxation of controls on border trade with China in the far northeast. In this region, the DPRK province of Ryanggang and the Chinese Yanbian Korean Autonomous Prefecture shared economic problems such as sparse population, poor infrastructure, rough terrain and harsh climate. They also shared a legacy of development as one economic unit under the Japanese as well as strong cross-border family, business and personal ties.[20] Despite these affinities, however, political disputes between the two countries limited cross-border contacts until the signing of a border trade agreement between the two sides in February 1982. Contact then gradually expanded during the 1980s with a number of measures aimed at facilitating the flow of people and goods.[21] As the 1990s began, a rapid and lucrative increase in economic penetration into Ryanggang took place, mainly driven by means of cross-border smuggling syndicates led by Chinese–Koreans.[22]

Like all DPRK state policies, the tactical measures outlined above took as their first principle the defence of the country's socialist system. As a result, no public debate on economic issues emerged, standing orders for low-level cadres to report any private economic activity remained in place, and these were backed up by the formation in 1992 of special 'groups for the eradication of anti-socialist activities'. Anti-market campaigns continued throughout the early 1990s, and the fact that such campaigns met with indifferent success was not by design but rather because the government had lost the capacity for proactive enforcement.[23] Moreover, an important criterion for new forms of economic activity became the extent to which these could be concealed from the population at large. This could be accomplished either geographically by confining such activities to remote areas such as the northeast, or else procedurally by allowing, for example, foreign investment and merchandise to enter the country with their point of origin concealed. Thus, inter-Korean trade could flourish as long as the goods involved did not overtly display their southern origin and as long as capital investment from the South remained concealed.[24]

Meanwhile, however, such measures had little impact on the broader picture, where the gap in performance between the DPRK and the ROK economies continued to grow as high growth rates in the ROK and stagnation in the DPRK was rendering the DPRK grossly inferior in all sectors except the military.[25] By 1990, ROK annual GDP exceeded the DPRK's GDP tenfold, and the annual increase in ROK GDP was greater than the entire DPRK GDP (Namkoong, 1995a: 6). This disparity had obvious and severe consequences for their military rivalry and for the economic and political influence that the two countries could exert regionally and globally. ROK economic performance had, for example, been a prime reason for awarding the 1988 Olympiad to Seoul, and had also been a principal reason why China and the Soviet Union had entered into relations with Seoul.

The South–North dialogue resumes

After the DPRK unilaterally withdrew from existing dialogues in January 1986, the inter-Korean dialogue entered a new phase marked by low-level official contact, occasional high-level secret contacts and an active exchange of talks proposals.[26] These were years of success for ROK diplomacy and the DPRK had no interest in contributing to this aura, preferring to talk when it believed its opponent was under pressure or else was disposed to offer unilateral concessions. In the meantime, Pyongyang was not averse to applying judicious measures of violence, as was the case with the 1983 Rangoon bombing.

A low point was accordingly reached with the detonation of a time bomb on board Korean Airlines Flight 858 over the Andaman Sea on 29 November 1987 with the loss of 115 lives. At a press conference in Seoul on 15 January one of the agents subsequently captured stated that acting on official DPRK orders she had planted a bomb on the aircraft.[27] The DPRK vehemently denied complicity, maintaining as it had in the case of the Rangoon bombing that the ROK itself had planted the bomb to embarrass the DPRK (*PT*, 30 January 1988). Notwithstanding, a wide spectrum of governments and organisations around the world found the evidence detailed and convincing, and, amid yet another chorus of international condemnation, once again the DPRK found itself subject to an array of international sanctions.

By now, however, developments in ROK domestic politics were beginning to have a significant impact on inter-Korean relations. In February 1988, President Roh Tae Woo was inaugurated as President of the Republic of Korea after an improbable series of events. Coming from a military background, he was readying himself to take over and rule in a similar, authoritarian manner to his predecessor and colleague Chun Doo Hwan after election through an indirect electoral college system that ensured success to the ruling party nominee. However, the holding of the ruling party nomination convention in June 1987 also triggered off widespread anti-government demonstrations that brought about the downfall of the Fifth Republic shortly afterwards. This led to the promulgation of a new constitution that provided for the election of the president by direct popular vote. The election duly took place in December 1987 and, due to the splitting of the opposition vote between long-time bitter rivals Kim Young Sam and Kim Dae Jung in the first-past-the-post system, Roh was successful with only 36 per cent of the vote. Thus, Roh, who had been poised to become president under the old system, became president under the new system and entered office carrying considerable political baggage. In an effort to counterbalance this, he sought a breakthrough in inter-Korean relations, and also concentrated on improving relations with China and the Soviet Union in a policy that became known as Nordpolitik. In adopting this strategy, he perceived and acted upon the diplomatic dividend accruing to the ROK through continuing rapid economic growth, the now-imminent Seoul Olympiad and the on-going process of economic reform in both the Soviet Union and China.

Roh's first major initiative towards the North came in the form of his July 1988 Six Point Declaration, in which the ROK defined the DPRK not as an adversary but as part of 'a single nation community' and sought to develop relations on this basis.[28] Accordingly, the ROK would promote a broad programme of exchanges, including concerted action via Red Cross talks to resolve humanitarian issues affecting separated families and the opening of trade relations. It would also drop its objections to other nations trading with the North in non-military goods, end diplomatic rivalry, seek to cooperate with the DPRK internationally and assist the DPRK to improve its relations with ROK allies such as Japan and the US.

In October 1988, Roh expanded further on these themes in an address to the United Nations General Assembly, and in September 1989 he made a further detailed policy statement in which he proposed that the two Koreas work towards final unification via an interim, loose union to be called a Korean Commonwealth.[29] This proposal was essentially an elaboration on a number of themes that had long been an established part of ROK policy.[30] Its basic assumptions were gradualist, looking at reunification as a long drawn-out process requiring some interim governmental structure to oversee the process, integrationist in its expectation that the Commonwealth would aim to lay the groundwork for the emergence of a single social and political system, and democratic in its advocacy of full reunification validated through a general election. The DPRK response was truculent and deeply suggestive of wounded pride at the on-going erosion of its diplomatic base, but after a number of counter-proposals aimed past, and not at the South, Pyongyang finally entered into a substantive negotiation process, and in July 1990 the two sides reached agreement to hold prime ministerial level talks. With this agreement, a new phase of high-level talks began.

The first session of Prime Minister-level talks took place in Seoul in September 1990.[31] The symbolic significance was for outside observers to debate, but the fact remained that the two interlocutors were essentially bureaucratic–technocratic appointees of their respective leaders, not substantial power wielders in their own right, and neither party brought anything substantially new to the talks. Instead, each side concentrated on presenting its own agenda for dialogue and these agendas contained little if any overlap.[32] Nor were the atmospherics very encouraging, with the Pyongyang print media reporting the proceedings with the ministerial titles of ROK delegation members placed in inverted commas.

Eventually, though, the two sides made unexpected progress at the fourth round of the Prime Ministerial talks, held in Pyongyang during October 1991, and produced an agreement to negotiate what was to be officially titled an Agreement Concerning Reconciliation, Non-aggression, Exchanges and Cooperation between the South and the North.[33] The two sides then quickly produced a mutually acceptable text for the agreement, which was signed in December 1991. The agreement foresaw the setting up of a number of civil and military committees to give effect to its provisions, including a South–North liaison office, a South–North Political Subcommittee and a South–North Exchanges and Cooperation Subcommittee, all within the framework of continuing prime ministerial talks. As 1991 drew to a close, the North–South talks had passed through the first stage of negotiation and had established substantial machinery to deal with inter-Korean reconciliation.

However, as with the 1972 Joint Communiqué and the 1984–5 talks, once again initial procedural agreement marked the high point of negotiation, after which momentum was rapidly lost. Whereas the South interpreted the agreement as a specific framework for confidence-building measures, the North interpreted it as a broad agreement that could accommodate its two-tier talks strategy of negotiating a peace treaty and troop withdrawal with the US and then negotiating a political settlement with the ROK.[34] The wording of the agreement was vague enough to accommodate both these widely differing interpretations and, in the absence of agreement on more fundamental issues, it was incapable of providing a framework for sustained, productive negotiation. Thus, by the end of May 1992, the atmosphere of the negotiations had cooled considerably.

ROK patience finally gave out in June 1992 and in a wide-ranging statement, Seoul accused the DPRK of a series of actions that placed the talks in jeopardy. These actions included the infiltration of armed troops into the DMZ in May, attempts to circumvent the established intergovernmental channels and bring political pressure to bear in Seoul by organising a 'pan-national rally' of youth and students in Pyongyang with the joint participation of DPRK students and ROK dissident students, and the issuing of numerous invitations to ROK businessmen to visit the North and undertake individual joint ventures outside the framework of the Agreement.[35] By October 1992, it was clear that no progress in the military talks was to be expected, and this state of affairs, coupled with the exposure of a major DPRK spy ring in the South and growing international suspicion that the DPRK was actively pursuing a nuclear weapons programme, led the ROK and the US to announce they would resume their annual Team Spirit military exercises in 1993 after suspension in 1992.[36] The North reacted by advising that all dialogues would be stalemated and the implementation of all South–North agreements would be suspended for the duration of the exercises (*PT*, 7 November 1992). Pyongyang duly kept its word, and the ninth round of prime ministerial talks, scheduled for Seoul in December 1992, did not take place.

The level and frequency of inter-Korea negotiation then sank to a ten-year low in 1993. The DPRK announced its intention to withdraw from the Nuclear Non-Proliferation Treaty in March, became openly dismissive of the value of any further negotiation with Seoul and thereafter made direct bilateral discussions with the US the chief focus of its diplomacy. The prime ministerial talks did not reconvene and the two sides reverted to sporadic official contact at more junior levels. Negotiations reached a new low point on 19 March 1994 when the DPRK delegation leader walked out of negotiations, famously declaring, 'If a war breaks out, Seoul will be turned into a sea of fire.'[37] In this context Kim Il Sung's agreement during talks with former US President Jimmy Carter on 16–17 June to a summit meeting with ROK President Kim Young-sam was a surprising development which seemed at odds with prevailing DPRK policy towards the ROK. Preparations began, but whether the talks would have ever taken place – last-minute cancellation of scheduled talks was a standard DPRK tactic – let alone achieved anything, became moot when Kim's death on 8 July brought about the suspension of all inter-Korean negotiations.

Rearguard action: the DPRK and regional diplomacy, 1988–94

Meanwhile, in the late 1980s, the basis for relations between states in the Northeast Asian region underwent fundamental change as a result of far-reaching changes in the international economic and political order. When the new order more or less settled into place, the Soviet Union was gone, old ideological ties had been weakened and economic pragmatism had been affirmed. However, through all of this, the DPRK emerged with ideology intact and with a decidedly unpragmatic economic policy, such that China, the ROK and Japan essentially rallied to Pyongyang's aid, stating that they did not wish to see total collapse in the North. If this was a victory for the North, then it was a hollow one, but it reflected an increasing awareness among the DPRK's adversaries that inducing collapse was a bad option for fear of unpredictable consequences. The DPRK itself, of course, was well aware of this strand of thinking and viewed it as a paradoxical source of negotiating strength-in-weakness, which in fact it was.

This process of transformation gathered pace in March 1985 when Mikhail Gorbachev became CPSU General Secretary and began to initiate radical change to traditional Soviet policies of global ideological and military rivalry with the US. By the end of 1988, he had enunciated a new basis for foreign policy, which included the freeing of international relations from ideology, the acceptance of greater political freedom in Soviet Bloc countries and an end to the arms race. As the Soviet Union put these principles into effect during 1989, the Cold War ceased, global ideological competition effectively ended, many regional disputes that had been sustained by Cold War exigencies became more susceptible to negotiated settlement, and efforts to manage or at least contain the economic crisis afflicting the Soviet Union and Eastern Europe became a major focus of Western diplomacy.

The Soviet retreat from ideological and military contention with the West and its emphasis on economic issues inaugurated a new era in the East Asia region. US–Soviet confrontation in the region gave way to measures of cooperation, including unilateral arms cuts. Similarly, Mikhail Gorbachev's Vladivostok speech in July 1986 inaugurated a renewed process of Sino–Soviet rapprochement. The Soviet Union backed up the new priority accorded to the economic development of the Soviet Far East by a significant expansion of Soviet economic diplomacy in the region (Roy Kim, 1987: 382–3) and this in turn underscored the need to revise its policy on non-recognition of the ROK. Meanwhile, much of the same economic logic applied to China's ROK policy and, as a result, Beijing opted to seek a significant improvement in its relations with Seoul. Accordingly, during 1987 significant changes in Chinese and Soviet policies towards the ROK began to occur, gathering momentum in the 1988 Olympiad year.

The Seoul Olympiad took place without incident from 17 September to 2 October 1988 and, as the ROK anticipated, the event gave substantial impetus to the ROK's drive for acceptance by the Soviet Bloc and China. Accordingly, Gorbachev's Krasnoyarsk declaration in September 1988 signalled Moscow's preparedness to develop economic relations with the ROK and a series of incremental steps led to the establishment of full diplomatic ties in September 1990. Earlier that month, Soviet Foreign Minister Eduard Shevardnadze had effectively altered the basis for Soviet–DPRK relations when he officially notified Pyongyang that large-scale Soviet investments in the DPRK economy would be suspended, that military aid would be cut sharply, and that future bilateral trade would have to be conducted in hard currency. The DPRK reacted strongly to this development and openly threatened to proceed with the production of nuclear weapons since the Soviet nuclear umbrella afforded by the 1961 mutual defence treaty was now useless.[38]

Soviet criticism of many aspects of DPRK economy and society now increased in visibility and intensity via a series of electronic and print media commentaries. The general purpose seemed to be to apply pressure to Pyongyang to begin a liberalising process, but it also indicated Moscow's displeasure at the extreme language now being used by Pyongyang to denounce Soviet policies.[39] The DPRK had ample opportunity to respond in kind during 1991 when Gorbachev paid an official visit to the ROK in April, where he announced Soviet support for Seoul's position on separate UN entry for the two Koreas. DPRK–Soviet relations in all fields contracted sharply and reached their nadir when the DPRK gave overt support and encouragement to the leaders of the August 1991 coup against Gorbachev. Then, as the nuclear issue grew more and more salient during 1992–93, Moscow added its weight to international pressure on the DPRK, but the collapse of the previous Soviet–DPRK relationship left it with little leverage in Pyongyang. The cool and formal state of relations was perhaps best illustrated when the Russian Prime Minister – and not President Yeltsin – sent condolences to his opposite number after Kim Il Sung's death in July 1994.

Meanwhile, in 1988 China, Pyongyang's last remaining big power patron, also undertook a fundamental reassessment of its policy towards the ROK, which involved establishing parameters for moving towards diplomatic relations.[40] The Chinese timetable was upset by the June 1989 Tiananmen Square incident, and more broadly by the concern they felt at the speed with which communism had collapsed in Eastern Europe during 1989, but the tempo of contacts between the two countries began to pick up in 1990. In October 1990, the two governments announced that they would exchange semi-official trade offices with consular functions. The ROK office in Beijing opened in February 1991, but this did not produce any public protest from the North, while Pyongyang also accepted the establishment of full China–ROK diplomatic relations in August 1992 with considerably more grace than it had displayed in the case of the Soviet Union.[41]

The DPRK, the US and Japan

The international situation in 1988–9 held opportunities as well as dangers for the DPRK, for in the light of the changes in the region, both the US and Japan regarded the continuing isolation of the DPRK as undesirable, and now sought to engage Pyongyang in productive dialogue. The immediate objective of both Japan and the US was to secure both an unequivocal DPRK acknowledgement of the ROK as a legitimate negotiating partner and an irreversible commitment to the resolution of the Korean conflict by negotiation. And, of course, both sought an end to Pyongyang's unnatural and potentially dangerous isolation.

The chief impediment to DPRK dialogue with Japan and the US was, as usual, ideology. The Kimist worldview identified US imperialism and Japanese militarism as immutable threats to the Kimist state, and it projected this view with a rhetorical intensity that often beggared belief.[42] While these views were often expressed in a more understated manner in some quarters of the DPRK government, there was never any doubt that they devolved from the deep personal conviction of Kim Il Sung. Nor was there any doubt that through constant, mind-numbing repetition, over time this conviction became deeply ingrained in the Party and the bureaucratic elite. Thus, the conceptualisation, let alone the discussion, of less extreme views and strategies was all but impossible. The DPRK constantly projected a profound belief that the re-emergence of Japanese militarism was only a matter of time, and that the US controlled the decision-making process in both Seoul and Tokyo, and so it approached negotiations accordingly.

In dealing with the US, the DPRK carried heavy historical and ideological baggage. It had suffered immense physical damage during the Korean War, primarily through intensive US bombing, but Kimist propaganda had greatly exaggerated the very real dimensions of that suffering. Harrowing stories of US war atrocities, including wildly fraudulent claims of widespread civilian massacres and use of chemical and biological warfare, featured heavily in the ideological education of all North Koreans,[43] and for decades the DPRK media had portrayed the US as perpetrators of heinous crimes on a daily basis and on a global scale. The crude, racist invective that they habitually directed towards the US and the blood-frenzy they displayed towards US forces in a long list of military incidents, culminating in the Panmunjom axe killings in 1976, reflected the space allotted to the US in the Kimist narrative, but while it may have served to stiffen DPRK morale, gains in this direction were more than cancelled out by the arguably greater stiffening effect they had in Washington, and especially within the US military. Without question, more tempered behaviour would have been infinitely more difficult for the US to handle, but in an era when the value of US commitments in the Asian region as a whole was routinely and deeply questioned in the US, a broad domestic consensus on the US role in Korea held firm, not the least because of DPRK actions.[44]

In April 1987, Washington made a tentative gesture towards Pyongyang by relaxing its policy on contacts with DPRK diplomats.[45] Regular diplomatic contact – the first-ever such contact – began at counsellor level through each country's Beijing mission in December 1988, where officials met at an average of three- to four-month intervals in the years following 1988. The issues for the US were progress in the DPRK's dialogue with the ROK, other confidence-building measures on the Korean Peninsula, DPRK disavowal of the use of terrorism and the return of MIA remains. Nuclear transparency and the sale of missile technology were soon added to the list. For the DPRK the issues remained, as always, the withdrawal of US forces from Korea and the negotiation of a DPRK–US peace treaty.[46] However, despite periodic positive gestures, such as in 1991, when for the first time the DPRK handed over MIA remains of some of the 8,000-plus US servicemen still missing from the Korean War, throughout this period it remained clear that the DPRK had no intention of moderating its long-standing demand for direct negotiations with the US on troop withdrawal from the ROK.

The nuclear issue swiftly came to overshadow relations. After the results of an initial high-level meeting held on 22 January 1992 in New York between KWP International Bureau Chairman Kim Yong-sun and US Under-Secretary of State for Political Affairs Arnold Kanter were deemed satisfactory by the North (*PT*, 1 February 1992), the dialogue was essentially placed on hold until evidence of DPRK responsiveness on the nuclear issue was forthcoming.[47] In addition, the US continued to place a series of other conditions on the improvement of relations, including improvements in human rights and the cessation of missile system exports to the Middle East. In this atmosphere, the dialogue did not go beyond continuing counsellor-level contacts in Beijing.

The Japanese effort to initiate a dialogue with Pyongyang was more substantial. In addition to supporting the ROK's Nordpolitik initiatives,[48] Japan also felt the need to support broader post-Cold War diplomatic strategies in the region by contributing to a settlement in Korea. The continuing situation where Japan and the DPRK had virtually no communications links of any kind and no mechanisms for resolving trading, consular, fishing and other disputes was not only anomalous but potentially dangerous, given the DPRK potential for posing a strategic threat to the Japanese islands.[49] Like all the DPRK's would-be dialogue partners, Japan hoped that expanded diplomatic contacts might induce more realism into Pyongyang's perception of the outside world, and so reduce this threat. Moreover, Tokyo wished to close the books on the 1910-45 era by reaching agreement on compensation, as it had done when it normalised relations with the ROK in 1965.

Tokyo first signalled its willingness to open talks with the DPRK by allowing a KWP delegation to enter Japan to attend the national convention of the Japan Socialist Party in February 1989, and in September 1990 an unprecedented joint parliamentary mission led by senior Liberal Democratic Party figure Kanemaru Shin visited Pyongyang and signed an eight-point joint declaration which covered compensation not just for the colonial period but also for what were termed 'abnormal relations' in the post-1945 period. The declaration also endorsed the concept of one Korea, the need for peaceful reunification and urged the two governments to hold talks on diplomatic recognition. However, after examining the text of the Joint Declaration, Tokyo concluded that Kanemaru had exceeded his brief in signing a declaration unduly favourable to the interests of the DPRK, especially in its acknowledgement of Japanese responsibility for post-1945 events.[50] The net effect was that when the talks on the normalisation of relations began, the DPRK insisted on tying the talks to the declaration, but the Japanese government presented a significantly modified agenda. The talks quickly stalemated and, as occurred so widely elsewhere, eventually fell victim to growing concern over the DPRK's nuclear programme, before ceasing entirely in November 1992.

The limitations of DPRK diplomacy were also exposed at the United Nations in 1991 when the ROK stepped up its long-standing campaign for separate, full UN membership for the two Koreas. The North had opposed this as an unacceptable manifestation of a two-Koreas policy, although its opposition was grounded in the far more pragmatic assessment that the internationalist ROK had far more to gain than the DPRK did by dual entry. In the past they had been supported by the threat of a Chinese and/or Soviet veto should any application reach the Security Council, and as late as November 1989, the DPRK appeared to have firm Chinese backing for its stance (Samuel S. Kim, 1994: 35). However, as China moved to establish official relations with the ROK, Beijing's position became untenable, and Chinese Premier

Li Peng confirmed the withdrawal of the Chinese veto during his visit to Pyongyang in May 1991. After waging a vigorous media campaign in which it warned of unspecified dire consequences if simultaneous UN entry were to go ahead, the DPRK then bowed to the inevitable with an announcement on 27 May that it would also seek separate UN admission (*PT*, 1 June 1991).[51]

The DPRK's nuclear programme

While there were various strands of tactical compromise in the DPRK's foreign policy, after 1989, Pyongyang's underlying strategic intransigence gained its fullest expression in Pyongyang's programme to acquire nuclear weapons. We are concerned here with what is known about the development of the programme up until the end of 1994.

The DPRK began a modest programme of nuclear research under Soviet auspices in the 1960s, but the foundation of its weapons programme was laid in 1980 when construction commenced at Yonbyon on a 5 MWe reactor fuelled with natural uranium, moderated with graphite and capable of generating 20–30 MW of thermal power.[52] This reactor, which was capable of producing small amounts of plutonium, began operation in 1986. Meanwhile, construction of a second reactor at Yonbyon with a capacity of 50 MWe began in 1984 with a scheduled completion date of 1995 (Oh and Hassig, 1994: 235). International fears over Pyongyang's nuclear intentions were initially allayed when the DPRK acceded to the Nuclear Non-Proliferation Treaty (NPT) in 1985, and also because the programme appeared to be under some form of Soviet control and supervision.

However, beginning in 1989, US and ROK sources began to express concern about the configuration of buildings in the Yonbyon complex, most notably the size of the reactor itself and the construction of what appeared to be a reprocessing plant. To such concerns were added the fact that the DPRK had not signed the NPT safeguards agreement with the International Atomic Energy Agency, a requirement for international inspection to take place, and the fact that the DPRK possessed all the natural resources necessary to make weapons-grade plutonium.

In response to pressure, in February 1990 the DPRK advised the IAEA that it would sign a safeguards agreement if the United States gave legal assurances that it would not resort to a nuclear threat against the DPRK. By Pyongyang's definition, this involved withdrawal of tactical nuclear weapons from the South, removal of the US nuclear threat to the North, simultaneous inspections in the South and in the North, and no further international pressure on the DPRK over the nuclear issue. However, the IAEA rejected this linkage, and throughout 1990 international pressure on Pyongyang built up steadily. In particular, future economic and diplomatic gains that the North hoped to make with Japan, the US, and other Western nations became unambiguously contingent on it signing the safeguards agreement and allowing inspection.

By this stage the DPRK was, of course, facing a complicated international situation. It had begun its nuclear weapons programme years before the collapse of the Soviet Bloc could ever have been imagined, but now that this had occurred, the acquisition of nuclear weapons acquired a special significance in Pyongyang. The announcement of the establishment of full diplomatic relations between the ROK and the Soviet Union in September 1990 was of particular importance since it meant that the 1961 DPRK–Soviet mutual defence treaty became ineffective. Thus, in public statements and official meetings with the Soviets on the eve of the Seoul–Moscow announcement, the DPRK stated that it would need to take measures to obtain 'weapons for which we have so far relied on the alliance', a clear reference to nuclear weapons. The second half of 1990 also saw the build-up to the Gulf War following the Iraqi invasion of Kuwait in August 1990, and with the launching of Operation Desert Storm in January 1991, the DPRK had the opportunity to observe the awesome power and reach of US diplomacy and military technology when it was unchecked by global competition with the Soviet Union, and this would have given it considerable pause.

The period 1991–4 was characterised by continuing cat-and-mouse manoeuvring, involving the DPRK, the US and the IAEA.[53] Initial signs seemed hopeful, but ultimately this led to a major crisis in March 1994 when the IAEA pronounced the results of the latest of a series of inspections unsatisfactory after the DPRK had imposed on-site restrictions that prevented the team from verifying that no nuclear material had been diverted for reprocessing into weapons-grade plutonium since the last inspection in February 1993.[54] This led the US to discontinue on-going bilateral negotiations with the DPRK and to refer the matter to the UN Security Council. On 31 March the President of the Security Council issued a statement urging the DPRK to comply with the IAEA inspection regime. Pyongyang rejected the request and the issue began to move towards a further crisis point in early May when it announced that it would soon begin unloading spent fuel rods without IAEA supervision, thus destroying evidence of suspected weapons-grade plutonium conversion. In May, the UN Security Council moved closer to approving economic sanctions against the DPRK, when it unanimously approved a statement by the President of the Security Council warning Pyongyang that unloading the rods without IAEA supervision might lead to further Security Council action. The DPRK quickly rejected the letter, stated that the application of economic sanctions would amount to 'an act of war', and in June it proceeded to withdraw from the IAEA.

Confrontation, possibly military, with the US seemed inevitable until the visit of former US President Jimmy Carter to Pyongyang on 15–19 June for talks on the nuclear issue. Carter visited Pyongyang at the DPRK's invitation as a private citizen but with President Clinton's approval, and he obtained Kim's agreement to a freezing of the unloading process in return for cessation of sanctions talk and a return to negotiations with the US. After a delay caused by Kim's death in July, negotiations resumed in August, and in October 1994 the two sides signed what is known as the Agreed Framework,[55] whereby the DPRK agreed to remain in the NPT and to return eventually to the IAEA inspection regime. The US agreed to broker the provision of two light-water reactors (LWRs) for energy production in the North, fund compensatory annual deliveries of 500,000 tonnes of fuel oil, take steps to normalise diplomatic relations, and to further the causes of peace on the Korean Peninsula and nuclear non-proliferation. A new era in DPRK–US engagement began.

The setting of an obsessively secretive state and an isolated leadership with singular convictions as the nature of international relations has naturally led to a number of often sharply differing interpretations of Pyongyang's nuclear intentions. As evidence of strong DPRK intent first emerged in the early 1990s and as initial scepticism gradually gave way, some focused attention on the DPRK's nuclear programme as the development of a 'nuclear card', to be exchanged for diplomatic and economic benefits (Chung-In Moon, 1993; Byung-Chul Koh, 1994) while others saw the nuclear option not as a bargaining tool per se, but as a counterweight to growing ROK conventional military superiority (Mack, 1991; Byung-Joon Ahn, 1993).

In time, this led to a basic divide between those who saw the containment of the DPRK nuclear programme within existing international norms as achievable through negotiation and threat-reduction measures, and those who essentially did not. The former view fundamentally foresaw the possibility of a win–win outcome and interpreted the consequent, obvious failure of negotiations primarily in terms of shortcomings in foreign policy processes and attitudes in Washington, Seoul and Tokyo, leading to misunderstanding and missed opportunity (Hayes, 2003). The latter view essentially saw the DPRK's nuclear programme as so fundamental to the DPRK's security, if not its very self-identity as a state, as not to be susceptible to meaningful accommodation. Such a view interpreted negotiation failures primarily in terms of DPRK bad faith as it played for time in developing its nuclear arsenal. The former view is open to charges of unwarranted optimism and a fundamental exaggeration of the DPRK's preparedness to be a rational actor, while the latter is open to charges of undue pessimism and reductionism.

The spectre of a country reducing itself to Third World penury and yet still allocating an astounding proportion of state resources to the acquisition of nuclear weapons in pursuit of a strategic vision that it alone shares is, of course, puzzling in the extreme. How, then, to account for it? In a DPRK context it is always useful, if not essential, to begin with the perspective of Kimist ideology. Kimism has always struggled mightily to exclude foreign influence from its own defence calculations, and therefore conceptually the possession of nuclear weapons serves this core objective, to the extent that it is difficult to conceive of such calculations being challenged by any other objective unless the DPRK fundamentally redefines itself and becomes a participatory member of the broader international community, something that historically it has never sought to do. Strategically, since the very identity of the DPRK state and the survival of its leadership is inextricably bound up with the continuation of struggle against a broad array of powerful enemies, the acquisition of nuclear weapons appears to offer greater hope in this struggle than would otherwise have been possible. Possession of nuclear weapons guarantees at least stalemate, and hence continuing survival until the tide turns. How much greater sense of hope and purpose this option has given the leadership may be judged from the spectre of the DPRK maintaining its quixotic confrontation with its southern neighbour in unchanging fashion, dismissive of the vast superiority enjoyed by the ROK in all major indices of state power.

Then there is the peculiar psychological attraction of the weapon itself. Its symbolism is powerful, and in many countries development and possession of nuclear weapons has tended to take on a life of its own, claiming privileged status and overriding the frequently more pragmatic claims of conventional alternatives. Achievement in this area of high technology seems to symbolise an ultimate form of success in military technology, often assuaging nagging doubts in the national psyche, and becoming a source of self-gratification, self-congratulation and self-reassurance – to a France or a UK as much as an Iran or DPRK. For the DPRK, which ardently desires to achieve its own version of modernisation, nuclear weapons – 'the nuclear treasured sword' in the later words of Kim Jong Un – are in the same category as Pyongyang's monumental architecture in projecting the image of accomplishment and grandeur, while they also appear to symbolise one area where, in a field otherwise strewn with failures, at least here they have succeeded. Nuclear weapons stand as perhaps the supreme symbol of the DPRK's triumph in pursuit of its dysfunctional version of modernity.

Within this broad strategic picture, the actual contours of DPRK nuclear policy become easier to identify and lesser tactical demarches fall more neatly into place. We now have behind us some twenty-five years of negotiation history, punctuated so far by five underground DPRK nuclear tests at the time of writing and with the certain promise of more to come. This has been coupled with major progress towards acquiring various means of delivery, backed up by a diplomatic strategy that has succeeded in ensuring that the DPRK is able to pursue its programme without fear of foreign intervention, and is limited only by its own material means and priorities. This in itself is indicative of a fixed underlying strategy, but the present outcome has not been reached in lineal fashion, and in particular DPRK thinking and action has been influenced by a number of events significant to it over this period, including the fall of the Soviet Union, Operation Desert Storm, the Arduous March famine, internal economic collapse and regroup, and the Arab Spring. Moreover, as an integral part of its national security calculations, the DPRK perceives the nuclear issue as a means of driving a wedge between the US and the ROK, and to a lesser extent Japan. Here, the calculation appears to be that if the DPRK can induce the US to conclude that the defence of the ROK is not worth the cost, and if significant numbers of South Koreans can be brought to the conclusion that it is not worth living with an indefinite nuclear threat hanging over them, then this could be a game-changer. This scenario advances hopes of achieving a favourable bilateral channel of dialogue with Washington, thus boosting domestic morale, diminishing the sovereignty of the ROK and potentially causing friction between the ROK and the US, whose relationship Pyongyang fundamentally misunderstands in the first place.

This potent combination of technological achievement, projection of regime prestige, strategic utility and ideological dysfunction helps explain why the importance of nuclear weapons transcends politics, the military or indeed any sectional interest and even arguably 'rationality' itself, and goes to the very self-definition of the DPRK as a state. This places the debate in an infinitely broader dimension to shallow speculation on the DPRK playing a 'nuclear card', or else that the leadership was pursuing this programme to placate putative military 'hardliners', the latter view a particular curiosity not only because the entire programme has been directed with considerable initiative by the Kims from its inception, and they are the last people to feel the need to placate anyone in such a manner, but also because a credible DPRK nuclear deterrent would arguably diminish the military by diminishing the role of conventional weapons in the DPRK's overall military posture. Instead, since it is dismissive of the economic well-being of its people as an end in itself, fixed in its view of the international system as a hindrance to its core mission, inured to hardship and isolation, and patiently willing to accept small and piecemeal concessions from the US along the way, in accepting the October 1994 Agreed Framework the DPRK accepted what on the surface appeared to be major concessions, but this was deceptive, for the agreement did not – could not – deliver what Pyongyang assessed as its absolute priority – nuclear-backed survival. The agreement was always a means to this further end.

Concluding remarks

As the Soviet Bloc collapsed, those in the KWP and government elite who chose to do so could probably see that their country was facing a profound crisis from which there seemed no way out. An unreformed DPRK seemed manifestly incapable of sustaining itself, let alone realistically pursue its major goal, but the process of reform elsewhere had been inexorable, forcing regimes well beyond intended limits. Communist reformers in Europe had invited criticism and had intended no more than disavowal of a few side effects of authoritarian Party rule that were hurting their prerogatives, but instead, ordinary people had spoken out against the very foundations of political power in their countries, against the core features of the dictatorship of the Party and against many of the policies that flowed from them. They had served a log of claims on their oppressors that included the right to choose their own representatives, to be free from political surveillance and to openly debate social and political issues, the right to complain and register dissent, the right to be treated with respect by those in authority, to have fundamental control over their daily lives, to be better informed, to have more consumer goods, to have access to information both frivolous and serious from the outside world, and to travel and see foreign sights for themselves. Here, then, was convincing evidence of the impossibility of repudiating select parts of an ideology that had long presented itself as monolithic truth and of the futility of acknowledging even limited forms of accountability where for decades such regimes had held themselves unaccountable.

Soviet Bloc communists lost heart and lost power for a number of reasons. The more humane among them simply grew more and more repelled by the repressive means employed to achieve the objectives of the state, and they were encouraged in such thinking by the remorseless reality check presented by the open societies and market economies on their borders and by the cascading leaks in their own information firewalls, the effects of which simply grew more and more severe as time went by. The cynicism and demoralisation of erstwhile true believers that gradually took hold within the Soviet Bloc also arose from the fundamental placement of Marxism within the broader tradition of European political thought, and within this tradition it had long become painfully clear to Marxists that in practice their sublime ideology was deeply flawed. However, they could not simply give up and somehow they had to go on, giving ground and adopting expedients. Hence the Khrushchev Thaw, goulash communism, the Prague Spring, and finally *glasnost* and *perestroika*, until the Soviet Union essentially lost hope and lost the will to continue.

No such doubts or scruples were allowed to surface within the DPRK, where Kimist triumphalism still held sway, the will to isolate and brutalise the population remained strong, and the firewall against the dangerous reality check of the ROK, Japan and, increasingly, China remained all but impermeable. Nor was there an avatar regime or political tradition to serve as a yardstick of success or failure, for the Neo-Confucian past was now a thoroughly foreign country and North Koreans were unaware of it except in the survival of some scattered items of social behaviour and etiquette, while the DPRK's leaders held themselves thoroughly unaccountable to any vestige of its moral values. This meant that in Pyongyang the only questions asked were tactical, not strategic, for Kimist logic, Kimist strategy and Kimist objectives were beyond challenge, and the struggle, like life itself, had to continue. Decades of militarism and policies predicated on the profound belief in the rectitude of Kimist ideology had created severe dysfunction, but even if, like their European counterparts, some grew to harbour doubts – clearly the journey of a Hwang Jang-yop was not a solitary one – they could not go back, for then they would have to acknowledge the failure of their life's work and the failure of the ideology and the policies that had given decisive shape to almost every aspect of the world around them. And, having spent a lifetime brutalising others, why would that not in turn be their fate if they relinquished power? In this manner, the DPRK continued to face the post-Cold War world with Party and government institutions, senior personnel and ideology essentially unchanged since the 1960s.

While the Stalinist–Maoist doctrine that a modern economy could be built by an isolated and highly regimented population, devoted primarily to heavy industry, military production and hero-worship became outmoded and began to be set aside in the Soviet Union in the mid-1950s and in China in the 1970s. In the DPRK, Kim Il Sung lived on in self-imposed isolation, and so both the doctrine and the ideology that reinforced the state remained essentially intact. 'The mystery is why the North Koreans did not understand the historical magnitude of the change around them', observed Marcus Noland in 2011.[56] But while on one level it presents as a mystery, it is far less so when one reminds oneself, as one constantly needs to, that Kim truly and unshakably believed that the system he had created would achieve his central goal, and hence it needed to be enforced and defended down to the last detail. The DPRK leadership accordingly dwelt in a very different mental world. It was a world that dismissed capitalist economic development as illusory. This conviction did not result from rational analysis, but from Kim's self-delusion, which was buttressed not just by ideological hostility towards market economics, but also by next to no understanding of the underlying concepts of such economics.[57] In particular, improving the material lives of people as an end in itself was quite alien to his own experience, and on some level he quite possibly perceived it as a source of threat since it lessened their degree of dependence on the state — that is, him. Instead, Kim's conception of economic activity was that it could be purposeful only if it was entirely controlled and directed towards military goals determined by ideology and genius-leadership.

Placing no intrinsic value on capitalist economic achievement, Kim was therefore supremely confident of the DPRK's innate superiority to the ROK system and that just left the harnessing of his system to military production as the way forward. Accordingly, his was a world in which the yardstick of economic progress was overwhelmingly a military yardstick, and as long as he believed the economy could continue to funnel resources through to the military, then it was more or less fulfilling its purpose. Characteristically, then, as the potential of his conventional weaponry to force the issue faded, and then as he reached his manpower limits, Kim had no hesitation in turning to nuclear weapons, for it opened up a whole new range of options, again nullifying the weight of capitalist economics. While no longer able to press for victory, if all went well, then at least he could achieve indefinite stalemate and hence survival, which was at least acceptable because he was unshakeable in his belief that in the longer run the tide of history would run in his favour.

While in the early 1990s one frequently heard predictions of the DPRK's impending significant adjustments to the new regional and global order, these have repeatedly been confounded. Dialogue with the ROK, Japan and the US excited media interest, but such talks led nowhere, even though the ROK was offering massive economic investment, Japan was standing poised to negotiate a multi-billion dollar settlement for reparations arising from the 1910–45 colonial era, and the US was prepared to relax long-standing restrictions on trade and other contacts with the DPRK. This was because none of these three adversaries could give the DPRK leadership and elite what it truly wanted, which was the right and the material means to safeguard its fundamental identity as a righteous war-making state and, as the ubiquitous Party slogan put it, the right to 'live in our own way'. Thus, talk of the likelihood of the DPRK emulating aspects of China's economic reforms remained unfulfilled, and instead almost all sectors were gutted to support the military and especially the nuclear weapons programme, while the search for new sources of revenue to at least partly replace lost Soviet inputs was prioritised. When mixed with rigid ideological conviction and praxis, various forms of cognitive bias such as groupthink and wishful thinking, the reinforcement of orthodoxy through state terror and the profound resultant inability to conceptualise alternatives, these new inputs somehow suggested viability, if only through the further impoverishment of the people, who in any event were there to be called upon to offer the sacrifice of soldiers in wartime.

Finally, we need to factor in the extent to which all these calculations filtered through the ageing mind of Kim Il Sung. Here we find evidence that a limited intellect, physical isolation, paranoia, an overbearing, browbeating personal manner, the corrupting effects of sustained power without accountability, firmly established megalomania, unsophisticated adherence to an ideology that consecrated revolutionary violence and stressed the historical inevitability of the global victory over imperialism, and blind insistence on a manifest destiny that gave him a significant role in this victory had all clearly combined to leave Kim, by now well into his seventies, frozen in the past, giving him the illusion of control over events and depriving him of any real capacity for self-reflection and self-correction. The results were, of course, catastrophic. Economic dysfunction left people increasingly more vulnerable, their poverty contrasting painfully with massive expenditure aimed at projecting a message of power and grandeur through staged spectacles and grotesque monumental architecture, including the spectacle of billions of dollars lavished on an essentially meaningless World Youth and Students Festival in 1989 as a riposte to the Seoul Olympics, the unfinished and unfinishable 105-storey Ryugyong Hotel, rows of other empty hotels and facilities built for non-existent tourists, somehow expected to be drawn to visit the DPRK by the power, prestige and magnetism generated by the Great Leader, and a slew of other monuments reached through broad, empty streets.

The transcripts of Kim's discussions and meetings with foreign leaders and visitors during this period make depressing reading, as a pedestrian intellect carelessly deals out half-truths and distortions at will to friend and foe alike in a manner that thoroughly reflected the mental world of a person who had not had to suffer contradiction for the best part of forty years. Thus, to a Soviet delegation in 1985 he declared that if the ROK and the US attacked the North, 'a mighty partisan movement will rise up in the South' (Volkogonov, 1999: 418). Likewise, in a 1991 interview with a Japanese publisher, we see him soberly likening ROK anti-tank traps on the southern side of the DMZ to a ROK equivalent of the Berlin Wall designed to prevent southerners coming north as refugees and northerners going south in comradeship,[58] while also in

1991 we find him in formal meetings with the Chinese leadership offering fantasy figures on DPRK economic performance, which the Chinese found sufficiently insulting to their intelligence for them to say so to other diplomats.[59] Kim began the task of convincing others by convincing himself, and in reading the treatises and interviews of both Kims during this era, and in observing policy outcomes, we find no grounds for doubting the sincerity of their constant professions of faith in ultimate success, which seemed to grow more and more shrill as the material base for achieving reunification on their terms dissipated.

Notes

1 For fuller details of Politburo changes throughout this period, see Buzo (1999: 165–9, 206–11).
2 The Party, of course, gave no explanation for the dismissal, but strong evidence points to O's advocacy for a leaner, more efficient KPAF, and his displeasure at the large-scale redeployment of troops to civil construction projects on the grounds that it was disrupting military preparedness (Mansourov, 2004: 25). The latter is especially plausible because such practices were already widespread in the DPRK (Buzo, 1999: 166). O's fall from grace was not total, however, and after a period in obscurity under Kim Jong Il, he rose again to become a member of the inner circle and one of the four regents appointed by Kim to support Kim Jong Un upon the latter's succession in 2011.
3 'Younger' is, of course, a strictly relative description here. If we assume that the earliest officer candidates in 1945 were about twenty years of age, then at the time of O's dismissal, the post-war generation comprised all military officers under the age of 60.
4 One ignores the ideological pronouncements of such regimes at one's peril, no matter how fantastical they may sound. The key argument advanced by Kim Jong Il at this time is therefore worth quoting at length: 'The socio-political organism needs a focal point which has unified command of the activities of the social community. Just as a man's brain is the centre of his life, so the leader, the top brain in a socio-political community, is the centre of the life of this community. The leader is called the top brain of the socio-political organism because he is the focal point which directs the life of this organism in a unified manner . . . Since the leader is the centre of the life of a socio-political community, revolutionary duty and comradeship must also be centred on the leader. Revolutionary duty and comradeship find their most noble expression in the relationship between the leader and his men. Loyalty to the leader and comradeship towards him are absolute and unconditional because the leader, as the top brain of the socio-political organism, represents the integrity of the community' (*PT*, 1 August 1987). See *PT*, 19 March 1988 for a summary of the theory. For subsequent passing references to it in the Kim's speeches and writings, see *PT*, 9 December 1989 and *PT*, 26 May 1990. For analysis, see Byung-Chul Koh (1991: 3–4) and Jae-Jean Suh (1994: 29–32). The metaphor is strongly reminiscent of the pre-Second World War Japanese imperial rescript to military officers which stated: 'We are your Commander-in-Chief. Our relations with you will be most intimate when we rely on you as our limbs, as you look up to us as your head' (Eckert, 2016: 141).
5 Gause (2015: 53) cites a number of high-level DPRK defectors in maintaining that 'By the late 1980s and early 1990s, Kim Jong-il's apparatus was reportedly bugging Kim Il-sung's offices and determining which reports [Kim] would see. In this way, Kim Jong-il was increasingly responsible for running the regime while

142   *Tactical retreat: 1987–94*

limiting Kim Il-sung's situational awareness.' Testimony from the high-level defector Hwang Jang Yop and from Jang Jin Sung, who lived among the elite before defecting, also states that the younger Kim began to shunt his father aside towards the end of the latter's life (for example, Jang 2014: 138). Testimony from such quarters should, of course, be taken seriously, but cautiously. In his post-defection writings, Hwang was not always a free agent, while the pronounced levels of animosity he directed towards Kim Jong Il must raise doubts as to his objectivity on this issue. Meanwhile Jang, while something of an insider, was not a political analyst, and was several steps removed from the inner sanctum, which is an exceedingly long remove in DPRK court politics terms. His accounts essentially pass on what may well have been court rumours or even post-defection constructs and, like those of Hwang, remain in the realm of intriguing speculation. The above 1992 quote from Kim Il Sung does not support the hypothesis of Kim Jong Il in control, and one cannot imagine the older Kim agreeing to having such words placed in his mouth. Of course, court intrigue has no rule book, but even if Hwang and Jang were somehow describing the situation accurately, and Kim Jong Il was in fact more fully in charge against the will of his father than is currently believed to be the case outside the North, such an arrangement had no discernible impact on policy, which remained consistent with long-standing Kimist parameters.

6 For the text of Prime Minister Yi Kun-mo's speech to the SPA announcing the plan, see *PT*, 25 April 1987. For sector-by-sector analysis, see Komaki (1987: 14–15) and Uehara (1987:20).

7 This much could readily be gleaned from the outside at the time. For an account of the debates inside the DPRK Administration Council at the time, based on Soviet Embassy sources, see Mansourov (2004: 24–5).

8 In a sign of things to come, from defector testimony Lankov and Kim (2008: 68–69) detail the rise of a number of informal economic practices in the late 1980s as local communities attempted to deal with the food shortages that grew out of the Soviet withdrawal and the collapsing Public Distribution System. One practice was to cannibalise factory inventories and barter them for food. There was also an unannounced increase in the size of private farming plots, which were universally (but of course only privately) acknowledged to be more productive than collectively farmed land.

9 Economic statistics during this period, such as those of the *Economist Intelligence Unit*, show a balance of trade in favour of the Soviet Union, but it is doubtful that the Soviets derived much benefit from their trade with the DPRK. The Soviet export figures are inflated by inclusion of items such as oil, coking coal, industrial equipment and textiles provided largely on credit to the DPRK for the processing of materials for re-export to the Soviet Union (Zhebin, 1995: 735). Zhebin also criticises what he terms 'the DPRK's selfish approach to, and its interest in gaining unilateral benefits and advantages from its relations with the Soviet Union, and cites falsification of statistics and repeated non-delivery of contracted goods as standard DPRK practices during this period.

10 Kim Jong Il's views on this subject, on the decadence of Western society, and on the course of world history since 1945 emerge with exceptional clarity in his 1987 treatise 'Let us march forward dynamically along the road of socialism and communism under the unfurled banner of the anti-imperialist struggle'.

11 Kwang-Yong Kim (1994: 98) quotes a survey of firms interested in doing business with the North conducted in 1991 by the Korea Trade Promotion Corporation (KOTRA) which revealed the following major sources of motivation:
In order to secure a bridgehead for future advancement: 41.5 per cent.
Interest in cheap labour: 31.5 per cent.
Interest in exploiting natural resources: 24.4 per cent.

12 For estimated DPRK trade volumes with major trading partners during 1990–4, see Namkoong (1996: 230).
13 For details on the DPRK's missile systems trade, see Pollack (2011).
14 For an account of what is known about the origins and development of Bureau 39, see Kan et al., (2010: 8ff.).
15 See, for example, Wyler and Nanto (2008: 4) and John S. Park (2009).
16 For the text of the Administration Council decision establishing the zone, see *PT*, 1 January 1992. The zone covered 621 square kilometres and was to be supported by the declaration of Rajin, Sunbong and Chongjin ports as free trade ports. In the zone, 'foreigners are allowed to establish and run various forms of business including co-production, joint venture and foreign-funded business and engage in service business of various forms' with their capital and income protected under DPRK law.
17 In a survey of 116 foreign investment projects initiated in the period 1984–93, Namkoong (1995b: 468) found that they totalled US$150 million and that in 90 per cent of the cases, the foreign partner was from the pro-North section of the Korean community in Japan. By sector, they comprised light industry (35 per cent); retail stores including shops and restaurants (30 per cent); agriculture (11 per cent); metal and machinery (8 per cent) and mining (7 per cent). Namkoong contrasts this with the $7.46 billion in foreign investment attracted by Vietnam in the period 1986–94.
18 A UNDP-sponsored meeting in Pyongyang in October 1991 established a management committee to conduct a feasibility study of the plans submitted by China, Russia and the DPRK, with the aim of advancing a master plan acceptable to all parties by June 1993. For further information, see Si-Joong Kim (1996).
19 Nevertheless, the Rason FETZ project was never short of enthusiastic spruikers: 'By 1996, North Korea could be on the cover of *Newsweek* as the new Vietnam' was a typical quote at that time (*The Financial Times*, 23 June 1994). But given the near-total lack of institutional or personnel moves to support the initiative, it is not surprising that not much has changed in twenty-five years. For an account of a recent visit to the area, see Frank (2014). For a more detailed analysis of the situation as of November 2015, see Abrahamian (2015).
20 For a useful account of the political and economic situation along the border during the 1990s, focusing on the refugee phenomenon, see Lankov (2004).
21 For details, see 'Order on the Border', *FEER*, 20 March 1986.
22 Because of the illegal nature of most of the transactions involved, there is little literature on this subject. According to one estimate, by the mid-1990s the trade had grown to involve up to 100,000 people, some of whom traded in major commodities including lumber, automobiles and artefacts. Estimates of its annual value vary from $30 million to $300 million, compared with a reported $550 million in official DPRK–China trade in 1995. See 'Barter on the Border', *FEER*, 10 October 1996.
23 Based on defector testimony, Lankov and Kim (2008) provide a detailed picture of the rise of private economic activity in the early 1990s. The backdating of the emergence of crisis-like economic conditions and the associated emergence of private markets is an important issue in studies of this period, underlining as it does the extent to which the leadership had time to see the trend and take corrective action, but chose not to. For an introduction to significant ROK scholarship on the earliest signs of such emergence, see Ward (2014).
24 For further details, see Hy-Sang Lee (1994: 199–202).
25 For a detailed, sector-by-sector comparison of ROK and DPRK economic capability as of 1992, see Namkoong (1995a).
26 For details of these moves, see Buzo (1999: 175ff.).

144 *Tactical retreat: 1987–94*

27 The woman, Kim Hyon-hui, recounted how she and an accomplice, assuming false identities as Japanese nationals, had planted the bomb while en route from Baghdad to Abu Dhabi where they had disembarked. The pair aroused suspicion while waiting for a connecting flight out of Abu Dhabi and were arrested. The woman's companion died after swallowing a suicide pill but she herself was arrested, interrogated and handed over to the ROK authorities. Eventually, she admitted she was the daughter of a DPRK diplomat who had been recruited for special operations by the KWP in 1980. For official ROK documents relating to the incident, including Kim Hyon-hui's statement, see *KWA*, 1988, 12(1): 181–184. For reports on the incident, see 'The Pyongyang factor' and 'Seeking forgiveness', *FEER*, 28 January 1988, and *KH*, 22 January and 9 February 1988.
28 For the text of this declaration, see *KWA*, 1988, 12(3): 627–30.
29 For details and analysis of this proposal, see Hakjoon Kim (1992: 594–597).
30 For detailed analysis, see Byung-Chul Koh (1989) and Sang-Woo Rhee (1991).
31 For speeches and news conference transcripts, see *KWA*, 1990, 14(4): 568–577.
32 For analysis of the prime ministerial talks, see Dae-Sook Suh (1990: 617–0).
33 See *KWA*, 1991, 15(4): 757–71.
34 Kim's hostility to confidence-building measures was well known and long established, and had again been amplified in his New Year Address on 1 January 1991. The relevant portion read: 'We deem it necessary to settle the humanitarian question of visit and exchange, but cannot compromise with the attempt to delay the settlement of the question of peace, the military question, which is more pressing. Home-town visits or economic exchange, to be effective, require before anything else that the daggers hidden in the bosom should be thrown away and that the fear of invasion from the south or 'invasion from the north' should be dispelled. Evading the settlement of the military question and insisting only on exchange in the situation of our country where there is a real danger of war, is in fact tantamount to wishing no peace, no normal visit or no exchange itself.' (*PT*, 1 January 1991)
35 For the text of this statement, see *KWA*, 1992, 16(2): 378–80.
36 For the official ROK Government statement on the uncovering of a 62-man DPRK spy ring on 6 October and a statement of the ROK–US position on the DPRK's nuclear policy, see *KWA*, 1992, 16(4): 757–764.
37 This statement was widely quoted in the international media at the time. For its context, see *The Korea Times*, 21 March 1993.
38 Boulychev (1994: 103–4) gives a vivid account of the state of Soviet–DPRK relations at this stage: 'When Soviet foreign minister E. Shevardnadze arrived in Pyongyang at the beginning of September 1990, and tried to explain why the USSR cannot avoid diplomatic normalisation with South Korea, he received very harsh treatment and a well-prepared answer with a whole set of menaces [*sic*]. They included recognizing the Soviet republics (at that time still a part of [the] Soviet Union) as independent states, setting up relations with Japan and joining Japan's positions on the "Northern territories." Pyongyang also pointed out that the setting up of relations with the "enemy" would "take away any meaning" from [the] alliance treaty and, therefore, would force the DPRK to "produce different kinds of weapons." This was the most ominous threat of all [because] it was the first time that Pyongyang's hitherto top secret nuclear program was brought into the open.'
39 See, for example, *PT*, 6 October 1990: '"Diplomatic relations" bargained for dollars', which described Soviet–ROK negotiations as 'characterised by hypocrisy and betrayal urged by double dealing.' On the ROK agreement to extend $2.3 billion in economic assistance to the Soviet Union, Pyongyang alleged that 'south Korea is not in a position to issue such a colossal sum of money. It is highly probable that it will come from the special fund of the US imperialists for disorganizing

socialism'. On the other hand, Boulychev argues that the DPRK had good reason to feel aggrieved, for Soviet policy on Korean issues in the *perestroika* era was in a confused and contradictory state. The more conservative Soviet Ministry of Foreign Affairs dealt with Pyongyang, while Gorbachev's staff forced the pace on recognising the ROK. The result was that many significant steps were taken without consultation or advance warning to Pyongyang (Boulychev, 1994: 100ff.).

40 According to Hua Di, who was a foreign affairs adviser to Deng Xiaoping at the time, in the autumn of 1988 Deng approved a policy that set three preconditions for establishing diplomatic relations with Seoul: a corresponding move by the Soviet Union, the suspension of the annual Team Spirit exercises and the withdrawal of US nuclear weapons from the Korean Peninsula. Deng saw the latter two as concessions to Pyongyang in order to make DPRK acceptance of the Chinese move easier (Hua, 1991: 31). They were subsequently dropped.

41 For details of the China–ROK negotiations, see Chae-Jin Lee (1996: 122–8).

42 And, of course, still does. In his keynote speech to the 7th KWP Congress in May 2016, Kim Jong Un was still castigating Japan for 'its greed for reinvasion of the Korean Peninsula'. See: www.kcna.co.jp/item/2016/201605/news07/20160507-19ee.html (accessed December 2016).

43 Again, it is far too common to find observers prepared to be either bemused, adopt an attitude of moral equivalence, or else, more insidiously, assume such propaganda rests on some significant kernel of truth. A useful reality check of just what is involved here is the following description of the Sinchon Museum of War Atrocities by Erich Weingartner (2015). The museum is a destination for all North Koreans as well as for foreigners taking the Panmunjom tour, and it continues to play a leading role – arguably *the* leading role – in promoting these images. Weingartner writes as follows: 'The Sinchon Museum of American Atrocities is a memorial dedicated to what North Korea claims are the 35,000 victims of an American massacre during the Korean War. The Kim Jong Un regime completely rebuilt and redesigned the museum in one of its many beautification projects. While the old site housed exhibits of photographs, documents and paintings, the new museum, inaugurated in June of this year, has life-sized, detailed representations in sculpture and three-dimensional scenery of uninhibited violence being perpetrated by American soldiers, with sneering – presumably South Korean – collaborators looking on. As visitors move between scenes, each complemented by screaming sound effects, their senses are assaulted by what I can only describe as a pornography of violence: women having spikes nailed into their heads; breasts being cut off; children being torn from mothers' arms; mothers and children burned alive, buried alive and tossed from a bridge; men being blown up by dynamite inside caverns – the horrors are unrelenting in number and variety.'

44 For a perceptive description of the DPRK attitude to the US, see Zweig (1989: 77–8).

45 For details, see *KWA*, 1987, 11(1): 172–4.

46 On the earlier history of US–DPRK relations, see Scalapino (1983) and Byung-Chul Koh (1984). For further details on the US–DPRK dialogue after 1988, see Sung-Joo Han (1991), Chae-Jin Lee (1994) and Eberstadt (1995).

47 As an insight into DPRK thinking, *The Wall Street Journal*, 8 June 1994 related how at the Kim-Kanter talks, Kanter 'delivered a carefully scripted message: North Korea could participate in the Asian economic miracle if it would drop its nuclear ambitions. Then Kim Young Song (*sic*), a senior North Korean, offered this idea: The U.S. and North Korea should team up against the real threat to the region, Japan. Mr. Kanter was stunned, and the Americans wondered how they could do business with a regime so isolated that it proposed an alliance against a critical U.S. ally.' It is hard to credit that Kim Yong-sun, who presented as a skilled, urbane negotiator, could possibly have himself held such views. It is far easier to credit

146   *Tactical retreat: 1987–94*

   that the DPRK record of conversation from this meeting would, of course, go immediately to Kim Il Sung, and hence would need to show that Kim Yong Sun had presented this idea to the Americans – that is, if he were to remain alive and in his job.
48 These initiatives meant that long-established ROK opposition to the notion of expanded Japan–DPRK contacts was no longer a major factor, and by the middle of 1988 the ROK was, in fact, encouraging such contact. The scope and significance of this change in ROK policy was considerable and is worth noting, especially in view of the later common narrative of Sunshine Policy advocates that significant change in attitudes towards the North only began substantially with them. Japanese officials confessed that in discussions with ROK officials they had been 'taken aback by the boldness of the ROK's unilateral and unsolicited gesture of support [for Japan–DPRK contacts]'. See AA Cable from Tokyo to Canberra, 12 July 1988: CRS A1838; 3125/11/87.
49 In addition to the burden of history, the issue of relations between the two countries was complicated by periodic 'abductions' of Japanese citizens by DPRK agents and the DPRK detention since 1983 of two crew members from a Japanese fishing vessel *Fujisan-maru* in an attempt to secure the return of a DPRK soldier who had sought asylum in Japan after stowing away on the same vessel during an earlier voyage. The humanitarian issue of consular access to the Japanese wives of Korean residents in Japan repatriated to the DPRK was a further significant issue. For a detailed account of DPRK–Japan relations from 1960 to 1977, see Jung-Hyun Shin (1981). On relations in the 1980s, see Jung-Hyun Shin (1986) and Hong-Nack Kim (1983, 1994a, 1994b).
50 For the text of this agreement, see *PT*, 29 September 1990. On 10 October 1990, *The Japan Times* published an 'inside account' of the events leading up to the signing of the joint declaration. According to this account, there were 'sharp disagreements' between the Japanese and DPRK parties until the final moments before the signing. In this account Kanemaru emerges as having insisted on acceptance of the post-war compensation concept in order to resolve disagreements among the Japanese delegation. At this, 'Officials of the North Korean Workers' Party reportedly were delighted at the Japanese concession. They described the outcome of the talks as nearly 100 per cent in their favor.' See 'Japan–N. Korea talks controversial until the end', *The Japan Times*, 10 October 1990.
51 For a more detailed account of the ROK's campaign for separate UN membership, see Samuel S. Kim (1994: 34–40).
52 On the background to the DPRK's nuclear programme, see Bermudez (2015). For negotiations during the period 1989–92 in particular, see Mazarr (1992).
53 For a summary of moves during this period, see Buzo (1999: 225–229).
54 For the 21 March 1994 statement of IAEA Secretary General Hans Blix, see *KWA*, 1994, 18(1): 154.
55 Its full title is *Agreed Framework between the United States of America and the Democratic People's Republic of Korea*.
56 Quote available at: www.theatlantic.com/business/archive/2011/12/how-kim-jong-il-starved-north-korea/250244/ (accessed September 2016).
57 It was a faintly surreal experience to sit in the DPRK Foreign Ministry reception room in September 1975 and have an ambassador-level Foreign Ministry official conduct animated pantomimes such as pricking balloons and operating invisible puppet strings in an endeavour to explain to me why the ROK economy was about to collapse.
58 This bizarre perspective merits elaboration: 'U.S. President Bush cheered the removal of the Berlin Wall, but he does not even mention the existence of the concrete barrier that divides the north and the south of Korea. The South Korean authorities have camouflaged the concrete barrier and refuse to allow the public

to see it. This reveals their intention to keep Korea divided. However, the existence of the concrete barrier on the southern side of the Military Demarcation Line cannot be concealed. Last year, on the initiative of the International Liaison Committee for the Reunification and Peace of Korea, an international investigation commission to confirm the existence of the concrete wall composed of prominent figures from many countries came to our country, took photographs of the wall and showed them to the world.' (*PT*, 8 June 1991)
59 AA cable from Beijing to Canberra, 13 November 1991: CRS A1838; 3107/40/91.

References

Abrahamian, Andray (2015) *Tumen Triangle Tribulations: The Unfulfilled Promise of Chinese, Russian and North Korean Cooperation*. US–Korea Institute at SAIS: Washington, DC.

Ahn, Byung-joon (1993) Arms control and confidence-building on the Korean Peninsula, in *Asian Flashpoint: Security and the Korean Peninsula*, Andrew Mack (ed.), Allen & Unwin: Australian National University, Department of International Relations, Canberra, pp. 97–112.

Bermudez, Joseph S. Jr (2015) *North Korea's development of a nuclear weapons strategy*. US–Korea Institute at SAIS: Washington, DC.

Boulychev, Georgi D. (1994) Moscow and North Korea: The 1961 treaty and after, in *Russia in the Far East and Pacific Region*, Il-Yung Chung and Eunsook Chung (eds). The Sejong Institute: Seoul, pp. 81–118.

Bracken, Paul (1998) How to think about Korean unification, *Orbis*, 42(3): 409–22.

Buzo, Adrian (1999) *The Guerilla Dynasty: Politics and Leadership in North Korea*. I.B. Tauris: London.

Department of Foreign Affairs and Trade (DFAT). Commonwealth Record series A9737, Correspondence files, annual single series 1990–; Commonwealth Record series A1838, Correspondence files, multiple number series, 1948–89, recorded by the Department of Foreign Affairs from 1970–87 and thereafter by DFAT. All files consulted were made available to the author under the Special Access provisions of Section 56 of the Archives Act, 1983.

Eberstadt, Nicholas (1995) *Korea Approaches Reunification*. M.E. Sharpe: Armonk, NY.

Eckert, Carter, J. (2016) *Park Chung Hee and Modern Korea: The Roots of Militarism, 1966–1945*. The Belnap Press of Harvard University Press: Cambridge, MA.

Frank, Ruediger (2014) Rason Special Economic Zone: North Korea as it could be, available at: http://38north.org/2014/12/rfrank121614/ (accessed October 2016).

Gause, Ken E. (2015) *North Korean house of cards: Leadership dynamics under Kim Jong Il*. Committee for Human Rights in North Korea: Washington, DC.

Han, Sung-Joo (1991) The Korean triangle: The United States and the two Koreas, in *North Korea in Transition*, Chong-sik Lee and Se-Hee Yoo (eds). Institute of East Asian Studies, University of California: Berkeley, CA, pp. 43–53.

Hastings, Justin V. (2014) The economic geography of North Korean drug trafficking networks, *Review of International Political Economy*, 22(1): 162–93.

Hayes, P. (2003) DPRK briefing book: Bush's bipolar disorder and the looming failure of multilateral talks with North Korea, available at: http://nautilus.org/publications/books/dprkbb/multilateraltalks/dprk-briefing-book-bushs-bipolar-disorder-and-the-looming-failure-of-multilateral-talks-with-north-korea/ (accessed February 2017).

Hua, Di (1991) *Recent Developments in China's Domestic and Foreign Affairs: The Political and Strategic Implications for Northeast Asia.* Strategic and Defence Studies Centre: Australian National University.
Jang, Jin-song (2014) *Dear Leader.* Rider Books: London.
Kan, Paul Rexton, Bechtol, Bruce E. Jr and Collins, Robert M. (2010) *Criminal Sovereignty: Understanding North Korea's Illicit International Activities.* Strategic Studies Institute: Carlisle, PA.
Kim, Hakjoon (1992) *Unification Policies of South and North Korea 1945–1991: A Comparative Study.* Seoul National University Press: Seoul.
Kim, Hong-Nack (1983) Japan's policy toward the Korean Peninsula since 1965, in *The Two Koreas in World Politics*, Tae-Hwan Kwak, Wayne Patterson and Edward A. Olsen (eds). The Institute for Far Eastern Studies, Kyungnam University: Seoul, pp. 305–30.
Kim, Hong-Nack (1994a) Japan's North Korea policy in the post-Cold War Era, *Korea and World Affairs*, 18(4): 669–94.
Kim, Hong-Nack (1994b) Japan and North Korea: Normalization talks between Pyongyang and Tokyo, in *Korea and the World: Beyond the Cold War*, Young-Whan Kihl (ed.) Westview Press: Boulder, CO, pp. 111–32.
Kim, Il Sung (1992) *Reminiscences with the Century 1.* The Foreign Languages Publishing House: Pyongyang.
Kim, Kwang-Yong (1994) Inter-Korean economic cooperation – current status and future prospects, *East Asian Review*, VI(3): 91–110.
Kim, Roy U.T. (1987) Gorbachev's Asian policy and its implications for peace and unification of Korea, *Korea Observer*, XVIII(4): 380–408.
Kim, Samuel S. (1994) The two Koreas and world order, in *Korea and the World: Beyond the Cold War*, Young-Whan Kihl (ed.). Westview Press: Boulder, CO, pp. 29–68.
Kim, Si-Joong (1996) The Tumen river area development program: The present status and future prospects, *The Economics of Korean Reunification*, 1(1): 105–19.
Koh, Byung-Chul (1984) *The Foreign Policy Systems of North and South Korea.* University of California Press: Berkeley, CA.
Koh, Byung-Chul (1989) Seoul's new unification formula: An assessment, *Korea and World Affairs*, 13(4): 656–71.
Koh, Byung-Chul (1991) Political change in North Korea, in *North Korea in Transition*, Chong-sik Lee and Se-Hee Yoo (eds). Institute of East Asian Studies, University of California: Berkeley, CA, pp. 1–15.
Koh, Byung-Chul (1994) A comparison of unification policies, in *Korea and the World: Beyond the Cold War*, Young-Whan Kihl (ed.). Westview Press: Boulder, CA, pp. 153–66.
Komaki, Teruo (1987) Economic trends in North Korea and the Third Seven-Year Plan, *China Newsletter*, 70: 12–15.
Komaki, Teruo (1992) North Korea inches toward economic liberalization, *Japan Review of International Affairs*, pp. 155–74, Summer.
Lankov, Andrei (2004) North Korean refugees in Northeast China, *Asian Survey*, 44(6): 856–73.
Lankov, Andrei and Kim, Seok-hyang (2008) North Korean market vendors: The rise of grassroots capitalists in a post-Stalinist society, *Pacific Affairs*, 81(1): 68–9.
Lee, Chae-Jin (1994) The United States and Korea: Dynamics of changing relations, in *Korea and the World: Beyond the Cold War*, Young-Whan Kihl (ed.). Westview Press: Boulder, CO, pp. 69–82.

Lee, Chae-Jin (1996) *China and Korea: Dynamic Relations*. The Hoover Press: Stanford, CA.

Lee, Hy-Sang (1994) Economic factors in Korean reunification, in *Korea and the World: Beyond the Cold War*, Young-Whan Kihl (ed.). Westview Press: Boulder, CO, pp. 189–216.

Mack, Andrew (1991) North Korea and the bomb, *Foreign Policy*, 83: 87–104.

Mansourov, Alexandre (2004) Inside North Korea's black box: Reversing the optics, in *North Korean Policy Elites*, Ralph Hassig (ed.), available at: www.brookings.edu/wp-content/uploads/2016/06/oh20040601.pdf (accessed October 2016).

Mazarr, Michael J. (1992) North Korea's nuclear program: The world responds, 1989–1992, *Korea and World Affairs*, 16(2): 294–318.

Moon, Chung-In (1993) The political economy of security on the Korean Peninsula in the regional context, in *Asian Flashpoint: Security and the Korean Peninsula*, Andrew Mack (ed.). Allen & Unwin: Australian National University, Department of International Relations Canberra, pp. 113–36.

Namkoong, Young (1995a) A comparative study on North and South Korean economic capability, *The Journal of East Asian Affairs*, IX(1): 1–43.

Namkoong, Young (1995b) An analysis of North Korea's policy to attract foreign capital: Management and achievement', *Korea and World Affairs*, 19(3): 459–81.

Namkoong, Young (1996) Trends and prospects of the North Korean economy, *Korea and World Affairs*, 20(2): 219–35.

Oh, Kongdan (1990) North Korea in 1989: Touched by winds of change?, *Asian Survey*, XXX(1): 74–80.

Oh, Kongdan and Hassig, Ralph C. (1994) North Korea's nuclear program, in *Korea and the World: Beyond the Cold War*, Young-Whan Kihl (ed.). Westview Press: Boulder, CO, 233–52.

Park, J.S. (2009) *North Korea, Inc.: Gaining Insights into North Korean Regime Stability from Recent Commercial Activities*. United States Institute for Peace: Washington, DC.

Pollack, Joshua (2011) Ballistic trajectory: The evolution of North Korea's ballistic missile market, *Nonproliferation Review*, 18(2): 412–29.

Rhee, Sang-Woo (1991) From national unification to state unification: A realistic design for one Korea, in *North Korea in Transition*, Chong-sik Lee and Se-Hee Yoo (eds). Institute of East Asian Studies, University of California: Berkeley, CA: 129–37.

Scalapino, Robert A. (1983) North Korean relations with Japan and the United States, in *North Korea Today: Strategic and Domestic Issues*, Robert A. Scalapino and Jun-Yop Kim (eds). Institute of East Asian Studies, University of California: Berkeley, CA, pp. 331–350.

Shin, Jung-Hyun (1981) *Japanese–North Korean Relations: Lineage Politics in the Regional System of East Asia*. Kyunghee University Press: Seoul.

Shin, Jung-Hyun (1986) North Korea's relations with Japan: The possibilities for bilateral reconciliation, in *North Korea in a Regional and Global Context*, Robert A. Scalapino and Hongkoo Lee (eds). Institute of East Asian Studies, University of California: Berkeley, CA, pp. 240–262.

Suh, Dae-Sook (1990) Changes in North Korea and inter-Korean relations, *Korea and World Affairs*, 14(4): 610–25.

Suh, Jae-Jean (1994) Ideology, in *Prospects for Change in North Korea*, Tae-Hwan Ok and Hong-Yung Lee (eds). Institute of East Asian Studies, University of California: Berkeley, CA.

Uehara, Takashi (1987) North Korea's external trade in 1986, *China Newsletter*, 70: 16–21.
Volkogonov, Dmitri (1999) *The Rise and Fall of the Soviet Empire*. HarperCollins: London.
Ward, Peter (2014) Before the collapse: The micro-foundations of marketization in North Korea, available at: http://sinonk.com/2014/05/27/before-the-collapse-the-micro-foundations-of-marketization-in-north-korea/ (accessed February 2017).
Weingartner, Erich (2015) The long road to reconciliation: reflections on a visit to the Sinchon Museum, available at: http://38north.org/2015/11/eweingartner 112715/ (accessed September 2016).
Wyler, Liana Sun and Nanto, Dick K. (2008) *North Korean Crime-for-Profit Activities*. Congressional Research Service: Washington, DC.
Zhebin, Alexander (1995) Russia and North Korea: An emerging, uneasy partnership, *Asian Survey*, XXXV(8): 727–39.
Zweig, David (1989) A sinologist's observations on North Korea, *Journal of Northeast Asian Studies*, VII(3): 62–82.

6   Triage: 1994–2004

Introduction

On 9 July 1994 the DPRK media announced that Kim Il Sung had died of a heart attack the previous day. The country subsequently entered into a three-year period of state mourning, and with normal public Party and government activities suspended, it became difficult for outside observers to detect movements in policy and personnel matters. Talk of military coups, revolts, assassination attempts and impending collapse abounded in the international media, but in time it became clear that despite the country's deep economic crisis, arrangements for the succession of Kim Jong Il had gone relatively smoothly. By the time Kim Jong Il emerged and assumed the position of KWP General Secretary in October 1997, it was also clear that he would do little to change the hallmark policies of his father. He would rule by cult of personality through existing ideological parameters, avoid any substantive economic reform measures and direct the country towards nuclear weapon-backed survival on its own terms. In the meantime, though, the younger Kim had to deal with the challenge of the creeping advance of the catastrophic Arduous March famine. The famine took at least one million lives, thus affording Kim Il Sung the somewhat grisly fortune of passing from the scene before the full effect of decades of his economic policies became clear.

    Kim Il Sung's passing also immediately focused on the future direction of the country, for to most observers Kim's passing meant the passing of the person who had so thoroughly shaped the nation in a feat of willpower that it seemed unsustainable without him. After Stalin, the Soviet Union had recoiled from the excesses of Stalinism, post-Mao China had done likewise, and it seemed to contradict logic that Kim Jong Il could succeed in maintaining the style and substance of his father's rule. After all, he was a different person from a different generation with different life experiences, a different personality and with different psychological drives, and set against the real possibility of total economic collapse, many outside observers anticipated that early and significant change would occur.

    However, this was a significant misreading of the situation for a number of reasons. First, not enough was known about the dynamics of power in the

DPRK to support any definitive judgement predicting either imminent collapse or long-term viability. Moreover, from a distance it was hard for outsiders to see that the DPRK state was based on a genuine historical narrative, and although this had been grossly distorted by Kimism, with the distortions enforced with an extraordinary degree of ideological intensity and relentless state terror, this narrative still elevated the regime out of the category of simply one man's tyranny and into the level of a distinctive system shaped by colonial experience, ideology and war, in which a highly disciplined elite pursued specific goals that it was prepared to defend uncompromisingly. Outsiders also tended to place too much weight on what we might term the pragmatic perspective, and so they could not comprehend why this elite did not simply admit obvious defeat and renounce its dysfunctional policies instead of continuing to inflict horrendous, seemingly invidious suffering on the population. But the main reason for misreading the DPRK's prospects was that Kim Jong Il was a shadowy figure and the full range of his abilities was unknown.[1] Given this vacuum, people had over-fed on propaganda highlighting eccentricities and barbarities, and ridiculing everything from his appearance to his dress to his extravagant lifestyle, and therefore many were well schooled into believing that he was at best a mediocrity or a buffoon, a pale shadow of his father. In the event, though, he proved to be anything but, as he embarked upon a seventeen-year period of rule during which he quickly grew to exercise unchallenged political control, defend Kimism and manage the country's various crises through complex and demanding times.

So where did the DPRK stand in 1994? Inside the impregnable fortress of the North basic human services such as healthcare had atrophied, rations distributed through the Public Distribution System, which constituted at least half of total wages (Lee *et al.*, 2008: 25), had dwindled drastically, the ongoing decline of living standards had gathered pace, and the general loss of social morale and discipline had become more palpable, marked by steadily increasing levels of corruption, workplace asset theft and expanding private economic activity in defiance of official sanctions. Just around the corner a reckoning was at hand, and millions of people were about to pay a terrible price for the pursuit of quixotic ideological objectives they had no part in determining. Outside the DPRK's borders, Pyongyang's ongoing efforts to destabilise the ROK continued to be ineffective. The economic battle had long been lost, as had the arms race and the battle for hearts and minds, which just left the application of sporadic, special operations military pressure, intended to boost the morale of true believers and to extract economic concessions in return for cessation. China remained the DPRK's only significant ally – a major regional power, but one that applied very clear limits to the type of support it was prepared to offer.

However, this catalogue of failure did not mean that the DPRK state was veering towards significant policy change, let alone collapse. Rather, it was adjusting to a policy of resolute survivalism. It still had in place a determined, ruthless leader who showed no sign of losing his nerve, and it still possessed a coercion and control system functional enough to ensure that it only had to deal with petty, apolitical forms of dissent and disobedience. This meant that although the system-defending revenue-raising measures of the early 1990s had not gone close to replacing lost Soviet inputs, to some extent they had enabled continued core funding for the military, and especially for the ongoing nuclear weapons programme. The first nuclear test was still some twelve years away, the creation of a credible nuclear threat much further out than that, and there were many uncertainties surrounding the programme – finance, human resource availability, access to technology and the ultimate strength of countervailing international diplomatic and military pressure, to name just a few. However, sufficient encouragement was present for the leadership to persevere and play for time while it pursued what promised to be a game-changer. In truth, it believed it had nowhere else to go.

Externally too, the situation was far from hopeless. Opportunities to exploit marginal weaknesses in their adversaries' strategies had always existed, and as the 1990s progressed the DPRK had good reason to believe that useful dividends could be garnered from this quarter. First, for very different reasons, their adversaries were also playing for time, with the US in particular negotiating loose outcomes, their acuity blunted by the sure and certain faith that these outcomes would probably never need to be honoured since the collapse of the DPRK regime was at hand.[2] Second, in the mid-1990s the DPRK realised that the international community could not just stand idly by and watch a mass starvation, and so it was able to turn over a significant amount of the responsibility for feeding its own people to a number of international relief agencies, most notable the World Food Programme.[3] Finally, in 1998 the new ROK President, Kim Dae Jung, initiated his Sunshine Policy, which proceeded to deliver substantial economic benefits to the North with no strings attached.

However, the full effect of many of these benefits and windfalls lay in the future when in 1994 Kim Jong Il assumed full power, and in seeking to understand DPRK actions during the ensuing decade it is useful to consider the fundamental policy options he faced. Briefly, there were three broad options: to pull back from total Kimist control and seek an alternative form of legitimacy, as the Albanian communists, for example, had unsuccessfully attempted to do through elections in 1991; to maintain Party control but accept significant, open-ended market-enabling reforms as the Chinese Communist Party had done, or else to uncompromisingly defend the system. However, any pull-back from Kimism would have required Kim Jong Il to turn his back on all he had thought and done essentially since he was a child, and even if he were attracted to this option, then still-recent events in the former Soviet Bloc, not to mention the Albanian case itself, were in themselves powerful disincentives, for it was clear that there was no future for either him or the Party if he chose that path.

Pursuing the Chinese option of economic reform while retaining political hegemony was likewise unrealistic, and those who saw this as a possible option tended to ignore the profoundly differing historical and ideological traditions of the two parties, not to mention the vast differences between the two countries' economies: the DPRK was not, and simply never could be anything resembling some little China. And even if by some calculation the ideological and political disincentives to China-style change were not strong enough, the sheer scale of the economic challenge itself was overwhelming, for the economic differentials between the DPRK and its neighbours, most notably the ROK, had blown out to daunting proportions.[4] Thus, it was hardly surprising that Kim Jong Il chose the option that in any case his whole-life experience would have pressed him to choose: play for time, seek nuclear-backed survival through defending the essentials of the Kim Il Sung system by any means necessary, and derive comfort from the steadfast ideological conviction that difficulties would not last and that somehow the tide would eventually turn against the enemy.

In this manner the defining characteristics of the Kim Jong Il era emerged. Politically, it was distinguished by the maintenance of Kim's unchallenged personal authority through the rigid application of Kimist ideology with its lynchpin personality cult, by the continued enforcement of a rigorous coercion and control system, and by the co-opting and suborning of the military elite through a new military-oriented state policy framework known as *son'gun* ('placing the military first'). From this flowed a distinctive decision-making apparatus and a highly idiosyncratic economic structure whose central purpose was to fund the core prerogatives of the military and the elite through a rigorous marshalling of domestic resources and the extraction of revenue from the international community by a variety of means both legitimate and illegitimate. Economically, Kim struggled to preserve as much of the Kimist economic system as possible, and he succeeded in ensuring that the DPRK remained essentially cut off from the international economy, except for approved foreign currency transactions conducted by members of the elite. In addition to the regime's criminal enterprises and arms dealing, foreign transactions featured mainly informal trade in consumer and light industrial goods with neighbouring Chinese provinces across the Yalu, as well as a substantial trade in minerals.

Socially, however, this period in DPRK history told a different story, for change took place in a manner that marked a significant retreat from the Kimist ideal. This was because the famine largely destroyed the basis for the intensely mobilised daily life hitherto led by most North Koreans, and because the appalling scale of human suffering during the famine had brought with it a final revelation to many ordinary people of the mendacious, pitiless system they lived under. Most importantly, with the government having told the people to fend for themselves during the famine, it was now increasingly forced to acknowledge the informal economic practices that had emerged throughout the country as a result. Many people were no longer under close and direct government control, and by necessity went about their daily lives with greater and greater degrees of autonomy. Unintended, a different species of civil society had come into existence, and while it continued to be hemmed in by the government, and even if the ultimate consequences of this development remained unclear, what was done could not be undone, and in any case the government no longer had either the power or money to undo it. Acceptance of this informal market sector was a bitter ideological pill to swallow, and moves towards grudging acceptance were almost immediately followed by a slow, insistent process of clawback, aimed at re-establishing desirable levels of central control.

Understanding Kim Jong Il

As our narrative reaches the point where Kim Jong Il assumes supreme leadership of the DPRK, it is useful to consider the man and his method of rule more closely. In previous chapters we have already discussed key aspects of Kim Jong Il's career up to his public emergence in 1980, and in particular we have noted the building of a powerful personal secretariat, based on the KWP's Organisation and Guidance Department (OGD) and deployed in a wide variety of key agitprop activities. After 1980, Kim duly became the junior member of a duumvirate with his father, the two apparently cooperating rather seamlessly in pursuit of the father's objectives. His milestone fortieth birthday in 1982 became the occasion of the publication of his major ideological work *On the Juche Idea*, and on his fiftieth birthday in 1992 his father relinquished to him the position of Supreme Commander of the Korean People's Armed Forces. Outside North Korea, the media consistently portrayed him as a mentally unbalanced tyrant, leading an extravagant, dissipated lifestyle while people starved, while within the DPRK his vices remained private, of course, and his many ascribed virtues remained extravagantly public.

By the time of Kim Il Sung's death, the OGD was primed to become an omnipotent superstructure of political control and coercion, overhanging the Party and all functions of government, capable of cutting across rigidly separated existing lines of Party, military and governmental authority, and ensuring that no single centre of potential power could rival Kim Jong Il's access to crucial information. At the centre, where the lines finally met and the total picture became clearer, Kim Jong Il ruled as a micromanager, his authority reinforced through rigid ideological discipline backed up by the cult of personality established by his father and, of course, derived from Joseph Stalin, the great avatar of such cults. He continued, however, to remain in the shadow of his father's cult, rather than advance his own. Perhaps he was shrewd enough to see that this was the best strategy, for he could never compete with his father's aura, and perhaps he saw that the simplistic nostrums of Juche ideology contained all he needed for effective ideological control.

Kim Jong Il chose not to reverse the steady decline of the Korean Workers' Party as an all-powerful ruling party, and so the Party continued to wither on the vine. Public reference to whatever activities it conducted ceased, while the biannual plenary sessions of the Central Committee ceased to be held,[5] and appointments to the highest ranks such as the Politburo ceased to be made until, as we shall see, very late in his period of rule Kim decided to resurrect it to support his son Kim Jong Un through the succession process. And so the once omnipotent Party became a web without a spider, as Kim's omnipotent, omniscient personal secretariat essentially took over the Party's role of providing definitive ideological guidance to government.

How did Kim reach policy decisions? The essential flavour of individual authoritarian systems of rule lies in their combination of formal and informal channels of power and influence. This is, of course, especially true in the DPRK whose Leninist–Stalinist tradition produced an elaborate machinery of government that tended to conceal the extent to which the DPRK system is in fact poorly institutionalised, often chaotic, and riven with informal channels and personal networks of influence and power that enable North Koreans high and low to somehow do business within it, but more obviously despite it. Just as any formal description of how the ROK is governed is grossly incomplete without reference to the myriad overlapping networks of elite interest that operate behind and within formal institutions, so any description of how Kim Jong Il ruled is incomplete without noting a similar phenomenon in the North, whereby Kim first sought detailed information and policy input from designated individuals and groups who lacked clear institutional affiliations and then decided on courses of action.[6]

Observers have speculated that Kim was still subject to pressures from formal institutions such as the military, the Party or the bureaucracy, as represented by the Cabinet (until 1998 the Administration Council), or from factions and sectional interest groups representing views ranging from 'hard line' to 'moderate'.[7] Among quite a few others, the US journalist Mike Chinoy (2008: 8), for example, notes that 'On my visits to Pyongyang in 1995 and 1996, North Korean officials hinted at differences between "moderates" in the Foreign Ministry and "hard-liners" in the military who were sceptical that the North was gaining anything from the accord' and relates that Kim Jong Il said something similar to Madeleine Albright during their November 2000 meeting (Chinoy, 2008: 31). Such remarks require careful consideration, for to take them at face value is to fly in the face of practically everything that is known about the DPRK system, especially the rigid discipline it enforces when talking with outsiders. To begin with, we are of course safe in assuming the ordinary workings of competition between rival bureaucracies – turf wars – but once one ascends to the higher reaches of power and decision-making, we are equally safe in asserting that in the Kimist system formulation and execution of core state policies does not reflect trade-offs or internal stakeholder policy debate in any form that outsiders might recognise as occurring in their own political systems.

Policy discussion and final decision-making has always issued from the painstaking application of rigid ideological formulae to given situations. At this level the penalty for even minor infractions of ideology, standing leadership instructions or court protocol, let alone for signs of independent thinking, was severe, for always lurking behind the words and deeds of the elite is the awareness that like their Stalin-era Soviet counterparts, they are the most monitored group in the country (Collins, 2015: 63). Kim Jong Il may have been hampered by the country's chronic lack of resources in the execution of policy, but protracted observation of the DPRK's political culture leaves little room for doubt that while for all sorts of reasons the DPRK advanced counter-productive policies, Kim faced few constraints during the actual decision-making process, for he was self-disciplined enough, able enough and ruthless enough to enforce his personal authority.[8]

In the event, Kim proved to be a well organized, disciplined leader. The overwhelming evidence of his pre-1994 writings and public utterances showed that he was anything but pragmatically oriented, for he consistently stressed the subservience of technology to ideology in a manner essentially indistinguishable from his father. A related facet of this was Kim's barely concealed disinterest in economic affairs. This was perhaps most famously displayed in the transcript of his 1996 Kim Il Sung University talk (q.v.), but was on display on various other occasions and, of course, it is reflected in the actual record of his economic decision-making. He was far from erratic, though, and may fairly be described as dedicated, ruthless, an exceptionally able strategist, heedless of the suffering his policies were inflicting, and focused on military production and preparedness to the marginalisation of all other facets of economic management and human need. It was the supreme misfortune of practically all North Koreans that he proved to be so adept in pursuing such objectives.[9]

The source that attests most eloquently to Kim Jong Il's ability is the accumulated testimony of Kim's foreign interlocutors during the brief period during 1999–2001 when he personally conducted diplomatic negotiations with the US, the ROK, the EU, Japan and Russia. By this time sections of the international media had long waxed fat on images of violent, capricious behaviour and a dissipated, sybaritic lifestyle, to the extent that in media briefings some of Kim's interlocutors, among them seasoned foreign politicians, envoys and negotiators, felt strangely obliged to tell of their surprise that Kim Jong Il did not conform to the images that this media itself had fomented on the flimsiest of evidence in the first place.[10] What they had witnessed, in fact, were polished performances in which Kim carefully prepared himself, displayed a clear, uncluttered mind and intellect, exhibited a mastery of detail and a strong fixity of purpose, made no moves to accommodate any agenda but his own, and above all knew the strengths and limitations of his own system and how far he could go with them. And while he evidently enjoyed playing the gracious host on such occasions, he did not stray beyond the strict confines of his brief and, unlike his father, he was sufficiently in control of his ego not to seek the international limelight. No sooner had he charmed and bluffed a succession of foreign visitors than he vanished forever from the diplomatic frontline, having achieved what he could to buy time and deflect attention, and having assessed that further possibilities for such personal diplomacy would dry up as the DPRK's nuclear weapons programme advanced. The international media were left to resurrect again their usual errant themes, and a quick survey of Kim Jong Il's obituary articles will give the gist of such themes.

Putting the military first: Kim Jong Il consolidates

The death of Kim Il Sung brought no immediate change to state policies. The country entered into a three-year period of mourning, during which the pre-arranged succession of Kim Jong Il proceeded smoothly, and no purges, dismissals or demotions of senior cadres or other signs of a power struggle in Pyongyang took place.[11] The fact that Kim Jong Il did not immediately take up the posts of State President and KWP General Secretary left vacant by his father's death aroused speculation on possible limits placed on Kim Jong Il's authority by other forces within the Pyongyang hierarchy, but this line of speculation did not explain why assuming these posts was essential to the exercise of effective political control in Pyongyang. Nor did it satisfactorily explain the juxtaposition of any serious power struggle with the consistent public media emphasis on Kim Jong Il's virtue and authority, including the unambiguous public designation of Kim as 'Supreme Leader of the Party, State and Army'. The notion that Kim could project his cult of personality through the media but not have effective control of the reins of power was, of course, illogical in the setting of the DPRK. During the period of mourning, then, Kim Jong Il continued to release his periodic rescripts on ideology, and almost every issue of every major publication in the DPRK continued to extol his virtues in characteristically extravagant terms.

The most noticeable development in the immediate aftermath of Kim Il Sung's death was the almost immediate expanded public profile of the Korean People's Army, and this quickly grew into Kim's hallmark militarist *son'gun* framework.[12] This process began almost immediately after Kim Il Sung's death, with the DPRK media rapidly devoting considerable energy to praising the KPA, whose leaders now received very public promotions and honours, including the unprecedented status of a higher listing than the alternate members of the Politburo at full gatherings of the country's leadership. The DPRK later dated the inception of *son'gun* to January 1995 when Kim Jong Il paid a surprise New Year call to soldiers at a military outpost, rallying and encouraging them with his solicitude and in turn being inspired by them, and calls to many other posts followed as the concept of *son'gun* took shape in Kim's mind (Dae-sook Suh, 2002: 151).[13] The first specific media references occurred in May 1998 before *son'gun's* full-scale unveiling later that year. Within a comparatively short period of time, *son'gun* had become the means by which Kim customised the governmental structure and placed his distinctive stamp upon the DPRK – in ideological, institutional, policy and personnel terms.

Over the years the DPRK has presented the ideological underpinnings of *son'gun* in characteristically trenchant commentaries of little explanatory power, but the fundamental concept underlying such commentary was that the military was not just an instrument for defending the state. Rather, the military stood for something infinitely grander than this – no less than the embodiment of the state's highest values, a symbol and principle of unity above and beyond class interest or indeed any other interest including Party interest, for its calling and its training gave it a special insight into the nature of the sacred mission of defending the leader and the state. Thus, instead of the military serving the people, state and even Party, it should be the other way around: the state and the lives of the people should be ordered around support for the military. Meanwhile, when taken in conjunction with Kim Jong Il's Theory of the Leader, the elevation of the military and its separation from the working class removed practically all remaining vestiges of adherence to Marxist–Leninist principles (Frank, 2005: 286ff.).[14]

Institutionally, the *son'gun* framework took shape at the first session of the Tenth Supreme People's Assembly in September 1998. Kim Jong Il had already assumed the position of General Secretary of the KWP in October 1997, but with the Party mothballed, the convening of the newly elected SPA provided the real venue for a series of defining moves. In addition to the military almost doubling its SPA representation, an amended constitution proclaimed Kim Il Sung as Eternal President,[15] and designated the Chairman of the National Defence Commission, a position Kim Jong Il had already held since 1992, as the new supreme leadership position. Hitherto, the NDC had been a somewhat obscure SPA committee, but now that the military was specifically elevated above the Party (and of course the Cabinet) in importance, the NDC effectively replaced the KWP's Central Military Committee, and more broadly the Politburo itself, as the public expression of political leadership.[16] These moves reflected two key elements in the symbolic dimension of Kim Jong Il's rule – namely, he always remained within the comforting carapace of his father's ideological legacy, and while he never donned a military uniform, he always cloaked himself in the mantle of the military.

The signs of increased status for the military noted above were now buttressed by signs of real power. Sitting on the ten-member NDC were only two other civilians apart from Kim – Yon Hyong-muk and Chon Pyong-ho. Yon was present ex officio as the Prime Minister while the Commission was bedded down and Chon was practically a military man with a long career in the policy area of military procurement. They sat alongside seven senior military commanders, only one of whom, Kim Ch'ol-man, had held Politburo rank at the time of Kim Il Sung's death. This was a leadership group of ageing but still influential figures, not a ceremonial gathering, and they represented a broad range of expertise, including general staff, the political and security apparatus, logistics and the military economy. More to the point, they stood at the centre of powerful networks of patronage and mentoring – 'the elite of the military elite' (Bermudez, 2004: 7). During the Kim Il Sung years such active duty military commanders were notable by their absence from active participation in state and Party functions, but now they advanced into the limelight, delivering public reports on major issues, becoming highly visible in accompanying Kim Jong Il on his inspection tours and, in the case of Vice-Marshal Cho Myong-nok, going to Washington in 2000 for face-to-face talks on missile issues. Moreover, the absence of subsequent structural tinkering or of sudden, unexplained changes in the status of key personnel in the period following 1998 suggests that the military more or less got what it wanted and Kim Jong Il got what he wanted at the first attempt.[17] The smooth embedding of this major new system contrasts with the more uneven pattern of his son's initial appointments during 2012–14, and reflects Kim's careful preparation and adroit control of the DPRK decision-making structure, all the more noteworthy given his lack of a military background.[18]

A number of overlapping factors contributed to the triumph of such unbridled militarism. First and foremost, as we have seen, the DPRK had been a highly militarised state practically from its inception in 1945, and certainly since the adoption of Equal Emphasis in 1962. After the 1967–8 purges, there were no countervailing civilian forces left to inhibit what had become an ongoing, leadership drive towards further militarisation, and thus *son'gun* was a logical incremental step.

Second, an institutional vacuum had to be filled. The KWP was no longer very relevant, both because the downfall of the Soviet Bloc meant that Party to Party fraternal relations were no longer significant except with China, and because the collapse of the planned economy meant that the technocratic rump of the Party was now even less relevant. Moreover, Kim Jong Il had never had much time for the Party, and so he was not interested in maintaining its paramount status, especially as this would require the painstaking task of

Table 6.1 Changes in the DPRK leadership rankings: 1994–8

	Kim Il Sung's Funeral Committee, July 1994	*First session of the 10th SPA, October 1998*
Kim Jong Il	1	1
Kim Yong-nam	8	2
Hong Song-nam#	17	3
Yi Chong-ok★	4	4
Pak Song-ch'ol★	5	5
Kim Yong-ju★	6	6
Cho Myong-nok+	85	7
Yi Ul-sol+	77	8
Kim Il-ch'ol+	90	9
Yi Yong-mu+	55	10
Kye Ung-t'ae	10	11
Chon Pyong-ho+	11	12
Han Song-ryong	12	13
Kim Yong-ch'un+	88	14
Yang Hyong-sop	19	15
Ch'oe Tae-bok	15	16

Source: DPRK media

Notes:
+ = active duty military commander, appointed to the NDC in 1998.
# = ex-officio ranking as Premier.
★ = deceased, retired or otherwise no longer active by 1994.

engineering substantial generational change in its senior ranks, for, like the Soviet Union Politburo in the 1980s, these ranks were by now stacked with seriously ageing mediocrities. Many were there for little obvious reason other than that they were Kim Il Sung's loyal anti-Japanese guerilla comrades, strangely resembling a College of Cardinals, but otherwise virtually non-functional. It was far simpler to let it continue to wither and bypass it with a group more relevant to the handling of the key policies of the day.[19]

Third, and allied to this, it was now wise for stability to award senior military commanders political power and a public presence commensurate with their military rank, especially since after elevating O Kuk-ryol in 1980 (and dismissing him in 1988), Kim Il Sung had not admitted any military figures trained in the post-war period to full membership of the Politburo, reflecting his discomfort around senior commanders who lacked a guerilla background. After all, who knew more about military matters than Kim?

Fourth, with the collapse of the state sector, major economic power increasingly resided within the military economy, and this elevated its role in economic decision-making.

Fifth, Kim Il Sung had died in the midst of an on-going international crisis precipitated by the DPRK's nuclear weapons programme and amid uncertainty as to the final outcome of this contest, highlighting the role of the military was appropriate on many levels, especially in building morale.

Sixth, and while this factor is hard to calculate, over the previous decade or so leading commanders and strategists of the Korean People's Armed Forces (KPAF) had seen all remaining hope of reversing the verdict of the Korean War disappear and their fundamental mission had changed from inflicting defeat to avoiding defeat. No soldier likes a defensive role, and so in such circumstances Kim may well have judged it wise to emphasise a new, proactive role and paramount status for the military.

Seventh, despite the gutting of other sectors to maintain the military, allocations were still not enough to prevent the on-going degrading of the KPA. Although it was hard to actually quantify, but evident to their US and ROK adversaries, both in terms of weaponry and in terms of training resources, the KPA began to fall further and further behind the US and ROK forces in the 1990s. All Kim could do was slow down this process and compensate with asymmetrical weapons, but meanwhile he could also offer senior commanders compensatory rises in prestige and public visibility.

Finally, and perhaps most importantly, *son'gun* issued from Kim Jong Il's personal conviction that this was the best option. It was not prised out of him by military lobbying or pressure; he never played the role of the military wannabe, nor did he act out of any perception of weakness in his power base. Rather, he himself was convinced that *son'gun* offered the best survival strategy, for himself, his class and his country.

Along with expanded military input into a whole range of state policy issues, the most important consequences of *son'gun* were economic, because now, quite explicitly, the already sizeable military economy was prioritised, and so presumably it no longer had to compete with civilian sectors for budgetary allocations, for the latter now effectively received the left-overs.[20] In actual fact, this was not a major step, because the military, featuring the fourth largest standing army in the world, was already a powerful, ubiquitous presence throughout the country, its economic filaments stretching far and wide in the domestic economy due to its sizeable food, clothing, housing, equipment procurement and logistic needs.[21] Major infrastructure decisions involving transport, communications and power-generating assets were already tilted towards it, and it also claimed many of the best and the brightest minds in the country. Its major manufacturing plants, some of which were quite sophisticated, to judge from their products, comprised an economy within an economy, one which was uniquely placed to engage in extensive foreign currency transactions, certainly to the benefit of the bankrupt, autarkic DPRK economy, but above all to the benefit of the military itself.

At the same time, however, *son'gun* led the DPRK further and further away from the adoption of a modern economic structure, and this provides the essential background for viewing the management of the DPRK economy under Kim Jong Il, and subsequently under Kim Jong Un, and especially for viewing putative moves towards reform. Terms such as 'creative' and 'modernisation', and especially the emergence in early 1998 of the slogan *kangsong t'aeguk* ('strong and prosperous nation') with its strange evocation of the state-defining Meiji Japan slogan *fukoku kyohei* ('rich nation, strong military'), are part of Pyongyang's own economic narrative during this period, but the actual economic record presents them as essentially meaningless slogans in an economy that remained profoundly and determinedly anti-modern.

Economic collapse

As the 1990s progressed, the central pillars of the DPRK economy all but collapsed, as did the social security and health systems as well as the Public Distribution System (PDS), the system that had long kept people alive, for they were almost totally dependent on this system as their only source of food, fuel and other basic daily items.[22] The system-defending measures of the early 1990s had generated sufficient revenue for the leadership to feed the military and court economies without too much evident disruption, but there appears to have been almost nothing left over to maintain either the state economy or essential social services. The state therefore proceeded to abdicate the remaining vestiges of its duty of care towards its citizens, and by the mid 1990s DPRK economic practice had produced a fragmented economic structure comprising a number of largely separately functioning parts.[23]

At the apex stood the military economy, its needs accorded absolute priority by the leadership, and accounting for anywhere between 30 per cent and 50 per cent of all production, the proportion blurred by the widespread interpenetration of civilian and military economic activity, and constantly rising as it maintained its share of the national wealth while the share of other sectors fell.[24] Of equal standing was the court economy, which attended to the needs of the leadership and the Party, government and military elite. Best visualised as a series of concentric circles of increasing privilege and usually decreasing productivity, this economy ranged from the petty privileges accorded to lower level cadres, who with their dependants numbered three million or so, to an inner core comprising several hundred senior cadres, all of whom were to be housed, fed and clothed at a level of comfort far above that of ordinary people, and finally to the well-chronicled extravagances of the extended Kim household itself. This economy also extracted resources to feed the Kimist cult, ranging from public celebrations and distribution of food and other forms of largesse to the general population to mark key anniversary dates, to monumental prestige architecture. All told, it required a sizeable budget, some of it clawed back from its chief beneficiaries via 'loyalty payments' from senior cadres, chiefly earned by their privileged access to foreign currency transactions and major rent extraction activities.[25]

The third economy comprised foreign trade in illicit items, which tended to be quarantined off, both because of the extent to which its proceeds fed the court economy and because of the highly specialised skill sets required to produce items such as counterfeit currency, cigarettes, front-shelf pharmaceuticals such as Viagra, and drugs such as heroin and methamphetamine, and then liaise with international criminal syndicates for their effective sale. The income of such operations was, of course, both unquantifiable and fluctuating, but was generally estimated to be in the several hundred million dollar range. Counterfeit US dollars were believed to bring in $15–25 million in their heyday, although since 2011 their production appears to have been curtailed. Likewise, the DPRK appeared to pull back from the large-scale international drug trade about 2005 (Chestnut, 2007: 83; Hastings, 2014: 1), although it was still being implicated in occasional large-scale trafficking in 2013. Regarding scale, we are on firmer ground with tobacco products, for the 1,300 incidences of seizure of DPRK-sourced Marlboros reported by US authorities up to 2003 indicate a major international operation (Chestnut, 2007: 92). A sub-branch of this illicit economy perpetrates fraudulent insurance claims, claimed by one former regime insider who used to process these claims to be the largest of all generators of foreign currency for the regime (Kim Kwang-jin, 2011).[26]

Originally, the state economy with its monopoly control of heavy industry had represented the gateway to advanced economic status and had been central to the country's economic policies immediately after the Korean War. However, this sector was increasingly made subject to the demands of the military economy in a process that proved to be irreversible, and in fact grew more severe in the 1990s as a coherent non-military industrial base came to be assessed as an unaffordable luxury. The Soviet exit brought about a fundamental breakdown in the procurement and distribution process for raw materials, deprived the DPRK of most of its Soviet Bloc export market[27] and severely depleted its technological base. Without such resources and markets, many major industries all but ceased to operate, in many cases being abandoned as useless by the central government as desperate workers stripped of their assets and inventories for onward bartering and sale. By the end of the decade the planned economy was by some estimates running at less than 50 per cent of capacity and accounting for less than 50 per cent of total economic output.

The final form of economic activity constituted private economic transactions. The DPRK had always been distinguished by the extent of the power it exercised over its citizens in their daily lives, and traditionally it had been able to almost totally suppress such activity. However, as economic conditions worsened during the 1980s, its first line of defence against such activity, comprising the local officials, cadres and local neighbourhood committees (*inminban*) crumbled and became complicit. Small markets selling agricultural produce from private plots increasingly appeared in country areas, typically operating on three days or so a month, probably on a rotating basis as was the traditional practice pre-1945. They were allowed to expand modestly as part of the government's early response to food shortages (Haggard and Noland, 2007: 33), and then expanded rapidly in the 1990s as the government lost substantial control of food procurement and distribution. By 2002, there were an estimated three hundred such markets, selling daily necessities and raw materials alongside food sourced from foreign aid supplies, private plots, illegal hillside cultivation and various leakages in the state procurement and distribution network. Meanwhile, the government's longstanding neglect and failure in the light industry sector opened things up for trade in daily necessities and household goods, including clothes, shoes, utensils and basic appliances. Retail services also became involved, from small shops to transport and accommodation.

Gradually, external parties – namely, the Chinese – became involved in the supply of an ever-expanding range of goods such as prestige rice cookers and other household appliances, designer clothes, tradesmen's tools, industrial kitchenware for restaurants, and raw materials such as textiles for clothes manufacture, leather for shoe and clothing manufacture, and sugar for sweets manufacture. Many entrepreneurs required labour in various forms, and so the markets also became de facto labour exchanges.[28] Finally, the breakdown of the state procurement and distribution system prompted factory managers to become informal market participants, seeking machinery, spare parts and maintenance services to keep their own plants running and also to enable them to enter into new fields of marketised production, and so a further level of market sophistication unfolded. While most of this trade remained petty, and at best never moved beyond the consumer and light industrial level, it is easy to see how during this period by some estimates such markets grew to account for up to 30 per cent of all economic activity and were accessed by 80–90 per cent of the general population.

These different parts of the DPRK economy did not come into being overnight, nor is it likely that such a structure was in any way consciously planned for, although a splintered economic structure strangely mirrors the separated lines of authority in the military and Party bureaucracies, and probably serves the regime's overriding internal security interest. They probably emerged as the weight of past government decisions grew heavier, alternatives narrowed down and desperate exigencies arose. Little is known about their inner workings or their interrelationships, both horizontal and vertical, but the weight of evidence suggests little horizontal communication between them, with the various threads of control only bound together at a senior governmental level. Moreover, in the absence of legislative and judicial clarity, at every Party and governmental level, taxes, levies, rents, bribes and other fees were exacted and extracted as the price of doing business in a grossly inefficient, rampantly corrupt system. However, the point that appears to escape most observers who subscribe to the narrative that the DPRK has been constantly seeking ways and means to reform its economy is that this structure remained in place throughout the Kim Jong Il years and endures to this day under Kim Jong Un, and so it is clearly an accepted and acceptable outcome. Such as it was, post-1991 Kimist-style 'reform' *has* in fact occurred, and this is the result.

The Arduous March famine

Over an extended period of time, depriving the civilian economy, and especially the agriculture sector, of productive investment inputs necessarily had its outcome in falling output and in the exacerbation of pre-existing and widespread food shortages, triggering the collapse of the PDS in many areas. Widespread flooding in August 1995 is often seen as the trigger for full-blown famine,[29] but the first requests for international food aid had already gone out to meet the annual spring shortage, or 'barley hump', in early 1994 (Haggard and Noland, 2005: 14), before the situation then spiralled out of control with deaths reaching their peak in early 1997, gradually ameliorating by 2000 to a new normality in which approximately one million people were dead, deaths by starvation were still occurring but at a much lower rate, while malnutrition affected millions more. Agricultural policies remained virtually unchanged.

The DPRK refers to this period as the Arduous March[30] and people generally refer to it as a famine because this is the less emotive term, but in all honesty it had many of the characteristics of a starvation, for it was the conscious withholding of food from people so as not to compromise the leadership's authority and its chosen military priorities. At the very least, humanity owes it to the millions of dead and still suffering North Koreans to say as much. This outcome was not for the purpose of just wantonly inflicting pain and distress, but these deaths were collateral damage from the policies of a regime which, if it had elected to prioritise the saving of human life, had ample time and means to take corrective action by releasing food from stockpiles or negotiating the necessary commercial imports to cover the immediate shortfalls and then deploying the military in distribution. However, the regime had been hollowed out to the extent that it was almost entirely devoid not just of the type of disaster prevention and response planning infrastructure that is expected of modern states, but was also now bereft of the basic mentality required to perceive and act on simple human need. Again, one thinks of the guerilla mindset and the ruthless, perverse priorities and values that have issued from it.

Our focus here lies primarily with cause, response and effect.[31] Here we find that the long-term causes of the famine lie in the agricultural policies of the previous decades. The backdrop here was the Soviet model and legacy, founded on collectivisation, reinforced by Stalinist dogma, and characterised by top-down management, the rejection of many traditional farming practices as 'backward' and their substitution for 'scientific' methods, which generally entailed numerous expensive and unproductive inputs, including the over-use of chemical fertilisers and the inefficient application of mechanisation, in the belief that these would result in higher yields. A further debilitating factor was the legacy of 'transformationism', a fetishist outlook that seemed inseparable from the core messages of Marxism–Leninsm, and which hubristically cast man as the master of nature, thus producing a series of unsustainable, ecologically disastrous practices, including overcropping, deforestation and excessive interference with natural water courses.

In the DPRK we see the Soviet model played out in a somewhat less sophisticated, and hence more extreme form. As we have previously noted, Kim Il Sung had little understanding of agriculture and was alienated from the peasantry, and so for reasons of economic ignorance, ideological dogma and political control, Kimism organised farmers as though they were industrial workers. Removing farmers from both their individual attachment to and strong knowledge of specific plots of land removed a great deal of incentive and expertise as farmers became disincentivised work team members, and many farms were structured like industrial workplaces, their fields excessively strewn with soil-impoverishing chemical fertiliser and subject to poor crop rotation practices in pursuit of over-optimistic production quotas mandated from afar by central planners. By the early 1990s, the predominantly fuel-based fertiliser plants were idle, there was no fuel for the motor pumps on farmers' irrigation works, and many of their surrounding forested hills had been denuded and sown with illegal crops, producing a further set of debilitating problems, including erosion and the silting-up of water courses. Moreover, since these outcomes were fundamentally the result of the implementation of Kim Il Sung's 1964 *Rural Theses*, they could not be meaningfully addressed, for this system was set in stone, and so moving beyond peripheral tinkering and realignment represented – and still represents – anathema.

As to the government's response, we have come to understand that the deeper tragedy of the Arduous March famine was that the enormous loss of life had more to do with the actions of the central government than it did with the actual size of the harvest. At the centre of the tragedy lay the failed Public Distribution System, under which food was to come to the people, like rations delivered to a field army, and due to rigid internal controls on human movement, the people could not go to the food. Thus, when nothing came to them, people died in huge numbers where they lived, especially in the major industrial cities of the northeast such as Hamhung and Chongjin (Demick, 2009). Where people did not simply wait for death, as so many did, the picture at the local level that emerges is one of widespread economic anarchy. Not only did individuals resort to pilfering, bartering, selling possessions and then engaging in other types of small-scale economic activity, but as the local administration itself collapsed, local officials reacted to looming starvation, including their own, by commandeering – that is, looting – state assets, including factories and warehouses, and allowing others to do likewise, for sale or exchange in the informal markets. 'There was so much looting of state property, you could hear people dragging wheelbarrows around throughout the night' is one memorable refugee quote, all the more significant for coming from Sariwon, a major city centrally located in a fertile region about 70km south of Pyongyang, where the government could easily have intervened, had it chosen to.[32]

The government's response also meant that the impact of the famine on fundamental state policies would be minimised, especially as they affected the all-embracing Kimist definition of national security and survival. In other words, dealing with the famine would be conducted in accordance with the normal business of government. Major domestic stockpiles reserved for the military or else earmarked for the Pyongyang-based elite would not be touched even fleetingly, for while tapping into them could have resulted in the major saving of life elsewhere, it would have left the military in a temporary state of vulnerability.[33] Likewise, food aid was to be treated as an economic resource, and as aid flows increased, commercial food imports decreased as the government, long schooled in external predatory behaviour, identified the economic dividend in using international aid to subsidise other priorities.[34]

Food aid sources also fluctuated with a pronounced linkage to the political calculations of both donor country and DPRK politics. In general, the DPRK benefited from this process, for just as donor fatigue began to set in and levels of food aid from initial large-scale donors such the US and the EU levelled off and even fell post-2000, policy changes in China and the ROK led to significant increases from this quarter. With their non-intrusive, undemanding ways, these two were in fact more desirable partners, and had the effect of encouraging DPRK resistance against the internal monitoring requirements of the World Food Programme and others (Haggard and Noland, 2007: 7).

Ideology also mandated that the DPRK would not attempt any meaningful reform of now dysfunctional Kimist agricultural policies, for raising food production by providing incentives to production, such as by giving farmers more control over the entire agriculture process, from crop selection and raising to produce marketing ran counter to the self-proclaimed 'infallible' pronouncements of Kim Il Sung in this domain. The force of entrenched attitudes rendered even marginal reassessment of the system all but inconceivable to policy makers, and so significant adjustment remained anathema – a typical example of the way in which the Eternal President of the Republic continued to rule the country from his mausoleum.[35]

In directing this response, Kim Jong Il was rather less challenged by these events than might be supposed. Some portrayed him as paralysed and unable to take hold of the situation,[36] and the ostensible transcript of a speech he gave to senior cadres in December 1996 at Kimilsung University is often cited in support of this interpretation. The key section reads as follows:

> At a time like this with the overall political situation so complicated, I can't solve all pending problems and take charge of day-to-day management of the economy as well. I alone am responsible for major sectors, including Party and military affairs. If I became involved in running the economy it would cause irreparable damage to the revolution and construction. When he was alive, the Leader [Kim Il-sung] told me on no account to get involved in economic work. He repeatedly said that if I did so I would not be able to handle Party and military affairs properly. In the current situation we face, since the most important task is strengthening the military, I have been providing frequent on-the-spot guidance to military units. It is the workers and economic administrators who must take responsibility for economic affairs.[37]

Questions must inevitably attach themselves to the accuracy of an unofficial transcript of unclear origin, believed to have been brought to the South by the defecting KWP Party Secretary Hwang Jang Yop in February 1997.[38] It has been read as self-justificatory, but one cannot imagine that a leader of Kim Jong Il's mettle would demonstrate such weakness of spirit, especially before such an audience. Read more in the context of the times and Kim's policies, it is more convincing to see it as the statement of a clear, brutal strategy that more or less explains the trajectory of the famine: regime survival – and therefore the survival of the way of life enjoyed by all those present – superseded *all* other objectives.

By 2004, the DPRK's actions, strategies and their outcomes left few in any doubt as to the ruthless determination and effectiveness of DPRK policies. Meaningful agricultural reform had not occurred and would not occur, food production levels still approximated the levels of the early 1990s, outright famine conditions had not recurred, though further significant deaths were to occur in 2008 after a bad harvest in 2007 and vulnerability levels remained high. However, with a decade of experience in food supply management now behind it, the DPRK had good reason to believe that it would be able to get by without significant compromise to its system. Thus, while Kim Jong Il did not direct a timely response to the famine and did not preside over any real amelioration of the food supply situation, these were not his objectives. In the desperate calculus of the time and within the constraints of the Kimist system, he achieved what to him was the more important objective of containing the potential of this situation to threaten broader policy objectives.

Despite all the resources available in the modern world, devastating famines have periodically broken out in fragile states in decades past, most notably in the Horn of Africa. Warfare, administrative breakdown, blight and changing climate patterns have all played their role in elevating these events to the status of major disasters. In the case of the DPRK, though, none of these factors intruded. Instead, a pre-existing fragile food supply situation became a catastrophe and was prolonged due to calculated, calibrated government policies and priorities. Nicholas Eberstadt's description of the DPRK as 'the first urbanized literate society in human history to suffer famine during peacetime' (Eberstadt, 2009: xi) is as telling an epitaph as is needed.

The state fights back: the July 2002 measures

The reactivation of a formal governmental structure in 1998 fed a broader sense that the worst was over and that the government could begin a cautious programme of reassertion amid a changed and precarious situation. By 1999, signs of economic stabilisation were also emerging after successive years of GDP contraction, and this established a platform from which the leadership could come to grips with the collapse of the state economy and the growth of the informal economy. The first substantial shot in the campaign to bring the state back in came via a series of measures taken in July 2002, usually referred to as the '7.1 Measures for the Improvement of Economic Management' (*7.1 kyongje kwalli kaeson choch'i*). Their unifying thread was the standard need of governments everywhere to raise revenue and cut expenditure, and they featured three chief components: the legitimisation of some forms of private economic activity, the remonetising of the economy by means of a significant devaluation of the North Korean won with associated major hikes in official wages and prices, and the devolution of economic decision-making in some state-owned enterprises.

The protracted decline of the DPRK economy had already pared down the income flow from state-owned enterprises, and this process had gathered pace after the mid-1990s, especially when the government lost its control over grain procurement and tax collection at the local level during the chaos of the famine. Lee and Yoon (2004: 47–48), for example, estimate the decline of revenue during 1994–98 at around 50 per cent, from $19.2 billion to $9.1 billion, and the persistence of low-key civil disobedience, the on-going dysfunction of the state economy and continuing high military priorities seem to have ruled out any major drive to retrieve these assets in the short term. This left divestment of liabilities as a key alternative, and accordingly both the subsidising of state-owned enterprises and the funding of the PDS system, the latter alone absorbing an estimated 12–14 per cent of the budget, were curtailed.[39]

Regarding private economic activity, some redrawing of boundaries was unavoidable since people would now have to provide for themselves what government no longer could. The structure of the informal marketplace was already in place, and so co-opting it must have seemed like the easiest path to the government's objective, especially since co-opting enabled closer political control and hence ideological threat containment. In addition, there were already enormous amounts of money circulating in the markets which could be sopped up as revenue. Thus, the authorities slowly moved from informal tolerance of food markets as a necessary evil during the famine to formal tolerance of general markets (Lee and Yoon, 2004: 49–50; Lee Kyo-duk *et al.*, 2008: 35; Kim and Yang, 2015: 19). By the end of 2003, there were over thirty large-scale markets, defined as those with over 500 registered vendors (Mansourov, 2004: 1). They were far from backstreet affairs, but were well defined, well structured and well appointed, with fixed stalls and facilities for vendors and visitors alike (Ward, 2014).

However, in order to effectively buy and sell in these markets people needed a stable circulating medium, which meant that the economy would have to be significantly monetised. This represented no small leap of the imagination, for practically throughout its entire life the DPRK had functioned with a demonetized economy in which the circulation of money was marginalised since people laboured for the state and instead of being paid salaries they were issued with rations and coupons. In any case, they had little use for money as they had virtually no access to consumer goods.[40] The major remonetisation instruments employed by the government in July 2002 consisted of intertwined major wage rises to augment the money in circulation and even greater price rises, ostensibly in order to stimulate consumption and hence production, but also to relieve the government of the burden of the highly subsidised prices at which it made available basic goods and services. Remonetisation would also soak up some of the idle currency that had accumulated during more than a decade in which there was basically nothing to buy, and it would also not have escaped attention that this would curb the power of the private market entrepreneurs by biting into their working capital, which of course was held in cash. Prices for basic goods and services now broadly reflected marketplace prices, a typical case being rice, which rose by a multiple of 550 (Frank, 2005: 296), while major wage rises in theory enabled people to cope with these rises, although in quite a differential manner, for the rises favoured government and military personnel, as well as workers in key revenue-raising sectors such as mining.

The third major component of the 2002 measures allowed more enterprise-level decision-making, the actual effects of the measures depending on the nature of the enterprise concerned. Strategically important industries such as steel and metallurgy remained on a short leash, but for light industry and industries with a service interface opportunities opened up. Thus, with the planning process so broken down, typically the government simply endorsed the ingenuity that managers and workers had displayed during the previous decade, for what management did in pursuit of central planning objectives was no longer as important as what they could actually remit to the central government. This meant that they were able to seek out ways and means of increasing production while retaining a good deal of any profit. Therefore, once they had made show of fulfilling undemanding, unsupervised production quotas, they were able to pursue other avenues of commerce, relying on a more incentivised workforce who were now paid wages that reflected the economic value of their work more accurately.

The case for assessing the July 2002 measures as significant reforms is dubious at best and has not been borne out by subsequent events.[41] Rather, they were conceived and executed from within the logic of Kimist ideology as forced adjustments taken without any intention of proceeding towards an open-ended 'reform' stage, with all the intimations of significant ideological or political compromise that such reform would, of course, entail.[42] Thus, no changes to either the sclerotic financial and banking system, the government structure or key personnel accompanied the new measures, no discernible public debate emerged to rally people behind the measures, and again when we look at actual policy outcomes we see that no liberalising trends flowed from them. Most important, there was no opening of the economy to substantial foreign inputs, and so increased inputs had to come from wealth somehow generated from within the slender resources of the impoverished, essentially autarkic domestic economy.

Quite the contrary, then, the July 2002 measures marked the launching of a campaign of reassertion by the Kimist state, essentially endeavouring to control the informal market by acknowledging and allowing space for the major practices that had grown up piecemeal over the previous decade. However, alignment of government policy with market forces was not the intention: the government simply saw no other option for restoring fundamental viability to its finances. And, of course, re-establishing fundamental viability could equally establish a pathway back to resurrecting the centrally planned economy.[43] Policy makers and Kimist stakeholders had been convinced against their will that something had to be done, and they were far from enthusiastic about the situation, especially the loss of control over people's lives that it represented. This helps explain why the subsequent story of the July 2002 measures is not one of flow-through effect, but one of a protracted campaign directed by Kim Jong Il against the further spread of marketisation.

Furthermore, these measures came, of course, less than four years after Kim Jong Il had set in place the profoundly anti-modern *son'gun* framework, anti-modern because no would-be modernising state in the modern world has ever achieved its goals on the back of a militarised economy and society.[44] The harmful effects of *son'gun* economics are manifold and obvious. First, with their heavy infrastructural and material industrial needs – steel, metallurgy, electronics – they skew basic economic priorities, distort distribution and bleed their civilian counterparts. Second, while the military can be a source of foreign currency earning, it also must absorb much of what it earns in sourcing advanced components and technology and in R&D investment in order to maintain the production of market competitive products. Third, much of military weaponry production is highly specialised and isolated from the mainstream economy, and so there is little human resource or technology spill-over, not just in terms of their products but in terms of their distribution systems and their workplace culture. Finally, a bloated military that almost totally deprives the economy of the productivity of most young men between the ages of 20 and 30 constitutes an enormous drain on the country's human resources. Thus, any move towards 'reform' by its very nature would have led away from, and undermined *son'gun*, and it would have made no sense for the leadership to think in these terms only four years after installing *son'gun* at the very centre of national life. In short, when seen in context, the July 2002 measures could hardly be other than what in fact they were: rather blunt, grudging, system-defending instruments.

Social change

The growth of private economic activity did, however, begin a process of significant social change which has radically redrawn the boundaries between DPRK state and society, changing many aspects of life in the North and potentially posing a long-term threat to Kimism. The essence of this change was the collapse of Party authority at the local level, where cadres were increasingly forced to go against Party policies to deal with problems of survival in what Everard aptly termed 'effectively an act of mass civil disobedience' (Everard, 2011). This also meant the loss of many of the social inhibitions enforced minutely through the coercion and control apparatus, for people were no longer confined to their workplace and locality. Instead, they moved about and interacted far more freely in the new marketplaces, and since a majority of the population now survived and earned a living by informal market activities, although they were surrounded by uncertainty, they became more and more autonomous in their daily lives.

Working life for many people also changed. Attachment to a state-allocated job in a specific workplace was still a necessity for the distribution of rations, but for most workers there were no duties to perform and no meaningful wages to be paid. Thus, the practice also emerged whereby workers paid a set fee to the management to remain on the company's books in order to collect rations and avoid detection, but were otherwise absent from work in order to work in the informal sector in a practice described as 'daylighting' – doing a second job, but doing it not by moonlight but in broad daylight (Lee *et al.*, 2008: 28; Joo Hyung-min, 2010: 132; Choi Changyong, 2013: 664). Refugee evidence suggesting that 35–40 per cent of the entire workforce engaged in this practice (Lee *et al.*, 2008: 39) and its necessity was underlined by the fact that while the PDS notionally continued, figures given to missions by the Food and Agricultural Organisation (FAO) throughout this period place the ration at somewhere between 25 and 50 per cent of the minimum daily caloric requirement.[45] This short supply meant that in order to live, people had no choice but to supplement their state-generated income by participating in the informal market. No wonder, then, that refugee accounts from the mid-1990s onwards demonstrate an almost uniform 60–80 per cent participation rate in the informal market (Haggard and Noland, 2010; Joo Hyung-min, 2010: 114; Kim and Yang, 2015: 34).

Information exchange also now grew horizontally, not exclusively vertically, as people who had previously been strangers talked of business conditions, money-making opportunities, and ways and means of avoiding harassment from authority. There were even refugee anecdotes from former law-enforcement officers recounting how they learned to play the informal market and access escape routes from talking with prisoners and detainees in their charge (Choi Changyong, 2013: 660–2). A further facet of this was the growth of new commercial alliances between market players who had knowledge and expertise, and bureaucrats who had insider trading knowledge and who could also provide protection. To the financier of major private market transactions, or money master (*donju*), facilitation of transport, advance notice of grain shipment arrivals, advance warning of crackdowns, and above all the fireproofing of profits through access to foreign currency were vital and well worth paying for.

Another major feature of life in the post-famine era was the exponential growth of institutionalised corruption, to the point where it became accepted as an integral part of the governmental process and was informally systematised (Young-ja Park, 2015: 143). The origins of such corruption lie in the historical Marxist–Leninist disdain for 'bourgeois legalism' and the resultant weakness of legal checks and balances within the system. Now with the breakdown of law and order and of centrally enforced discipline, and with the inability of the government to pay its employees a living wage, further opportunities arose. Civil and criminal law exist, of course, in the DPRK, but they lack detail and are supplemented by a widespread system of ad hoc but legally enforceable proclamations within state organisations, the enforcement of which lies in the hands of its functionaries (Young-ja Park, 2015: 135). Corruption therefore thrived in an environment characterised by wide discretionary powers and limited oversight, as citizens sought out such officials for protection in a broad range of activities relating not just to business activities but to daily life issues.[46] Meanwhile, however, the *gulags* remained intact, state violence against citizens was still routine and harsh, and the country was still sealed off from the outside world.

It remains difficult to assess the long-term significance of these developments. Regarding corruption, at the very least we may be looking at another important source of system resilience, for it does enable various tasks of both government and the market economy to be performed with what one might term pragmatism. Moreover, testimony from defecting former senior cadres suggests that for most government employees corruption constitutes an overwhelming proportion of their total income, thus further relieving the government of a financial burden. The other side of the coin is that such practices postpone the injection into the system of even a modicum of transparency and rule of law, without which no base for major economic reform can be secured. However, as long as domestic reform and interaction with the global economy remain non-priorities in Pyongyang, the authorities probably perceive that there are more positives than negatives in this state of affairs.[47]

Thus, at this stage of the DPRK's story we are often observing favoured entrepreneurs with little technical expertise, in a close and corrupt relationship with the authorities and the ruling party-based elite, both parties being essentially rent seekers with sparse skill-sets, concluding shady, low-tech deals in expensive salons and coffee shops to pay bribes and gain lucrative privileged import licences for the on-sale of goods to a captive market or otherwise to circumvent a hostile system. In the wake of the July 2002 measures, then, mainstream capitalism in the DPRK had apparently advanced to the stage reached by the ROK in the 1950s under Syngman Rhee, while the late deindustrialisation of the 1990s had yet to become the prelude to even later reindustrialisation.

Nuclear negotiations: the Agreed Framework and KEDO

The Arduous March famine played out against the broader background of the DPRK's negotiations with outside parties over its nuclear weapons programme. These negotiations entered a new phase in October 1994 with the signing in Geneva of a crucial Agreed Framework between the DPRK and the US. The first-ever bilateral US–DPRK agreement, it contained four provisions, comprising one operational provision to address the immediate crisis and three highly aspirational provisions devoted to broader issues.[48] The former addressed the immediate cause of the specific crisis – namely, the DPRK's withdrawal from the IAEA in June 1994 and the imminent further download of weapons-grade plutonium from its Yongbyon reprocessing facility. It did so by securing DPRK agreement to stop downloading the plutonium, to shut down and dismantle the facility, and to safely dispose of the spent fuel from the reprocessing operations there. In return, and ostensibly in compensation for lost possibilities of power generation at Yongbyon, the US was to broker a deal subsequently involving the ROK and Japan to build two light-water nuclear reactors, and in the meantime also to provide up to 500,000 tons of heavy fuel oil per annum, well over half the DPRK's estimated needs.[49] In addition, the three aspirational provisions committed the two sides to move towards the full normalisation of relations, to cooperate to achieve 'peace and security on a nuclear-free Korean Peninsula' and to strengthen the international nuclear non-proliferation regime. There was no mention, nor were there any subsequent discussions on how these objectives might be progressed.

The aspirational provisions were, of course, quite unattainable. For example, the DPRK's long-standing definition of 'fully normalised relations' meant US military withdrawal from the ROK and a dismantling of that portion of the US military posture in Japan which was unilaterally defined by the DPRK as a threat to its security – all to be carried out without reciprocity over ROK security since the DPRK maintained that its dealings with the ROK were none of the US's business. And if somehow relations ended up being normalised, then this would mean that the ROK would no longer be the puppet of an enemy but the ally of a 'friend', and this would make a nonsense out of the DPRK's basic claim to be the one true, authentic Korean state, for US and ROK enmity was essential to this claim. The agreement's two-track design, with milestones in LWR construction linked to milestones in dismantling nuclear facilities, was also unrealistic for the same reason, for again it relied on a non-existent willingness to engage in reciprocity. Moreover, the agreement lacked any semblance of bipartisan support in the US Congress, and so Republican Party opposition after gaining control of Congress in November 1994 meant that the Clinton administration largely forfeited the power to make good on its promises to the DPRK. As Stephen Bosworth, the first CEO of the Korean Peninsula Energy Development Organization (KEDO), later observed, 'The Agreed Framework was a political orphan within two weeks after its signature.'[50] Thus, it was not surprising that the Clinton administration quickly ceased to invest time and political capital in what was clearly a losing cause, as its pragmatic interest lay increasingly in deflecting attention away from it.

On the other side, Pyongyang soon made it clear by its actions that it viewed the actual conclusion of the agreement as a victory in itself – which in many ways it was, as Robert Gallucci, the US signatory to the Agreed Framework, subsequently effectively confirmed.[51] The DPRK could therefore be well satisfied with its achievement and walk away with its gains at any stage, for, contrary to outside party assumptions, these gains did not necessarily include future power output from the two LWRs: the subsequent course of events renders it doubtful that the DPRK ever entertained any clear idea how to actually bring them on line, any more than it had had a clear idea how to utilise its imports of advanced technology plants during 1972–4. The gains did, however, include the heavy fuel oil, the buying of time, the establishing of Pyongyang as a dialogue partner with a reluctant US thus undercutting the ROK, the raising of its own status, and the much-needed boost these outcomes gave to Party and military morale. They also included embroiling the US, the ROK and Japan in a joint project whose timing and phasing the DPRK exercised final control over, thus enabling it to engender and exploit tensions and difficulties between these three key adversaries.

This was probably the limit of Kim Jong Il's Agreed Framework ambitions, for a DPRK in which the terms of the agreement had been carried out would have been a DPRK that had changed utterly, and from Kim's perspective not for the better. To begin with, it would possess a security posture heavily degraded from nuclear weapons-capable independence to non-nuclear regional interdependence, and this would have stood every tenet of Kimism on its head, to the extent of changing the very identity of the DPRK state. Moreover, just commissioning the two LWRs would have been impossible without Pyongyang becoming enmeshed in a sea of international compliance issues and agreements covering the operation of such facilities, and it would also have automatically entailed joining and then seeking billion-dollar loans from international agencies such as the Asian Development Bank and World Bank as the only possible means of connecting output from the LWRs to what passed for the national grid. These are, of course, two institutions that Pyongyang has not joined to this day. In short, the expectation of such a major departure from the fundamental Juche principles of economic autarky for the sake of the output from two LWRs made no policy sense. And so it is that the substantial LWR construction site at Kumho lies abandoned.

Perhaps the most important component of the DPRK's negotiating success was that in agreeing to eventually dispose of its processed nuclear waste, most likely to a European destination, Pyongyang was well aware that neither the US nor any other outside party had precise knowledge of the amount of plutonium it still held.[52] Thus, while the DPRK's adversaries believed the economic inducements on offer were real inducements, Pyongyang was to demonstrate that it was only interested in what could be accommodated within its existing policy goal of achieving nuclear weapons-based survival and security. This should have been clear from the 1990 Kim Il Sung–Kanemaru negotiations with Japan, where Pyongyang walked away from a potential multi-billion dollar normalisation of relations settlement rather than countenance renegotiation of an unworkable agreement, and was also about to become clear again from its various responses to the economic spin-offs from the ROK's Sunshine Policy. In sum, although at different levels and at different times DPRK negotiating and implementing behaviour was not without peripheral, tactical flexibility, and although its grievances at the US's sporadic performance in ensuring the fuel oil deliveries arrived in an orderly manner were quite real, Pyongyang viewed the agreement implementation phase more as a pay-off phase than as a further engagement and cooperation phase, and its compass always swung away from more pragmatic considerations such as power generation and normalisation of relations with the US, and back to maintaining ideological rectitude, working towards nuclear weapons capability, and maintaining military and diplomatic pressure against the ROK.

After protracted and discursive negotiations, the DPRK finally accepted two ROK-designed LWRs, and in December 1995 signed a supply agreement with KEDO. A ground-breaking ceremony was held in August 1997, and meanwhile the North began to take delivery of its KEDO-sponsored 500,000 tonnes of heavy fuel oil per year. But although Pyongyang was in theory engaged in a billion-dollar project that could eventually lead to the renovation of its dysfunctional power grid, it did not allow this to interfere with the military's on-going programme of special operations against the South. Hence, in 1996 a DPRK submarine ran aground off the ROK east coast while landing an infiltration team, thus precipitating a protracted land pursuit and fire-fight with numerous casualties. Then in August 1998, the North test-fired a celebratory Taepo-dong medium-range missile which overflew northern Japan and landed in the Pacific Ocean some 1,500 kilometres away.[53] Both actions seriously affected US, ROK and Japanese domestic political opinion towards the entire KEDO operation, for while under the Agreed Framework the DPRK was still at liberty to work on missile delivery systems, under any calculus that included a will to progress the Agreed Framework, both actions were unnecessary and inflammatory. These incidents underlined the two-track nature of DPRK policy: in their eyes the Agreed Framework was a bilateral DPRK–US issue, and how Pyongyang chose to act towards the ROK and Japan was irrelevant to it.

Most important, the DPRK utilised the Agreed Framework window of opportunity to work on other key aspects of nuclear weapons technology, especially highly enriched uranium (HEU) production. This highly sophisticated programme originally grew out of the synergies of the DPRK and Pakistan nuclear programmes, whereby DPRK missile technology was considerably advanced over Pakistan, but it lagged behind in weaponisation technology. Its inception is commonly dated to Pakistan Prime Minister Benazir Bhutto's December 1993 visit to Pyongyang and the process of technological exchange that ensued,[54] although the DPRK is believed to have only gained access to what it needed from Pakistan's technology via the rogue Pakistani nuclear scientist A.Q. Khan during 1997–8. Thereafter, the DPRK soon developed a sophisticated HEU research programme aimed at mastering a complex and expensive weaponisation technology. Some have linked this development to DPRK disillusionment over the implementation of the Agreed Framework, but almost certainly far less ruthlessly survivalist states that the DPRK would not have passed up the opportunity of developing HEU technology in such circumstances. However, this move necessarily left an international money and procurement trail, many elements of which were gradually picked up by US agencies, and by mid-2002 the broad internal consensus of the US intelligence community was that the DPRK had moved beyond HEU research and design to production capacity (Chinoy, 2008: 91). This more or less sealed bipartisan agreement in Congress that the DPRK was a bad faith negotiator, and in turn this sealed the fate of the Agreed Framework.

In 1998, however, the US was unaware of the DPRK's HEU plans, and so it remained focused on Pyongyang's missile programme. Here, the August 1998 missile incident led Washington to a further comprehensive North Korean policy review carried out by former Defense Secretary William Perry. Published in October 1999, it sought to address a number of developments since 1994. Foremost among these were the DPRK's ballistic missile development work, indications that the DPRK was continuing with nuclear weapons-related work, the DPRK's economic collapse and humanitarian crisis, the emergence of the ROK's Sunshine Policy and a hardening in Japanese policy towards the North due to the missile issue. Taken together, these factors constituted a new framework of negotiation centring on comprehensive missile containment and aiming at offering the DPRK strong security, and economic and diplomatic incentives to discontinue its nuclear weapons and missile development activities, including its lucrative export trade in missile systems. This in turn led to a flurry of diplomacy in the last months of the Clinton administration, including direct talks between Secretary of State Madeleine Albright and Kim Jong Il, but ultimately the two parties could not find enough common ground to achieve progress.[55]

Some observers have claimed to detect significant movement in DPRK policy at this time (Kartman et al., 2012: 106; Mansourov, 2003: 94), but if so, either the message did not get through to the US or it was half-hearted and tactical to begin with. The US ultimately adopted the latter view, and this probably does not represent one of history's great missed opportunities, not the least because there is little support for this interpretation of impetus towards change elsewhere in DPRK policy. Quite the contrary, prioritising the military through the proclamation of the *son'gun* framework in September 1998 and simultaneously committing to a major, expensive HEU production programme also in 1998, do not sit in any logical relationship with a policy of opening up to the world, nor do they suggest any departure from a DPRK strategic mindset that had been entrenched for decades.

The advent of the Bush administration in January 2001 impacted US policy considerably. Yet another review combined demands for progress on the Agreed Framework, acceptance of international surveillance of missile programmes, a ban on missile exports and 'a less threatening conventional military posture' into a set of conditions to be met by the DPRK in return for moves towards normalisation. This fairly expressed the US interest, but it was clearly aimed past and not at Pyongyang, suggesting that the US believed it held the whip hand in the face of what it still believed to be the DPRK's impending collapse. The fact that George W. Bush personally and publicly used harsh and personal language to criticise Kim Jong Il further underlined the administration's hardened mindset, but such language was also unnecessary and self-indulgent.[56] Broader events in the shape of the September 11 2001 terrorist attacks then intervened, and the following January, in his State of the Union address, Bush designated the DPRK, Iran and Iraq as an international 'axis of evil'. Official-level exchanges became more and more terse, and in October 2002 US negotiators advised their DPRK counterparts of their conclusion that the DPRK had been running an HEU production programme, an interpretation the DPRK did not attempt to dispute.[57] On 13 November further shipments of heavy fuel oil were suspended pending clarification of the North's HEU activities, and this led Pyongyang to announce on 21 November that the Agreed Framework was now a dead letter.

It will be clear from the various levels of complexity outlined above that it is simplistic in the extreme to apportion blame for the collapse of the Agreed Framework to any one overriding factor. The positions adopted by the US Republican majority Congresses and the Bush administration come under particular scrutiny and are often cited as a major factor, but this assumes that the Agreed Framework was inherently viable in the first place, and this is debatable. Concluded reluctantly by the US and cynically by the DPRK, it was close to the best deal on offer, but it was not a framework to resolve the issue so much as an expensive exercise in delay that suited both parties since both believed that time was on their side – the US because it believed that time brought DPRK collapse closer and the DPRK because it believed time brought nuclear weapons-guaranteed survival closer. In this context Republican misgivings were understandable, even if the broader partisan agenda that fed these misgivings at times did them little credit. Hindsight has only made clear what the DPRK's adversaries do not appear to have been sufficiently aware of at the time, that in agreeing to the terms of the Framework, the DPRK was not turning a corner, nor was it adjusting to the post-Cold War world. It believed it had won this particular battle and was demanding the spoils of victory.

Viewing the DPRK as an aggrieved partner to the Agreed Framework is therefore awkward. In some aspects it may have been, but such a view needs to persuasively explain why it was also a heedlessly inflammatory partner, which also did next to nothing to assist the processes that KEDO had to undergo to deliver its side of the bargain. It also needs to offer a more convincing and less patronising explanation than simple ignorance of international norms in explaining why Pyongyang regarded the various technical obstacles encountered by KEDO as adversarial opportunities to apply pressure, especially through vehement complaints over construction delays that had arisen for quite practical or rational reasons. Most important, LWR construction never reached the point that would have triggered DPRK full compliance with its IAEA safeguards agreement under the Agreed Framework, and rather than simplistically assert that the DPRK kept its side of the bargain, it is more accurate to say that Pyongyang was never called upon to keep any end of its bargain, other than routine inspections of facilities that were not subject to the freeze.[58]

Many years on, when we see the Agreed Framework in perspective, we see a mixture of success and failure for both sides. Fundamentally, prior to the 1994 crisis, the Clinton administration had allowed non-proliferation rhetoric to run ahead of its actual power to do anything about the situation, and it was now forced to back down from threats of action through the United Nations Security Council that it could not realistically back up. It thus sought the best face-saving deal it could, because the alternative of unrestricted DPRK production of plutonium was a considerably worse option, and the result was of necessity a somewhat imperfect document. The construction of two extraordinarily complex billion-dollar facilities in a remote area north of Wonsan in what was now essentially a Third World country in technological and infrastructure terms would have been challenging enough even under the best of circumstances, but beyond that, there was simply no basis in trust or good will to broker this project, let alone agree to an accompanying set of major aspirational objectives.

Thus, for the DPRK success was measured by the time it gained to work on other components of its nuclear weapons programme, the valuable oil subsidy it extracted and the fact that it succeeded in retaining a part of its pre-1994 plutonium stockpile. Since it placed little or no value on the two LWRs on offer, it was at best calculatedly and fundamentally ambivalent as to the outcome to their construction. Meanwhile, the US measured its success by its extrication from a confrontation that could only have ended badly for all concerned. The agreement applied a circuit-breaker, saved face, and over time the US slowly came to terms with its limited power where the DPRK nuclear weapons programme was involved. If nothing else, the outcome of the Agreed Framework established that there was no point in threatening the DPRK, and so it was better to opt for virtually open-ended multilateral discussions. Out of this process came the Six Party Talks process (2003–9), which was tacitly designed to massage the issue but to lead nowhere. In this manner the US began to adjust awkwardly and resentfully to the revelation of its impotence, but at least it was no longer likely to embark upon the type of catastrophic action taken against Iraq, the DPRK's co-tenant on the axis of evil.

The Sunshine Policy

During this period we also see signs of significant DPRK diplomatic engagement, comprising substantial missile talks with the US, DPRK–ROK and DPRK–Russia summits in 2000, and in leadership talks with the EU (2001) and Japan (2002, 2004). These policy démarches encouraged speculation at the time that Kim Jong Il was seeking to implement more outward-looking diplomatic and economic policies, but they accomplished little, and were in any case contradicted by the thrust of on-going DPRK domestic policy. However, with the ROK more substantial talks were held and substantial agreements entered into during the years of the Sunshine Policy framework (1998–2007), such that for some it appeared that the two Koreas were at last adopting enduring, fundamental principles of mutual non-aggression and cooperation.

After breakdown in 1992, the inter-Korean talks again entered hibernation. Pyongyang's outright rejection of Red Cross talks proposed by Seoul in August 1994 reflected a lack of interest in renewed dialogue in the immediate post-Kim Il Sung period, and a series of incidents during the 1994–97 period of mourning marked a continuing deterioration in inter-Korean relations. The September 1996 submarine incident, and a further DPRK incursion and exchange of fire in the DMZ in July 1997 again emphasised the continuing stand-off, and although inter-Korean famine-related economic exchanges continued and expanded during 1997, political and military tension remained high.

This was the background against which the Kim Dae Jung Administration took office in February 1998, whereupon Kim immediately enunciated his Sunshine Policy,[59] which proactively sought engagement with the North based on the principles of no tolerance for DPRK armed provocations, no ROK efforts to undermine or absorb the North, and active ROK attempts to promote reconciliation and cooperation between the two Koreas. The policy elicited little response from Pyongyang in its first two years before Kim Jong Il suddenly agreed in April 2000 to receive Kim Dae Jung in Pyongyang for a summit meeting in June. This meeting produced a communiqué vague enough to accommodate both sides' positions, and also produced agreements on a wide range of economic and other intergovernmental initiatives, but as was the case with similar predecessor agreements, during the ensuing months negotiations on major elements of implementation quickly stalled. In the face of a further serious naval clash in the Western Sea in June 2002 and revelations concerning the North's clandestine highly enriched uranium programme shortly after, public support in the South for the Sunshine Policy declined sharply, and by the end of 2002 the process was essentially moribund. Ambivalence, if not hostility, now characterised the popular mood in the South, and continuing intransigence characterised the policies of the North. Kim's successor, Roh Moo-hyun, maintained the thrust of the policy during 2003–8, and contacts – at times substantial contacts – continued, culminating in Roh's visit to Pyongyang in October 2007 during his last weeks in office, but this visit generated no further momentum and Lee Myung-bak officially disavowed the policy when he took office in February 2008.

Discussion of many aspects of the Sunshine Policy belongs primarily in the field of ROK domestic politics, and its contours have much to do with the conflicted personality and ambitions of Kim Dae Jung, but they also reflect evolving ROK attitudes towards reunification which had been taking shape since the 1970s when the ROK first began to move away from its reflexive anti-communist mindset, and which became more salient in the aftermath of the country's reversion to democracy in 1987. Living with the live issue, dealing with the North on a regular basis, debating it in an ever-widening circle of government, military, academic and international contexts had gradually produced a sophisticated, substantial pool of knowledge and expertise vis-à-vis the North. At the same time, of course, reunification issues were not quarantined from broader partisan politics in the South, and politicians tended to see reunification policy through the prism of their broader interests and convictions. Opposition circles tended to be critical, often sharply so, of what they saw as a national policy still too narrowly tied to the military–security perspective, and they aggressively believed that a grander process of outreach to the North was bound to, more than was likely to, achieve a major breakthrough. All parties, however, shared the usually unspoken conviction that the North faced an invidious future and would therefore be inclined to respond to ROK overtures, a perspective that reflected the palpable sense of self-confidence that the ROK had derived from its economic achievements, but which was also tinged with a sense of patronisation, if not triumphalism as well, for the sun clearly shone from the South. Kim Dae Jung's mindset emerges in his reported remark to then US Senator Joe Biden in 2000 that 'North Korea is like a mold. Sunshine is the disinfectant' (Chinoy, 2008: 55).

Our focus, though, is not on the ROK, but on Pyongyang's response to this policy and what it tells us about the DPRK's outlook at this point. The first point to note here is that the Sunshine Policy did not come at a time of Pyongyang's own choosing, and in fact was arguably inconvenient. In early 1998, the very survival of the Kimist state still hung in the balance, the peak of the famine had only just passed, Kim Jong Il had only just assumed the position of KWP General Secretary the previous October, he was fine-tuning the *son'gun* policy framework and, most importantly, was still engaged in the more preferable strategy of negotiating directly with the US over the implementation of the 1994 Agreed Framework. Moreover, the long-term effect of the country's economic collapse on the DPRK's overall military assets was still far from clear, although during 1998 it had managed to find the resources to initiate pursuit of its expensive highly enriched uranium project and to seek major military purchases abroad.[60] Thus, there was little that direct negotiations with the South at this time could contribute to this mix, although this did not preclude tactical engagement, especially when substantial and uncomplicated economic benefits were clearly on offer. This highly tactical response was widely overlooked as Pyongyang's adversaries believed that its economic collapse was leading it towards substantial engagement, a strange and wishful perspective that contrived to believe that the weaker the DPRK became, the more willing it would be to negotiate the shape of its future.

Somewhat concealed under the prevailing rhetoric was the fact that almost all the major Sunshine Policy principles were, in fact, highly consistent with standing ROK policy in previous administrations, and when the ROK sought to re-engage the DPRK under the new policy in 1998, their proposed point of departure – summarily rejected by the North as a dead letter – was the implementation of the December 1991 agreement. The sole exception to this consistency was the stated goal of seeking 'reconciliation' instead of 'reunification', but this was a realistic word choice since the latter looked more and more like an absorption strategy, given the gross economic disparities that had developed between the two states. Thus, the Sunshine Policy's hope was to achieve in the long run a 'de facto, if not necessarily institutional, unification in which people, goods and services could freely flow in and out across the DMZ' (Moon, 2012:17). What made the policy different, therefore, was not so much its principles but its implementation strategies, specifically its willingness to pursue economic cooperation measures independent of progress in the core military–security area, and its adoption of increasingly flexible interpretations of what might constitute acceptable DPRK reciprocity.

It was inevitable that the DPRK would probe the new policy and assess its possibilities, and so in April 1998 the two sides held officials' talks in Beijing, the first talks at this level for four years, but without substantial outcome. By August 1998 the DPRK had clearly determined the need to test the limits of the ROK's no-tolerance policy regarding armed provocation, and so it proceeded with its on-going missile test programme with its intermediate range Taepo-dong missile test. It also activated its Northern Limit Line strategy, leading to a major ROK–DPRK naval confrontation in June 1999, in which the ROK navy sank one DPRK navy torpedo boat and damaged five others.[61] When the clash did not derail the Sunshine Policy, the chief lesson for Pyongyang was that the ROK was working from an ill thought-out strategy, for it had begun by fully showing its cards and without generating a national consensus, leaving Kim Dae Jung, always a divisive figure in ROK politics, vulnerable since he was under strong domestic political pressure to show early results from his policy.[62] This left the North in a much stronger bargaining position than many could possibly have imagined.

A key point of pressure for the North was Kim Dae Jung's open and avid pursuit of a summit meeting, and in April 2000 Kim Jong Il acceded. A series of officials' meetings in April–May prepared for a 13 June 2000 meeting in Pyongyang, and by now the DPRK demonstrated its bargaining strength by demanding a last-minute ROK payment of $500 million on pain of cancelling the proposed meeting. Kim Dae Jung, feeling the hand of history on his shoulder, complied.[63] The summit thus became the first face-to-face meeting between the leaders of the two Koreas. Of itself it was, of course, rich in symbolism, but its five-point Joint Declaration was considerably short on substance, only agreeing that there was an unspecified 'common element' in the two sides' differing reunification formulae, and that reunification efforts should tend 'in that direction'. This was not very encouraging because previously the two sides had at least been able to agree on the same formula, such as the 4 July 1972 declaration that 'a great national unity, as a homogeneous people, shall be sought first, transcending differences in ideas, ideologies and systems', before advancing differing, mutually exclusive interpretations of such formulae. Otherwise, the agreement confined itself to humanitarian issues such as separated family reunions and the release of unrepentant communists from the ROK jails, and a series of unspecified exchanges in the economic, social and cultural spheres, to be determined through later talks at the ministerial level. Kim Jong Il undertook to visit Seoul 'at an appropriate time', while military–security and human rights issues were not mentioned.[64]

Initially, the two sides appeared to be making more progress than was achieved in the 1972–3, 1984–6 and 1990–2 negotiation processes. A brisk tempo in family reunion visits was initiated in August 2000, as was a series of ministerial-level talks to discuss and implement joint governmental projects, while agreement in principle to begin work on a joint industrial zone in Kaesong was also reached. September brought further reunion arrangements, agreement to allow the first-ever mail communication, the commencement of ROK work on the reconnection of the Seoul–Pyongyang–Sinuiju railway, confirmation of sorts for a Kim Jong Il visit to Seoul in 2001, and Kim Dae Jung's announcement of his intention to revise the ROK's National Security Law, which was a longstanding DPRK demand. Defence ministerial talks the same month, however, were less successful, with the DPRK not attracted to a number of ROK confidence-building proposals. This turned out to be the first and only such meeting.

Thereafter, the tempo of meetings and exchanges slowed markedly, partly indicating the DPRK belief that it had already given sufficient value back for Kim Dae Jung's summit payment and that it had exhausted most of the potential of its tactical démarche. Of particular relevance was the intensive phase of DPRK–US negotiations over the DPRK's missile programme which began with the October visits of Vice Marshal Cho Myong-nok to Washington and US Secretary of State Madeleine Albright to Pyongyang. Thus, by spring

2001 the initial momentum from the talks was all but spent. Kim Dae Jung's visit to Washington in March 2001 for talks with newly inaugurated George W. Bush was pivotal, for it confirmed that at this juncture the US, with an inexperienced president and a strong neo-conservative influence in foreign policy, had little support to offer for Kim's chosen strategy. Kim was therefore reminded in rather forthright fashion that the US, not to mention the international community at large, also had interests at stake, most notably nuclear non-proliferation, and he was pressured to adopt more rigorous standards of reciprocity in dealing with the North. Kim acceded and thereupon indicated that 'flexible dualism' would be replaced by 'comprehensive reciprocity', a stricter standard that had no appeal to the North.

Sunshine Policy partisans unequivocally assert that the US's hard-line policy was instrumental in causing the DPRK to withdraw from engagement with the South (Moon, 2012: 2), but Pyongyang's policies depended on a good deal more than who occupied the White House. In particular, the strong differences in policy towards the North between the ROK and US that were vented during Kim's visit afforded the DPRK the opportunity to wedge this relationship, and to emphasise again the ROK's 'puppet' status. Pyongyang therefore resolved to intensify attacks on the US–ROK relationship, renew military pressure in the South through a series of incursions south of the Northern Limit Line (NLL), while it nonetheless sought to preserve the maximum possible economic benefit from the Sunshine Policy under these settings. In a sign of things to come, in May 2001 Kim Dae Jung made a public plea to Kim Jong Il to commit to his promised reciprocal visit to Seoul, at the same time announcing that there would be no joint celebration of the first anniversary of the June 2000 summit. In painful counterpoint, three days later a DPRK patrol boat conducted a further incursion south of the NLL, the second that month and the seventh that year (Manyin, 2002: 18).

Successive delays now characterised meetings and projects, a trend broken only by a brief, tactical display of revived initiative in early September 2001. This occurred on the eve of a state visit to the DPRK by Chinese President Jiang Zeming, the first by a Chinese paramount leader since 1982, and since a more conciliatory tone towards Seoul accorded with Chinese interests, it was probably crafted to aid the tone of the talks between Jiang and Kim. In addition, the North was also undoubtedly influenced by the fact that its preferred interlocutors in the South were in serious domestic political trouble. In August 2001, some more radically inclined members of a ROK delegation of 311 religious, labour and civic activists to Liberation Day celebrations in Pyongyang had breached established and stipulated ROK protocol, and attended ceremonies and visited localities in an overtly pro-North context, causing a major political uproar in the South. The incident helped crystallise disillusionment in the broader ROK community at the returns from the Sunshine Policy, and in early September Kim Dae Jung's junior coalition ally broke ranks and supported a National Assembly motion of no-confidence against the minister seen as the Sunshine Policy's chief architect, Unification

Minister Lim Dong-won. Lim's fate was now effectively sealed (he resigned in December) and so there was no further point in Pyongyang being conciliatory. With almost unseemly haste, Pyongyang then seized upon the heightened security measures being put in place by the ROK in the immediate aftermath of 9/11 as constituting an obstacle to further talks.[65]

By January 2002, Kim Dae Jung was in the last year of his term of office, and his domestic political standing had been deeply eroded by corruption scandals, by the fracturing of his ruling coalition over Sunshine Policy issues and by general popular disenchantment summed up by a series of unfavourable by-election results. Throughout the year, residual public support for the Sunshine Policy continued to erode in the light of a second serious NLL naval clash in June 2002 which killed thirteen DPRK and six ROK sailors, and also with the revelation in November of the DPRK's clandestine highly enriched uranium programme. The Roh Moo-hyun administration took office in 2003, but while it essentially maintained continuity with Kim's policies, to all intents and purposes momentum had been lost and this phase of inter-Korean contact had ended.[66]

The balance sheet for this phase of negotiation was understandably highly favourable to the DPRK. This outcome was quite expected in the short term by proponents of the Sunshine Policy who openly argued the merits of a give-first-ask-later strategy. Although military–security issues were, of course, fundamental to the ROK, the Kim Dae Jung administration's chosen strategy of postponing discussion of substantive issues and its confusion over the concept of reciprocity kept such issues off the agenda, and so, with the exception of the largely symbolic cross-border rail linkage issue, they were barely discussed. All mention of human rights in the North was likewise shamefully absent.[67] Meanwhile, as previously noted, the DPRK continued to benefit from ROK food aid, much of which went directly into the government's distribution channels, a practice which undermined the World Food Programme monitoring efforts and was also in violation of ROK international obligations (Haggard and Noland, 2005: 23). The one arguable humanitarian success was that the tempo of separated family reunions accelerated markedly, with eighteen face-to-face and seven video reunion events involving 21,000 individuals held between 2000 and 2013, although it should be added that the DPRK refused to institutionalise the process, retained tight control over it and extracted heavy payments from the ROK for each reunion event.

The major benefit of the Sunshine Policy to the DPRK was, of course, in the economic sphere, and so this was the longest-lasting area of cooperation to emerge out of the 2000 summit. The most visible projects were the Hyundai Asan Kumgang-san tourist venture and the Kaesong Industrial Zone, but they also involved a range of smaller private sector activities. The Kumgang-san venture was not formally part of the Sunshine Policy, although it required final approval from the ROK government before it was launched in November 1998. This came after the better part of a decade of path-breaking personal diplomacy by North-born Hyundai patriarch Jung Ju-yong, and although it was formally a business venture, it could hardly be measured in these terms. Coldly viewed, though, Jung's idealism was roundly exploited by the North, which extracted nearly $1 billion in licensing fees from the Hyundai subsidiary Hyundai Asan for the venture. Hyundai finally closed down the project after the July 2008 shooting death of a South Korean tourist who had strayed marginally outside the area's security zone, whereupon the North resumed the entire complex and associated infrastructure.[68]

The Kaesong Industrial Zone was similarly lucrative, as well as furnishing a useful point of pressure against the ROK. Also established under Hyundai auspices, it was essentially a haven for ROK sunset industries, where a North Korean workforce assembled South Korean components, chiefly in the areas of textiles, garments, footwear and light industrials. The zone opened in December 2004 and delivered upward of $100 million per annum to the DPRK, most notably through the payment of wages directly to the northern authorities, only a fraction of which reached the actual workers. By 2009, its high point, the Kaesong Industrial Zone (KIZ) had grown to account for over half of inter-Korean trade, employing a northern workforce of some 40,000 (Lim, 2009). However, to represent this as an example of inter-Korean cooperation represented a considerable stretch, for on whatever yardstick one chose to employ – economic cooperation, technology transfer, political symbolism, workers' rights – it represented the corralling of low and mid-tech ROK economic activity into an environment where economic activity was controlled, often extortionately, by the DPRK. The zone survived a number of inter-Korean crises and a number of unilateral DPRK imposts, but the ROK finally withdrew in February 2016 after the fourth DPRK nuclear test, and at the time of writing it remains closed.[69]

In summing up the Sunshine Policy period, the DPRK's actions during 2000–2, not to mention its general approach to the ROK in the context of KEDO, indicate a strong consistency with its traditional objectives of doing whatever ideology permitted them to do to degrade the coherence of the ROK government by emphasising both Seoul's inability to provide for the security of its citizens and its abject dependence on the United States. On the ROK side, the force of political ego and ambition fuelled the conviction of Sunshine Policy proponents that they could succeed with essentially the same deck of cards as their predecessors, and this led to a chronic inability to draw up firm bargaining positions and develop strategies that served their strengths and recognised their limitations.[70] We have previously noted that no basis of mutual trust existed to support the ambitions of the DPRK–US Agreed Framework, and this applies equally to the Sunshine Policy. This circumstance could not be altered by 'reimagining' a context in which such mutual trust did exist, nor could such trust be created out of unilateral concession-making by the ROK. In recasting the DPRK as a malleable entity capable of being drawn into the world of the ROK's preferred realities, it was, of course, easy to get lost in a hall of mirrors, mistaking quantity for quality, tactical feints for strategic purpose, symbolic for substantive progress and blindly insisting that it was just a matter of time before the policy would bear full fruit. In the final analysis, then, it was the Sunshine Policy's faulty conceptual foundations, its poor strategic insight and the extent to which in execution it mixed principle, political self-interest and wishful thinking that determined its outcome. Defenders, if we may call them such, would argue that the ultra-flexible negotiating positions were the price one had to pay to substantively engage the North, but on this occasion flexibility accommodated lack of principle and lack of clear strategic thinking. Of the many epitaphs that have been written of it, the observation that such a policy needed statesmen but got politicians still seems appropriate.[71]

Concluding remarks

For all the speculation that preceded it, Kim Il Sung's death had little impact on the march of events in the DPRK. The fact that it occurred on the eve of the famine has naturally led to speculation as to whether he would have handled things differently, and such speculation is also extended to other major areas of state policy. Popular biographies and obituaries often favour accounts of how their subjects' lives were just about to take a significant turn, usually in some kind of positive direction, when death intervened, and Kim has sometimes attracted similar coverage, especially in view of his agreement just before his death to meet with Kim Young Sam, but in Kim Il Sung's case, asking an octogenarian dictator with his track record to somehow adopt a reverse course on pragmatic grounds is, of course, fanciful. And from the son, what the North Koreans actually got was entirely consistent with the father's life-long thoughts and behaviour, for the son, like the father, was a callous man who in his intellectual isolation insisted on the absolute priority of the leadership's military prerogatives. This is the framework within which we follow Kim Jong Il through the Arduous March famine, *son'gun*, the cat-and-mouse game with the nascent informal economy and his various diplomatic dealings.

The calculus of what represents success and what represents failure in Pyongyang often appears obscure, if not obscurantist. Nevertheless, to a considerable extent by 2004 Kim Jong Il's option of staying the course had been vindicated in the eyes of the elite. First and foremost, the widespread, confident predictions of collapse had been confounded, the country's food supply had more or less returned to pre-famine levels of shortage, and in good part this outcome seemed to come down to force of will on the part of the leadership and to uncompromising reliance on the strengths of the remorseless, resilient system created by Kim's father. Dealing with the socioeconomic side-effects of the famine remained deeply problematical, but acting from the premise that the Kimist state could no longer generate the resources to perform its basic duty of care toward its citizens *and* maintain its chosen military posture, Kim Jong Il reluctantly accepted a reduced state role in which at least for the time being ordinary citizens would have to be allowed to trade in daily necessities with each other. In this frame of mind the regime stumbled into unchartered territory. Extended internal deliberations then produced the July 2002 measures, the outcome of a things-must-change-in-order-to-remain-the-same strategy, under which the government remained in control of a revised, remonetised system in which 'modernisation', as the DPRK understood the term, was ostensibly part of the agenda, but paradoxically reform was not. And so the economy remained essentially autarkic, and the Party and government elite continued to exercise decisive control over the fate of the market economy sector.

In government affairs, Kim Jong Il by-passed the KWP in favour of the *son'gun* framework, and erected a revised and coherent system of government centred on the National Defence Commission to deal with changed circumstances. In political terms, he accomplished the considerable feat of installing a new military elite over the top of his father's ex-guerilla elite without disturbing the latter. This reflected the fact that Kim was in no doubt that for the DPRK to live in nuclear-armed rejection of the international order, the formalisation of the military's paramount status was necessary. It is also important to note that the move in itself was profoundly anti-modern, especially in endorsing a military-based economic structure that led diametrically away from any possibility of reform.

Kim also parried the threat of a hostile international order, foremost by his strategically adroit handling of the twin challenges of the Agreed Framework and the ROK's Sunshine Policy. The DPRK extracted significant benefits from the Agreed Framework, the most important of which was the time it gained to make further progress in its nuclear weapons programme with reduced external pressure. Also useful from its perspective were the fuel oil shipments and the opportunities afforded in negotiations to discomfort its adversaries, taunting the ROK by constantly portraying it as a backward puppet state and wedging the ROK–Japan–US alliance. Success in the latter endeavour, however, was limited, for while the ROK and Japan resented various aspects of the US role in KEDO, they both stayed the course. Similarly, Kim gained substantial tangible rewards from participation in various Sunshine Policy activities, with direct cash transfers, plus the isolated, politically sanitised and easily reversible Kumgang-san and Kaesong Industrial Zone projects reaping well over a billion dollars, all gained without obliging the DPRK to make other than vague, tactical commitments. Other benefits, perhaps esoteric to outside eyes but important in the North, were that Pyongyang's adroit handling of the ROK's Sunshine Policy initiatives had revealed and exploited radical-conservative fissures in the hitherto united Seoul front to inter-Korean negotiation, and had caused further tension between ROK leftists and the US, where the Bush administration was called upon to shoulder chief blame for the Sunshine Policy's lack of success. Pyongyang had also validated the 1997 activation of the Northern Limit Line naval strategy as a useful, effective and consequence-free means of applying military pressure to the South, a strategy to which Kim would return again soon.

Kim Jong Il eventually retired from the Sunshine Policy table with his substantial winnings, an outcome that served the continuing capacity of the DPRK to 'Live in our own way' and also demonstrated its underlying fear of and contempt for the ROK by inflicting upon it the loss of face which comes with policy failure. With the 2016 closure of the Kaesong Industrial Zone, every major initiative begun under the Sunshine Policy has now ended. Some Americans and South Koreans seek to assign responsibility to their respective governments for unfavourable outcomes in dealing with North Korea, and in the matter of the fate of the Agreed Framework and the Sunshine Policy George W. Bush and Lee Myung-bak attract considerable partisan attention, while the careful questioning of DPRK motives is often buried beneath the robust belief that Pyongyang indeed wanted to change if only its adversaries had been able to come up with and deliver the right deal. However, this perspective routinely patronises the DPRK leadership as willing to seek an alternative to the country's established identity, when the evidence of decades is that its thoughts run on a very different track. Moreover, this perspective tends to overlook the role played by deeply flawed US and ROK negotiating premises in dealing with the North, for there was more than enough to ensure failure in ill thought-out, overly ambitious gambits that papered over profoundly differing aims and objectives.

Unlike his adversaries, the most striking characteristic of Kim Jong Il during these years was consistency, for his conduct of state affairs evinced no strategic uncertainty or hesitation, but rather conviction and coherence amid dire choices. This owes much to the tightly interlocking nature of all facets of DPRK state policy, but we should also be in no doubt as to the strength and depth of Kim Jong Il's convictions and how closely they coincided with those of his father's. There are significant areas of Kim Jong Il's psychology that are obscure, but the well-springs of such callous certitude, reminding us as they do of his father, probably run deeper than just the closeted upbringing of a princeling or some twisted form of filial piety, much less the specific circumstances in which he exercised power. In the end, his accumulated record shows him to have been remarkably faithful to his father's vision, and if Kim Il Sung was a guerilla by sustained early practice in life and also a convinced Stalinist to the end, then his son was also a convinced Kimist. This perspective helps us to understand the rational basis for his choices, and in turn may help us to understand why the famine and economic collapse of the 1990s did not lead to reform. And now the years after 2004 were to again affirm just how far from reform Kim's thoughts ran.

Notes

1 'He was then and he is now a man of mystery' was how Jimmy Carter put it in a 2000 interview reminiscing on his 1994 visit to Pyongyang, during which his request to meet Kim Jong Il was turned aside (*KH*, 6 August 2000). US Secretary of State Madeleine Albright later revealed that prior to her December 2000 visit to Pyongyang 'for the most part, our intelligence had told us that he was a recluse

and that he was crazy' (Chinoy, 2008: 18). Happily, on her return she was able to assure a dinner of North Korean experts that 'This guy is not a nutcase' (Chinoy, 2008: 32). In perspective, Albright was, of course, referring to the leader of a small, weak nation who by this time had mounted and sustained a major and continuing security and foreign policy challenge to the US for a number of years, and so this involved a glaring underestimation. Albright's visit appeared to help, though, and by 2001 there were more balanced assessments, such as that given by then Deputy CIA Director John E. McLaughlin in 2001: 'It is easy to caricature [Kim Jong Il] either as a simple tyrant blind to his dilemma or as a technocratic champion of sweeping change. But the extreme views of him tend to be the product of bias, ignorance, or wishful thinking. The reality is more complex. At home, he has shown his hard side through his purges of the elite, his light regard for the suffering of ordinary Koreans, and the swift destruction of any expression of popular discontent. Abroad, he has shown his pragmatic side through his willingness to engage old enemies and his skilled brinkmanship as he does so.'See: www.cia.gov/news-information/speeches-testimony/2001/ddci_speech_04172001.html (accessed September 2016).

2 Collapsist literature from this period is represented in its most cogent form by Eberstadt (1995, 1999). See Harrison (1998: 61) for a range of quotes from senior US political and military figures predicting or assuming collapse. The US CIA's internal assessment in 1997 was that 'given the multiple problems confronting Kim Chong-il's regime, there may be only a brief window of time to consider how to deal with the probable reality that the North will experience a "hard landing". The prospect of achieving either a "soft landing" or a "no landing" appears illusory without a regime change in the North.' See: http://nsarchive.gwu.edu/NSAEBB/NSAEBB205/Document%20No%2014.pdf (accessed July 2016). Less common was consideration of the implications of DPRK survival, and here Levin (1997) provides a comprehensive discussion, many points of which are obviously still relevant today.

3 Haggard and Noland (2007: 85–6) estimate the value of non-Chinese food aid to the DPRK during 1996–2005 at *c*. $2.4 billion.

4 With reference just to the ROK, in December 2001 the ROK National Statistical Office released comparative statistics for the ROK and DPRK. Among the starker disparities were national income ($455 billion to $17 billion), per capita income ($9,628 to $757), a trade ratio of 139: 1 ($333 billion to $2.4 billion) and an export ratio of 244: 1, which meant that the ROK exported more in thirty-six hours than the DPRK did in a full year (Foster-Carter, 2001).

5 Plenary sessions originally performed major decision-making functions, both in the USSR and in the DPRK. Their significance declined with the growth of the Kimist autocracy, but they continued to be held, usually biannually, up until the death of Kim Il Sung. For more on the historical work and role of KWP plenums, see Scalapino and Lee (1972: 727) and Dae-sook Suh (1981: 277).

6 Various detailed, necessarily speculative accounts of Kim's actual work style exist. Bermudez (2004:1–4) provides one of the more illuminating, detailed accounts.

7 Among more prominent commentators, see Pinkston (2003) with his postulation of various stakeholders in the policy-making process, and the 'institutional pluralism' described by McEachern (2008, 2010). Scalapino (1998: 2) was probably nearer the mark when he observed: 'Spotty evidence suggests that the differences among leaders of North Korea have existed, at least over timing and tactics, some of them requiring very high-level decisions. Indeed, North Korean sources have recently made such assertions to the United States, but to what extent this information is part of the bargaining game – with the implication that 'moderates' must be supported lest 'hard-liners' gain greater authority – is unclear. Stronger evidence points to sharp rivalry for turf and recognition at horizontal levels, for example, between party and governmental agencies. In sum, the power structure is

undoubtedly tight but less than monolithic.' Hwang Chang-yop, of course, dismissed the existence of such entities as 'moderate' and 'hard-liner' out of hand.
8 For a conflicting view, see McEachern (2008, 2010), who rejects the totalitarian and personalistic models in favour of the DPRK as 'a state characterized by institutional pluralism' (McEachern, 2008: 239). Here, however, we accept the thrust of Geddes's work on authoritarian states, especially her comment that 'Because so much power is concentrated in the hands of one individual in personalist regimes, *he generally controls the coalition-building agenda [as well]*' (Geddes, 1999:18 – italics added). In a similar vein, particular mention should be made of Kim Kap-sik (2008) and his description of the *suryong* (leader) system, and the detailed work on this topic by Gause (2014) and his hub-and-spoke model for Kim Jong Il's leadership style, which places Kim at the hub and a number of constituencies at the rim, most prominently the Kim and partisan families, the military, the Party, the Cabinet and the various security services, their reporting leading directly to the hub with little horizontal communication. There was never any doubt which was hub and which was spoke: the actual wielding of power and influence was clearly confined to the after-stage of policy implementation, not formulation.
9 For more detail on the range of skills employed by Kim in maintaining his authority, see Byman and Lind (2010), especially their summation: 'Kim Jong-il's meticulous use of the tools of authoritarianism reveals him to be a skilled strategic player. The revulsion people feel for his regime, which has the blood of millions on its hands, should not obscure the strategic logic that its brutality follows.' (Byman and Lind, 2010: 75)
10 They range from US Secretary of State Madeleine Albright to EU Commissioner Chris Patton to a number of Russian, Japanese and ROK interlocutors. ROK impressions are, of course, of particular interest, especially those of Lim Dong-won in 2000. See Oberdorfer (2001: 338) for the gist of Lim's report to Kim Dae Jung after his first meeting with Kim Jong Il. For comments after Albright's 2000 visit from Wendy Sherman, see: http://thecable.foreignpolicy.com/posts/2011/12/19/wendy_sherman_on_kim_jong_il_smart_witty_and_humorous (accessed August 2016) and from Charles Kartman, see: www.pbs.org/wgbh/pages/frontline/shows/kim/interviews/kartman.html (accessed February 2017). Of particular interest is the following comment in 2011 from Georgy Toloraya, a Korean policy specialist, who had significant access to Kim Jong Il at this time: 'I was impressed how this particular Korean was different: he emanated charisma and intellect, looked free and relaxed. His speech was fast and witty, he seemed to draw on enormous resources of intellect and had a remarkable memory on almost any subject (one exclusion might be modern economics, in which he, it seemed, was not so very interested, regarding it just as a tool for rich Westerners to extract profits from their fellow compatriots and poor countries).' Available at: http://38north.org/2011/12/gtoloraya122811/(accessed November 2016).
11 Reports of military plots and attempted military rebellions and coups became rife during this period. Almost all are unverifiable, and many represented ROK disinformation or else unfounded media assumptions that any sort of self-defined unusual behaviour detected in the North represented a coup attempt. The most prominent in this genre involved a major revolt believed to have been planned by VI Corps in the northeast in 1996 where the famine had hit hardest, which was reportedly discovered and suppressed before it began. This is believed to explain why the VI Corps no longer exists. See 'Remembering the coup d'etat in 1996' at: www.dailynk.com/english/read.php?cataId=nk02100&num=7321 (accessed August 2016) for details. Bermudez (2001: 319) attributes the dissolution of VI corps to a major corruption scandal and surmises that an earlier 'coup' in 1993, often referred to in the literature, especially in collapsist scenarios, was probably a similar corruption case. Given the level of misperception and disinformation that

abounds concerning the DPRK, it is usually better practice to accord greater credence to less sensationalist interpretations. On this score it is worth noting Russian specialist opinion that the younger Kim's rise did not cause any particular dissent within the military (Levin, 1997: 163).
12 And this meant corresponding inactivity in state institutions. New elections for the Supreme People's Assembly were postponed from 1995 to 1998, the KWP held no plenary sessions and no significant activity by the Administration Council was observed. We are left to conclude that government proceeded by behind-the-scenes activity, overseen by Kim's personal secretariat.
13 This is almost certainly disingenuous. The speed with which the DPRK media took up what were in effect *son'gun* themes makes it clear that Kim Jong Il had already conceived of something very similar to *son'gun* before his father's death.
14 In passing, we may also note the emergence in the 1990s of other ultra-nationalist themes, long adumbrated, during this period as the regime sought more persuasive themes in their agitprop. These included the DPRK describing itself as 'the great Mt Baekdu state', the Kim family as 'the peerlessly great persons of Mt. Baekdu' and the country's revolution as 'the juche revolution pioneered from Baekdu'. For extended discussion of these themes, see Myers (2011).
15 For analysis of the 1998 constitutional changes see D.K. Yoon (2003). With the presidency now non-functioning, the SPA Central People's Committee, essentially a ratifying body for the president's decisions with a membership drawn from senior Party and Administration Council members, sometimes referred to as a 'super-Cabinet', also passed out of existence. Other powers and duties of the president were redistributed, and on paper the Administration Council, now renamed the Cabinet, gained more authority, but its most significant portfolios still consisted of various second-tier economic and civilian industrial portfolios, while major military, security and foreign affairs issues continued to be dealt with elsewhere, either in the NDC or Kim's personal secretariat.
16 Table 6.1 demonstrates the significant changes that had taken place between 1994 and 1998. Significant features include clear evidence that old comrades of Kim Il Sung such as former Premier Yi Chong-ok, former Foreign Minister Pak Song-ch'ol, Kim Jong Il's uncle Kim Yong-ju and long-time Politburo member Kye Ung-t'ae were to retain public positions of honour and ceremony, but that only Kim Yong-nam remained active in the functioning of government. The ranking of Hong Song-nam was an ex-officio ranking stemming from his appointment as premier, a long-established DPRK practice for the government's senior bureaucrat, and this left a leadership absolutely dominated by ageing but still active military figures who had been allocated significantly lower places in the hierarchy under Kim Il Sung.
17 The 1998 *son'gun* settlement was also reflected in the pattern of Kim Jong Il's public appearances. Long described as 'reclusive', but perhaps more accurately and neutrally described as averse to unnecessary public appearances, as indeed was Stalin, during 1998–2005 the frequency of such appearances increased from an unreclusive once every five days to once every three days, with a pronounced emphasis on appearances in a military context surrounded by uniformed officers (Gause, 2006: 9). Again, it had been a rarity for his father to be presented in this way, but it reinforced Kim's image as a commander-in-chief actively working to protect a country under siege.
18 It practically goes without saying that this was not a relationship that relied on trust, for there is good evidence to suggest that Kim deployed the same sort of multiple, overlapping security reporting structure against the military as he did in all other domains. Other coup-proofing measures included staffing key positions with family members, blood relatives and closely bound loyalists; maintaining sizeable parallel armed forces such as the Guard Command and the Pyongyang

Defence Command, to be deployed against regular forces in the event of a coup; frequent and judicious rotations of key commanders to prevent the building of any power base; and the creation of an institutional structure designed to minimise horizontal information flows. For details, see Gause (2006: 12), and especially Byman and Lind (2010: 66–68).
19 During the 1994–7 Period of Mourning guerilla generation representation in the Politburo continued to shrink with the death of elderly members such as O Chin-u in February 1995 and Ch'oe Kwang in February 1997. With Ch'oe's death, the last surviving cadre of the Kim Il Sung guerilla generation still actively exercising power passed from the scene.
20 A typical expression of this prioritisation can be found in a 3 April 2003 *Rodong Shinmun* commentary: 'Once we lay the foundations for a powerful self-sustaining national defence industry, we will be able to rejuvenate all economic fields, to include light industry and agriculture and enhance the quality of the people's lives.' See Eberstadt (2004: 78) for discussion.
21 Bermudez (2001: 41–3) gives a brief description of the astounding variety of these needs, which leaves no doubt as to their enormous economic consequences.
22 In refugee interviews, a majority concurred that the PDS had already collapsed in their local districts prior to the actual 1994–7 onset of the famine (Haggard and Noland, 2005: 14).
23 Disaggregations of the DPRK economy differ chiefly in the significance and autonomy they assign to the court and illicit sectors. Habib (2011), for example, includes both, Tara O (2015) combines the two, while Lee and Yoon (2004) include neither.
24 The military economy is sometimes confusingly called 'the second economy', a term in wide use elsewhere, especially in Soviet studies, to indicate private economic activity. The DPRK term seems to have devolved from the Second Economic Committee, the KWP committee established in the wake of the 1962 Equal Emphasis policy to oversee the military economy. For details of the history and function of this committee, see: http://nkleadershipwatch.files.wordpress.com/2009/10/thesecondeconomiccommittee.pdf (accessed November 2016).
25 According to a former DPRK trade official, Kim Kwang-jin, the foundations for the court economy were laid in 1974 when Kim Jong Il ordered the establishment of the entity known as Bureau 39. For a detailed account of his insider experience in Building 39, see Kim Kwang Jin (2011). Also see Green and Denny (2017).
26 For details of these activities, see especially Chestnut (2007) and Hastings (2014). Regarding the disappearance of the counterfeit dollars, see: https://news.vice.com/article/north-koreas-counterfeit-benjamins-have-vanished (accessed July 2016).
27 According to the figures of Eberstadt (2015: 44), this was a market that had produced a trade surplus of about $4.6 billion in the DPRK's favour during 1985–93, not to mention many other forms of subsidy and assistance during the life of the Soviet Union. By contrast, the corresponding figure for trade with Russia during 1994–2002 was $0.4 billion.
28 For details of the many forms that the shadow labour economy took during these years, see Hyung-min Joo, 2010: 130–2.
29 Haggard and Noland (2007: 33–8) discuss this issue at length, and the gist of their conclusion is that the floods were a minor factor, prone to exaggeration by Pyongyang since citing the natural origins of the crisis deflected attention from the role played by agricultural policy. In particular, they cite Noland *et al.* (2001) to the effect that restoration of the flood-affected land and capital 'would have had a minor impact on the availability of food' for the crisis was far more widespread and deep-seated than this.
30 The term 'Arduous March' itself is a euphemism drawn from Kim Il Sung's guerilla years, when Japanese military pressure, some say after the 1937 Bochonbo raid, forced him and his group into an extended and arduous retreat march.

31 The literature on the Arduous March famine has grown broad and deep over the years, though it necessarily has important gaps. A short list of major works would include the economic perspective of Haggard and Noland (2005), the NGO experience related through Flake and Snyder (2003) and the human experiences related through Demick (2009) and Fahey (2015).
32 This description is drawn from the work of ROK academic Joung Eun-lee, which is in turn based on refugee interviews. See Ward (2014).
33 A policy specifically defended by Kim in his December 1996 Kim Il Sung University speech (q.v.).
34 This trend may be observed in literally graphic form at Haggard and Noland (2005: 15).
35 Meanwhile, domestic propaganda explained the famine as resulting from two causes – economic blockade and the local manifestation of a global phenomenon. Myers (2011: 120) provides the following quote from a North Korean short story set in 1997:

> It had been a hard year. The continuation of the imperialists' blockade, and, on the world's stage, war and strife, starvation and extreme poverty, historically unprecedented oppression threatening all mankind – it had been a year in which these things had enveloped the world like a black cloud.

36 Foster-Carter, for example, finds Kim assailed by '[a] mixture of panic, myopia and bile'. Available at: www.keia.org/sites/default/files/publications/aps_foster-carter_0_0.pdf (accessed October 2016). Samuel Kim (1996: 64) assessed that: 'With Kim Jong Il apparently unable and/or unwilling to take command over the sinking ship of state, the center remained largely paralyzed and rudderless, agreeing only on tightening up military controls to keep a lid on food riots and other expressions of popular discontent.'
37 Author's translation of the text in the July 1997 edition of *Wolgan Choson*.
38 I have been unable to determine to my own satisfaction the precise route Kim's words took to the publicly available printed version of them, and therefore prefer to believe that he said something like this, rather than that he used these precise words. But there can be little doubt that the words reflected his thoughts at the time.
39 The 12–14 per cent figure is cited by Hale (2005: 829) from the work of Ruediger Frank.
40 Eberstadt (2010) helps place this into perspective in observing that 'apart from Pol Pot's Cambodia, no other modern government has come so close to completely demonetizing a national economy'.
41 There is little point in analysing the analysts on this point. Since no DPRK public official or media outlet ever put the case that the July 2002 measures constituted reform, external observers who detected it at the time relied on oblique hints gleaned from parsing the 1998 constitutional changes, the pattern of DPRK leadership visits to major Chinese economic and business centres (as though to see is to be converted) and by specific interpretations of DPRK domestic media commentaries. Such arguments, though, are contradicted by the DPRK's actual deeds, while Pyongyang's rhetoric represents the employment of traditional DPRK revolutionary transformationalist rhetoric, not to describe a reform process but to buttress a quite different, reactionary intellectual framework in which, for example, *son'gun* itself is routinely described as 'revolutionary'.
42 Since the word 'reform' recurs with some frequency in our narrative, and is generally used in a loose fashion in the literature, it should be stated that the definition adopted here is the standard one from Janos Kornai (1992): 'in order to be called a reform, changes need to be sufficiently deep and radical, and they must affect the first three blocks of the main line of causality, namely ideology and

43 political power, property rights, and coordination. A reform thus amounts to a change of the economic system, although it not necessarily means an immediate regime change.' These blocks, of course, remain in place in the DPRK.
43 A point recognised by Eberstadt (2004: 81): 'It is important also to recognize just what this July 2002 package does not signify. To begin with, it does not represent an unambiguous move toward market principles in the DPRK economy. To the contrary: remonetisation of the domestic economy would likewise be a sine qua non for the resurrection of the DPRK's badly broken central planning mechanism.'
44 For further discussion along these lines, see Lee and Yoon (2004: 48–54). For the unhappy post-1991 fate of the Soviet Union's military–industrial sector and its attempts to adjust to an emerging market economy, see Tikhomirov (2000), especially pp. 17–24.
45 See, for example, the report of the 2004 mission at: www.fao.org/docrep/007/j2972e/j2972e00.htm and for subsequent years at: www.fao.org/country profiles/index/en/?iso3=PRK
46 Defector testimony lists a number of arrangements that become possible when senior patronage was forthcoming, including murder case plea bargaining, favourable handling of drugs charges, securing overseas employment and matriculation to favoured universities. The following refugee testimony provides an intriguing glimpse of the extent of the phenomenon: 'They give the right to process drug dealing cases to the Ministry of State Security for them to run a drug crackdown squad. Then all bribes related to drug cases belong to the Ministry of State Security. The Ministry of the People's Armed Forces is in charge of car dealing. Drug dealing which involves a lot of bribery belongs to the Ministry of State Security; so instead, they let the Ministry of the People's Armed Forces have authority over car dealing. This is how they allocate rights.' (Young-ja Park, 2015:146)
47 The DPRK currently ranks 167th on the Transparency International Corruption Perceptions Index, tying for last with Somalia and trailing such troubled jurisdictions as Afghanistan, Iraq and South Sudan. See: www.transparency.org/country/#PRK_DataResearch (accessed October 2016).
48 The full title of the Agreement was *Agreed Framework between the United States of America and the Democratic People's Republic of Korea*. The full text may be found at: https://web.archive.org/web/20031217175315/http://www.iaea.org/Publications/Documents/Infcircs/Others/infcirc457.pdf (accessed September 2006).
49 All too transparently, this was a disproportionate inducement, reflecting the US's weak bargaining position. Even if Yongbyon were capable of feeding significant power into the system, the DPRK's power grid was heavily degraded and in need of an investment in grid renovation costing upward of $1 billion (Kartman *et al.*, 2012: 36) and this, of course, applied equally to the future output from the LWRs. The agreement did not mention this issue, nor did the DPRK display any significant awareness of it. Moreover, the US agreed to LWRs on the grounds that it was more difficult to extract weapons-grade material from them – difficult, but not impossible. In fact, given the relative sizes of the Yongbyon and LWR reactors, the potential plutonium production capacity of the LWRs was considerable.
50 See 'Rummy's North Korea Connection' at: http://archive.fortune.com/magazines/fortune/fortune_archive/2003/05/12/342316/index.htm (accessed September 2016).
51 In 2003, Gallucci stated that 'If we didn't do a deal, either we would have gone to war or they'd have over 100 nuclear weapons' (ibid.). It would, of course, have been a war of choice, not necessity, and in passing we may note the highly rhetorical nature of the figure of 'over 100 nuclear weapons'. Recent credible estimates vary, but are far short of this alarmist figure. They include 21–37 (Asher, 2013); 10–16 (Albright, 2015) and 5–27 (Hayes and Cavazos, 2014).

196 Triage: 1994–2004

52 Estimating the amount of plutonium secreted by the DPRK prior to 1994 is a highly speculative and necessarily politicised exercise. Albright and Brannan (2007) cite the CIA as positing a worst case of 10kg, with the IAEA and the US Joint Atomic Energy Intelligence Committee (JAEIC) assessing considerably less. This compares with a declared stock of c. 27–9kg. It takes about 5–7kg to manufacture a single bomb and the DPRK's secreted stock was probably around this mark. For details of these and other estimates, see Niksch (2006).

53 This was six days before the first session of the 10th Supreme People's Assembly, where Kim Jong Il was confirmed in the supreme leader position of Chairman of the National Defence Commission.

54 For the text of a 2004 interview giving context to this visit from Benazir's point of view, see www.digitalnpq.org/global_services/global viewpoint/02-17-04.html (accessed September 2016). For an account of the DPRK's HEU programme, see Chinoy (2008: 88ff.).

55 For Albright's account of these negotiations, see Albright (2003: 455–72). Especially useful is the US National Security Agency Archive text *Discussions between Secretary of State Madeleine Albright and North Korean Leader Kim Il Jong, October 22–25, 2000*, available at: http://nsarchive.gwu.edu/NSAEBB/NSAEBB164/Discussions%20between%20Secretary%20of%20State%20Albright%20and%20Kim%20Il%20Jong.pdf (accessed November 2016), whose extended quoting of Kim Jong Il is of particular interest.

56 Chinoy (2008: xx) lists 'pygmy', 'tyrant' and 'spoiled child' among Bush's public epithets. In a widely quoted interview in August 2002 with Bob Woodward, Bush stated 'I loathe Kim Jong Il. I've got a visceral reaction to this guy because he's starving his people'.

57 Some doubt still surrounds the actual words used by the DPRK, but most parties accept their import. For a detailed account of this episode, see Chinoy (2008: 135–137).

58 The timing of full compliance was defined under Article IV.3 as 'when a significant portion of the LWR project is completed but before delivery of key nuclear components'. What the DPRK may or may not have done had this point been reached is unknowable. Incidentally, far from being strict or harsh, this formula, arguably negotiated by the US in some haste, brought forth objections from the IAEA for being too lenient since it excessively postponed assessment of just how much plutonium the DPRK had already downloaded.' (May, 2001: 18)

59 The policy's official title was Policy of Reconciliation and Cooperation toward the North (*taebuk hwahae hyomnyok chongch'aek*), but Kim Dae Jung preferred the term 'Sunshine Policy'.

60 In 1996, the DPRK had attempted to purchase 133 MiG-21 fighter aircraft from Kazakhstan before the deal was called off due to US intervention. In 1999, it renewed its endeavours, again unsuccessfully. See: www.globalsecurity.org/military/world/centralasia/kazak-airforce.htm (accessed November 2016).

61 The Northern Limit Line (NLL) represents the ROK's military demarcation line in the Western (Yellow) Sea and runs north of five islands which are ROK territory under the 1953 Military Armistice Agreement, but are actually north of the 38th parallel. The DPRK has never recognised the NLL line, which was in fact unilateral in origin, but except for a brief period in 1973 had never overtly disputed it or made it a focus of military pressure before June 1999, when it evidently decided to wedge this issue in what is often referred to as the First Yonp'yong Sea Engagement (*Cheil yonp'yong haejon*) by initiating a firefight south of the NLL. For a June 2016 summary on the NLL from the North's perspective, see Peace on the Korean Peninsula and the 'Northern Limit Line', available at: www.nknews.org/2016/06/peace-on-the-korean-peninsula-and-the-northern-limit-line/ (accessed October 2016).

62 When DPRK military pressure made it clear that reciprocity would not be forthcoming, Kim Dae Jung could not, of course, resile from his basic policies without massive loss of face, and so he resorted to what became known as 'flexible dualism', under which Seoul would accept an unchanging DPRK in the short term against the possibility of future changes. Kim articulated four key components in this: approach the easy tasks first and leave the difficult ones for later; seek economic cooperation first and political agreement later; involve ROK NGOs first and the government later; give first in order to receive later (Moon, 2012: 26). For an account of the evolution of these modifications during 1998–2000, see Shinn (2001: 15).
63 In February 2003, an independent presidential counsel appointed by Roh Moo-hyun under pressure from the National Assembly reported that of $500 million transferred to Pyongyang just before the summit, $100 million was government money, and a significant proportion of the rest was Hyundai money borrowed from a state-run bank. As a footnote, the DPRK attempted a similar extortion tactic during the Six Party Talks on the eve of the signing of the breakthrough February 2007 agreement, but was unsuccessful in the face of the calculated indifference of the other parties as to whether the agreement was signed or not (Buszynski, 2013: 141–2). It is, of course, interesting to speculate what a more principled ROK government committed to harder bargaining might have achieved.
64 The text of the Joint Declaration may be accessed at: www.usip.org/sites/default/files/file/resources/collections/peace_agreements/n_skorea06152000.pdf.
65 One might add that in evidently seeking to support the architects of the Sunshine Policy, the North was not motivated by any sense of warmth, goodwill or respect for Kim. See Myers (2011: 159–60) on how in its domestic coverage the DPRK media routinely denigrated Kim in a crude and contemptuous manner throughout this period.
66 For a useful summary of the continuities in the South–North dialogue between the Kim Dae Jung and Roh Moo-hyun administrations, see Manyin *et al.* (2005: 6).
67 In a notable display of moral relativism, in a 2001 speech to the American Enterprise Institute Kim responded to criticisms on this score by stating: 'To affront North Korea with human rights issues in their face, with criticism, would not be wise – the greatest human rights issue on the Korean Peninsula is that of the 10 million members of the separated families.' Quoted in Sung-Yoon Lee (2010).
68 Initial indications were that DPRK officialdom was taken unawares by this incident in which a 53-year-old woman was shot twice, allegedly in a poorly signposted area, but the modalities for dealing with it to the ROK's satisfaction were awkward, especially the demand for a joint investigation, and may have involved an unacceptable acknowledgement of responsibility and expression of contrition. The DPRK therefore opted to stand on its dignity. Estimates of the loss of revenue to the North varied, with $20 million per annum a widespread consensus number. See 'South Korean tourist fatally shot at Kumgang' at: www.nkeconwatch.com/2008/07/21/south-korean-tourist-fatally-shot-at-kumgang (accessed August 2016).
69 The KIZ was by no means the sole venue for private ROK firms seeking to do business in the North during the early 2000s. For absorbing case studies of six ROK firms directly engaging with the North, see Tait (2003).
70 One is reminded of former ROK Prime Minister Lee Hong-koo's remarks at the time of the proclamation of the Sunshine Policy in February 1998: 'In North–South relations, 90 per cent depends on North Korea. It doesn't depend so much on who is in [the] Blue House.' See 'South Korea's New President Appeals to North to End Decades of Division', available at: www.nytimes.com/1998/02/25/world/south-korea-s-new-president-appeals-to-north-to-end-decades-of-division.html?pagewanted=all (accessed October 2016).

71 For an exhaustive, avowedly partisan defence of the Sunshine Policy, see Moon Chung-in (2012). For a critique, see Lee Sung-Yoon (2010).

References

Albright, David (2015) *Future Directions in the DPRK's Nuclear Weapons Program: Three Scenarios for 2020*, US-Korea Institute at SAIS, February 2015, available at: http://38north.org/wp-content/uploads/2015/02/NKNF-Future-Directions- 2020-Albright-0215.pdf (accessed October 2016).

Albright, David and Brannan, Paul (2007) *The North Korean Plutonium Stock, February 2007*, available at: www.isis-online.org/publications/dprk/DPRKplutoniumFEB.pdf (accessed January 2017).

Albright, Madeleine (2003) *Madame Secretary: A Memoir*. Hyperion Books: New York.

Asher, David L. (2013) *Pressuring North Korea: The Need for a New Strategy*, Testimony before the House Foreign Affairs Committee, 5 March.

Bermudez Jr, Joseph S. (2001) *Shield of the Great Leader: The Armed Forces of North Korea*. Allen & Unwin: Sydney.

Bermudez Jr, Joseph S. (2004) 'Information and the DPRK's military and power-holding elite', in *North Korean Policy Elites*, ed. Ralph Hassig. Institute for Defense Analyses, available at: www.brookings.edu/wp-content/uploads/2016/06/oh200 40601.pdf (accessed June 2016).

Buszynski, Leszek (2013) *Negotiating with North Korea: The Six Party Talks and the Nuclear Issue*. Routledge: London.

Byman, Daniel and Lind, Jennifer (2010) 'Pyongyang's survival strategy: Tools of authoritarian control in North Korea, *International Security*, 35(1): 44–74.

Chestnut, Sheena (2007) 'Illicit activity and proliferation: North Korean smuggling networks', *International Security*, 32(1): 80–111.

Chinoy, Mike (2008) *Meltdown: The Inside Story of the North Korean Nuclear Crisis*. St Martin's Press: New York.

Choi, Changyong (2013) 'Everyday politics' in North Korea, *The Journal of Asian Studies*, 72(3): 655–673.

Collins, Robert (2015) Regime leadership and human rights in North Korea, *International Journal of Korean Studies*, XIX(1): 621–96.

Demick, Barbara (2009) *Nothing to Envy: Ordinary Lives in North Korea*. Spiegel and Grau: New York.

Eberstadt, Nicholas (1995) *Korea Approaches Reunification*. M. E. Sharpe: Armonk, NY.

Eberstadt, Nicholas (1999) 'Self reliance' and economic decline: North Korea's international Trade, 1970–1995, *Problems of Post-Communism*, 46(1): 3–13.

Eberstadt, Nicholas (2004) North Korea's survival game: Understanding the recent past, thinking about the future, in Chung-yong Ahn, Nicholas Eberstadt and Young-sun Lee (eds), *A New International Engagement Framework for North Korea? Contending Perspectives*. Korea Economic Institute of America: Washington, DC, pp. 63–116.

Eberstadt, Nicholas (2009) *The North Korean Economy: Between Crisis and Catastrophe*. Transaction Publishers: New Brunswick, NJ.

Eberstadt, Nicholas (2010) *The North Korean Economy in 2010*, available at: www.aei.org/publication/the-north-korean-economy-in-2010/ (accessed July 2016).

Eberstadt, Nicholas (2015) *North Korea's 'Epic Economic Fail' in International Perspective*. The Asan Institute for Policy Studies: Seoul.

Everard, John (2011) *The Markets of Pyongyang*. Korea Economic Institute, Academic Working Paper Series, 6(1).
Fahey, Sandra (2015) *Marching through Suffering: Loss and Survival in North Korea*. Columbia University Press, New York.
Flake, L. Gordon and Snyder, Scott (eds) (2003) *Paved with Good Intentions: The NGO Experience in North Korea*. Praeger: Westport, CT.
Foster-Carter, Aidan (2001) North Korea–South Korea relations: On, off, on again, *Comparative Connections*, 3(4), available at: https://csis-prod.s3.amazonaws.com/s3fs-public/legacy_files/files/media/csis/pubs/0104qnk_sk.pdf (accessed August 2016).
Frank, Ruediger (2005) Economic reforms in North Korea (1998–2004): Systemic restrictions, quantitative analysis, ideological background, *Journal of the Asia Pacific Economy*, 10(3): 278–311.
Gause, Ken E. (2006) North Korean civil–military trends: Military-first politics to a point. Strategic Studies Institute, available at: www.strategicstudiesinstitute.army.mil/pdffiles/pub728.pdf (accessed August 2016).
Gause, Ken E. (2014) North Korean leadership dynamics and decision-making under Kim Jong-un: A second year assessment, available at: www.cna.org/CNA_files/PDF/COP-2014-U-006988-Final.pdf (accessed October 2016).
Geddes, Barbara (1999) Authoritarian breakdown: Empirical test of a game theoretic argument, available at: http://eppam.weebly.com/uploads/5/5/6/2/5562069/authoritarianbreakdown_geddes.pdf (accessed February 2017).
Green, Christopher and Denny, Steven (2017) Pockets of efficiency: An institutional approach to economic reform and development in North Korea, in *Change and Continuity in North Korean Politics*, Adam Cathcart, Robert Winstanley-Chesters and Christopher Green (eds). Routledge: London, pp. 95–108.
Habib, Benjamin (2011) North Korea's parallel economies: Systemic disaggregation following the Soviet collapse, *Communist and Post-Communist Studies*, 44: 149–159.
Haggard, Stephan and Noland, Marcus (2005) *The Politics of Famine in North Korea*. US Committee for Human Rights in North Korea: Washington, DC.
Haggard, Stephan and Noland, Marcus (2007) *Famine in North Korea: Markets, Aid and Reform*. Columbia University Press: New York.
Haggard, Stephan and Noland, Marcus (2010) *Political Attitudes under Repression: Evidence from North Korean Refugees*. East–West Center Working Papers, Politics, Governance and Security Series No. 21.
Hale, Christopher D. (2005) Real reform in North Korea? The aftermath of the July 2002 economic measures, *Asian Survey*, 45(6): 823–84.
Harrison, Selig (1998) US policy toward North Korea, in *North Korea after Kim Il Sung*, Dae-Sook Suh and Chae-Jin Lee (eds). Lynne Riener: Boulder, CO, pp. 13–32.
Hastings, Justin V. (2014) The economic geography of North Korean drug trafficking networks, *Review of International Political Economy*, 22(1): 162–93.
Hayes, Peter and Cavazos, Roger (2014) North Korea in 2014: A fresh leap forward into thin air? *Asian Survey*, 55(1): 119–31.
Joo, Hyung-min (2010) Visualizing the invisible hands: The shadow economy in North Korea, *Economy and Society*, 39(1): 110–45.
Kartman, Charles, Carlin, Robert and Wit, Joel (2012) *A History of KEDO 1994–2006*. Center for International Security and Cooperation: Stanford, CA.
Kim, Kap-sik (2008) Suryong's direct rule and the political regime in North Korea under Kim Jong Il, *Asian Perspective*, 32(3): 87–109.

Kim, Kwang-jin (2011) The defector's tale: Inside North Korea's secret economy, *World Affairs*, September/October 2011, available at: www.worldaffairsjournal.org/article/defector%E2%80%99s-tale-inside-north-korea%E2%80%99s-secret-economy (accessed November 2016).

Kim, Samuel S. (1996) North Korea in 1995: The crucible of 'our style socialism', *Asian Survey*, 36(1): 61–72.

Kim, Suk-jin and Yang, Moon-soo (2015) *The Growth of the Informal Economy in Korea*. Korea Institute for National Unification Study Series 15–02, Seoul.

Kornai, Janos (1992) *The Socialist System: The Political Economy of Communism*. Clarendon Press: Oxford.

Lee, Kyo-Duk et al. (2008) *Changes in North Korea as Revealed in the Testimonies of Saetomins*. Korea Institute for National Unification: Seoul.

Lee, Sung-Yoon (2010) Engaging North Korea: The clouded legacy of South Korea's Sunshine Policy, available at: www.aei.org/wp-content/uploads/2011/10/2AOLeeApril2010-g.pdf (accessed November 2016).

Lee, Young-sun and Yoon, Deok-ryong (2004) The structure of North Korea's political economy: Changes and effects, in *A New International Engagement Framework for North Korea? Contending Perspectives*, Chung-yong Ahn, Nicholas Eberstadt and Young-sun Lee (eds). Korea Economic Institute of America: Washington, DC, pp. 45–62.

Levin, Norman D. (1997) What if North Korea survives?, *Survival*, 39(4): 156–74.

Lim, Kang-taeg (2009) South and North Korea's economic relations seen through statistics: The past and the present, and the future, in 2009 International Conference on Humanitarian and Development assistance to DPRK, available at: www.ncnk.org/resources/publications/2009-international-conference-on-humanitarian-and-development-assistance-to-dprk-current-humanitarian-situation-and-international-cooperation (accessed July 2016).

McEachern, Patrick (2008) Interest groups in North Korean politics, *Journal of East Asian Studies*, 8(2): 235–58.

McEachern, Patrick (2010) *Inside the Red Box: North Korea's Post-Totalitarian Politics*. Columbia University Press: New York.

Mansourov, Alexandre (2003) The hermit mouse roars, *Asian Affairs: An American Review*, 30(2): 88–95.

Mansourov, Alexandre (2004) Inside North Korea's black box: Reversing the optics, in *North Korean Policy Elites*, Ralph Hassig (ed.), available at: www.brookings.edu/wpcontent/uploads/2016/06/oh20040601.pdf (accessed October 2016).

Manyin, Mark E. (2002) *North–South Korean Relations: A Chronology of Events in 2000 and 2001*. Congressional Research Service, The Library of Congress, Washington, DC.

Manyin, Mark E., Chanlett-Avery, Emma and Marchart, Helene (2005) *North Korea: A Chronology of Events, October 2002–December 2004*. Congressional Research Service: Washington, DC.

May, Michael (ed.) (2001) *Verifying the Agreed Framework*. Center for Global Security Research, Livermore, CA.

Moon, Chung-in (2012) *The Sunshine Policy: In Defense of Engagement as a Path to Peace in Korea*. Yonsei University: Seoul.

Myers, B.R. (2011) *The Cleanest Race*. Melville House: New York.

Niksch, Larry A. (2006) *North Korea's Nuclear Weapons Program*. Congressional Research Service: Washington, DC.

Noland, Marcus, Robinson, Sherman and Wang, Tao (2001) Famine in North Korea: Causes and cures, *Economic Development and Cultural Change*, 49(4): 741–67.

O, Tara (2015) Understanding the nature of the North Korean regime: A foundation to engagement and coercion discussions, *International Journal of Korean Studies*, XIX(1): 36–60.

Oberdorfer, Don (2001) *The Two Koreas: A Contemporary History*. Basic Books: New York.

Park, Young-Ja (2015) Informal political system in North Korea: Systematic corruption of power-wealth symbiosis, *International Journal of Korean Unification Studies*, 24(1): 123–56.

Pinkston, Daniel (2003) Domestic politics and stakeholders in the North Korean missile development program, *The Nonproliferation Review*, 10(2): 1–15.

Scalapino, Robert A. (1998) Introduction, in Dae-Sook Suh and Chae-Jin Lee (eds), *North Korea after Kim Il Sung*. Lynne Rienner: Boulder, CO, pp. 13–32.

Scalapino, Robert A. and Lee, Chong-sik (1972) *Communism in Korea Part 2: The Society*. The University of California Press: Berkeley, CA.

Shinn, Rinn-Sup (2001) *South Korea: 'Sunshine Policy' and Its Political Context*. Congressional Research Service, The Library of Congress: Washington, DC.

Suh, Dae-Sook (1981) *Korean Communism 1945–1980: A Reference Guide to the Political System*. The University Press of Hawaii: Honolulu.

Suh, Dae-sook (2002) Military-first politics of Kim Jong Il, *Asian Perspective*, 26(3): 145–67.

Tait, Richard (2003) Playing by the rules in Korea, *Asian Survey*, 43(2): 305–28.

Tikhomirov, Vladimir (2000) *The Political Economy of Post-Soviet Russia*. Palgrave Macmillan: Basingstoke.

Ward, Peter (2014) After the collapse: The formalization of market structures in North Korea, 1994–2010, available at: http://sinonk.com/2014/06/09/after-the-collapse-the-formalization-of-market-structures-in-north-korea-1994-2010/ (accessed September 2016).

Yoon, D.K. (2003) The constitution of North Korea: Its changes and implications, *Fordham International Law Journal*, 27(4): 1289–305.

7 Regroup and strike: 2004–11

Introduction

In terms of his own objectives, Kim Jong Il completed his first decade as leader with a mixed record of relative success abroad, but more qualified success at home. This latter assessment may present to some as a gross understatement for a leader who had just presided over the famine deaths of a million of his countrymen, but it also underlines the extent to which Kim was a leader like no other in a state like no other. Therefore, most important from his perspective was that he had navigated the uncharted waters of the hereditary succession and had established his own autocracy. The loss of life during the famine had been horrendous, but after the starvation reached a peak in early 1997, the food situation stabilised and its potential for causing unrest receded, with the manipulation of international food aid playing a crucial role in alleviating immediate pressures. Most important from Kim's point of view, the impact of the crisis on basic military priorities, and especially on the nuclear weapons and missile programmes had been cushioned, and by 2004 the country was close to conducting its first nuclear test.

By 2004 Kim indisputably ruled in his own right, on his own terms, and through both the workings of his own secretariat and the *son'gun* framework for dealing with issues of state, he had placed his own distinctive stamp on government. He had preserved his father's legacy and during testing times had held both foreign influences and challenges to modify the founding ideology of the Kimist state to a minimum. With his power base, his ideological line and the policies that flowed from this securely in place, in the seven years that were left to him Kim continued to deal with major security and economic policy challenges from a position of increasing strength, with no observable tentativeness, ill-discipline or inconsistency. Any sense of gratification, though, would have been tempered by awareness that the management of the post-famine domestic economy within Kimist parameters posed different, more subtle and more intractable challenges than Kimism had ever previously had to confront. Throughout his entire career Kim had been adamant in maintaining the subservience of economic activity to ideology, and so being forced to co-opt and rationally assign an economic role to private economic activity that challenged this ideology was a bitter pill to swallow. The limit of his thinking was how to cope with it as a necessary evil, and at the first opportunity he proceeded to go on the offensive, progressively reshaping and restricting market activity during 2004–11, while reserving its choicest pickings for the elite.

All this was to change in August 2008 when Kim suffered a debilitating stroke. The structure of government he had built around him was sturdy enough to carry on as usual in the months that followed as he achieved a substantial recovery. Kim's illness, however, did cause him to firm up plans for the succession and in an immediate after-effect his third son, Kim Jong Un, stepped into the public arena after an abbreviated process of behind-the-scenes preparation. In addition, moves made in a number of policy areas indicated that more hard-line policies were adopted as the succession plans took hold. The father had calculated that his own customised hub-and-spoke structure for micromanaging government would not form a stable power base for his son, who because of his inexperience would need to rely more on delegated authority, and this led him to restore to prominence the Korean Workers' Party, beginning with a Third KWP Conference in September 2010. The day before the conference, Kim Jong Un's name was mentioned in the public media for the first time with the announcement of his promotion to the rank of General, reflecting the fact that in the *son'gun* era the regime's self-defined criteria for leadership began with military leadership. Like his father before him, the younger Kim moved swiftly and smoothly into the public space allotted to him under regime protocol, and by the time Kim Jong Il died of a heart attack in December 2011 at the age of 69, Kim Jong Un had decisively emerged as the designated successor.

Meanwhile, Kim's foreign policy continued to reap somewhat paradoxical gains. The Agreed Framework had collapsed in 2003, and the inter-Korean dialogue inspired by the ROK's Sunshine Policy had also lost momentum by this time, but from Pyongyang's perspective both had served their respective purpose and were now things of the past as the DPRK prepared for the greater challenge of life as a nuclear-armed outlaw state. The US's aggressive stance towards Pyongyang after 2000 had led nowhere, and it was now substantially distracted by its wars in Afghanistan and Iraq. Washington therefore decided that multilateral pressure to curb the DPRK's nuclear programme was a better option, and so also in 2003 the protracted Six Party Talks process involving the US, the DPRK, the ROK, China, Japan and Russia began. Like the Agreed Framework, this process itself was an indication of DPRK success, for Kim knew that unlike the 1990s, any threatening course of action among five partners with such diverse national interests was now distinctly unlikely. Even more important, the DPRK had survived when its adversaries had predicated their basic assumptions on a hoped-for regime collapse. This would clearly not take place as predicted, and so they were tipped into an on-going, intractable strategic and policy vacuum.

Domestic politics

The Tenth Supreme People's Assembly (1998–2003), the first under the *son'gun* system, duly completed its five-year term, and after elections in August 2003 the Eleventh SPA (2003–8) convened in September. Despite the pre-eminence of the National Defence Commission, nominally an SPA committee, overall the SPA exercised little power, and essentially remained a rubber stamp legislative body, for Kim Jong Il wanted fewer, not more institutions capable of exercising real power under him. Nevertheless, during this period of hibernation for the Korean Workers' Party, analysts turned towards the SPA for signs of the direction Kim was headed in. The public architecture of power with its associated rituals is always important in regimes dominated by ideology, not so much for what it reveals about policy debate, development and execution, for these take place elsewhere. Rather, its importance lies in the symbolic domain, where it gives a tangible form to this ideology, confirming and celebrating to its leadership and elite such themes as triumph, domination, solidarity and loyalty. In the SPA, it was clear that the mature Kim Jong Il's *apparat* was significantly different in structural terms from that of his father, but its overall purpose had changed surprisingly little, since both men's structures were modelled on military command structures in times of war, and were designed to maximise the Leader's freedom to manoeuvre and centre all significant decision-making on him and his staff. The major themes struck at the SPA's one-day session were therefore stability and continuity with past practice, with the brief, cursory attention given to economic matters providing no support for perennial external speculation that reform was on the agenda. The major policy focus rested on the country's nuclear weapons programme, helpfully described as 'a self-defensive means to repel a U.S. preemptive attack and ensure peace and stability in the Korean Peninsula and the region'.[1]

The traditional heavy turn-over of SPA deputies also took place, with 49 per cent of the incumbents ceding their positions, most likely because of the need to spread what was basically a major honour as widely as possible. By contrast, though, comparison of the leadership line-up at the opening ceremony to the first session of the tenth and eleventh SPAs revealed virtually no change during the period 1998–2003, which of course also gave the lie to predictions of any reformist intent. Three elderly National Defence Commission members, Ri Ul Sol (aged 82), Paek Hak Rim (85) and Kim Chol Man (85) stepped aside, while the Cabinet appointments, headed by the appointment of Pak Pong-ju to replace Hong Song Nam as Premier, were routine. The session telegraphed no new policy directions, nor did any subsequently emerge. The period of the 11th SPA (2003–9) was thus uneventful, with Kim Jong Il presiding over a stable, though not static, leadership configuration, marked by routine appointments and departures. In particular, the office of Premier was routinely rotated, from Pak Pong-ju (2003–7), to Kim Yong-il (2007–10) to Choe Yong-rim (2010–13), but as in the ROK, such appointments were essentially managerial and the incumbents had little or no role in shaping major policies.

This relatively uneventful period came to an end in August 2008 when Kim Jong Il suffered a major stroke and disappeared from view for several months. The effect of this on government immediately became a matter of strong speculation, and when one examines Kim's moves over the ensuing months, it appears that unlike some authoritarian leaders, he had accepted that he was not immortal and that he needed to hasten to secure the family succession. His own succession had been a struggle, achieved via a long process of emergence under his father at a time when the very concept of hereditary succession was anathema to many members of the Party. Now, however, his success in inheriting power and wielding it effectively in pursuit of family and elite interests meant that his designated successor would face an easier time. In fact, his dilemma was of a somewhat different kind, for at some point he and his counsellors concluded that his two older sons, Jong Nam and Jong Chol, lacked the requisite abilities for leadership, prompting him to reach past them to his third son Jong Un.

During this period one finds the media, especially the ROK media, and even the work of more serious analysts littered with references to court politics and factions forming in Pyongyang depending on which son one supported (Gause, 2006: 3). However, there is no compelling evidence that either older brother ever seriously sought to become the focal point of a power play in the demanding game of Kimist politics. Kim Jong Nam evinced an engaging charm and a refreshing degree of normality in his various YouTube interview clips, but he clearly lacked ambition and seriousness of mind, and until his very public death in February 2017 he devoted much energy to the pursuit of shadowy business deals with Chinese partners and a self-indulgent social life, also with Chinese partners.[2] Kim Jong Chol was less conspicuous, but likewise his father did not appear to regard him as leadership material, and again, this was a judgement his lifestyle seemed to confirm. Since this was not the Choson Dynasty and Kim Jong Il was not bound by custom to anoint his oldest son, he appears to have exercised his judgement that Kim Jong Un offered the best chance for a successful transfer of power, and so even in advance of his father's illness, Kim Jong Un began to receive the type of situational awareness training undergone by his father in the early 1960s, first by receiving specialist instruction from Kim Il Sung University tutors and then by various forms of attachment within his father's secretariat in a clear process of preparation for future leadership.[3]

Although Kim Jong Il's stroke had changed the calculus, succession planning was far from a rushed process. This is partly because Kim appears to have already been thinking about the succession some time before his illness[4] and because he pursued the goal of a smooth succession of family power in a clear-sighted manner, involving political, institutional, personnel and policy moves. In the political sphere, significant changes to the National Defence Commission in April 2009 marked the assumption of formal roles by trusted *consiglieri* such as O Kuk-ryol and Chang Song-t'aek, and in due course were followed by the convening of the Third KWP Conference in September 2010, at which the installation of a new Politburo formalised many of the roles being played by senior cadres, while Kim Jong Un was given public status as the heir-apparent in much the same way as his father at the Sixth KWP Congress in 1980. In policy terms, one needs to be careful not to explain all policy moves during this period in terms of the succession, but moves in a number of different areas contrived to place the DPRK in what can only be described as semi-lockdown mode, including the tightening of internal security appointments, the reassertion of traditional ideological parameters such as Chollima, and a renewed assault on the markets with a major and confiscatory currency realignment in November 2009. Externally, this period was marked by withdrawal from the Six Party Talks and by an unprecedented display of military aggression directed at the ROK around the Northern Limit Line in March and November 2010.

In personnel terms, one of the earliest pointers to Kim Jong Il's revised thinking came in April 2009 when the new 12th SPA convened for its first session and appointed a new NDC which reflected both specific change brought about by Kim's stroke as well as long-term developments. A broadening of areas of expertise, especially in internal security appointments (Chu Sang-song and U Tong-ch'uk), was noticeable, probably reflecting Kim's sense that the external threat had eased, but the internal situation in the era of private markets required heightened vigilance. However, the most salient move was the appointment to the NDC of O Kuk-ryol and Chang Song-t'aek, by any standards two of the strongest wielders of power behind the scenes since Kim Il Sung's death. Under Kim's personalised system, power was delegated directly from the Dear Leader, and so given their close ties to him there was arguably

Table 7.1 National Defence Commission membership: 1998–2009

	1–10 SPA, 1998	1–11 SPA, 2003	1–12 SPA, 2009
1	Kim Jong Il	Kim Jong Il	Kim Jong Il
2	Cho Myong-nok	Cho Myong-nok	Cho Myong-nok
3	Yon Hyong-muk	Yon Hyong-muk#	Kim Yong-ch'un
4	Yi Yong-mu	Yi Yong-mu	Yi Yong-mu
5	Kim Yong-ch'un	Kim Yong-ch'un	O Kuk-ryol★★
6	Kim Il-ch'hol	Kim Il-ch'ol	Chon Pyong-ho
7	Yi Ul-sol★	Chon Pyong-ho	Kim Il Ch'ol
8	Chon Pyong-ho	Ch'oe Yong-su##	Paek Se-bong
9	Paek Hak-nim★	Paek Se-bong	Chang Song-t'aek★★
10	Kim Ch'ol-man★		Chu Sang-song★★
11			U Tong-ch'uk★★
12			Chu Kyu-jang★★
13			Kim Chong-gak★★

Source: DPRK media.

Notes:
★ retired 2003; # died with state funeral 2005; ## not reappointed, rumoured to have been purged in 2004 (Gause, 2012: 137); ★★ new appointees

little need for either man to hold senior, public positions during this time, other than for prestige reasons. However, their appointments at this time indicated that Kim Jong Il had begun the process of providing institutional support for his son's leadership. In short, when the son eventually came to power the father wanted him to look around the room and be assured of continuity and loyalty with O and Chang present.

Although periodic mention has already been made of O Kuk-ryol, to this point we have not had cause to mention the role of Chang Song-t'aek, husband of Kim Jong Il's sister Kim Kyong-hui, the only Kim family member of Kim Jong Il's generation to be actively involved in politics at a senior level. Both husband and wife located themselves at the centre of the power structure, exercising broad, shadowy power and influence, with Chang initially becoming influential at some point in the early 1990s after becoming head of a section within the Organisation and Guidance Directorate, known benignly as the Administration Department, which was responsible for the oversight of judicial and internal security agencies (Gause, 2015: 195). Amid the chaos of the time, Chang contributed substantially to Kim Jong Il's consolidation of power and expanded his influence by playing a leading role in foreign revenue raising, principally for the court economy. He was also clearly a man of substance, impressing the South Koreans who met with him when he visited Seoul in 2002.

Royal in-laws or court favourites are rarely popular no matter what the historical time or place, and so Chang appears to have caused considerable resentment elsewhere in elite circles. In 2004 his rise was briefly checked in what presents as a bureaucratic turf war between his power base within the OGD and other powerful forces within the leadership group, and he was consigned to a period of arrest and re-education (reports on the degree of severity differ) before he re-emerged in March 2006 with enhanced authority over the country's internal security agencies. The OGD's Administration Section was detached from the parent body and became a powerful separate and rival Party Department headed by Chang, the new arrangement reflecting a general tightening process associated with the on-going, sustained crackdown on private economic activity. Kim clearly believed that Chang offered a degree and type of loyalty above and beyond that of other senior cadres.[5] Promotion to the NDC followed in the wake of the 2009 SPA election, where his appointment as Vice Chairman made him by far the leading civilian on the Commission, and along with Kim Kyong-hui, O Kuk-ryol and Ch'oe Yong-hae, he was one of four regents designated by Kim to guide Kim Jong Un in the initial stages of succession. To Chang's cost, the younger Kim, once in power, proved to have a mind of his own when it came to accepting guidance.

Strategy in the 1970s had dictated that Kim Jong Il's rise had to be at the expense of the Party, but now the opposite tack emerged: Kim's son's accession would to some extent bring back the Party. Accordingly, in September 2010 Kim convened the Third KWP Party Conference, the first to be held since 1968, eighteen years after the last known plenary meeting of the Party Central

Committee, and thirty years after the last Party Congress, despite a Party constitutional requirement to convene every five years. Like his father during the 1970s, by this time Kim Jong Un had passed through a period of behind-the-scenes emergence, and he now became a public figure with the announcement the day before the Party Conference of his promotion to the rank of general.

Once the conference opened, its first order of business was the reconstitution of the Party leadership, by then formally consisting of a skeleton crew of some four or five surviving octogenarians, so that it would be ready to resume its function of ideological and political oversight throughout government and society in ways that supported the leadership. Thus, 124 full members and 105 candidate members were elected to the Central Committee, and 17 full members and 15 candidate members to the Politburo. At the apex, Kim Jong Il was re-elected First Secretary, the position he first assumed in 1997, heading a five-man Presidium, comprising President of the SPA Presidium and nominal Head of State Kim Yong-nam (82), Premier Ch'oe Yong-nim (80), NDC Vice Chairman Cho Myong-nok (82) and KPA Chief of General Staff Yi Yong-ho (68). Succession strategy called for Kim Jong Un to establish some kind of credibility in military affairs as a priority, and so while there was no place yet for him in the Politburo hierarchy, he was appointed as Vice-Chairman of the Party's Central Military Committee (CMC), second only to his father. The significance of this appointment was that reconstitution of the KWP meant reconstitution of the CMC as the centre of political control over

Table 7.2 KWP Politburo elected, 28 September 2010

Rank	Name	General area of expertise
1	Kim Jong Il	All
2	Kim Yong-nam	Party organisation, foreign relations, nominal head of state
3	Ch'oe Yong-nim	Administration – Prime Minister
4	Cho Myong-nok	Military – NDC Vice Chairman
5	Yi Yong-ho	Military – Chief of General Staff
6	Kim Yong-ch'un	Military – KPAF Minister
7	Chon Pyong-ho	Party affairs, military procurement
8	Kim Kuk-t'ae	Public security
9	Kim Ki-nam	Media and propaganda
10	Ch'oe Tae-bok	Indoctrination and education
11	Yang Hyong-sop	Party organisation
12	Kang Sok-ju	Foreign policy
13	Pyon Yong-nip	Science
14	Yi Yong-mu	Military – NDC Vice Chairman
15	Ch'u Sang-song	Minister for Public Security
16	Hong Sok-hyong	Economy
17	Kim Kyong-hui	Family – aunt of Kim Jong Il

Source: *The Pyongyang Times*.

the military, in effect superseding the NDC. Accordingly, he then accompanied his father on a series of well-publicised military unit inspection visits and field guidance tours, on which he was listed behind Presidium members but ahead of ordinary Politburo members.

The new Politburo was not a complete reflection of who were the major power brokers in Pyongyang, nor did it signal its re-emergence as a paramount decision-making body. Rather, it reflected the Party's prevailing institutional status and authority as a pre-eminent institution within the leader-oriented system, sited in the midst of the labyrinthine Pyongyang power structure. Thus, Ch'oe Yong-nim sat in the Presidium *ex officio* as Prime Minister, but the infinitely more powerful O Kuk-ryol was not named to the Politburo, despite his former Politburo status in the 1980s and his current status as a close Kim family adviser and a vice-chairman of the NDC. Similarly, Chang Song-t'aek received only Candidate Politburo status. Meanwhile, other noticeable themes in these appointments were advanced age and representation from a broad cross-section of Party activity, including media and propanganda (Ki Ki-nam), science (Pyon Yong-nip) and the Kim family (Kim Kyong-hui). The importance that Kim Jong Il attached to internal security was reflected in the appointment to the Politburo of two leading cadres in this area, Kim Kuk-t'ae and Ch'u Sang-song, while the military had a smaller representation than might be expected in this era of *son'gun*, consisting of the top two NDC members, Cho Myong-nok and Yi Yong-mu, the Chief of General Staff Yi Yong-ho and the KPAF Minister Kim Yong Ch'un, none of whom for differing reasons had far to go before the end of their careers. The near-total disinterest in active economic oversight was also made clear with the only appointee from the field of economic management, Hong Sok-hyong, ranked 16th and soon to be dropped.

In summing up these institutional developments, we find that when Kim Jong Il came to power he dealt with his father's geriatric Politburo by leaving it in place while confirming his personal secretariat as the real locus of decision-making, overlapping with the NDC on military matters. He thereby showed respect for the surviving guerilla elders because those who were still there in 1994 had in turn supported his succession. He also reflected the reality that the key Party function of liaison and fraternal relations with other Marxist–Leninist parties was no longer relevant, and instead rewarded the type of leaders he believed he needed in a time of crisis – that is, active duty military commanders. Now in 2010, as this generation of military commanders was itself seriously ageing, as the country's strategic situation had improved with clear evidence that its adversaries were unable and unwilling to act militarily against the country's nuclear weapons programme, and as the Party was no longer recognisable as the Party whose foundations he had attacked in the 1970s, he again adopted a similar strategy, this time shifting the locus of decision-making back to the Party without disrespecting the members of the NDC. The stage was being cleared for Kim Jong Un to surround himself with new men to meet changing circumstances.[6]

The result was that when Kim Jong Il died of a heart attack on 17 December 2011, aged 69, and his son, while still young and as unknown a quality as his father had been at the time of accession, assumed power with the task of mastering a labyrinthine, demanding power structure, he had the benefit of a solid policy framework and the presence around him of experienced, loyal counsellors, mostly hand-picked by his father.

The state versus the markets

Kim was, of course, quite perceptive in seeing regime threat in the rise of private economic activity, for it reflected the eroded control of party and government over DPRK society. Gerontocracy, cronyism, nepotism, bureaucratism, profound corruption, obsession with esoteric ideology and insulation from the economic and social consequences of bad policy-making dating well back into his father's time were only the most salient of the characteristics that over time had produced a strong disconnect between the Party centre and the periphery, where local officials became increasingly unresponsive to Party directives, which were generally causing more and more suffering not to faceless 'enemies' and 'traitors' but to people they personally knew. The evidence of refugees suggests that the reputation of the Party fell drastically during the famine as local officials became the official face of the organisation that was delivering starvation (Lee *et al.*, 2008: 11), and with the erosion of the Party at the local level came the erosion of the tight driving reins of the coercion and control apparatus. Thus, while the *gulags* remained well populated, the expanding net of corruption made it more and more possible for people to avoid conflict with authority.[7] And so, throughout the 2000s we see growing private space carved out by the private economic activity which the overwhelming majority of the population now engaged in.[8] Major symptoms included expanded freedom of internal movement, continuing illegal crossings of the Chinese border by foragers and refugees, the widespread circulation of prohibited video material and now-rampant corruption in myriad forms. They help us to understand the spirit of the age and the specific contours of Kim Jong Il's war on the markets.

The economic measures taken on 1 July 2002 had provided the necessary framework for the government to use the market to restore government finances, and in the years that followed the leadership acted to further extend its economic reach through a very broad array of policy measures, some petty, some basic, but all designed to bring the state back into people's lives. Fundamentally, the government wanted more revenue, less expenditure, and more control over both the economic life of the country and the daily activities and thoughts of its people. What it wanted, though, mattered less and less as one descended to the local level, for there it no longer had the resources to control the basic productive and distributive functions of local markets, and although it still had formidable powers of repression and punishment, it could only apply these in sporadic fashion, usually to make examples out of a few minor players who lacked the protection of more powerful interests.[9] A cat-and-mouse game developed which uncomfortably resembled its equivalent in the natural world.

There was no sustained follow-up to the July 2002 measures of the type that might indicate commitment to a new direction – no fine-tuning, no campaigns, no significant media editorials or commentaries, no personnel shifts, no movement elsewhere in the realm of public policy – and this all points to the nature of the measures as a one-off move and not part of an on-going economic agenda. For a while after implementation, though, the regime appeared to benefit from the more rational organisation of the informal markets, in which operators could for the moment pursue their daily activities with enhanced security. Moreover, the range of goods and services expanded as what were previously designated as 'farmers' markets' (*nongmin shijang*) were now designated 'comprehensive markets' (*chonghap shijang*), where not only foodstuffs but also daily necessities, services and labour were exchanged. Established by decree in March 2003, the state itself sold goods in these markets, but more typically administered them, maintained surveillance and extracted fees for its services (Lee *et al*., 2008: 35).

However, unintended side-effects soon emerged, for with its intense concentration on raising revenue and divesting itself of unwanted, unaffordable expenditure, and with its characteristic ideological myopia in economic matters, the government had underestimated the scale and diversity of the markets, especially in an environment where local level officialdom was no longer either willing or able to act as a brake on such activity. The government thus faced the increasingly uncontrollable circulation of people, goods and even ideas, and this prompted successive campaigns and measures of strike-back, pursued by means of a staggered, piecemeal campaign involving government edicts, enforcement of pre-existing regulations temporarily in abeyance, exemplary punishments usually by public execution[10] and low-level harassment measures.[11] What is striking about the pushback is that over a period of four years from 2005 to 2009 it was extraordinarily comprehensive, taking in state security personnel harassment of market dealers, public education campaigns and vigilante activities directed against regime-defined 'anti-social' market activities, increasingly rigorous control of movement across the Chinese border, the closure of specific, major markets that had developed wholesale transaction characteristics such as the major produce market at Pyungsung in June 2009, crackdowns on the circulation of illicit video materials and repeated edicts restricting market trading days and hours, incorporating restrictions on who could trade, what they could trade in, how they could travel, where they could stay, how goods could be transported and how much they could charge.[12] If rigorously enforced, these moves would have essentially returned the economy to the later years of the Kim Il Sung era, but while that was no longer possible, there is no doubting what the desirable policy direction was.

The first major constriction on the markets began with the attempted reinstitution of the cornerstone Public Distribution System (PDS) with the banning of the sale of rice through the market system in late 2005. This measure was a major counter-stroke as it reaffirmed Kim's belief in the validity of the PDS not so much as a means of feeding people: if it did so, then well and good, but it operated foremost as a means of establishing strong control over people's movement and over their daily lives in general. It achieved this because distributions took place through people's state-determined place of employment, and so workers were forced back to their designated place of work, despite having little or no work to do there since the state sector still remained largely dysfunctional, and economic units often had neither raw materials to process, machinery and equipment to process it with, nor functioning distribution channels to place their products in. However, the measure was only partly successful as a food distribution measure because enough food was simply not available,[13] and even less successful as a control mechanism because workplaces continued to accept 'daylighting', or management-sanctioned absenteeism, for the purpose of market activity. This emphasised that the government could not change the basic equation, which was that people could not survive on the reduced PDS, which was why markets were necessary in the first place. With no new inputs, private food market transactions had to continue if further mass starvation was to be avoided, and with it came subtle, widespread forms of non-compliance that the government was unable to eradicate.

However, the markets were still the victims of their own success, and so other measures restricting private economic activity were soon brought to bear. During 2004–9 a series of edicts criminalising broad areas of market activity were issued (Haggard and Noland, 2012: 660), and beginning in 2008 the government increasingly deployed its domestic security agencies in a broad crackdown aimed against private-invested companies, effecting major shutdowns which appeared to focus on those engaged in foreign currency transactions, especially in processed foodstuffs (Kim and Yang 2015).[14] Meanwhile, the periodic crackdowns on the circulation of foreign video material intensified, especially from late 2007, while it became increasingly difficult for ordinary North Koreans to cross the border to China, a common foraging expedition, and so the numbers of North Korean illegals in China dropped accordingly.[15] At the same time, though, the evidence from refugees, visitors, residents and even satellite imagery is that where markets continued to serve their original intended purpose, they thrived, and this reflected the government's intended message that there were strict boundaries, within which marketeers would be largely left alone.[16]

The government's pushback finally culminated in the major domestic currency readjustment of 30 November 2009. This was essentially an exercise in demonetisation, perhaps more accurately 're-demonetisation', designed to soak up the large amounts of cash circulating in the markets, and so curb their activity. In the move, the North Korean won was devalued by a multiple of 1:100 on short notice and there was highly restricted convertibility from the old to the new currency.[17] This was followed up with an edict outlawing foreign currency transactions in the markets, again with the intention of forcing entrepreneurs out of private business and back into the state sector by depriving them of operating capital. The move essentially completed the reversal of the July 2002 measures, which were deemed to have served their purpose, a policy objective made clear not only by the policy itself but by various public and semi-public pronouncements accompanying the measure,[18] and also by a variety of supporting measures and campaigns, including the reassertion of state control over land that had fallen into private food cultivation and livestock-raising use, and the curbing of inter-enterprise transactions.

This readjustment was, of course, highly ideological, for in cramping the market the government was again seeking to drive people back to the still-dysfunctional state sector. And while the state sector was clearly, however delusionally, intended to be the winner, the collateral winners were foreign currency holders, which obviously meant the Party and government elite and especially the traders allied to the elite who dealt in Chinese yuan and/or US dollars with business partners across the border. The losers, of course, were those among the market entrepreneurs whose links with the bureaucracy were not strong enough for them to hold their assets in foreign currency and secure for them the usual advance notice of policy change, and who thus lost their chief circulating medium and most of their operating capital. This in turn meant that wholesale traders in both China and the DPRK withheld supply and hyperinflation ensued,[19] in many cases quickly annulling the effect of the revaluation. As transactions across the board were affected, it soon became clear that in its ideological haste, characteristic economic policy hamfistedness and overall mindset of unaccountability, the government had once again seriously misjudged the scale and nature of its unwanted symbiotic relationship with the private market.

Eventually, the ructions proved wide and deep enough to secure a rapid and in time almost total back-down, possibly a unique example of Kimist policy reverse-course, which could only have come from pressure within sections of the elite. The back-down began with the raising of the convertibility ceiling and the extending of selected compensatory (but inflationary) wage rises, and progressively over the ensuing months the official markets were allowed to resume their normal operations, with only the smaller, informal traders, the so-called 'frog market vendors', unable to avoid the full consequences of the revaluation (Everard, 2011). Another index of the strength of reaction against the revaluation was the demise of a senior cadre, Pak Nam Gi, Director of the Planning and Financial Department of the Central Committee of the Workers' Party, who had reportedly played a leading role in formulating this policy and who disappeared from public view at this point. This particular battle in the Kimist war on its citizens ended in retreat.

In sum, a number of major economic trends stand out during the period 2002–11. First, the leadership displayed clear and consistent determination in rejecting reform options in favour of salvaging what it could of the pre-famine state-dominated order of things.[20] The case for detecting either reform or reform countermanded is not credible, both because the anti-reform policy outcomes themselves are clear, and also because such postulations involved a considerable misreading of policy, beginning with a tendency to take regime rhetoric at face value, to misinterpret its intention and context, or else to ignore the direct anti-reform statements of the very officials who were meant to be part of the reform process.[21] And while the July 2002 remonetising measures were significant, this was so only in the context of a regime forced to address unwanted economic side effects of the famine, and they did not challenge basic Kimist principles. Nicholas Eberstadt (2010) detects 'hesitant economic experimentation' during 2002–9, which seems a fair summation if we accept that the aim of the experimentation was to achieve better outcomes from within existing parameters and not to disturb the parameters themselves. On the basis of the relatively high degree of competence in economic management displayed by other regional players, including the ROK, Taiwan, China and, at least until the 1990s, Japan, it is always tempting to impute something of this capability to the DPRK. However, the DPRK has always been fundamentally committed not to the traditional aims of modern economic policy-making, but to the pursuit of quite different policy outcomes, in which economic growth and efficiency do not figure as ends in themselves.

Second, and allied to this, throughout this period the DPRK remained strongly autarkic, with the severely restricted trade along the Chinese border, illicit forms of international trade, the declining arms trade, and the growing trend of selling North Korean labour to international labour brokers the only significant interface with broader foreign markets. It remains the case that neither the deaths of one million citizens, the continuing impoverishment of many of those still living, nor the steady delivery of the country into the status of an economic dependency of China have constituted sufficient motivation to force pragmatic re-evaluation of this cornerstone of Kimism, and so thinking cannot develop past the guerilla-like conviction that the external environment is inherently threatening.

Third, as though hypnotised by its nostalgia for the demonetised past, throughout this period the government made no serious attempt to defend the stability of the North Korean won, which, of course, remains a fundamental requirement in any process of economic reform. Hence, Pyongyang's extreme tolerance of inflation and its willingness to see what has become the 'yuanisation' of large sections of the non-state sector, where the yuan has increasingly become the preferred currency, even for small market vendors (Green, 2013); a trend that is by no means restricted to the border areas. This wholesale, invited invasion by a foreign currency underlines yet another singular, anti-modern feature of the DPRK economy.

Finally, any description of the DPRK economy during this period would be incomplete without taking note of its impact on the look and feel of Pyongyang. As early as the mid-2000s, visitors' reports suggested that downtown Pyongyang was beginning to gain a cosmopolitan edge, where foreign designer clothing, accessories and personal items were appearing, along with small businesses, including coffee shops, bath houses, spas, and both Korean and foreign restaurants.[22] The wealth and consumerism that this spoke of was generated through economic possibilities undreamt of even a decade earlier, ranging from such small consumer-oriented businesses to the import and sale of Chinese consumer goods, and major construction and infrastructure operations, all of which had to be carefully negotiated through alliances with the bureaucracy. But the dark, empty mausoleum-like quality of the capital even a few years previously (Smith, 2011) had been tempered not with trickle-down economics but with a manufactured cosmopolitanism that was nonetheless bizarre in its fundamental disconnect with the lives of quiet despair lived by most North Koreans away from such intermittent bright lights, for meanwhile the story for many people continued to be one of privation and official harassment encountered in their daily efforts to survive.

Nuclear success and the Six Party Talks

The decade-long US–DPRK bilateral nuclear talks process had come to a rancorous end in November 2002, after which the DPRK expelled the IAEA inspectors operating in North in December, restarted the Yongbyon reactor in February 2003 and completed its withdrawal from the NPT in April. The Bush administration thus found itself in the same cleft stick as the Clinton administration a decade earlier, for it could not influence DPRK policy either by threats or blandishments, and so while no one could ever publicly admit it, the only alternative was to put the best possible face on this incapacity by talking the issue to death in a multilateral forum. After extensive internal deliberations, in early 2003 the US tentatively returned to a less confrontationist policy framed around security guarantees and economic assistance. However, it refused to deal bilaterally with Pyongyang, a stance that seemed to be motivated by a strange mixture of principle, pique and, of course, Congressional pressure, where any agreement short of abject DPRK surrender of its nuclear assets stood little chance of ratification.

Meanwhile, China was sufficiently alarmed at the US's aggressive stance to adopt a more proactive diplomatic role. Beijing urged Pyongyang to moderate its insistence on bilateral negotiations and cajoled it into an April 2003 three-party meeting, representing it as essentially bilateral talks with the inclusion of the Chinese as facilitators. However, these talks made no progress and only appeared to underline the animosity between the DPRK and US, whereupon China accepted that it would have to cast the net further, in no small part because this would reduce the unwanted glare of the diplomatic spotlight it found itself in as the sole facilitator. It therefore invited the ROK, Japan and Russia into the process, and somehow convinced the DPRK that this format would still provide ample opportunity for progress on its bilateral agenda with the US.[23] For its part, Pyongyang appears to have concluded that while such talks offered little that it didn't already have, they might present some opportunities for economic gain, which in fact subsequently proved to be the case, and that meanwhile such a format would not obstruct its on-going nuclear programme. As a result, in August 2003 the Six Parties met for the first of six rounds of talks held during six years, 2003–9, before adjourning indefinitely following a unilateral DPRK withdrawal.

It was noteworthy that the DPRK should commit to such a forum in the first place, and of course it did so in accordance with its fundamental maxim of only negotiating from a position of strength. In this case, strength came from a number of sources that were characteristically underestimated by its adversaries. Essentially, since its vital interests did not in any way depend on a positive outcome, all it needed to do was to reapply the tactics of the Agreed Framework era – to see what was on offer, utilise delaying tactics, avoid specifics, unilaterally change negotiating positions and apply judicious pressure.[24] But in addition it also benefited from the relative weakness of the US, its chief adversary, for in their different ways and in accordance with their different interests, China, Russia, the ROK and Japan each had broad misgivings on US policy, beginning with the Bush administration's highly confrontationist approach, but also taking in the US's broader unilateralist approach in foreign relations. These misgivings became more pointed when the issue narrowed down to the North's denuclearisation, a goal that the US pressed with a vehemence that no other party shared, for while obviously deeply concerned, the other parties were far more accepting of the status quo of a DPRK progressing towards nuclear weapons capability because they attached greater importance to maintaining their own lines of influence with Pyongyang, rather than simply siding with the US in what they tended to assess was gross overreach in pursuit of a lost cause. In this manner, the US diluted its diplomatic strength, rendering itself deaf to policy nuance and often consigning itself substantially to ineffective isolation within the talks framework.

In addition, the US was out of step with specific partners on specific policy matters. It was clearly at odds with the ROK and its Sunshine Policy, which it had treated with considerable insensitivity, and it also clearly overestimated the lengths to which Beijing was prepared to go to secure a denuclearised North. The Chinese role was, of course, pivotal, for its national interest was vitally engaged, but the US did not properly factor in decades of evidence that while the Chinese government as a whole would probably prefer to live without a Kimist DPRK, there was no such entity as the Chinese government as a whole: influential sections of it were deeply invested in the DPRK on a number of levels – military, historical, ideological and, increasingly, economic – and China was not about to embark upon a radical departure from its established policy when it could not see what the practical outcome would be, other than a probable heightening of policy disharmony within CCP ranks and a dangerously uncertain future for the DPRK. Finally, US relations with Russia, which had reached a high point of strategic cooperation in 2003 in the wake of 9/11, were about to enter into a long process of deterioration, precipitated by the evolution of Putinism, but also assisted in the first instance by the US withdrawal in 2002 from the Anti-Ballistic Missile Treaty it had concluded with the Soviet Union in 1972, and then by the further extension of NATO eastwards to cover the Baltic States in 2004.

Thus, the Six Party format constituted little improvement on the pre-existing situation, and from the outset appeared extremely unlikely to achieve any commitment to concerted action. After three rounds of talks in which the participants duly walked over familiar ground and chewed over familiar proposals, a major breakthrough appeared to beckon in September 2005 when the US position shifted on a key component – the DPRK's right to a non-military nuclear programme, specifically the development of light water reactors for power generation. Negotiations then quickly produced a Six Party Joint Statement on 19 September in which the DPRK agreed to abandon its nuclear weapons in the light of a US affirmation that it had no intention of attacking or invading the DPRK, and would also 'take steps to normalise their relations subject to their respective bilateral policies'. The Six Parties further recognised the DPRK's right to a civilian nuclear programme, and agreed to provide major energy assistance in the form of an unspecified number of light water nuclear reactors and the provision by the ROK of 2,000 MW of electricity annually.[25]

This agreement revisited much of the ground covered in the 1994 Agreed Framework, but while the actual achievement of the agreement was noteworthy, not only did the devil lie in the detail, but there were many familiar holes in it, and so it had a short active life. Neither side was strongly invested in this new development, and the US in particular was reluctant, having been shoe-horned into it by Chinese pressure (Buszynski, 2013: 98). Clearly as well, the DPRK commitment was transparently tactical since the fate of KEDO had already effectively established that LWR-generated power was a low priority in Pyongyang, for as we noted in the previous chapter, the operation of LWRs requires accession to various international agreements with significant inspection and reporting requirements. Moreover, not only had the DPRK continued to assign a low priority to the maintenance of even a passable electricity grid, but reliance on ROK-sourced electricity supply, if it ever came to pass, would similarly open up the DPRK to multiple breaches of its economic firewall, and would indicate DPRK willingness to engage in a major strategic and economic transformation. The clear evidence from across broad areas of domestic policy-making and behaviour is that this was not in DPRK thinking at this time.

The fundamental negotiating issue was now the DPRK demand that LWR construction precede disarmament, and so when the Six Parties met in November 2005 to progress the agreement, there was immediate and diametric disagreement with the US on this point. The DPRK thereupon applied pressure from a radically different direction by raising the tangential issue of sanctions levied by the US Treasury against some North Korean trading companies for alleged involvement in weapons of mass destruction (WMD) technology transactions with Middle East clients and against the Banco Delta Asia of Macau, a major conduit for passing the DPRK's counterfeit US bank note product into international circulation.[26] The DPRK refused to return to the talks until the sanctions were lifted, and as the US refused to do so, action on the terms of the September joint statement stalled.

All the while, the DPRK nuclear programme continued to make progress, first to a series of missile tests in July 2006, which among other things ended an eight-year self-imposed test moratorium, and then to the important milestone of a first nuclear test in October 2006. In itself this test, which was widely assessed to have been only partially successful,[27] meant little since a long path still lay ahead in converting a controlled nuclear explosion into credible weaponry, but the DPRK had affirmed to itself that it was on the right track, and this in itself could only have been an enormous boost to morale when one considers all that had occurred during the previous fifteen years.[28] Pyongyang had also definitively reaffirmed its continuing willingness to seek its ultimate destiny outside the established international order, and while UN condemnation and sanctions duly followed, they of course had little effect, vindicating the North's maintenance of economic isolation.

As the significance of the test sank in, major ramifications emerged elsewhere. In the first place, in the ROK it discredited the Roh Moo-hyun administration and all those who had argued that the DPRK could be dissuaded from its nuclear ambitions by 'the right deal' – the right mix of security and economic guarantees whose advantages would outweigh the perceived advantages to the DPRK of becoming a nuclear armed state. The Bush administration also suffered damage as its negotiating strategy had been definitively revealed as ineffective in preventing this ultimate outcome, and in particular the credibility of the unilateralist neoconservative camp suffered. They were, in any case, in full retreat with the on-going Iraq debacle, and after significant Republican losses in the November 2006 mid-term elections, George W. Bush came to seriously review his options. This involved a return in January 2007 to the bilateral negotiation option he had repeatedly rejected from the beginning, with US face being saved by the concoction that the talks were not really bilateral since they were still under the umbrella of the Six Party Talks format.

On the basis of ensuing bilateral US–DPRK talks held in Berlin in January 2007, the Six Parties again convened in February and reached a further agreement, which was in essence a substantial revival of the 1994 Agreed Framework. Presented as an implementation plan for the September 2005 agreement, and thus given the title *Initial Actions for the Implementation of the Joint Statement*, the agreement was couched in the same mould of security and economic incentives, including 'emergency economic assistance' of 50,000 tons of heavy fuel oil in return for denuclearisation, with the major point of interest, as always, being verification of existing stocks of plutonium.[29] This was an especially sensitive issue, for the DPRK had managed to retain some plutonium in 1994, and now it had had a further thirteen years in which to plan how to do so again. Most important, the action plan did not mention the North's HEU programme, whose existence was not in doubt, but which the DPRK had always denied.[30]

Negotiations on implementation proceeded throughout 2007. In further bilateral negotiations, duly tabled at the Six Party Talks in September, the

DPRK committed to the disabling of Yongbyon and the provision of a list of all its nuclear programmes by the end of the year, while the US authorised the first shipment of 50,000 tons of fuel oil under the agreement, and also initiated moves to remove the DPRK from both the list of sanctioned states under its Trading with the Enemy Act and its list of states sponsoring terrorism, a far cry from Pyongyang's subsisting former status as a member of the axis of evil.[31] The DPRK list finally emerged in June 2008 and despite IAEA misgivings about its comprehensiveness, the US accepted it subject to some points of clarification, and proceeded to present its preferred verification procedures to the DPRK. Intense negotiations on a number of verification issues were still on-going when Kim Jong Il suffered his stroke in mid August, but this did not impact upon the larger picture, in which the DPRK again assessed that the US needed this agreement to work more than the DPRK did, and so it again applied pressure. By November, the DPRK had been removed from the state sponsors of terrorism list, but the US was still far away from agreement on an acceptable verification procedure, having only been able to negotiate access to DPRK-declared nuclear sites, with undeclared sites – precisely the ones most under suspicion – accessible only by mutual consent, and with only ambiguous assurances regarding sample taking. There were to be no further concessions on offer from the DPRK when the Six Parties met in December 2008, deadlock prevailed, and the Initial Actions plan, like the 2005 Joint Statement, became a dead letter. The final act came in April 2009 when the DPRK test-fired a three-stage rocket, ostensibly as part of its space programme, an act that drew down further UN Security Council sanctions on DPRK trading firms. Pyongyang responded by leaving the Six Party Talks, rubbing it in by conducting its second nuclear test in May.

The Northern Limit Line

The DPRK's lockdown mentality was also reflected in Pyongyang's calculated escalation of tension with the ROK along the Northern Limit Line, where after an extended period of inactivity, two major incidents occurred in 2010. The first occurred in May 2010 with the sinking of the ROK navy corvette *Cheonan* off Baengnyeong Island in the vicinity of the NLL, with the loss of forty-six ROK servicemen's lives. The incident soon became enveloped in waves of speculation and disinformation, but the most credible explanation, reflecting the findings of an international panel of experts, remained that the *Cheonan* had been sunk by a torpedo fired by a DPRK submarine.[32] There was no doubt, however, about the origins of the artillery shells that struck Yeonpyeong Island, another ROK island near the NLL on 23 November the same year, killing two ROK servicemen and two civilians. This was the first DPRK shelling of ROK territory since the 1953 Armistice, and was clearly a carefully calculated operation that seemed to come from nowhere, was not accompanied by any follow-up demands, and appeared to achieve no objective other than to demonstrate that the DPRK could carry out such operations with impunity. The timing, a fortnight after Seoul had hosted a G20 summit, should also be noted, for this was consistent with the DPRK's past record of offering dampeners just as Seoul was basking in international attention, past examples including the October 1984 Rangoon bombing as Chun Doo-hwan embarked on his first major regional tour, the November 1987 bombing of Korean Airlines Flight 858 in the lead-up to the Seoul Olympics, and the June 2002 NLL firefight on the eve of the final of the ROK–Japan co-hosted World Cup. The most credible, though nonetheless somewhat incredible, explanation appeared to be that this was foremost a live firing exercise undertaken as part of Kim Jong Un's training in situational awareness, coming as it did two months after his appointment to the Party's revived Central Military Committee.

Concluding remarks

In assessing Kim Jong Il, we find that he was remarkably successful in achieving a demanding set of goals with very limited means. It is easy to dismiss this achievement on the grounds that these goals seemed to defy the many rational assumptions we make about how nation states should behave in the modern world and how it should treat its people. However, in so doing we become blind to many important, inconvenient facts in the DPRK narrative, beginning with the conviction of its leaders that state survival depends on uncompromising isolation and non-participation in the international community, which in turn opens up many opportunities for rogue state behaviour. Kim's various achievements far transcend the rat-like cunning model of intelligence usually ascribed to him, for he was clearly a very able strategic thinker, especially when it came to foreseeing the end game. Within the exacting DPRK system, which requires the leadership to practise constant, measured vigilance that still somehow manages to avoid falling into the irrationality of paranoia, he largely made his own luck. His record in building the *son'gun* framework, managing generational change, maintaining elite solidarity, and controlling the senior military and civilian cadres around him virtually without resorting to purge or terror compares more than favourably with his father's less disciplined ways. Throughout his reign there was no doubt who was in charge: for better or for worse – mostly worse as far as ordinary citizens were concerned – he *was* the leader.

In dealing with his external adversaries, Kim certainly had the good luck to deal with a number of poor strategists and short-sighted thinkers, and this suited his basic survivalist goal of playing for time while he acquired a game-changing nuclear arsenal. It is ironic in view of the preponderant role that ideology played in DPRK calculations that his adversaries, whether US neoconservative rightists or ROK leftists, should also have been so tossed around by their own ideologically derived convictions, and were thus driven to place the DPRK into self-serving conceptual frameworks that ultimately led to policy failure. And so such people invented 'carrots' and 'sticks'; they posited pragmatism and reform agendas in Pyongyang where none existed; they saw China as a willing collaborator; they based strategy on imminent economic collapse on no basis of evidence other than extrapolation of statistics and 'logic'. They then even queried whether the DPRK leadership was 'rational' when it did not conform to their expectations. This in turn led them to constantly overestimate their strength and to overplay their cards in pursuit of the breakthrough 'deal', all the while being chronically distracted by the complexities of their own open societies and political processes, and being blinkered both by their own agendas and by their very limited conceptual understanding of the DPRK state. This was the fundamental source of such good luck as Kim Jong Il encountered in this sphere, but we should be clear that whether in diplomacy or war, good luck is, of course, usually the residue of good strategy. Notwithstanding the ideological constraints he was working under, including his own set of personal ideological convictions, Kim appeared to know far more clearly what he wanted and what he needed to do in order to get it, and the story of his success unfolded accordingly.

Regarding economic policy and the issue of reform, Kim Jong Il's view of the North Korean people, their role in DPRK society and ultimately the purpose of government itself, did not change, and so fundamental economic policy did not change. Thus, for all his occasional talk about becoming a 'strong and prosperous nation' and pursuing 'modernisation', in the end Kim toyed with the present and the future from within a political culture and mindset that kept him firmly anchored in his father's past. And again, one confronts the awkwardness of somehow imputing reform intentions to a government while ignoring not only actual policy outcomes such as achieving nuclear-armed status, but also the evidence of regime rhetoric, the implications of the *son'gun* structure of government, the pattern of senior appointments, and especially ignoring the total absence of public debate on the issue of economic reform. Moreover, one needs to ask just what the internal constituency for reform was. It certainly was not to be found within the ranks of the elite, with the probable exception of the occasional enquiring, doubting mind, because to such people reform represented a profound and unsettling threat to their privileged lives. Those not completely possessed by ideology had spent the better part of a lifetime learning how to play the Kimist game and survive and thrive, and to the extent that they could conceptualise what a reformed DPRK economy might look like, they believed it could deliver them nothing that they did not already have, or else they believed they could not survive in any other system. Outside the elite, it is fanciful to say the least to impute to the general population any concept of reform, for reform lay outside the existing system, and anything other than every outward show of enthusiastic acceptance of this system was a hazardous enterprise. We are left, then, with the only true backers of reform being those who lived elsewhere, and whether they wished the DPRK regime well or not, they were simply irrelevant to the debate.

So, when in 2011 we revisit the survivalist policy mix gradually adopted by the DPRK during the 1980s and early 1990s, we find that little had changed. The hallmark institutions of state and the dysfunctional architecture of the command economy were still in place in ways that nostalgic Stalinists would quickly recognise, while the market economy itself was strongly reminiscent of Lenin's 1922 New Economic Policy, having been adopted for broadly similar reasons: there was no other option if people were not to starve. A continuing prohibition on public or semi-public debate on economic reform remained in force, strong reliance on ideological incentives for the workforce existed alongside the burgeoning market sector, and the determination of the security and control system to brutalise and incarcerate ordinary citizens was not in doubt. The nuclear weapons programme was still being vigorously pursued, trading relations with the ROK had developed in a few select areas such as the Kaesong Industrial Zone and the Kumgang-san tourist precinct, but major ROK investment remained shunned. More broadly, the entire economy remained essentially autarkic, with most trade being conducted across the border with China in a highly contained fashion, with the maintenance of a broad suite of predatory and illegal international transactions, and with a continuing but tepid interest in Free Economic and Trade Zone (FETZ) strategies.

Significant changes had, of course, taken place in civil society, but it is important to place them in their proper context of a reluctant government giving way because it accepted that it had irretrievably lost the productive capacity and administrative competence to function without the acceptance of a controllable private economic activity sector, as long as this did not threaten the Kimist foundations of the regime. Whatever changes occurred were due foremost to the erosion of Party authority, and were the product of omission, not commission. The task of Kim Jong Il's successor would therefore be to ensure that the market sector, and more broadly civil society as a whole, remained tightly isolated and controlled, and that the revivified Party's control did not deteriorate further.

Nothing is ever likely to alter the harsh judgement of history on Kim Jong Il, for this is guaranteed by his inhumane conduct during the famine years, by economic management that prolonged Third World-like conditions of poverty and privation for the overwhelming majority of the population, by the horrendous scale of human rights abuse, deemed by the United Nations Human Rights Council in 2014 to constitute crimes against humanity, and by the potential global consequences of the DPRK's on-going nuclear weapons programme. Nevertheless, in 2011 his son and chosen successor, Kim Jong Un, inherited an essentially effective system for ruling the country, and at the time of writing continues to survive despite perennial speculation and predictions of systemic crisis and imminent downfall. The long-predicted collapse of the economy or the recurrence of famine-like conditions has not occurred, although the food situation remains endemically precarious,[33] and meanwhile the country's nuclear weapons and payload delivery programmes, both of which require exacting levels of scientific, technological and organisational skill, continue to make steady progress, impervious to outside pressure. From a purely Kimist perspective, when one sets aside all humanitarian considerations, as indeed Kim Jong Il himself did, much of what he actually achieved looks suspiciously like a Kimist definition of success.

Notes

1. See Kim Jong Il reelected Chairman of NDC at: www1.korea-np.co.jp/pk/ (accessed August 2016).
2. Mansourov (2004: 15) offers an interesting, detailed account of Kim Jong-nam's career up to 2003, recounting an almost clichéd take of a spoilt child who failed to live up to his father's expectations and was cast out.
3. The DPRK has no interest in catering for the international community's desire for precise information about Kim Jong Un's birthdate. ROK intelligence places it in 1984, and this is the date given by his aunt, who now lives in the US. See 'The secret life of Kim Jong Un's aunt, who has lived in the U.S. since 1998' at: www.washingtonpost.com/world/asia_pacific/the-secret-life-of-kim-jong-uns-aunt-who-has-lived-in-the-us-since-1998/2016/05/26/522e4ec8-12d7-11e6-a9b5-bf703a5a7191_story.html (accessed November 2016).
4. There are indications dating back to 2006 that Kim had decided on a hereditary succession, in both ideological terminology (Lee et al., 2008: 16) and in the inseparable issue of reviving the KWP where, as Frank observed, beginning in 2007 DPRK media references to him by the Party title of KWP General Secretary began to show a major increase (Frank, 2011).
5. For a detailed description of what is known of the new Administration Department's duties, see 'KWP Administration Department' at: https://nkleadershipwatch.wordpress.com/the-party/central-commitee-kwp-administration-department/ (accessed December 2016).
6. Kim's aims at the Party Conference obviously ran further than simply rearranging the institutional furniture. There were numerous, more subtle personnel issues to resolve, such as are common to the practice of politics everywhere – how to meet legitimate expectations, disrupt hostile coalition building, balance the distribution of power, retain loyalty, satisfy personal ambition etc. See Frank (2010) for more discussion along these lines.
7. On the basis of refugee interviews, the Seoul-based Database Center for North Korean Human Rights has detected a gradual decline in the number of refugees who had experienced or witnessed human rights abuses in the North from the 1980s to the present. For their general findings see: http://nkdb.org/en/database/findings.php (accessed August 2016). These statistics reveal marginal change, but given the widespread civil disobedience of the famine years one might have expected levels to rise if the authorities were still determined to enforce laws as written. This in turn indicates a declining will to enforce such laws, probably through an increased tendency to resolve issues by bribery before they reach the law enforcement level.
8. See Kyo-Duk Lee et al. (2008: 33). Interviews with refugees who escaped 1997–9 suggested that state-derived salary accounted for an average of 7.5 per cent of income and private transactions accounted for 91.1 per cent. This compares with a ratio 5.0 per cent to 88.1 per cent for the period 2004–6. Also see Haggard and Noland (2010a: 2), whose interviews with 300 refugees in 2008 showed that more than 70 per cent of respondents and more than 60 per cent of their spouses had engaged in private economic activity. Only 4 per cent stated that they had never done so.
9. See, for example, Haggard and Noland (2010a: 9), where they note the evidence of refugee surveys that smaller market players were especially targeted by the state, and so were significantly more likely to be subject to arrest and imprisonment. Everard (2011) describes a similar tactic.

10 It was, of course, a natural extension of the government's broad loss of authority throughout the country that the punishment system should also slip beyond control with predictable, horrific results. Refugees' accounts are peppered with accounts of marketeers suffering short, extreme periods of incarceration, enduring beatings and witnessing enforced starvation, torture and public executions. Haggard and Noland (2012: 661) describe 'a vast machine that processes large numbers of people engaged in illicit activities for relatively short periods, but which exposes them to terrible abuses while they are incarcerated'.

11 In almost all cases the primary sources for the information that follows do not include official government announcements but rather refugee network information and reflections on policy changes gleaned from foreign media in China and from pro-DPRK Japanese sources, which adhere to official lines but which could on occasion be more informative.

12 Lankov (2009: 60) provides an interesting example of this pressure at work in mid 2007:

> In summer 2007, government authorities attempted to introduce official caps on market prices as well as limits on the maximum amount of merchandise sold by a single vendor. These restrictions were especially noticeable in Pyongyang. For example, the price of octopus was limited to 2,200 won per kg, well below the market price of 3,700 won. The number of items each vendor was allowed to trade was also limited to fifteen, and the sale of more than 10 kg of seafood per day was prohibited.

13 One could never accuse the DPRK authorities of remaining on the back foot in the face of perceived ideological threat, and in this case they acted with exemplary haste, extrapolating on the relatively encouraging harvest results of 2001–5 for their calculations of how much the PDS could command. In the event, however, although initially the PDS revival appears to have been partially successful (Lankov, 2009: 59), the harvests of 2006 and 2007 were flood-affected and poor, and by 2008 the DPRK faced its most serious cereals deficit since 2001, further emphasising the importance of private market transactions for keeping people alive. For the FAO's assessment of the 2008 DPRK food situation, see Executive summary: Rapid food security assessment democratic People's Republic of Korea at: www.fao.org/giews/english/alert/dprk2008.pdf (accessed September 2016).

14 Also see Haggard and Noland (2010b: 3) for details of anti-reform measures enacted during 2008–9.

15 Lankov (2009: 64) cites both his own research and that of Yun Yo-sang in estimating that the number of North Korean illegals in Chinese border lands had fallen from c. 200,000 in 1998 to c. 30,000 in 2007. Not all of this decline can be attributed to improvements in the food situation, which, as we have seen, was still desperate in the northern DPRK provinces during 2006–8. Based on field research, Robinson (2013) gives figures of 75,000 in 1998, falling to 10,000 by 2009. We could account for the differences in raw numbers in any number of ways – definition, methodology, sample size, geographical range, but the point is that the reduction ratios remain similar.

16 It is worth noting that such pressure was not applied because of any improvement in the economy as a whole. Haggard and Noland (2009) and Eberstadt (2010) both view the period 2006–10 as a period of relative underperformance after the initial period of recovery in the early 2000s. This tends to suggest that the government's zest for placing ideology before economic pragmatism was undiminished.

17 Haggard and Noland (2010b: 6) calculate this limit through a number of metrics and conclude that the conversion limit 'appears quite low and probably hit a fairly wide swath of the population', an issue of significance in observing the popular

reaction. One of their metrics places the ceiling of permissible conversion close to the equivalent price of a 50kg bag of rice.
18 For samples, see Snyder (2010: 2).
19 Not only through the measure itself but through the loss of any confidence that the won had any underlying security or stability as a currency. It should be borne in mind that the Chinese yuan and US dollars were widely circulating in the market economy by now.
20 On this point Haggard and Noland (2010a: 9) present an interesting perspective when they note that policy since 2005 and especially since 2007 was 'essentially the reverse of the Chinese approach. In China, the market was allowed to "surround" the plan. Once plan obligations were fulfilled, production and consumption transactions occurred on market terms at the margin. Over time, growth increasingly occurred in response to market signals, even with public ownership of the means of production. The North Koreans appear to want to do the opposite. Authorities are seeking to reduce the scope of decentralised, market-oriented activity and are thus restricting the ability of the economy to respond to market signals and instead force development to occur according to state dictates.'
21 Hence, Chung-In Moon's comment in 2008, based on his years of interacting with DPRK officials: 'You have to be careful about not using the word "reform"; they are sensitive about that and prefer "modernize."' Available at: www.nytimes.com/2008/06/28/world/asia/28nuke.html?pagewanted=print (accessed July 2014). There is more than just semantics at work here, for what the DPRK evidently means by 'modernisation' is a process that occurs *within* the system, and stems from the fact that the vanquishing of 'backwardness' was a major reason why many Koreans rallied to the cause of the North in 1945. 'Reform', on the other hand, is an inconvenient reminder of how tragically wrong this cause has gone and that significant change from within is needed. And while selective quoting and misapprehension of Kim Jong Il's public statements during 2001–2 have convinced some that Kim had reform on his mind, one may, of course, find many examples to the contrary. See, for example, Oh and Hassig (2009: 76) who quote Kim Jong Il in October 2007 as maintaining that 'The market has generated into a place that eats away at our style of socialism'.
22 Among the most interesting and detailed accounts of daily life in Pyongyang at this time are Lankov (2007) and Everard (2012). Also see Haggard (2011) for a different view, based around what he terms 'the Pyongyang illusion'.
23 The Six-Party Talks represented an unprecedented way of seeking to deal with the North's nuclear programme, and the concept of such a 'multilateralisation' was arrived at by stages. Traditionally, the DPRK had always maintained a two-tiered bilateral talks policy, proposing to negotiate bilaterally with the US for a US troop withdrawal from the ROK, and then negotiate a peace agreement with the ROK. No other party needs be involved. Historically, the US and its allies had maintained that all negotiations were a matter for direct dialogue between the two Koreas, but then with the Cold War over, and with the ROK's encouragement, in 1990 Japan and the US initiated their respective bilateral talks processes with the North. These led nowhere before the US became embroiled once more in October 1994 through the bilateral Geneva Agreed Framework. A new phase of negotiation opened in April 1996 when the US and the ROK jointly proposed four-party peace talks, involving the US, the two Koreas and China as one of the original signatories to the 1953 Armistice Agreement. Pyongyang initially demurred, but in April 1997 attended a 'briefing session' on the four-party talks concept and then a preliminary meeting in August, but this again led nowhere, and there the matter rested until 2003, when four became six. Russia played only a minor role, as was perhaps to be expected given the scale of its interests, and for Japan, which had pursued a desultory involvement with the DPRK during the 1990s through its

tepid involvement in KEDO, the past abduction of Japanese citizens by DPRK agents had become such a major domestic issue by 2003 that Tokyo could not become an active participant in the Six Party Talks unless this issue was somewhere on the agenda, and when this proved to be impossible due to the absolute priority set by the DPRK on point-scoring where Japan was concerned, Japan retired to the diplomatic sidelines where it has remained ever since. A particular casualty was DPRK–Japan bilateral trade, which became negligible at this point.

24 See Buszynski (2013: 62–63) for a succinct analysis of the DPRK's negotiating strategy at this point.

25 The full text, titled *Joint Statement of the Fourth Round of the Six-Party Talks Beijing 19 September 2005* may be found at: www.state.gov/p/eap/regional/c15455.htm.

26 For details of these sanctions, see Rennack (2006). A particular feature of this action was the freezing of DPRK accounts worth some $25 million, most likely mainly working capital for the leadership and the elite, when the Banco subsequently defaulted. This issue was eventually resolved in March 2007 when the Treasury was overruled and the frozen funds were allowed to be transferred back into DPRK control, but the DPRK had suffered a blow since the episode could only have settled a general chill around other financial institutions disposed to deal with the North. See *Six Party Talks Break Down as N Korea Baulks on Funds* at: www.washingtonpost.com/wp-dyn/content/article/2007/03/22/AR2007032200160.html (accessed September 2016).

27 Those who watch these things believe that this test was at best a partial success, and that in fact it was another seven years before the DPRK managed a test that could be assessed as unambiguously successful (Lewis, 2015). See, for example, Siegfried Hecker's report, which includes Chinese nuclear specialist opinion that 'If the DPRK aimed for 4 kilotons and got 1 kiloton that is not bad for the first test. We call it successful, but not perfect.' Available at: https://cisac.fsi.stanford.edu/sites/default/files/DPRK-report-Hecker-06-1.pdf (accessed September 2016).

28 With this test the DPRK became the first, and so far the only, country to carry out a nuclear test in the twenty-first century.

29 The full text, titled *Initial Actions for the Implementation of the Joint Statement*, may be found at: https://2001-2009.state.gov/r/pa/prs/ps/2007/february/80508.htm

30 After emphasising evidence of a clandestine HEU program in 2002, the US now displayed a reluctance to maintain pressure on this front, giving rise to suggestions that it was deliberately soft-pedalling the issue so as not to jeopardise the chances of reaching a broader agreement. Finally, in September 2009 the DPRK acknowledged that it had an enrichment programme. In December 2010, the DPRK unveiled its pilot plant to a visiting US delegation. In the words of former Los Alamos National Laboratory Director, Siegfried Hecker (2010: 1): During my most recent visit to the Yongbyon nuclear complex, North Korean scientists showed me and my colleagues, John W. Lewis and Robert Carlin, a small, recently completed, industrial-scale uranium-enrichment facility and an experimental light-water reactor (LWR) under construction. I was stunned by the sight of 2,000 centrifuges in two cascade halls and an ultramodern control room . . . Although I and other nonproliferation experts had long believed that North Korea possessed a parallel uranium-enrichment program – and there was ample evidence for such a belief – I was amazed by its scale and sophistication.

31 For background to this removal, including the DPRK's links with Hezbollah, the Tamil Tigers and the Iranian Revolutionary Guards, see Manyin (2010).

32 Bechtol (2010) has presented what is probably the most detailed narrative of the incident, and this forms a useful background from which to view the many more interpretive versions of events. The question of the North's motivation is also of interest. The ROK assessment was that it was a form of retaliation (pique may also have been involved) for the recent refusal of the ROK, now firmly in post-

Sunshine Policy mode, to meet the DPRK's agenda for a resumption of some form of dialogue, Seoul having found Pyongyang's pre-conditional demand for food and fertiliser worth some $500–600 million excessive. The DPRK was always on the hunt for such supplies, and the breakdown of the Six Party Talks had precluded further supplies from this source. Behind-the-scenes talks were held during 2009 to find some formula for a resumption of dialogue, but by this stage, of course, the ROK had been burned rather too often to approach this formula for dialogue with enthusiasm. The talks petered out by January 2010, and since the basic DPRK formula was to seek economic incentives to refrain from aggressive behaviour, its inability to obtain these incentives on this occasion led to this show of aggression. For this ROK government account, see *Chosun Ilbo*, 'Cheonan Sinking Was "Revenge for Refusing Aid,"' 3 January 2013.

33 The reports of FAO missions to the DPRK throughout this period consistently reveal uncovered food deficits. For 2015, this amounted to 394,000 tons, or 7.3 per cent of an estimated total demand of 5.4 million tons. See www.fao.org/3/a-i5572e.pdf (accessed November 2016).

References

Bechtol, Bruce (2010) The implications of the Cheonan sinking: A security studies perspective, available at: www.marineclub.com/calendar/content/BruceBechtol IJKUS.pdf (accessed December 2016).

Buszynski, Leszek (2013) *Negotiating with North Korea: The Six Party Talks and the Nuclear Issue*. Routledge: London.

Eberstadt, Nicholas (2010) The North Korean economy in 2010, available at: www.aei.org/publication/the-north-korean-economy-in-2010/ (accessed July 2016).

Everard, John (2011) *The Markets of Pyongyang*. Korea Economic Institute, Academic Working Paper Series, 6(1).

Everard, John (2012) *Only Beautiful, Please: A British Diplomat in North Korea*. The Walter H. Shorenstein Asia-Pacific Research Center: Stanford, CA.

Frank, Ruediger (2010) Hu Jintao, Deng Xiaoping or another Mao Zedong? Power restructuring in North Korea, available at: *http://38north.org/2010/10/1451/* (accessed September 2016).

Frank, Ruediger (2011) The party as the kingmaker: The death of Kim Jong Il and its consequences for North Korea, available at: http://38north.org/2011/12/rfrank122111/ (accessed August 2016).

Gause, Ken E. (2006) North Korean civil–military trends: Military-first politics to a point. Strategic Studies Institute. Available at: www.strategicstudiesinstitute.army.mil/pdffiles/pub728.pdf (accessed August 2016).

Gause, Ken E. (2015) *North Korean House of Cards: Leadership Dynamics under Kim Jong Il*. Committee for Human Rights in North Korea: Washington, DC.

Green, Christopher (2013) Yuanization writ large: Daily NK confirms the rush to RMB, available at: http://sinonk.com/2013/04/19/yuanization-writ-large-daily-nk-confirms-the-rush-to-rmb/ (accessed July 2016).

Haggard, Stephan (2011) The Pyongyang illusion. Available at: https://piie.com/blogs/north-korea-witness-transformation/pyongyang-illusion (accessed November 2016).

Haggard, Stephan and Noland, Marcus (2009) North Korea in 2008: Twilight of the God?, *Asian Survey*, 49(1): 98–106.

Haggard, Stephan and Noland, Marcus (2010a) *Political Attitudes under Repression: Evidence from North Korean Refugees*. East–West Center Working Papers, Politics, Governance and Security Series No. 21.

Haggard, Stephan and Noland, Marcus (2010b) *The Winter of Their Discontent: Pyongyang Attacks the Market*. Peterson Institute for International Economics, Policy Brief No. PB10–1: Washington, DC.

Haggard, Stephan and Noland, Marcus (2012) Economic crime and punishment in North Korea, *Political Science Quarterly*, 127(4): 659–83.

Hecker, Siegfried S. (2010) What I found in North Korea: Pyongyang's plutonium is no longer the only problem, *Foreign Affairs*, 9.

Kim, Suk-jin and Yang, Moon-soo (2015) *The Growth of the Informal Economy in Korea*. Korea Institute for National Unification Study Series, 15–02, Seoul.

Lankov, Andrei (2007) *North of the DMZ: Essays on Daily Life in North Korea*. McFarland and Company: Jefferson, NC.

Lankov, Andrei (2009) Pyongyang strikes back, *Asia Policy*, 8: 47–71.

Lee, Kyo-Duk et al. (2008) *Changes in North Korea as Revealed in the Testimonies of Saetomins*. Korea Institute for National Unification: Seoul.

Lewis, Jeffrey (2015) *Revisiting the agreed framework*. Available at: http://38north.org/2015/05/jlewis051415/ (accessed September 2016).

Mansourov, Alexandre (2004) Inside North Korea's black box: Reversing the optics, in *North Korean Policy Elites*, Ralph Hassig (ed.), available at: www.brookings.edu/wpcontent/uploads/2016/06/oh20040601.pdf (accessed October 2016).

Manyin, Mark E. (2010) *North Korea: Back on the Terrorism List?* Congressional Research Service, The Library of Congress: Washington, DC.

Oh, Kongdan and Hassig, Ralph (2009) *The Hidden People of North Korea: Everyday Life in the Hermit Kingdom*. Rowman & Littlefield: Lanham, MD.

Rennack, Dianne E. (2006) *North Korea: Economic Sanctions*. Congressional Research Service, The Library of Congress: Washington, DC.

Robinson, Courtland (2013) The curious case of North Korea, in *Forced Migration Review*, 43, available at: www.fmreview.org/fragilestates/robinson.html (accessed September 2016).

Smith, Hazel (2011) Don't expect a Pyongyang spring sometime soon, available at: https://csis-prod.s3.amazonaws.com/s3fs-public/legacy_files/files/publication/pac1160.pdf (accessed June 2016).

Snyder, Scott (2010) North Korea currency reform: What happened and what will happen to its economy?, available at: www.asiafoundation.org/resources/pdfs/SnyderDPRKCurrency.pdf (accessed October 2016).

8 The young marshal takes command: 2011–16

Introduction

Two weeks after his father's death on 17 December 2011, at age 27 Kim Jong Un was named Supreme Commander of the Korean People's Armed Forces, thereby becoming the third leader of the Guerilla Dynasty. Immediately, many of the assumptions that were made when his father took over in 1994 surfaced again, for whatever his father might have done to ensure a successful transfer of power, change, whether intended or unintended, had to come. Not only the country's international rogue status, the dismal state of the economy and the abject poverty of most of the people demanded changes of policy, so the argument went, but again the case was put that the son's accession would bring change, for he was a different person from a different generation, with different life experiences, personality, needs and wants. And then, of course, he was exceptionally young, too young to be able to assemble a staff from his own generation whom he could truly trust, and surely too inexperienced to be capable of controlling the forces around him. With his father gone, people doubted that he would be able to control a phalanx of predominantly old men, most of them at least twice his age, and all of them hardened by decades of operating within a morally and ethically vicious world where they had been kept in line more by his grandfather's brutality, by his father's guile and by a nonpareil security and surveillance system, rather than by any institutional checks and balances within the system itself, let alone by moral scruple.

However, again predictions of basic change either by regime collapse or substantive reform have not been borne out. A number of years have now passed, and although we have no way of knowing how long Kim Jong Un will remain leader, he has already lasted longer than many had expected. From the little that we can deduce, Kim Jong Un and the people he has assembled around him appear to be capable of controlling and driving the DPRK system in its accustomed manner, while he also appears to possess the requisite sense of duty to maintain his inheritance and protect the interests of his family and class. He has taken on and so far prevailed against powerful individuals and interests, consolidating and adapting his father's institutional arrangements to suit his needs.

However, this degree of control has not been in the name of change, which so far has been minimal. Kim's policies have maintained the country's chosen means of nuclear-armed defence as well as its rigid isolation, while firmly rejecting the promotion of any economic policies resembling reform. And while he appears to have handled the social and political consequences of the ever-expanding sphere of private economic activity, both elite and non-elite, with more finesse than his father, levels of repression have not abated noticeably. Thus, to only a very limited extent has he been a different person living in a different time, with such change as there has been deriving chiefly from the on-going effects of decisions made by his father. The extent to which he owes his survival and success, such as it is, to his own ability, and the extent to which it derives from his father's legacy is still an open question, but meanwhile we continue to observe the on-going quixotic quest of the Kim family to preserve as intact as possible the legacy of Kim Il Sung.

Consolidation

Given the apparent lack of suitable family successors, a major expectation during Kim Jong Il's last years was that after his passing the DPRK leadership would be forced into a power-sharing arrangement (Haggard and Noland, 2009; Lee et al., 2008: 18). Initially, this appeared to be the case, for when Kim Jong Un inherited the DPRK leadership in December 2011, he was surrounded by the four loyalist 'co-regents' whom his father had informally installed around him for support – Ch'oe Yong-hae, O Kuk-ryol, Kim Kyong-hui and Chang Song-t'aek. Ch'oe Yong-hae and the aged O Kuk-ryol were two former princelings whose fathers had fought with Kim Il Sung in Manchuria in the 1930s, Kim Kyong-hui was Kim Jong Un's paternal aunt and her husband Chang Song-t'aek was the dominant regent by virtue of his intricate practical knowledge of the Kim Jong Il system. However, this arrangement was never designed as an on-going power-sharing arrangement. Quite the contrary, the DPRK defines its system as a *suryong* system, a leader-oriented system in which one genius-leader fashions and controls institutions to ensure he lies at the centre of all decision-making, and he has to have this power for the entire system to function.[1] It was therefore Kim Jong Il's intention that the regents should guide his son through to absolute *suryong* control. Due in no small part to Kim Jong Il's own acumen, this was a practical goal since his son possessed the enormous advantage of incumbency in what was increasingly a well-established system of hereditary family rule and one that most of the military and Party elite believed represented the best option for their continued privileged survival. With his legitimacy essentially beyond challenge within the elite, and with the police state apparatus neutralising any challenge from outside the elite, Kim Jong Un's initial hold on actual power appeared secure. Therefore, the major challenge did not lie in removal or overthrow, but in his ability to counter the emergence of people who might seek to work against him from within the *suryong* system, to curb his authority or else to otherwise manipulate him.

Kim Jong Un's first task was to place his own stamp on government and remove any vestige of alternative sources of power and leverage, and so during 2012–13 he moved first to confirm that a stable leadership transition had been effected and then to neutralise perceived threats to his authority. His first move was to convene a Fourth KWP conference in April 2012 in order to complete the work begun at the October 2010 Third Conference, where he had been given military status but no Politburo status. Kim now assumed the top Party position, First Secretary, with his father given the title of Eternal General Secretary, just as Kim Il Sung had been granted the title of Eternal President in 1998. Kim also moved up from Vice-Chairman of the Party's Central Military Committee to Chairman, thus completing his assumption of all significant Party positions,[2] while he also felt confident enough to make adjustments to the Politburo line-up drawn up by his father some eighteen months previously.[3] Otherwise, as befits such a convocation, little of a non-celebratory nature was either said or done and the DPRK media effusively endorsed the Conference outcome.[4]

His official status now confirmed, Kim Jong Un began to emerge as a leader who faced two major internal challenges to his power, one institutional and one individual. The institutional challenge lay in the legacy of the *son'gun* framework and especially in the power and influence of the military figures who were its chief stewards, while the individual challenge lay in the person of Chang Song-t'aek. From a broader perspective, while it involves something of an exaggeration to say that Kim entered office unprepared, he did begin his rule surrounded by his father's team and faced the inevitable personnel and institutional uncertainties involved with the transfer of autocratic power. Both Kim Jong Il's personal tendencies and the on-going major military threat to the country had validated *son'gun*, but now Kim Jong Un would need to redefine it, if he were to avoid becoming the puppet of the senior military commanders and their allies, all of whom owed their status to their support for, and their positions within, his father's system. In resurrecting and reinstitutionalising the Party, Kim Jong Il appeared to have understood that his micromanaging hub-and-spoke style of rule would not suit his less experienced son, who had not had an extended period of tutelage. However, his somewhat untimely death had now left Kim Jong Un with an unfinished edifice in which the *son'gun* generals remained in place, but it remained far from clear how influential they would be.

The specific legacy of *son'gun* was a powerful military state-within-a-state and an economy-within-an-economy that had largely ceased to be accountable to civilian authority except at the highest levels. Especially in economic matters, it had both an immense presence in the domestic economy, and it had grown to control a significant portion of the regime's hard currency transactions in such fields as mining, arms trading, chemicals and pharmaceuticals, to mention but a few. In these fields military-aligned trading companies were remitting proceeds back to the military, not to the hard-pressed central government, in a process that broadly resembled a similar trend involving the

People's Liberation Army in China during the 1990s, although in the setting of the DPRK's moribund economy the effects appear to have been more extreme, with some guesstimates placing the KPAF share of foreign currency transactions at around 70 per cent.

The type and extent of the impact that Kim Jong Un sought to have on this state of affairs is not clear, and we can only speculate on both the level of his desire to act and on the means at his disposal to act at the time. The military's economic power and its autonomous budget were long established, and clearly this system had its uses, for in a DPRK context it was arguably efficient since it funded core state defensive priorities but by-passed the transaction costs of channelling funds through the dysfunctional central bureaucracy. Kim also needed to tread warily because practically everyone around him, including all four regents, was heavily involved in such transactions, which were an important source of the kind of extreme wealth essential to influence peddling and power wielding in Pyongyang. Nevertheless, loss of too much revenue equated to loss of control and a broke government remained a weak government. Thus, a persistent theme emerged in Kim's early years whereby he looked for active serving military leaders who would accept that *son'gun* had to change, evolve and share its wealth more evenly.

The first stage of this search involved the replacement of the senior cadres that Kim had inherited from his father and who had embodied the very essence of *son'gun*. Comprising the seven men who had walked alongside Kim Jong Il's hearse on 28 December 2011,[5] within two years most had been reassigned or worse. Civilian octogenarians Ch'oe Tae-pok (83) and Kim Ki-nam (86) remained untouched, retaining their high Party rankings, and being listed at Nos 6 and 7 respectively in the Politburo elected at the Seventh KWP Congress in 2016, while the other civilian, Chang Song-t'aek, was living on borrowed time. Of the four military-security cadres, U Tong-chuk, head of the State Security Department, essentially Kim Jong Il's head of the secret police, disappeared from leadership gatherings in February 2012, KPAF Minister Kim Chong-gak was replaced in April, as was his successor Kim Yong-ch'un in November, following a brief tenure,[6] while Chief of General Staff, KWP Presidium member and regent, Yi Yong-ho, departed in apparently more acrimonious circumstances in July.[7] Thus, within a year the four top military figures had gone, taking with them significant numbers of protégés and members of shared networks.

This constituted the most significant mass departure since 1967–68, but the points of difference with those days were stark, for this was no winner-take-all purge. With the exception of Yi Yong-ho, the apparent exception of U Tong-chuk and the later exception of Chang Song-t'aek, the remaining four cadres were neither executed, imprisoned nor humiliated, while the senior military men among them were moved on to relatively insignificant but still honourable positions. These cases are significant pointers to an important facet of Kim Jong Un's professional attitude in dealing with senior military cadres, and are of course worth mentioning in view of the persistent, lurid and highly tendentious accounts, usually sourced from the ROK and avidly picked up by the international media, of Kim pursuing an alleged reign of terror.[8] It is an exceptionally ruthless system, but it has never been the setting for Caligula-like behaviour.

Kim's gathering sense that some senior military commanders were too old, too inflexible or perhaps were somehow uncomfortable with the new leadership also emerged a week before Kim Yong-ch'un's dismissal, when in a public speech delivered by Kim at Kim Il Sung Military University on 29 October 2012 he felt compelled to remind the audience that loyalty to the *suryong* system (i.e. his leadership) took precedence over all else, something that people had never previously needed to be reminded of.[9] At the same time, though, he clearly found that dismissing such cadres was easier than finding permanent replacements, and this produced an extended period of short tenure in the top positions of Minister for the KPAF, KPAF Chief of General Staff and KPAF General Political Bureau Director.[10] The reasons for this pattern are still unclear, but it is simplistic to merely ascribe it to some sort of unspecified power struggle, or to a putative struggle between 'moderates' and 'hardliners', terms that simply have no meaning when applied to Pyongyang politics from the outside. What does seem clear, though, is that the fundamental source of the conflict was not military strategy, for not only has there been strong continuity between the Kim Jong Il and Kim Jong Un eras in basic strategy, especially the DPRK's highly aggressive stance towards the ROK, but also the fate of the cadres discussed above would have been significantly harsher, and the actual execution of these strategies would have been significantly less consistent, if there had been genuine conflict over strategy at the senior level, for this would have amounted to insubordination.

Nevertheless, a specific aspect of the strategic dimension was present, albeit indirectly, and that was the status of *son'gun*. *Son'gun* was now a fifteen-year-old policy framework, but while many things had largely stood still in the DPRK during that time, the strategic situation had not, and so the hallmarks of *son'gun* as first advanced in 1998 no longer fully applied. In the interim, the Kimists had survived economic crisis and famine to achieve a measure of stability, the country had become a nuclear armed state, its missile technology had continued to grow, the threat of US-led military action to destroy the DPRK's nuclear weapons programme had receded, the importance of asymmetric assets had grown due to the on-going, irreversible degrading of the North's conventional assets,[11] the value of naval military pressure around the Northern Limit Line had become clear and the armed forces had extended their far-reaching, often corrupt access to foreign currency transactions. And, of course, the senior commanders who had presided over these changes were now significantly older. The presence of all these factors pointed towards reposturing, although it did not mean that the essence of *son'gun* would be challenged, for this could only occur in the context of a far-reaching change of ideology and policy in the direction of civilianisation, and this was not about to occur. This helps explain why Kim dispensed with senior officers but not with the underlying policy of *son'gun*.[12]

Having asserted his authority over the military, Kim turned his attention to Chang Song-t'aek, this strategy probably dictated by the calculation that Chang was the more difficult problem and would be easier to deal with after Kim's authority had been strengthened by bringing the generals more into line. Chang's threat was arguably greater because it lay on a number of levels, beginning with his command of the intricate Kim Jong Il system through the Party's Administrative Department, and the authority he had exercised within it going back twenty years or more, during which he was routinely referred to by analysts as the second-most powerful person in the country.[13] Chang does not appear to have always used this power very wisely and he antagonised other powerful interests, especially in the military, by the manner in which he utilised his Kim family connection to pursue his various agendas, amassing prodigious wealth which he retained in Chinese banks, rather than allowing it to return to the game (Collins, 2014; Gause, 2015: 49–59). Rather more serious, though, was the powerful role the Administrative Department exercised in overseeing the various internal security agencies and the fear among the elite that this power would have inspired.[14]

Kim Jong Il had already disciplined Chang once in 2004, probably reluctantly, and in allowing him to return to the centre of power by 2006 he demonstrated how indispensable he believed Chang to be. By itself, the extent of Chang's power and influence may well have been sufficient reason for Kim Jong Un to act against Chang, and he may have either perceived or accepted advice that he could never be sure that all the threads of power, especially as they related to external financial transactions and internal security issues, would pass through his hands and no one else's while Chang was still in the game. Kim's interest appears to have coincided with the broader elite interest that in purging Chang they would be free of a figure many of them disliked, they would be relieved of the anxiety of being purged themselves on the basis of internal security reports, they would possibly have access to the wealth brought back into the game by his demise and they would also pick up greater power amid the vacuum that Chang's departure would create.

In this manner, Chang became vulnerable. We do not know when Kim Jong Un actually decided to dispense with him, whether there was a tipping point or else just a slow and steady process, but once he did decide that Chang had to go, Chang's fate was sealed. In December 2013 he was publicly arrested in humiliating circumstances, subjected to some form of judicial process and speedily executed, taking with him an unknown but no doubt substantial number of aides, protégés and associates. Again, some saw this as indicating an on-going power struggle, but Chang could not have sought political power per se, for such power resided untouchably with the Kim family and he was only an in-law. We are talking, then, more of his seeking to maintain a heavy degree of influence over Kim Jong Un's decision-making, essentially acting as the power behind the throne through his control of the Administration

Department, but if this was his aim he would have needed to demonstrate to the elite that they stood a better chance of surviving and prospering with him controlling the under-experienced Kim. There is no evidence that he ever sought to make this case except by implication, but there is evidence that he would have lacked credibility if he had sought to do so, since he was neither well-liked nor trusted, and so he fell ignominiously, the surgical precision of his removal indicating that without Kim Jong Il his power base was fragile. Purges of Chang associates are believed to have occurred in the institutions that Chang controlled, but not a single Politburo member is reliably known to have shared his fate, leaving him as simply a rather spectacular loser in the game of court politics, after which people quickly moved on.

Was there a more substantial policy issue than just general court politics? Intuition would suggest there was, given such a public and exemplary punishment, unprecedented since the very different circumstances of Pak Hon-yong's show trial in 1953, but details are of course lacking. In mid-2014, a report surfaced stating that the specific issue that led to Chang's downfall was his management of economic relations with China. So the story ran, Chang had written to the Chinese leadership in early 2013 stating that he wished to empower Cabinet rule, sideline the authority of the Party and institute economic reforms, but the contents of this message had been leaked.[15] Despite his insistence that he acted with Kim Jong Un's approval, Chang's colleagues concluded that he had got too far ahead of the game in his cultivation of the Chinese leadership and Chinese economic interests, and moreover gave the impression of seeking to thwart Kim Jong Il's manifest intention to reinstate the Party, not sideline it, and this was grounds for exemplary punishment.[16]

The emerging framework: DPRK state policy under Kim Jong Un

Chang's downfall came at the end of an eventful year which began with a major, engineered escalation of tension with the ROK and the US during March–April 2013. Also in April, the first major sign that Kim Jong Un was beginning to shape his own policy agenda emerged with the enunciation of what has become Kim's hallmark *byungjin* policy framework – the simultaneous pursuit of nuclear weapons-backed military strength (*byung*) and economic development (*jin*). Less dramatically, events in May further advanced the pattern of frequent change in senior military appointments, and however unsettling such changes may have been to the principals involved, they were even more unsettling to the DPRK's adversaries, who struggled to understand the dynamics of power, and hence the command and control systems, in a nuclear-armed state.

Kim Jong Un's second year in power began with the resumption of Kim Il Sung's practice of delivering a New Year special address to the nation, discontinued under Kim Jong Il. Under Kim Il Sung these ritualistic messages had provided no guide to actual regime thinking, and this continued to be the case in 2013, for while the 2013 message attracted attention for what people asserted was its conciliatory content toward the ROK,[17] state policy was actually headed in quite a different direction. A much clearer guide to DPRK thinking was the sandwiching of this message between a further long-range missile test on 12 December 2012 and the DPRK's third nuclear test on 13 February.[18] On 22 January, the United Nations Security Council passed a resolution condemning the December test, drawing forth a robust DPRK response, which among other things took denuclearisation of the Korean Peninsula off the negotiating table.[19] Tensions then rose further in the wake of broad international condemnation of the DPRK's 12 February nuclear test as the DPRK responded to Park Geun-hye's 25 February inauguration as ROK president with ritualistic bellicosity, and on 7 March Pyongyang greeted the launching of the two month-long annual US/ROK military exercises known as Key Resolve/Foal Eagle with an unprecedented threat to conduct a pre-emptive nuclear strike against the US, maintaining that the US forces participating in the exercise possessed nuclear weapons and that, as had occurred in 1950, the UN Security Council's resolution on sanctions against the DPRK had provided the US with a *casus belli*. The DPRK further announced that it regarded the 1953 Military Armistice Agreement as null and void for the same reason.[20]

The following day the DPRK unilaterally abrogated all agreements and treaties with the ROK, including the 1992 Joint Declaration on the Denuclearization of Korea and closed the Panmunjom border crossing. A severing of the South–North hotline followed on 27 March, with the DPRK having earlier maintained that 'it is natural to cut the DPRK–U.S. military hotline in Panmunjom as . . . talking does not work on the war maniacs'[21] and on 30 March the DPRK declared that a 'state of war' existed against South Korea.[22] It logically followed that Pyongyang would therefore deny South Koreans access to the Kaesong Industrial Zone, which it duly did on 3 April, effectively closing the zone. The next parties to be involved were the resident embassies in Pyongyang, who were advised for their own safety to leave by 10 April, although the major missions declined and remained open. The DPRK media also advised foreign companies and tourists in the ROK to do the same.

Tensions remained high for the rest of the month, but with the conclusion of Foal Eagle on 30 April they began to subside and the parties moved into the post-crisis evaluation mode. The North was certainly not in conciliatory mode, for during May it carried out another series of short-range missile tests over the Eastern Sea. Also, in unstated retaliation against China for its supportive role in favour of United Nations Security Council (UNSC) sanctions during March, and especially the Bank of China's severing of ties with the DPRK's Foreign Trade Bank, on 5 May the DPRK seized a privately owned Chinese fishing vessel in the Western Sea and eventually returned it on 21 May after demanding US$100,000 in unspecified charges.[23] Then in August, the two Koreas undid the April closure by reaching agreement on the reopening of the Kaesong Industrial Zone, which duly took place the following month. However, agreement on further family reunions and a reopening of the Mount Kumgang tourist operation proved elusive, and the long hiatus in official talks continued.

This episode of manipulated tension, the first and so far the only one of its kind conducted on this scale in the Kim Jong Un era, is worth examining more closely, especially since it made a major contribution to Kim's international image as a reckless, bellicose leader. A first observation here is that there was little in the objective circumstances that could satisfactorily explain the DPRK's behaviour. The UN Security Council had passed resolutions condemning the DPRK's December rocket test and the February nuclear test, but it had also done so on prior occasions. Moreover, the US and the ROK had begun their annual Key Resolve/Foal Eagle military exercises on 1 March, but again there was nothing especially new in this development. Foal Eagle, which was first conducted in 1997, was large-scale, as its predecessor Team Spirit (1976–93) had been, and the DPRK had met these exercises with strong rhetoric in the past, but never on this scale. We therefore considerably underestimate DPRK threat assessment capabilities by believing that they could have soberly believed on such unremarkable evidence that a nuclear attack was imminent.

Moreover, it was clear that the DPRK itself did not believe its own assessment. In the midst of threats of pre-emptive nuclear strikes, severing of the hot line, abrogation of the Military Armistice Agreement, annulment of all treaties with the South, closure of the major economic asset of the KIZ, warnings to diplomatic missions in the North and to foreign businessmen and tourists in the South, and clear and public messages that war was only one command away, KWP and SPA meetings proceeded on 31 March–1 April with business-as-usual agendas that heavily featured economic issues, routine personnel adjustments and no hint of imminent conflict.[24] This suggests that the US and the ROK were probably not the only ones involved in military exercises at this time and that, as with the Yeongpyeong-do shelling in October 2011, the DPRK was conducting its own military exercise, manipulating and heightening tension to simulate an imminent nuclear war scenario in order to test its newly emerging military leadership team and its lines of communication in a higher state of alert than ever before. There was, after all, much to test in view of the various reshufflings of senior positions during 2012, and in view of the need to confirm that senior military commanders were in tune with a military command structure still in transition from the exclusively military leadership of the National Defence Commission to the Party-military leadership of the KWP Central Military Committee.

If this was the case, then we must allow that this was a carefully calibrated exercise and not just an episode of erratic, bellicose behaviour. And in the end, shortcomings in the command structure do appear to have been found, for soon after the end of Foal Eagle the pattern of reshuffling senior military commanders resumed. Although at the end of 2012, it appeared likely that permanent replacements had been found for the Kim Jong Il hold-overs occupying the top three positions of Chief of General Staff (Hyon Yong-ch'ol for Yi Yong-su), KPAF General Political Bureau Chief (Ch'oe Yong-hae as a permanent replacement for Cho Myong-nok, who had died in November 2010) and Minister for the Korean People's Armed Forces (Kim Kyok-sik for Kim Chong-gak), in the immediate aftermath of the March–April confrontation these arrangements were overturned, with Chang Chong-nam replacing Kim Kyok-sik as KPAF Minister, freeing him up to in turn replace Hyon Yong-ch'ol as Chief of General Staff, the job that would have come under most scrutiny in the simulated crisis, while Ch'oe Yong-hae remained in place.[25] Clearly, in some manner Hyon was found wanting, but not disloyal,[26] and was in fact recalled to serve as KPAF Minister in June 2014 before being replaced again and disappearing from public view in April 2015.

This process in turn reflected the emerging characteristics of Kim Jong Un's dealings with the military. The sidelining of his father's holdovers was an immediate priority, and in pursuing replacements the younger Kim and his core advisers appeared to adopt a chessboard approach, deploying loyal, responsive cadres, but not hesitating to shift and redeploy them in assembling a team capable of handling new strategic and political priorities to Kim's satisfaction.[27] Throughout this process, Ch'oe Yong-hae and O Guk-ryol remained constant presences, indicating their paramount status as Kim family *consiglieri*, and they were joined by Hyon Yong-ch'ol during 2012–15 and also by Yi Yong-gil. There appears to have been a considerable turnover in the senior ranks, but few outright, verifiable purges and certainly no reign of terror occurred at this level, with honourable retirements and reassignments to more junior positions as common as the outright disappearance of people, such as occurred with Yi Yong-ho. And while Kim also sought to both curtail the military's foreign currency operations and use the KPAF as an economic asset by involving the military in a range of non-military construction projects, it is more than likely that while such distractions from their core business of combat readiness would have caused grumbling in the ranks, they would not have induced significant unrest.[28]

The leadership itself seemed anything but distracted by the on-going aura of extreme threat, and among business-as-usual activities in a speech to a plenary session of the KWP Central Committee on 31 March 2013, Kim Jong Un articulated his major new *byungjin* ideological line.[29] The speech itself was virtually indistinguishable from speeches delivered by DPRK leaders in decades past, and most striking was the specific identification of *byungjin* with Kim Il Sung's 1962 Equal Emphasis policy ('With a gun in one hand and a hammer and sickle in the other!') which, as we have already noted, marked a fundamental turning point in the history of the DPRK, decisively turning it away from the possibility of evolving economically as a socialist developmental state and towards its current status as a specialised war economy.[30] The DPRK media always ritually reminded people of the various hallmark policies, movements and writings of the Kim Il Sung era, but this marked the resurrection of an old slogan that had received little attention over the ensuing decades.

Those examining Kim's speech for signs of change were therefore reduced to the usual game of parsing his words for nuances, but little was to be found there, for all policy pronouncements were solidly wrapped in the firm precedents set by his grandfather ('the Great Leader') and his father ('the Great General'), and thus any putative reformist intents were buried beneath a thick crust of precedent.[31] It was in this context that Kim made it clear that while he could do without his father's hold-over commanders, he fully endorsed his father's actual policies, and reserved specific praise for *son'gun*, thus confirming a huge policy overlap between *byungjin* and *son'gun*.[32] He was also unflinching on the country's nuclear programme – 'the nuclear treasured sword' – and on its centrality to national survival, promising further developments in weaponisation and miniaturisation, and enumerating various spin-off benefits from the program in the field of energy and in savings on conventional weapons expenditure.[33] References to economic issues were short and ritualistic, since the chief message was that 'The struggle to develop the economy and improve the people's living standards can be successfully carried out only when it is guaranteed by powerful military capabilities and nuclear armed forces.'

Orthodoxy was reasserted in other ways during 2013, most notably by the updating of the *Ten Principles on the Establishing of the Monolithic Ideology of the Party* in June. This was the fundamental ideological text for the entire country's mandatory daily study sessions that had first been compiled by Kim Jong Il in 1974, and it was now updated for the first time since then in order to raise Kim Jong Il's status by bracketing him with his father in many instances, as well as according greater status to the now-revived KWP (Tertitskiy, 2014; Green, 2017). In this manner one further brick was placed in position, and so by the end of 2013 key institutional, personnel and ideological adjustments appropriate to the new Kim Jong Un era had been made, a process in which the purging of Chang Song-t'aek concluded matters, rather than indicated on-going conflict. Kim had now effectively dispensed with the services of his regency group and cleared the way to implement whatever he meant by *byungjin*. However, to those looking for an agenda for change, the signs were not very encouraging, for all signs pointed away from leadership-managed change to a DPRK that would remain locked into Kim Jong Il's amalgam of nuclear-armed status, international isolation, Kimist mobilisation and rigorous denial of human rights, existing alongside constant railing against 'the imperialists' blockade' and the aspirational pursuit of becoming 'a highly civilised socialist nation'.

The sense that Chang Song T'aek's demise marked little more than the passing of the last Kim Jong Il era powerbroker rather than the clearing of the decks for a new beginning was then borne out during 2014–15 as the abiding characteristics of the DPRK leadership and economic systems took further shape, reflecting the internal conviction that the country was headed in the right direction, however much the outside world might beg to differ. *Byungjin* continued to be heralded and Kim Jong Un received long and effusive tributes to his genius, while depending on which sector of the state economy was involved, external observers professed to variously detect that economic change had occurred, or else had not occurred, or else had occurred and then been countermanded. In foreign relations as well, the DPRK continued to offer few avenues for dialogue with its adversaries, and relations with all comers essentially remained in a holding pattern. Opinion differed as to whether this static situation represented consolidation before engaging once again, or simply a manifestation of the serene DPRK elite conviction that this was how their 'perfect' world was meant to be shaped, but whereas the former view remained speculative, the latter view at least reflected what people could read, hear and see about them in the DPRK at this time.

In October 2015, the DPRK announced that the long-anticipated Seventh KWP Congress would be held in May 2016, some thirty-six years after the Sixth Congress. Preparatory campaigns immediately struck both a triumphalist and a retrospective note. The former was achieved through the detonation of the DPRK's fourth nuclear device on 6 January 2016 followed by a long-range missile test on 7 February, causing the ROK to respond by suspending indefinitely its participation in the Kaesong Industrial Zone and by initiating formal talks with the United States on the possible deployment of a Terminal High Altitude Area Defence (THAAD) missile defence system. Meanwhile, a retrospective note was struck through the Party's promotion of a 'speed battle', titled 'speed of the seventy-day battle', a quantitative production campaign of demonstrated economic inefficiency and ineffectiveness, but whose ideological roots lay deep in Chollima and in Kim Jong Il's eponymous 1974 campaign. Extending charity, one could say that this might have been more in the way of a tribute to Kim Jong Il than a sober reaffirmation of standing economic policy.

Taken together, these two strands struck an accurate key note for the Congress itself, which conformed to the character of its three immediate predecessors in 1961, 1970 and 1980 in that it was a celebration of intra-Party victories recently achieved, rather than a forum from which to announce anything of interest to the wider public, such as new policy directions. Thus, we find that the September 1961 Fourth KWP Congress of Victors was called some two and a half years after Kim Il Sung had vanquished the last of the non-partisan oligarchy members at the March 1958 First KWP Party Conference, the November 1970 Fifth KWP Congress fell two years after the purging of the last non-Kimist partisans during 1967–8, and the October 1980 Sixth KWP Congress convened two to three years after the purging of the last-known senior Party men to query the wisdom of the Kim Jong Il succession. Now the Seventh Congress convened some two and a half years after Chang Song-t'aek's purging.

The major revelation of the Congress was that Kim Jong Il's strategy of asserting Party authority over the KPAF was a far more ambiguous process than had generally been supposed, for the *son'gun* policy framework remained prominent. Through statements which noted the continuing special status of the armed forces such as 'The Party has developed into an invincible party with a solid mass foundation and powerful military foundation' and '[the Party] has trained the People's Army as a matchless revolutionary army of the Party remaining boundlessly loyal to it, and has let the People's Army become a strong pillar of the Party, thereby enabling it to perform a militant function and role as the powerful general staff of the *son'gun* revolution', the Party left no doubt as to the centrality of the military's role in policy-making.

In this manner, the relationship between *son'gun* and *byungjin* received clarification by implication, with the former emerging as the more fundamental concept. A typical formula emphasised that:

> By carrying forward the cause of the President [Kim Il Sung] under the wise guidance of Kim Jong Il, the KWP has firmly maintained the *son'gun* revolutionary line, the path of winning the steady victory of the Korean revolution, and [has] enforced *son'gun* politics in an all-round way. The KWP has bolstered the People's Army in every way, establishing state machinery centred on national defence and has transformed and adjusted all fields on the principle of *son'gun* as required by it.

By contrast, ritual references to the economy and to future economic planning were not linked to *byungjin*, and in fact, only brief, cursory mention was made of economic strategy, chiefly in the form of fleeting mention of a Five Year Plan with unspecified goals.

Unsurprisingly, appointments to the new Politburo reflected these themes. The new Central Committee was elected by the 3,467 delegates, 315 of whom were women, and evinced the usual high turnover, a reflection of the standard practice of sharing widely such a high honour. Out of the Central Committee's deliberations came a Politburo comprising nineteen full members headed by a five-man presidium and nine candidate members. Comparison with the pre-existing Politburo announced at the third Party Conference in 2010 showed a number of changes but no surprises. Hwang Pyong-so, a career civilian Party cadre before being parachuted into the senior ranks of the military in 2014 with his appointment to head the KPAF's General Political Bureau, received commensurate Party recognition, as did Pak Pong-ju, who received the customary ex-officio high ranking accorded to the Premier, and was also simultaneously appointed to the KWP Central Military Commission, reviving the practice of appointing the government's senior bureaucrat to the premier military committee.[34] Otherwise, appointments faithfully reflected the themes of the Congress, with the military retaining a reduced but still historically strong presence and with technocratic expertise concentrated in military-related industry.

In summing up the Congress, the only real surprise was the intensity of its retrospective character. Even allowing for the fact that this was the congress of a political party, and that the celebratory nature of the occasion called for

Table 8.1 Comparison of KWP Politburos: 2010 and 2016

Ranking	Politburo elected at 3rd KWP Conference October 2010	General area of expertise	Politburo elected at 7th KWP Conference May 2016	General area of expertise
1	Kim Jong Il	All	Kim Jong Un	All
2	Kim Yong-nam	Party organisation, foreign relations	Kim Yong-nam	Party organisation, foreign relations
3	Ch'oe Yong-nim	Administration – Premier	Hwang Pyong-so	Military
4	Cho Myong-nok	Military – NDC Vice Chairman	Pak Pong-ju	Administration – Premier
5	Yi Yong-ho	Military – Chief of General Staff	Ch'oe Yong-hae	Party/Military interface
6	Kim Yong-ch'un	Military – KPAF Minister	Kim Ki-nam	Agitprop
7	Chon Pyong-ho	Party affairs, military procurement	Ch'oe Tae-bok	Ideology and education
8	Kim Kuk-t'ae	Public Security	Yi Su-yong	Foreign relations
9	Kim Ki-nam	Agitprop	Kim P'yong-hae	Party organisation
10	Ch'oe Tae-bok	Education	O Su-yong	Technocrat – electronics industry
11	Yang Hyong-sop	Party organisation	Kwak Pom-gi	Technocrat – heavy industry
12	Kang Sok-ju	Foreign relations	Kim Yong-ch'ol	Military intelligence
13	Pyon Yong-nip	Science	Yi Man-gon	Technocrat – munitions industry
14	Yi Yong-mu	Military – NDC Vice Chairman	Yang Hyong-sop	Party organisation
15	Chu Sang-song	Public Security	No Tu-ch'ol	Government – Vice Premier
16	Hong Sok-hyong	Economy	Pak Yong-sik	Military – KPAF Minister
17	Kim Kyong-hui	Family – aunt of Kim Jong Un	Yi Myong-su	Military/Security
18			Kim Won-hong	Military/Security
19			Ch'oe Pu-il	Military/Security

Source: DPRK media.

expressions of pride in past achievements and avoidance of unpleasant memories, the KWP looked back over decades of disaster and underperformance and continued to find overweening comfort in them, with Kim Jong Un's speeches and their accompanying commentaries couched in terms indistinguishable in ideological content from the previous Congress thirty-six years ago, and once again giving the lie to any and all theories that the DPRK was seeking to alter its self-proclaimed sublime system. Retrospective themes resurrected at this time included Kim Il Sung's Democratic Federal Republic of Koryo, advocacy that the Cold War era Non-Aligned Movement, now basically a spent force, 'should be developed' and re-endorsement of Kim Jong Il's 1970s era Three Revolutions mantra. With its anti-modern view of modernity, this Congress was a gathering of people who believed that the good life they enjoyed could be sustained and prolonged indefinitely by the possession of nuclear weapons, by the on-going systematic committing of crimes against humanity against their own citizens, and by self-enrichment through profound endemic corruption and control of foreign currency transactions.

Some institutional loose ends were then tied up on 29 June when the Supreme People's Assembly met in its fourth plenary session, with the National Defence Commission being renamed the State Affairs Commission, and with Kim Jong Un being redesignated as Chairman of the new body. The NDC's designation as the supreme policy-making organ of the DPRK state in 1998 had essentially been a crisis management move as well as the supreme institutional expression of *son'gun*. It had begun with an almost exclusively military membership (the Premier Yon Hyong-muk was the only true civilian) but it gradually took in related fields, most notably internal security interests, in Kim Jong Il's last years. Now, as part of the general evolution of *son'gun* to a much broader role as the central organising principle for the allocation of state resources, even wider interests including the Cabinet (Pak Pong-ju),

Table 8.2 Members of the inaugural SPA State Affairs Commission, 2016

Name	Policy area
Kim Jong Un	All
Hwang Pyong-so	Military
Pak Pong-ju	Administration – Premier
Ch'oe Yong-hae	Party–military interface
Kim Ki-nam	Party – agitprop
Pak Yong-sik	Military – KPAF Minister
Yi Su-yong	Foreign relations
Yi Man-gon	Technocracy
Kim Yong-ch'ol	Military intelligence
Kim Won-hong	Security – Minister for State Security
Ch'oe Pu-il	Security – Minister for Public Security
Yi Yong-ho	Foreign relations – Foreign Minister

Source: DPRK media.

foreign policy specialists (Yi Su-yong and Yi Yong-ho) and civilian expertise (Kim Ki-nam and Yi Man-gon) were included, and with only three career military commanders (Pak Yong-sik, Kim Won-hong, and Ch'oe Pu-il) among twelve members, a more broad-ranging title was deemed appropriate. The change, while essentially semantic, constituted one more example of the institutional redefinition of *son'gun*, but not the dilution of its essence.

Economic policy

Well before now in our narrative, even the casual reader will have concluded that efforts to assess the state of the DPRK economy through the application of standard indices such as GDP, GDP per capita, sector performances and key foreign trade balances such as those with China have limited validity. This is because the information they may reveal on the vital signs of the economy clearly does not form the basis for such routine tasks of economic management as promoting the rational allocation of resources, providing feedback to sectors, enabling and coordinating long-term planning, and keeping foreign sources of investment and finance informed, let alone promoting the social well-being and quality of life, and hence the productivity, of its own citizens. Simply put, there appears to be little civilian economic activity in the DPRK that requires accurate statistical input and there is certainly no public acknowledgement of such a requirement. The state sector is no longer centrally planned in any meaningful way, with only a small number of enterprises functional, by at least one account estimated at about 30 per cent (Kim Tae Hong, 2012), and so planning on the basis of accurate statistics is of little help, although this does not necessarily apply to strategically vital industries, especially in the military sector, where different, far higher standards undoubtedly prevail. Moreover, in the monetised private sector, covering perhaps 30 per cent of all economic activity in the country, not only is most economic activity beyond government control, and hence beyond the capacity of the government to monitor, let alone quantify, but also many activities have been formally criminalised, and so most business decisions are made not in the light of informed commentary or accurate data, but on the basis of surreptitious informal, marketplace information, or else from information gleaned via a range of corrupt relationships with the authorities. Either way, a major priority of the market is to avoid or frustrate the gathering of accurate statistical information.

In its external economic relations, Pyongyang is still not seeking, and probably actually fears, the type of foreign investor for whom accurate data forms the basis for investment decisions and in fact has actively preyed on such people in the past. This is, of course, why foreign investors in the DPRK tend to be of the high-risk to low-technology variety, or else sourced from pro-North Koreans in Japan, or else they rely on close, corrupt relationships with government and Party entities for success. And so, by 2011 only two of China's top one hundred companies, both steel companies, had invested in trade with the DPRK (Thompson, 2011). In short, applying standard forms of economic analysis to the DPRK economy usually involves posing either irrelevant or unanswerable questions to dubious sets of rhetorical data, and it is therefore not surprising that even estimates from reasonably credible sources for economic growth during 2011–15 fluctuate wildly, from around the 1 per cent average range (Bank of Korea) to 3–4 per cent (Lankov, 2016) to 7.5 per cent for 2016 (Hyundai Research, Institute).[35]

At the time of writing, the most recent, reasonably comprehensive figures on the DPRK's foreign trade cover 2014.[36] By orthodox economic analysis, the overall profile is of an economy in the very early stages of modernisation, little changed from the DPRK profile in the 1970s and 1980s, with a relatively primitive manufacturing sector, a high dependence on exports of raw materials, and an almost complete absence of elaborately transformed manufactures, which therefore figure hugely in the country's imports. Actual volumes finally regained their best pre-1991 levels in 2010, but have more than doubled since then, mainly on the back of expanded mineral exports to China, suggesting that the DPRK has entered into a period of modest, stable economic growth, but one of debatable sustainability.

The most salient features in recent figures are the high deficit of $1.29 billion and the high level of dependence on China (90.1 per cent). The high dependence on China is relatively recent and has survived the downfall of Chang Song-t'aek and the loss of his role as a major economic facilitator. It is caused chiefly by the withdrawal of other traders, especially Japan, in compliance with UN sanctions, while further major factors have been the demand for DPRK minerals in China and the active Chinese role in building mineral extraction and transport infrastructure in the DPRK. Moreover, as Ward and Lankov (2016) point out, there is a sizeable component of soft, preferential trade involved, with UN sanctions applied very selectively by Beijing. Regarding the deficit, the figure appears to be alarming, given that the DPRK has virtually no means of debt financing, but historically the figure is not high, and it does not take into account the hundreds of millions of dollars that flow in annually in illicit transactions.[37] Another huge factor is remittances from abroad, from Koreans in the diaspora typically to family members in the North, and especially from the 60,000 or so North Koreans working overseas, a good deal of which goes to the government.[38]

What, then, can one say with confidence about DPRK economic policy under Kim Jong Un? We may, of course, begin with Kim Jong Il's bequest of a seriously eroded command economy in survivalist mode, not without some powers of adjustment to the market sector whose emergence it had been powerless to prevent, but otherwise so distorted and corrupted by expediency as to have seriously lost coherence in pursuit of non-military sector activities. In turn, Kim Jong Un has basically shown strong continuity with his father's policies in rejecting reform options, but to date his regime has shown itself to be far less rigid and less prone to intervention. Coherent economic planning is assumed to exist in the military sector but it is difficult to detect elsewhere, people still largely fend for themselves within market confines, autarky has been defended, while illicit trade including drugs, forgery and large-scale insurance fraud also continues. The major developments have been the development of a sizeable foreign market for DPRK labour, and the increasing blurring of cross-border trade with China, with thousands of North Koreans now working in Dandong, and with their output passing directly into the Chinese distribution system.[39]

Most importantly, while the profile that emerges from the trade figures is typical of countries in the early stages of industrialisation, including most of the DPRK's neighbours in now-distant generations past, the case of the DPRK is different, for it does not see this current structure as a stage of development on the way to an economic take-off point, as did its capitalist development state neighbours. Thus, in addition to quantification issues, interpreting the qualitative economic significance of GDP figures is problematic, for such figures do not indicate that a viable, open-ended growth strategy is in place. Instead, they currently reflect more or less the limit to which the leadership wishes the non-military sector to go, since at this level it meets their needs with a maximum of convenience and a minimum of threat. In other words, notwithstanding the vigour of the light industry sector, the development of advanced manufacturing, service and knowledge industries, not to mention international trade itself, does not loom large in current planning. There may well be advocates for such planning in Pyongyang, currently silent of necessity, and it becomes easy in the face of suave, flexible presentations by senior cadres to believe that reform is on the agenda somewhere, but in almost every conceivable way the leadership lacks the mindset and type of motivation that drove the ROK Third Republic under Park Chung-hee, not to mention other developmental strategies in the wider region. As matters stand, the DPRK economy is incapable of sustaining a growth rate comparable to its neighbours at similar stages in their growth trajectory.

Why continue to pursue this strategy? The answer is obviously that it must serve the leadership's purpose. No doubt many cadres are patriotic and would like to see a more successful, competitive economy, but for many more the situation is far from dire. Setting to one side the enormous ideological satisfaction some might gain from their belief, however fitful, that the country is fulfilling a mission of historical necessity, for now the DPRK appears to be paying its own way far more than it ever did in the first forty-five years or so of its existence, while at the same time financing nuclear weapons and missile programmes of ever-growing sophistication. Moreover, the strategy enables sizeable numbers of middle-ranking and senior cadres to amass fabulous sums of hard currency through institutionalised corruption, and this has been an important factor in ensuring elite loyalty. In turn, this means that the entire ruling class can look back at the events of the 1990s and feel a sense of security that the effect of possible future economic failure will again be felt not by them, but almost exclusively by the general population. This fuels a comforting sense of safety and unaccountability, and so while one sometimes hears the theory that since Kim Jong Un lacked legitimacy in the eyes of North Koreans, he has a proportionately strong need to gain such legitimacy by raising their standards of living (Hong-yung Lee, 2014: 89), this continues to be contradicted by policy objectives and outcomes, quite apart from obviously overstating the role public opinion or popular sentiment is allowed to play in these matters. Otherwise, while nuclear armed status is sustainable, and while life remains good for the elite, short-term exigencies will continue to drive out long-term strategic concerns, and so the case for change, much less reform, remains far less compelling than is often assumed.

These observations apply well to the agriculture sector. In China under Deng Xiaoping, meaningful reform in this sector telegraphed the regime's intention to pursue broader reform and eventually establish a more viable, rational economic structure, and in late June 2012 Kim Jong Un was believed by some to be following a similar path with a series of internal directives subsequently given the title June 28 New Economic Management Measures, or simply the 6.28 Policy, by outside observers. These measures achieved no public status, which in itself is an indication of their limited purpose, and are chiefly known through anecdotal evidence from people affected by them inside the DPRK, or else by aid worker and refugee accounts. From such anecdotes a picture emerged of efforts to reincentivise the farming workforce by stepping back slightly from Kim Il Sung's canonic 1964 Rural Theses. The two major methods applied have been the reducing of the size of the collectivised work teams, by several accounts from 10–25 to 4–6 (Sang-yong Lee, 2015), in order to retain the ideological commitment to collectivity but still seek increased productivity, and reducing the state share of the harvest to 70 per cent of the total. The workforce gets to keep 30 per cent and dispose of it as they wish, presumably through bartering or cash sale, or else as a source of loan collateral, possibly for productivity-enhancing investment. Collective farms were also able to manage their land with more autonomy, including the acceptance of private investment by agricultural entrepreneurs (Ireson, 2012), although this was an unlikely use of serious investment capital in the DPRK today, given the decrepit state of the sector and the investment options available elsewhere.

Opinions on the effect of these measures have naturally ranged from the sceptical (Ireson, 2014; Silberstein 2015a, 2015b) to the enthusiastic (Lankov, 2014),[40] to the euphoric (Hyundai Research Institute),[41] but the anecdotal nature of the evidence, as well as the inherent complexities of agricultural policy-making mean that assessment of policy outcomes is not a straightforward matter. FAO statistics, however, favour a more sober appraisal (see Table 8.3) and provide little evidence to support positive appraisal of the measures, with only marginal progress made on covering shortfalls.

First, one obviously needs to assess such outcomes against the intent and scope of the measures, and here we note that not only were the measures themselves introduced with an excessively modest lack of public proclamation, but also that at the time Kim Jong Un had been in power for just six months and was still nine months away from enunciating his *byungjin* vision. This was scarcely the time for major economic policy-making. Moreover, the measures

Table 8.3 DPRK food production, 2009–15: FAO assessments

Year	Total production	Import requirement	Planned imports	Pledged aid	Uncovered shortfall
2009	3.3	1.8	0.5	0.5	0.8
2010	4.5	0.9	0.3	n/a	0.5
2011	4.7	0.7	0.3	n/a	0.4
2012	4.9	0.5	0.3	n/a	0.2
2013	5.0	0.3	0.3	n/a	0.1
2014	5.9	n/a	n/a	n/a	n/a
2015	5.4	0.7	0.3	n/a	0.4

Sources: various files at www.fao.org

Notes: Denomination = million tonnes; estimated annual demand put at *c*. 5.4–5.5m tonnes

had quite limited objectives and had no intention of threatening the principle of collectivised agriculture. The reduction in the size of work teams seems to be confidently accepted by many observers as incentivising and productivity enhancing, but this is not necessarily so, especially as the smaller the teams the greater the need for support services, which were somehow expected to emerge from a sector which, like the rest of the economy, has been drastically hollowed out. The provision of meaningful technical support in the form of expanded rural extension services appeared to be absent from the policy mix, while a huge negative remained in the form of continuing reliance on the rickety state distribution system for seed, fertiliser and machinery fuel, potentially leaving the smaller teams vulnerable without the resources and flexibility that come with the larger work teams.[42]

Similarly, the 30 per cent crop retention measure has been confidently assessed as an incentive, but while outsiders usually cite this approvingly, they have no means of judging whether it truly represents a positive percentage, other than that it obviously appears to be better than nothing at all. The figure of 30 per cent was obviously not calculated with the welfare of the rural population in mind as an end in itself, but more likely represented an estimate of what was convenient to the government in order to get what it wanted. And, of course, 70 per cent of the crop is still acquired by the state at low, disincentivising prices and against the threat of forced levies.[43] Marketing of the 30 per cent is a further issue, for one must ask from what source would collective farm management access the commercial skills required for the fair marketing and selling their produce on the capitalist jungle of the open market without structures such as marketing cooperatives working on their behalf.

Taking a long-term perspective, the question of just what North Korean farmers themselves would confidently consider an incentive for them to increase production is similarly unclear, for reincentivising North Korean farmers with their set of lifetime experiences would not be an easy matter. While there may well be positive-minded would-be entrepreneurs in the farming communities who are looking for new opportunities to better their lives, far more commonly they are people who since 1945 have been beaten down, starved, repressed, hemmed in and made to feel vulnerable by the successive waves of debilitating policies that stemmed from Kim Il Sung's Rural Theses, and by outright predatory government behaviour. The DPRK's agricultural policy record is, of course, extremely bad, and it is probably a major misreading of rural worker psychology to assume that they would immediately respond positively to any new policy and produce more in the belief that the authorities had now somehow benevolently got it right. More likely reactions would be inertia and confusion, coupled with the assumption that if they produced more, the government would simply seize more in 'loyalty contributions' whenever the perceived need arose, as has been the case since the 1940s. Thus, one cannot simply assert with confidence that the 6.28 Measures in themselves are policies that might swiftly be embraced and be translated into sustained, increased productivity.[44]

Finally, a fundamental point that is usually overlooked is that one can only assess the success or otherwise of agricultural policy over a reasonable period of time. This is underlined by the uneven results since 2012, where the consensus is that the DPRK saw reasonable harvests during 2012–14 and a poor harvest in 2015, followed by serious flooding in the far north in 2016, whereupon the government again appealed for international aid. It is therefore far too premature to attribute the favourable 2012–14 returns to policy changes, as some have, rather than a broader set of causes, especially good weather patterns.[45] Allied to this, it is only when farmers sense that they really do have the sort of basic security that tells them they will continue to keep a reasonable proportion of what they grow that they will think of making productivity-boosting investments in the land, and such investments will obviously take time to flow through the system and bear fruit. And, of course, continuing collectivisation remains a profound disincentive to this ever occurring. In sum, then, it is still premature to proclaim that major change has taken place in agricultural policy and that this has been responsible for rising yields.[46] It appears more likely that the agricultural sector as a whole has received modest inputs but is still highly vulnerable, and that in 2016 most non-elite North Koreans still do not have enough to eat, and so for them 'food self-sufficiency' means access to survival rations.[47]

In the manufacturing sector, on 30 May 2014 the government was rumoured to have undertaken a similar incentivising initiative, usually referred to as the 5.30 Measures, in the state-owned enterprise sector, under which managers appeared to be given an extraordinarily wide latitude in running their businesses, including hiring and firing, wage structuring, raw materials purchasing and product marketing. Again, there was no formal announcement and evidence remained anecdotal, but there appears general agreement that within a matter of months it became clear that only very modest changes would be allowed to occur (Lankov, 2015). As usual, the absence of authoritative detail from the policy architects themselves makes it almost impossible to determine what was intended, whether the measures were intended to achieve a far more limited set of objectives, limited enough as to be almost invisible, or whether they were countermanded for unknown reasons. All that can safely be said is that the DPRK continues to lack a coherent non-military industrial policy, and that sporadic and uncoordinated efforts to encourage market-enhancing practices, such as under the 6.28 and 5.30 Measures, do not in themselves indicate a changing mentality, nor do they herald commitment to economic policy reform. Rather, they are revelatory of the government's fixed intention to maintain its dual structure of a military-dominated state sector supported by controllable marketisation (Song et al., 2016: 228).

The DPRK leadership's reluctance to obstruct the continuing flow-on effects of private economic activity hardly amounts to a reform agenda, and yet the common assumption that the DPRK is close to embracing a China-style opening still regularly surfaces (Lankov, 2014). As we have already observed, this is misplaced, for in terms of history, scale, structure and dominant ideology, the DPRK economy bears little resemblance to the Chinese economy. This means that while the DPRK has accepted a highly circumscribed light industrial-centred free market sector, not only is this very different from the Chinese whole-of-market acceptance of a 'market-oriented socialist economy', as the Chinese themselves describe it, but in conditions of nuclear-armed autarky no pathway exists for the DPRK market sector to access the capital and technology, let alone the export markets needed if it is to develop substantially in an open-ended Chinese direction. Thus, the purpose of such Kim Jong Un-sanctioned initiatives as the 6.28 and 5.30 Measures was to wring whatever can be wrought from the existing system without modifying it.

Finally, this entire process not only continues to be poorly managed by the central government, but it is also actively undermined from the centre in a number of other ways, including a deeply flawed set of state institutions, non-development of a rational banking and financial system,[48] continuing neglect of infrastructure,[49] the undermining of business transaction security through continuing criminalisation of large areas of private economic activity, the high tolerance for institutionalised corruption, the absence of legally defined property rights,[50] incoherent economic planning, absence of human resource planning and, of course, isolation from advanced foreign technology. The market in the DPRK remains a confusing, illogical world where all boundaries – financial, transactional, institutional, personal and legal – remain poorly defined.

Human rights

Like so many social causes and international issues, broader awareness of the extent of human rights abuses in the DPRK has moved to its own timetable, whereby serious abuses were known to have existed practically from the founding of the DPRK, but they lacked human faces and voices, and so monumental suffering continued amid near silence from the international community for decades. This situation gradually began to change during the

1990s with increasing numbers of North Korean refugees able to tell their stories and have these circulated internationally, whereupon a number of human rights groups focusing on the DPRK came into existence. Responding in no small part to pressure from a coalition of more than forty such groups, in January 2013 the United Nations Commissioner for Human Rights, Navi Pillay, called for an international enquiry into human rights offences committed by North Korea, estimating the population of political prison camps at 200,000, where people were subjected to 'torture and other forms of cruel and inhumane treatment, summary executions, rape, slave labor and forms of collective punishment that may amount to crimes against humanity'.[51]

In May 2013, the United Nations Human Rights Council appointed three leading international jurists to conduct a panel of investigation. The 372-page report of the panel, titled *Report of the Commission of Inquiry on Human Rights in the Democratic People's Republic of Korea*, was released in February 2014, and concluded that 'systematic, widespread and gross human rights violations have been, and are being, committed by the Democratic People's Republic of Korea, its institutions and officials' and in many cases these constituted crimes against humanity. It focused not just on the actual coercion and control apparatus, but more broadly on the extent to which such practices were an essential practice of government, which 'dominate every aspect of its citizens' lives and terrorises them from within'. The control of food distribution also figured prominently as a means of political control through 'discriminatory resource allocation that inevitably produces more unnecessary starvation among its citizens'.

Major practices included 'suppressing all political and religious expression that questions the official ideology, and tightly controlling citizens' physical movement and their means of communication with each other and with those in other countries', as well as discrimination on the basis of gender and *songbun* classification with the aim of blunting possible challenges to the political system. The keystone of the system was described as 'the vast political and security apparatus that strategically uses surveillance, coercion, fear and punishment to preclude the expression of any dissent', including the practice of foreign kidnappings which were 'unique in their intensity, scale and nature'. The report noted the decades of neglect that had gone before, and in addition to recommending a programme of reform to the DPRK as a United Nations member, it recommended that China should not engage in forced repatriation and extend normal refugee protections to North Koreans on its soil. To the international community, it further recommended that the issue should be referred to the International Criminal Court and that targeted sanctions be adopted against those most involved in these practices.

Upon its publication, the report achieved wide publicity and performed a valuable service in drawing attention to these abuses in such detailed and authoritative fashion, but to date this has been its only major achievement, for the path to the ICC lies through the UN Security Council, where it is stymied by a foreshadowed Chinese veto. In late 2016, Stephan Haggard was still referring to 'the ongoing international puzzlement about how to implement the Commission of Inquiry findings' and it would take a major and unforeseeable turn of events for the tormenters to ever have to face their victims.[52] Meanwhile, though, with obvious exceptions it is now a firm agenda item for almost all external parties in negotiations of any substance with the DPRK.

Foreign relations

By the time the Six Party Talks process broke down in April 2009, and probably for quite a while before this, the growing revelation of how little actual leverage the DPRK's adversaries possessed gradually had begun to hit home. The US tried engagement during the Clinton administration and confrontation during the Bush administration, and both policies still have their partisans, but neither had sufficient credibility to become the cornerstone of a non-partisan, persevering policy towards the North. Thus, after 2008 the US retreated to the inert diplomacy of the Obama administration's 'strategic patience' option of applying pressure to the DPRK chiefly through sanctions, but otherwise 'watching, waiting, and anticipating a collapse of North Korea' (Choi Jong-Kun, 2015: 57).[53] It is an undignified policy that goes against the grain of many US beliefs about its reach and power, and it surely faces attempts at modification at some stage under the Trump administration. The belief that the DPRK is still somehow close to collapse is especially an invitation for a more interventionist strategy, but the Six Party Talks trajectory suggests that this strategy is counter-productive as it leads to greater US isolation among the regional stakeholders.[54]

All eyes understandably remain focused on China as the neighbour with both the means and motivation to bring about regime modification in the DPRK. Here there is a certain ebb and flow effect at work in Chinese policy. During the early years of the Kim Jong Un accession relations remained tense, primarily over increased Chinese support for UNSC-mandated sanctions (Cathcart and Madden, 2012), but then rising China–US tensions, focused primarily on the South China Sea, but also on moves to deploy the THAAD missile defence system in the ROK, have caused a perceptible Chinese pull-back, and so currently the DPRK is benefiting from more benign Chinese policy settings. Clearly, the mental picture China still draws is of itself as a role-model and of the DPRK evolving into a 'Little China', sharing similar economic, political and strategic goals of denuclearised regional harmony, its economy more integrated into the region and especially into the economy of China's northeastern provinces. But for now it appears to have lost interest in proactively pursuing this agenda.

Relations with the ROK also reflected the DPRK's growing sense of security, for after the final demise of the Sunshine Policy in 2008, contact has been minimal. Initially, the Kaesong Industrial Zone continued to function as practically the only area of contact between the two states, while the major dynamic continued to be the steady disenchantment of ROK public opinion towards the North.[55] Lee Myung-bak's 'Vision 3000: Denuclearization, Openness' policy was peremptorily brushed aside by the North for reasons apparent in its title,[56] and quite apart from Lee's relinking of security and humanitarian issues to economic cooperation, his almost immediate slide in ROK public opinion polls to the 20–30 per cent range by May 2008 due to much broader issues gave the North no incentive to bolster his standing by dealing with him. Thus, the Lee administration became marked by continuing DPRK pressure on the ROK over Kaesong Industrial Zone issues, the closure of the Mount Kumgang operation after the shooting death of a tourist in July 2008, the general DPRK lockdown policy after Kim Jong Il's stroke in August 2008, the final breakdown of the Six Party Talks in April 2009, on-going missile tests and the DPRK's second nuclear test in May 2009, the sinking of the ROK corvette *Cheonan* in March 2010 and the Yeongpyeong-do shelling in November 2010.

Lee's successor Park Geun-hye took office in February 2013 and, as detailed earlier, was subject to an immediate and unprecedented show of military pressure. Under such conditions, there was no immediate scope for Park to place her own policy on the table, and so it was a further year before she announced her hallmark 'Trustpolitik' policy in March 2014. Not surprisingly, there was nothing new in this policy, which essentially returned to the pre-Sunshine Policy emphasis on confidence-building measures, especially in the economic sphere where it emphasised the smooth operation of the KIZ and proposed talks to restart the Kumgang tourist operation. In short, it offered nothing that Pyongyang could use. Finally, in February 2016, a further combination of DPRK nuclear and missile testing induced the ROK to take what was essentially the only retaliatory step left to it by shutting down the KIZ indefinitely on the grounds that the operation enabled the transfer of over $100 million annually into DPRK hands, and so indirectly supported the country's nuclear programme. Two-way trade, which as late as 2008 stood at $1.8 billion, or 32.2 per cent of the DPRK total foreign trade (Lim Kang-taeg, 2009:194), has shrunk to insignificance with the closure of the KIZ and one therefore looks forward to the advent of new leadership in the ROK as the next possible time for change. Otherwise, barring occasional tactical demarches, there is no other dynamic that seems likely to disturb the current indefinite freeze.

What, then, is the DPRK's strategy? Specialists tend to agree that the DPRK is now free to progress its nuclear weapons manufacture and delivery systems without fear of foreign military action and is constrained only by the limits of its own resources. We have therefore moved into a new phase in which most parties accept that it is no longer realistic to proactively seek the denuclearisation of the North, and so key international concerns revolve instead around assessing the DPRK's basic strategy, its coercive intent, its internal control mechanisms, its international proliferation potential and, of course, the extent to which the international system can continue to live with the nuclear-capable North. As usual, the DPRK offers little basic information on these issues, and so external commentary is more than usually speculative.[57] Notwithstanding images of erratic behaviour, though, the DPRK has developed and pursued a survival strategy with intense fixity of purpose over a period of some thirty-five years. It has forced its people to make enormous sacrifices, its tactics have evolved, it has learned a good deal about the international politics of nuclear weapons and it still has a long way to go. And while it would be a mistake to impute to Pyongyang any higher, more consistent levels of logical thinking on the management of this most illogical of weapons than has often been shown by other nuclear powers, as near as can be determined from the record, the DPRK broadly seeks the strongest possible deterrent arsenal to assure survival on its own terms, and the strongest possible retaliatory arsenal should it deem this survival to be directly threatened. Beyond these broad aims, though, considerable obscurity surrounds its strategic intentions and capabilities, raising unanswerable questions about the sophistication of its support capabilities, especially command and control mechanisms. The possibility of proliferation under the right conditions cannot be ruled out since the DPRK has already engaged in nuclear weapons technology cooperation with Iran and Syria. Meanwhile, we face the likelihood of the parallel development of more sophisticated weapons technologies, including miniaturisation, and mobile, silo and submarine launching platforms along with command and control capabilities of increasing sophistication.

Concluding remarks

How and to what extent has the DPRK changed so far under Kim Jong Un? When Kim became leader in 2011, his age drew widespread comment, mainly in the negative context of inexperience and perhaps a certain immaturity, and people believed his shortcomings would soon be exposed in the ruthless world of the DPRK politics. However, there have been other examples of young leaders in the modern world who have lasted the distance,[58] while immaturity, not to mention outright folly in office, is by no means the exclusive province of the young. Meanwhile, focusing on this side issue distracts from recognition of more important regime characteristics. Chief among these are a cohesive elite representing the dregs of a once-powerful ideological vision, an economy that continues to generate enough wealth for the government to operate and the continuing operation of a nonpareil coercion and control system, which ensures that this elite can continue, seemingly indefinitely, to be proofed against revolt or collapse, and also proofed against the unwanted influence of authentic modernity. The Korean Workers' Party has re-emerged, a greater civilian presence in external economic transactions has been noticed, the theatrics of the regime, most notably the nature of the public image Kim Jong Un seeks to project appears more civilian and quality-of-life oriented, but the backbone to the system remains military security.

Undergirding these hallmarks is *son'gun*, which retains the status given to it by Kim Jong Il as the paramount framework for state policy. In announcing his *byungjin* framework in March 2013, Kim Jong Un did not seek to bury *son'gun*, but in fact praised it as standing policy and repeated such praise at the Seventh KWP Congress in May 2016, indicating no current intention to roll it back. Kim has largely replaced the senior military hold-overs from the Kim Jong Il era who were its specific architects and servants, but their successors have given every outward sign that they support *son'gun*, and of course as military men they have every incentive to do so. Likewise, Kim does not yet appear to have made significant inroads in reasserting control over military-generated and controlled revenue. The external perspective suggests that little change has been made to the country's multi-headed economic structure in operation since in the 1990s, which in turn suggests that the military continues to operate as an almost separate economy. *Son'gun* also mandates the enforcement of the dour militarism that has characterised DPRK society since the 1960s, but while Kim has not embraced this, he has not rolled it back very far either. Many of his theatrics, including his beaming public persona and promotion of pet leisure projects such as the Munsu Wading Pool and the Masikryong Ski Resort near Wonsan, promote the sense that life has become better and gayer, as indeed it has for the privileged few, but most of this is part of the so-called Pyongyang Illusion and does not extend very far into life beyond foreign gaze. Fundamentally, however, *son'gun* buttresses the pursuit of the basic strategy of nuclear-backed isolation, and here Kim continues to operate in a manner that is essentially indistinguishable from his father's and grandfather's policies. Whether Kim wants to or is capable enough to seek change remains to be seen, but the evidence to date is that from the start he has sought to utilise *son'gun*, not roll it back, let alone institute significant reform.

Thus, very little has changed in DPRK politics, foreign relations or economic policy under Kim Jong Un. With the passage of time, the type of private economic activity that began to be tolerated fully fifteen years or so before he came to the leadership has become an increasingly accepted part of daily life and has grown in volume and sophistication, but one can only afford Kim negative credit for this in that he has not acted to repress it. He has basically accepted what his father accepted after the failed 2009 currency conversion, and there has been no repeat of his father's campaign of applying relentless constricting pressure on private market activity. But this market has not been allowed any formal role in what passes for the state economic planning process, nor has it been allowed to expand beyond its role of providing the light industry, food, consumer goods and miscellaneous services that for decades the government failed to provide, and so it constitutes no significant engine of growth that can prevent the DPRK from continuing to fall rapidly behind its neighbours. Moreover, the choicest pickings have been reserved for the elite, for in ways both great and small, they are the only ones with the full range and means to navigate their way through the bureaucratic maze and deliver for their clients.[59] The economy thus remains in an invidious hybrid state where change has come, but reform hasn't.

Widely differing assessments of the Kim Jong Un administration continue to characterise external commentary. The world being what it is, what matters most to it is the status and the strategic intention of the DPRK with its new defence assets, and here among the more informed, long-term observers one finds a typical spectrum, from those who find Kim more hawkish than his father (Toloraya, 2016), to more dovish outlooks, to the view taken here that there is strong continuity with past policies and micro-adjustment to an ever-evolving strategic situation. Such views all look at the same evidence but draw different conclusions for different reasons. Hence, the March–April 2013 war scare was either a quintessential display of 'irrational' DPRK threatening behaviour or else a response to perceived threat, or else a rationally designed war game designed to unnerve the incoming ROK president and also to test out the DPRK's changing command structure. To the rather simplistic question 'What do they really want?' we may well respond that the DPRK authorities appear to be quite willing to see the existing regional security framework overturned and that a heavy weight of past policy presses in on them to the extent that they seem unable to conceptualise alternatives. This in turn suggests that under Kim Jong Un the elite has no interest in altering the country's status as a rogue state dedicated to achieving the indefinite defence of their way of life.

Notes

1 For a more detailed examination of this system as it operated in the late Kim Jong Il era, see Kim Kap-sik (2008) and especially Gause (2015: 119–45).
2 In a complementary move two days later at the 5th Session of the 12th Supreme People's Assembly, Kim became First Chairman of the National Defence Commission with his father given the title of Eternal NDC Chairman. The SPA also ratified a number of changes to the 2009 Constitution in order to add laudatory references to Kim Jong Il and to define the DPRK as a nuclear-armed state. For details and commentary, see Green (2012a).
3 Ch'oe Yong-hae was appointed to the Presidium, Kim Chong-gak, Chang Song-t'aek, Pak To-jun, Hyon Ch'ol-hae, Kim Won-hong and Yi Myong-su to full Politburo membership, and Kwak Pom-gi, O Kuk-ryol, No Tu-ch'ol, Yi Pyong-sam and Cho Yon-chun to Candidate status. This represented a mixture of people on their way up and people who proved to be on their way out. In the absence of a full listing in the DPRK media, we can only speculate on removals, which appeared to have included the aged Chon Pyong-ho to honourable retirement, Kim Nak-hui and Yi T'ae-nam, who were probably Candidate members ex officio while serving as Vice Premiers, and U Tong-chuk, head of the State Security Department, who thus became the first of a series of Kim Jong Il hold-over military-security cadres to suffer significant demotion.
4 With the DPRK's Marxist–Leninist age now a distant memory, the Kim family were now 'the peerlessly great persons of Mt. Paektu', while in ideology Kim Jong Il was given implied equal status with his father. Also notable was that Kim Jong Un had showed no signs of distancing himself from *son'gun*. The relevant media commentary read as follows: 'His election as first secretary of the [KWP] is an expression of absolute support for and trust in the supreme commander of the Korean People's Army by all party members, servicepersons and other people.

He has developed the revolutionary idea of the peerlessly great persons of Mt. Paektu to glorify it as Kimilsungism-Kimjongilism with his gifted wisdom and through energetic ideological and theoretical activities and put forth unique ideas and theories of the revolution and construction and all other fields including politics, military affairs, economy and culture and successfully materialised them, thus making outstanding contributions to the Juche-based army building through his energetic Songun leadership.' (www.kcna.co.jp, 11 April 2012) [italics added]

5 Sometimes colourfully but misleadingly referred to as the Gang of Seven. They did not work as a 'gang' and would not have survived for very long if they had ever attempted to constitute a locus of power away from the *suryong*. At this point it is worth noting that by the late Kim Jong Il era, the definition of a military or security cadre had become increasingly blurred, as is shown, for example, by the awarding of what was essentially the courtesy rank of General to Chang Song-t'aek and Kim Kyong-hui. Therefore, in referring to cadres as 'military' or 'security' personnel, this is in the knowledge that it is often difficult to capture precisely what mix of civilian, career military and career internal security is involved in the résumés of the individuals concerned. Ch'oe Yong-hae is especially a case in point, for while his positions under Kim Jong Un placed him as head of the KPAF General Political Bureau, until 2010 his career had been in the civilian sector.

6 Gause (2015: 24–37) relates that Kim Yong-ch'un was appointed to a distinctly lesser post heading the KWP Department for Civil Defense, while Kim Chong-gak was appointed President of Kim Il-sung Military University. We may add that, unlike Ch'oe T'ae-bok and Kim Ki-nam, neither retained Politburo rankings at the Seventh KWP Congress, but both were named to Yi Ul-sol's funeral committee in 2015, a mark of respect.

7 See Gause (2015: 27–8). In Yi's case, there was no question of honourable retirement, probably because he had been too powerful. Yi was dismissed from all positions, has not re-emerged and has either been executed or else is in some form of rigorous, permanent confinement. There appear to have been policy issues involved, with Yi allegedly critical of the economic measures Kim is believed to have promulgated on 28 June 2012, especially as they related to the curtailing of the military's hard currency transaction conduits, but economic policy issues in themselves would not have been sufficient to secure his purging. More basically, Yi had been close to Kim Jong Il for quite a few years and was reportedly also close to Chang Song-t'aek – he would have had to have been – and now he was witnessing discomforting change. It would not have taken much for Kim to reach the conclusion that as his father's hold-over, Yi would prove to be more hindrance than help in the days ahead. Also see Gause (2015: 29) for an interesting, ROK-sourced detailed account of a showdown of sorts at the 15 July 2015 Politburo meeting at which Yi was purged. It should be viewed with circumspection since DPRK cadres are certainly not known for leaking such proceedings, especially in such detail. It should also be noted for the record that the story arrived in the South circuitously via a refugee group, NK Intellectuals Solidarity.

8 Imaginative touches, such as reporting the execution of former Chief of General Staff and Minister for the KPAF Hyon Yong-ch'ol in 2015 by anti-aircraft fire usually have little or no foundation in fact, but are repeatedly and enthusiastically passed on, especially since the DPRK, no doubt bemused, to the extent they could even care, has no interest in refuting such stories. See, for example, 'North Korea defence chief reportedly executed with anti-aircraft gun' at: www.theguardian.com/world/2015/may/13/north-korean-defence-minister-executed-by-anti-aircaft-gun-report, accessed July 2016. Moreover, there are cases where senior cadres have been pronounced purged on the basis of their absence from public ceremonies, only for them to subsequently reappear, seemingly none the worse for their experiences, as was the case with Yi Yong-gil, who somehow survived ROK

reports of his execution in February 2016. Since there appears to be no bottom to the market for such stories, the supreme irony is that it seems best to rely on the DPRK media for accurate, if sparse, information on this topic.

9   Green (2012b) carries the following quote from Kim: 'We do not need people who are not devoted to the Party and Suryeong, no matter how militaristic their disposition or excellent their tactical ability . . . Loyalty to Party and Suryeong are the very mark of an armed revolutionary. . . Historical experience has shown us that soldiers who are not devoted to the Party and Suryeong do not accomplish their mission as the warriors of a revolutionary army, and then fall as traitors to the revolution later on.'

10 The Ministry for the KPAF is the point at which the KPAF intersects administratively with the government and politically with the Party, and analogies are sometimes made with Ministries of Defence in other countries. It functions as an umbrella body for all operational and administrative functions. The General Staff is subordinate to the Ministry, and is the senior body responsible for all planning and operations work. The General Political Bureau is charged with ensuring the political and ideological reliability of the DPRK's armed forces, and while it is also in theory subordinate to the Ministry, in practice it operates separately with its own chain of command. For more detailed descriptions of these three positions, see Bermudez (2001: 25–34). For more up-to-date information, see Gause (2015).

11 For a succinct summary of what the US and ROK believe they know about the DPRK's substantial CBW assets, see Chanlett et al. (2016: 13) and its citations. For a recent US assessment of the DPRK's conventional assets, see the US Department of Defense report *Military and Security Developments Involving the Democratic People's Republic of Korea 2015*, especially pp.9–13.

12 We should note in passing Mansourov (2012a) and its detailed analysis of events during 2012, in which he assesses that Chang Song-t'aek was behind the military shake-up, replacing those dismissed with his own people in an endeavour to strengthen his power base. Actually, we don't know who was guiding Kim Jong Un's hand at this juncture, but apart from his closest staff advisers, in view of their pedigree and their continuing tenure in the inner circles of the Kim Jong Un court, it is more likely to have been a combination of Ch'oe Yong-hae and O Guk-ryol. If it had been Chang, the moves should have strengthened his position, whereas in fact they failed to prevent seemingly inexorable progress towards his purge, presciently predicted in Mansourov (2012b). Moreover, this analysis does not explain why putative Chang-engineered replacements, including Ch'oe Yong-hae and Hyon Yong-ch'ol, retained their status after Chang's demise.

13 The concept of a 'number two' makes no sense under the *suryong* system. However, it is not necessary to endorse such assessments to find them reasonably accurate in general terms – that is, that he stood at the very pinnacle of the DPRK power structure.

14 Gause (2015: 28) cites ROK intelligence sources for a story that U Tong-ch'uk's removal was engineered by Kim's aunt and regent Kim Kyong-hui, who somehow had discovered that on Kim Jong Il's orders U had been compiling secret dossiers on potential opponents of the Kim Jong Un succession. As usual, we can accord little or no credibility to this story as it stands since it claims knowledge gleaned from the innermost precincts of power in Pyongyang and is otherwise unsupported, but at the very least it is instructive as a reflection of why people fear the keepers of the secrets.

15 See 'Exclusive: Jang Song-thaek was executed following his letter to Chinese leadership', *New Focus*, 30 June 2014, at: http://newfocusintl.com/exclusive-jang-song-thaek-executed-followinghis-letter-chinese-leadership/ (accessed December 2016).

16 Chang was, of course, a most unlikely agent of reform, and we have no idea even as to whether what he had in mind could have been called 'reform' or a larger, more streamlined version of the prevailing system. Moreover, as we have seen, in 2004 he had crossed swords with the Cabinet bureaucracy, so it would not have made sense for him to seek to empower it now. One upshot worth noting in passing is that with Chang's demise economic relations with China entered an uncertain phase. The major monuments to this uncertainty include the still-born Hwanggump'yong-Wihwa Island SEZ on the Yalu, and the new road bridge across the Yalu at Dandong that was still unconnected on the DPRK side at the time of writing. I am grateful to Chris Green for helping me to connect the dots regarding the very considerable scale of Chang's Chinese connections and the consequences of his downfall.

17 Summed up in 'Signs of Change in Kim Jong-un's New Year's Speech', *Choson Ilbo,* 2 January 2013. For a contrasting, somewhat prescient analysis, see Jang Jin Song (2013), who concluded that confrontatory behaviour was imminent.

18 The missile test was the fourth attempt to launch a multi-stage rocket and appears to have been more successful than the previous three attempts in 1998, 2009 and April 2012, the latter timed to mark the one hundredth anniversary of the birth of Kim Il Sung.

19 See KCNA, 'DPRK Refutes UNSC's "Resolution" Pulling up DPRK over Its Satellite Launch,' 23 January 2013, at: http://webarchive.ssrc.org/NK/NKCHRON%202013.pdf (accessed October 2016).

20 See KCNA, 'Second Korean War Is Unavoidable: DPRK FM Spokesman,' March 7, 2013, ibid.

21 KCNA, '*Rodong Sinmun* on Halt to Activities of Panmunjom Mission of KPA', 13 March 2013, ibid.

22 Again, this was consistent with its earlier statement that 'It is necessary to eliminate everything lying in the way of starting a just war, revolutionary war to counter a war of aggression.' See ibid.

23 For an account of the incident leading up to the release of the fishermen, see 'North Korea Seized Chinese Boat', *The New York Times*, 19 May 2013, at: www.nytimes.com/2013/05/20/world/asia/north-korea-seized-chinese-fishing-boat.html?_r=0 (accessed September 2016). The DPRK was at pains to make its point and move on before Ch'oe Yong-hae arrived in Beijing on an official visit as Kim Jong Un's envoy on 22 May. The entire incident, of course, indicates the singular atmospherics in which the DPRK often elects to conduct its diplomacy.

24 The two meetings otherwise dealt with routine matters and appointments, including the ex officio promotion to full Politburo status of the new Premier Pak Pong-ju, the appointment of now-prominent military leaders Hyon Yong-ch'ol, Kim Kyok-sik and Ch'oe Pu-il as alternate members. The SPA meeting removed two demoted military leaders, Yi Myong-su and Kim Chong-gak from the NDC.

25 See Gause (2015: 35–36) for DPRK media references signalling these changes.

26 Gause (2015: 36) speculates that Hyon was a 'placeholder' until Kim felt ready and able to appoint Kim Kyok-sik as his preferred Chief of General Staff, but the timing suggests that Hyon's actual performance under war-game conditions was also a factor. Three months later, however, Kim Jong Un changed his mind and replaced Kim with Yi Yong-gil, who was fourteen years Kim Kyok-sik's junior and who had performed a senior role during the March/April 'crisis', during which corps commanders reported to him and he reported directly to the Chief of General Staff. The change-over appears to have been effected in an orderly manner through an August meeting of the Party's Central Military Committee, and health may have been a factor as Kim, 75 at this time, died of natural causes two years later. Like Ch'oe Yong-hae, Yi Yong-gil thus became a stable fixture at the very top

of the KPAF command structure and remains so at the time of writing, having meanwhile survived erroneous ROK reports of his purging in February 2016.

27 One characteristic that still eludes satisfactory explanation, but which does not appear to have had much impact on the larger web of events, is the pattern of minor rank promotions and demotions among the senior leadership, gleaned from the study of their uniforms on public occasions. See Gause (2015: 31) for details during 2012–13.

28 A crucial question for assessing the state of play between Kim and the military is the extent to which he has been able to roll back the military's domination of foreign currency transactions, but hard information is difficult to come by. Gause cites defector accounts to the effect that Kim has strengthened his control, effecting 'a restructuring of the lines of control over hard currency operations' (Gause, 2014: 165). If this is so, one would have expected greater signs of internal upheaval, for this is a high-stakes contest, but when one finishes examining the personnel movements in senior military ranks they seem rather less dramatic than often portrayed. And most significantly, if the military has, in fact, seriously ceded some of its prerogatives in this area, then as Haggard *et al.* (2014: 800) note, there does not appear to have been any related empowerment of civilian economic specialist cadres at senior levels of the Party or government.

29 For a translation of the speech, see www.ncnk.org/resources/news-items/kim-jong-uns-speeches-and-public-statements-1/KJU_CentralCommittee_KWP.pdf. For an accompanying commentary, see KCNA, 'Report on Plenary Meeting of WPK Central Committee', March 31 2013, http://webarchive.ssrc.org/NK/NKCHRON%202013.pdf (accessed October 2016).

30 The relevant portion of the speech read as follows: 'The strategic line on carrying out the economic construction and the building of nuclear armed forces simultaneously represents a succession to, and in-depth development of, the line of simultaneously developing economy and national defense, which was set forth by the great leader [Kim Il Sung] and thoroughly embodied by the great general [Kim Jong Il]. *At the fifth plenary meeting of the fourth party CC in December 1962, the great leader set forth the line on simultaneously carrying out the economic construction and national defense building, the first of its kind in history, and presented the revolutionary slogan called, A gun in one hand, and a sickle and hammer in the other!* It is because the leader clarified the simultaneous line and provided national defense capabilities for self-defense, along with the self-supporting national economy, that we were able to firmly defend the gains of the revolution without wavering in the face of the great upheaval of socialism collapsing in various countries.' [Italics added]

31 Without being too semantic, one might note that the catchphrase was '*byungjin*' and not '*jinbyung*', and that this was an accurate summation of Kim's priorities. The historically minded might be aware that even Meiji Japan, with its well-developed sense of external threat and militarist tendencies, opted to place the military second in its 'rich nation-strong military (*fukoku-kyohei*)' aspirational slogan.

32 'The great general achieved the great cause of nuclear weapons possession while leading the fierce anti-US nuclear war of confrontation to consecutive victories *with the outstanding military-first politics*, and provided a firm foundation for protecting the socialism of chuch'e and making a leap to the construction of a powerful state.' (Kim, 2013 [italics added]). Available at: www.ncnk.org/resources/news-items/kim-jong-uns-speeches-and-public-statements-1/KJU_CentralCommittee_KWP.pdf (accessed September 2016).

33 The serious intent of the nuclear and long-range missile aspects were emphasised at the SPA session on 1 April with a detailed ten-point declaration 'On consolidating North Korea's nuclear power status for self-defense' and the passing of laws establishing a National Space Development Bureau. For analysis, see Cheon Seong-whun (2013).

34 As had occurred when then-premier Yon Hyong-muk was appointed to the NDC in 1998. In passing, we may note that the ROK media among others quickly fastened on to Pak as 'a symbol of economic reform', again without supporting evidence and with reckless disregard for Pak's political health. See *Leadership shake-up adds to signs of change in N.K.* at: www.koreaherald.com/view.php?ud= 20120822000901 (accessed September 2016). As far as can be ascertained, Pak has never expressed any public opinions on the issue of economic reform, and if anything, the fact that his previous term as premier (2003–7) coincided with a steady tightening of regime control over private economic activity does not suggest reformist tendencies.
35 The Bank of Korea guesstimates annual GDP growth figures for 2007–15 as follows:

2007	2008	2009	2010	2011	2012	2013	2014	2015
–1.2	3.1	–0.9	–0.5	0.8	1.3	1.1	1.0	–1.1

Source: www.nkeconwatch.com/nk-uploads/GDP_of_North_Korea_in_2015_ff.pdf (accessed August 2016).

Having quite sensibly earlier concluded, 'Don't trust any figure relating to the North Korean economy that comes with a decimal point attached' (Noland, 2014), Noland (2015) comments in respect of the BOK's 2014 figures that, 'Given the anecdotal accounts of growing prosperity in Pyongyang and some other cities, the skepticism about the BOK's estimate is understandable and indeed, I suspect properly assessed the North Korean economy is growing faster – possibly much faster – than the BOK allows'. Lankov (2016) reaches a similar conclusion. It should be added that they do not reach this conclusion through detailed, empirical research but, as we have intimated, this may not necessarily be a bad thing. The Hyundai figure is cited at: www.economist.com/news/asia/21645252-tantalising-signs-change-are-emerging-whether-they-signal-more-profound-shifts-less (accessed November 2016). It is hard to avoid surmising that the considerably higher Hyundai figure reflects its desire to be positive, given its active business strategy towards the North.

36 The information in this section is drawn chiefly from Frank (2015) and IFES NK Brief No. 16–07–22.
37 A median figure would place illicit exports at *c.* 10 per cent of total exports (Noland, 2013), which means *c.* $300 million for 2014. However, we also need to factor in the increasing sophistication and hence undetectability of such transactions.
38 For details on the DPRK's foreign labour, see Chanlett-Avery *et al.* (2016).
39 For a detailed description of the intense and manifold light industrial activities around Dandong, see 'North Korea's Growing Economy – and America's Misconceptions About It', *Washington Post*, 13 March 2015.
40 Ireson's examination of the initial phase of implementation found evidence that the policy was 'confusing, internally inconsistent, applied in only a few test areas, and mostly applied half-heartedly. . . the conflict between economic efficiency and ideological control was resolved in favor of ideology, at the expense of any meaningful policy change' (Ireson, 2014). On the other hand, Lankov (2014) believed that 'while on paper, they did not look that ground-breaking, they represent a sweeping reform of agricultural management in the North'.
41 'Thanks to better harvests, the North Korean economy could grow by 7.5% this year, compared with annual growth of little more than 1% for a decade, reckons the Hyundai Research Institute, a think-tank in Seoul, the capital of South Korea. Asia's basket case could prove to be its fastest-growing economy.' See 'Spring release', *The Economist*, 28 February 2015.

In rather painful counterpart to such ebullience, a 2015 report by the World Food Program assessed that: 'more than 70 percent of the population in [the DPRK] is food insecure, with many people suffering from chronic malnutrition, from lack of essential proteins, fats, vitamins and minerals. This is particularly problematic for young children, pregnant women and nursing mothers, since good nutrition is crucial during the first 1,000 days of life. Diets are worse in towns and cities, where many rely on rural relatives, improvised "kitchen gardens" or market activities to supplement their PDS rations. In 2015, a WFP assessment indicated that stunting levels among children under five in WFP-assisted nurseries were moderate to high, with one in four children affected – a medium-to-high public health concern. Anaemia is widespread among young children and women of reproductive age; acute malnutrition, or wasting, affects four percent of children.' (www.wfp.org/countries/korea-democratic-peoples-republic, accessed November 2016)

42 And on this point the DPRK media itself has continued to point out the virtues of the larger work teams, the essential argument being that larger work teams enable a more even, diverse distribution of technical expertise throughout the collective. In this view, smaller work teams are inefficient and skill-impoverished. Whether so or not, the major point at issue here is that smaller work teams are still viewed as teams within the broader lens of traditional ideological commitment to collectivisation, not as a step on the way to privatisation. See IFES Brief 15–07–15 *North Korea Seeks Supplementary Measures for the Field Responsibility System* for quote from *Rodong Shinmun*, 10 July 2015.

43 For more information on these factors, see Ireson (2013). Meanwhile, the practice of passing any and all burdens down the line to the doorstep of the farmer was still evident in December 2015. See 'North Korean Authorities Fail Again to Distribute Crops Promised to Farmers' at: www.rfa.org/english/news/korea/crops-12212015150653.html (accessed September 2016).

44 One of the more compelling pieces of evidence for the limited effect of the 6.28 Measures actually comes from the FAO, which found no evidence of changes in the incentive regime for farmers a year after their introduction (Ireson, 2013). In its report *The State of Food Insecurity in the World for 2015* (p.15) it further noted: 'The only major exception to overall favourable progress in the [East Asian] region is the Democratic People's Republic of Korea, which is burdened by continuously high levels of undernourishment and shows little prospect of addressing its problems any time soon.' See: www.fao.org/3/a-i4646e.pdf (accessed January 2017).

45 Even so, reflecting the DPRK's standard man-is-the-master outlook, in 2015 the director of the Agricultural Research Institute of the Academy of Agricultural Sciences of the DPRK was quick to affirm the success of the new policy. In 2015, he was quoted in the pro-DPRK Japanese weekly *Choson Sinbo* as saying 'The effectiveness of field management system (*pojon*) from cooperative farm production unit system (*bunjo*) is noticeable and succeeded in increasing grain production despite the adverse weather conditions.' See *Despite Drought Last Year, Food Production Increased Due to Field Responsibility System*, available at: http://ifes.kyungnam.ac.kr/eng/FRM/FRM_0101V.aspx?code=FRM150710_0001(accessed January 2017).

46 For a useful commentary on how the DPRK agricultural situation has played out from the 6.28 measures to early 2016, see Noland (2016).

47 Of course, the picture is not uniformly bleak. It is helpful, though, to focus not so much on the alleged transformative powers of central government policy settings, but on modest, incremental inputs centring on technology that does not confront ideology. Here we find that improved strains have boosted rice yields, diminishing returns due to land impoverishment have been staunched by reductions in inappropriate winter barley planting in the southern regions, and there has perforce been less use of debilitating chemical fertiliser and more use of organic

fertiliser (Ireson, 2015, 2016). There are further potential small-scale gains to be had as these practices continue and spread.
48 According to one close observer, 'North Korea's banks are mere veneers. This hasn't always been so; up until the early 90s, North Koreans used them to deposit and withdraw their savings. The banks are desolate now; some banks in rural provinces go days without having even one visitor.' For more in this vein in an article dated October 2016, see http://newfocusintl.com/blackmarket-methods-investment-north-korea/ (accessed November 2016).
49 Although the nationwide mobile phone network appears to be a significant exception to this.
50 This requires qualification. The growing sense of security in the informal markets has led to the growth of petty forms of status quo recognition of property rights, such as with the privatisation of small areas of land for the purpose of kitchen gardens. In addition, significant mining and fishing operations also appear to operate with some form of tacit security afforded their assets, deriving in the long run from important patron–client relationship with high officials. In 2016, some limited forms of legal transfer appear to have been enacted – see: http://newfocusintl.com/exclusive-private-ownership-land-now-legal-north-korea/ (accessed December 2016). However, the ability of owners to enforce their rights through the legal system is probably still a long way off since the government is apparently aiming to perpetuate the denial of most types of formal property rights. The government remains the predator in this area, with power wielders able to seize assets at will, while bureaucratic facilitation of the technically illegal transfer of property rights remains an important source of corrupt money.
51 U.N. official urges scrutiny of North Korea, *New York Times*, 15 January 2013, available at: http://webarchive.ssrc.org/NK/NKCHRON%202013.pdf, accessed October 2016.
52 The literature on this topic is broad and diverse, ranging from scholarly works to first-accounts. Challenges to the authenticity of some of the latter periodically become news stories, and it seems clear that in some individual cases such challenges are warranted. In addition to the UN Report, useful sources for on-going up-to-date information include the Committee for Human Rights in North Korea (www.hrnk.org) and its publications, especially Hawk (2012), and the publications of the United Nations Human Rights Council, especially the UN General Assembly, Report of the Working Group on the Universal Periodic Review: DPRK, A/HRC/27/10/Add.1., 12 September 2014, which details the DPRK's on-going dealings with the UN on human rights issues and their initial reaction to the Report. Also see Cohen (2017) for a useful analysis of the state of play as of late 2016.
53 The only proactive move during this period came on 29 February 2012 when the US and DPRK agreed to a nuclear test moratorium in exchange for food aid. The deal quickly lapsed with a further DPRK missile test two months later.
54 Again, see Choi Jong-Kun (2015: 59–62) for a survey of US collapsist sentiment from the 1990s almost to the present. Choi further argues that 'strategic patience has deteriorated the quality of information on North Korea's nuclear programme and Pyongyang's intention on the nuclear endgame promotes', because it favours policy thinking on ways and means of moving the DPRK towards compliance at the expense of broader strategic thinking. Former CIA Director Leon Panetta's dismissive comment in his memoirs that 'the only three presidents [North Korea] has known have been father, son and grandson, each more eccentric than the last' (Panetta, 2014: 275) gives some idea of the need for such thinking.
55 By June 2009, only 22 per cent believed that the DPRK was a trustworthy negotiation partner, compared with 52 per cent after the June 2000 inter-Korean summit (Oh and Hassig, 2010: 94).

56 For an explication of this comprehensive policy which proposed to raise DPRK per capita income to $3,000 per annum through economic engagement, but which was conditional on resolution of the nuclear issue, see Suh Jae-jean (2009).
57 Summed up by Narang (2015:1): 'almost nothing is known about North Korea's nuclear arsenal or the doctrine by which those weapons might be employed'. Especially useful commentary may be found in the US–Korea Institute at SAIS North Korea Nuclear Futures series of commentaries, especially Shane Smith (2015) and David Albright (2015).
58 In the contemporary world, Cambodian Prime Minister Hun Sen, 32 when he assumed office 31 years ago in 1985, and Democratic Republic of the Congo President Joseph Kabila, 30 when he succeeded his assassinated father in 2001, come to mind as two examples of young leaders who made their way in comparably ruthless political worlds.
59 Green (2012c) provides an interesting example of how the average entrepreneur is stymied in this fashion by following the process of obtaining a mobile phone in the North. He concludes that the degree of investment in time and money needed in order to acquire such a basic tool of business would exclude many average market players. What operates even at this level would, of course, operate all the more so at higher levels of market activity.

References

Albright, David (2015) Future directions in the DPRK's nuclear weapons program: Three scenarios for 2020, US–Korea Institute at SAIS, February, available at: http://38north.org/wp-content/uploads/2015/02/NKNF-Future-Directions-2020-Albright-0215.pdf (accessed October 2016).

Bermudez Jr, Joseph S. (2001) *Shield of the Great Leader: The Armed Forces of North Korea*. Allen & Unwin: Sydney.

Cathcart, Adam and Madden, Michael (2012) Sinonk.com China–North Korea Dossier No. 3, available at: http://sinonk.com/wp-content/uploads/2012/08/sinonk-dossier-no-3-chinanorth-korean-relations-at-the-end-of-kim-jong-il-era.pdf (accessed January 2017).

Chanlett-Avery, Emma, Rinehart, Ian E. and Nikitin, Mary Beth D. (2016) *North Korea: U.S. Relations, Nuclear Diplomacy, and Internal Situation*. Congressional Research Service, The Library of Congress: Washington, DC.

Cheon, Seong-whun (2013) The Kim Jong-un regime's 'byungjin' (parallel development) policy of economy and nuclear weapons and the April 1st Nuclearization Law, available at: www.kinu.or.kr/upload/neoboard/DATA01/co13–11(E).pdf (accessed October 2016).

Choi, Jong Kun (2015) The perils of strategic patience with north Korea, *The Washington Quarterly*, 38(4): 57–72.

Cohen, Roberta (2017) A serious human rights negotiation with North Korea, available at: http://38north.org/2017/02/rcohen020117/ (accessed March 2017).

Collins, Robert M. (2014) North Korea's theatre of the absurd and the new number twos, available at: http://warontherocks.com/2014/02/north-koreas-theater-of-the-absurd-and-the-new-number-twos-3/ (accessed August 2016).

Frank, Ruediger (2015) North Korea's foreign trade, available at: http://38north.org/2015/10/rfrank102215/ (accessed December 2016).

Gause, Ken E. (2014) North Korean leadership dynamics and decision-making under Kim Jong-un: A second year assessment, available at: www.cna.org/CNA_files/PDF/COP-2014-U-006988-Final.pdf (accessed October 2016).

Gause, Ken E. (2015) *North Korean House of Cards: Leadership Dynamics under Kim Jong Il*. Committee for Human Rights in North Korea: Washington, DC.

Green, Christopher (2012a) North enshrines Kim's nuclear 'achievement', available at: www.dailynk.com/english/read.php?cataId=nk01700&num=9304 (accessed September 2016).

Green, Christopher (2012b) Kim regime facing military loyalty battle, available at: www.dailynk.com/english/read.php?cataId=nk00300&num=9983 (accessed August 2016).

Green, Christopher (2012c) Barriers to entry: Cellular telephony in the digital DPRK, available at: http://sinonk.com/2012/11/25/barriers-to-entry-cellular-telephony-in-the-digital-dprk/ (accessed July 2016).

Green, Christopher (2017) Wrapped in a fog: On the DPRK constitution and the Ten Principles, in *Change and Continuity in North Korean Politics*, Adam Cathcart, Robert Winstanley-Chesters and Christopher Green (eds). Routledge: London, pp. 23–38.

Haggard, Stephan and Noland, Marcus (2009) *Repression and Punishment in North Korea: Survey Evidence of Prison Camp Experiences*. East–West Center Working Papers No. 20. East–West Center: Honolulu.

Haggard, Stephan, Herman, Luke and Ryu, Jaesung (2014) Political change in North Korea: Mapping the succession, *Asian Survey*, 54(4): 773–800.

Hawk, David (2012) *The Hidden Gulag*, Committee for Human Rights in North Korea: Washington, DC.

Institute for Far Eastern Studies (IFES), North Korean GDP dropped estimated 1.1% in 2015. IFES NK Brief No. 16–07–22. Kyungnam University: Daegu, ROK.

Institute for Far Eastern Studies (IFES), North Korea seeks supplementary measures for the field responsibility system, IFES Brief 15–07–15. Kyungnam University: Daegu, ROK.

Ireson, Randall (2012) Agricultural reform again – or not?, available at: https://vtncankor.wordpress.com/2012/12/14/agricultural-reform-again-or-not-by-randall-ireson/ (accessed August 2016).

Ireson, Randall (2013) The state of North Korean farming: New information from the UN crop assessment report, available at: http://38north.org/2013/12/rireson121813/ (accessed August 2016).

Ireson, Randall (2014) Game-changing agricultural policies for North Korea?, available at: http://38north.org/2014/02/rireson022414/ (accessed August 2016).

Ireson, Randall (2015) Is the drought over?, available at: http://38north.org/2015/07/rireson071515 (accessed August 2016).

Ireson, Randall (2016) Why headlines about DPRK agricultural production miss the point, available at: http://38north.org/2016/05/ireson050616/ (accessed October 2016).

Jang, Jin-song (2013) Kim Jong-un's new year speech: What it really means, available at: www.nknews.org/2013/01/kim-jong-uns-new-year-speech-what-it-really-means-part-2-of-2/ (accessed October 2016).

Kim, Kap-sik (2008) Suryong's direct rule and the political regime in North Korea under Kim Jong Il, Asian Perspective, 32(3): 87–109.

Kim Tae Hong (2012) State to embark on swathe of forced mergers, available at: www.dailynk.com/english/read.php?cataId=nk09002&num=9868 (accessed September 2016).

Lankov, Andrei (2014), Reforming North Korea, available at: www.aljazeera.com/indepth/opinion/2014/11/reforming-north-korea-20141117121917871925.html (accessed August 2016).

Lankov, Andrei (2016) Kim Jong-un: What we know about the North Korean leader, available at: www.aljazeera.com/indepth/opinion/2016/01/kim-jong-north-korean-leader-160104121310318.html (accessed November 2016).

Lee, Hong-yung (2014) North Korea in 2013: Economy, executions, and nuclear Brinksmanship, *Asian Survey*, 54(1): 89–100.

Lee, Kyo-Duk et al. (2008) *Changes in North Korea as Revealed in the Testimonies of Saetomins*. Korea Institute for National Unification: Seoul.

Lim, Kang-taeg (2009) South and North Korea's economic relations seen through statistics: The past and the present, and the future, in 2009 International Conference on Humanitarian and Development assistance to DPRK, available at: www.ncnk.org/resources/publications/2009-international-conference-on-humanitarian-and-development-assistance-to-dprk-current-humanitarian-situation-and-international-co operation (accessed July 2016).

Mansourov, Alexandre (2012a) The Kim family reigns: Preserving the monarchy and strengthening the party-state, available at: http://38north.org/2012/12/amansourov 121912/ (accessed July 2016).

Mansourov, Alexandre (2012b) A dynamically stable regime, available at: http://38north.org/2012/12/amansourov121712/ (accessed July 2016).

Narang, Vipin (2014) *Nuclear Strategy in the Modern Era: Regional Powers and International Conflict*. Princeton University Press: Princeton, NJ.

Noland, Marcus (2013) North Korean illicit activities, Witness to Transformation blog, 11 March, available at: at https://piie.com/blogs/north-korea-witness-transformation/north-korean-illicit-activities (accessed August 2016).

Noland, Marcus (2014) BOK's estimate of North Korean national income, available at: https://piie.com/blogs/north-korea-witness-transformation/boks-estimate-north-korean-national-income (accessed November 2016).

Noland, Marcus (2015) Why is North Korea growing?, available at: https://piie.com/blogs/north-korea-witness-transformation/why-north-korea-growing (accessed November 2016).

Noland, Marcus (2016) The elusive charm of the 28 June reforms, Witness to Transformation blog, 12 January, available at: https://piie.com/blogs/north-korea-witness-transformation/elusive-charms-28-june-reforms (accessed November 2016).

Oh, Kongdan and Hassig, Ralph (2010) North Korea in 2009: The song remains the same, *Asian Survey*, 50(1): 89–96.

Panetta, Leon (2014) *Worthy Fights: A Memoir of Leadership in War and Peace*. The Penguin Press: New York.

Silberstein, Benjamin Katzeff (2015a) How bad is North Korea's food situation? Getting a grip on the numbers confusion, available at: http://38north.org/2015/12/bksilberstein120915/ (accessed January 2017).

Silberstein, Benjamin Katzeff (2015b) Why North Korea's supposed agricultural reforms may not actually be working after all, available at: http://38north.org/2015/06/bksilberstein061715/ (accessed January 2017).

Smith, Shane (2015) North Korea's evolving nuclear strategy, US–Korea Institute at SAIS, available at: http://38north.org/wp-content/uploads/2015/09/NKNF_Evolving-Nuclear-Strategy_Smith.pdf (accessed November 2016).

Song, In-Ho, Cho, Hye-Shin and Lee, Euna (2016) The past, present, and future of North Korean economy: An in-depth study on the North Korean constitution's economic clauses and the economic reality, *International Journal of Korean Unification Studies*, 25(1): 199–233.

Suh, Jae-jean (2009) The Lee Myong-bak government's North Korea policy: A study on its historical and theoretical foundation, available at: www.kinu.or.kr/upload/neoboard/DATA05/suh.pdf (accessed September 2016).

Tertitskiy, Fydor (2014) Evolution of party credo shows effort to elevate Kim Jong Il, the worker's party, available at: www.nknews.org/2014/12/the-partys-10-principles-then-and-now/ (accessed August 2016).

Thompson, Drew (2011) *Silent Partners – Chinese Joint Ventures in North Korea*. U.S. Korea Institute at SAIS: Washington, DC.

Toloraya, Georgy (2016) Deciphering North Korean economic intentions, available at: http://38north.org/2016/07/gtoloraya072616/ (accessed October 2016).

UN Office of the High Commissioner for Human Rights (OHCHR) (2014) Report of the detailed findings of the commission of enquiry on human rights in the Democratic People's Republic of Korea, A/HRC/25/63.

US Department of Defense, Military and security developments involving the Democratic People's Republic of Korea 2015, available at: www.defense.gov/Portals/1/Documents/pubs/Military_and_Security_Developments_Involving_the_Democratic_Peoples_Republic_of_Korea_2015.PDF (accessed November 2016).

Ward, Peter and Lankov, Andrei (2016) China and North Korea's economic future, available at: www.nknews.org/2016/02/china-and-north-koreas-economic-future/ (accessed August 2016).

9 Final perspective

The revolution that began in North Korea in 1945 displayed a blend of generic and specific characteristics. The generic lay in the lessons Kim Il Sung and his colleagues drew from the universal laws of Marxism, the revolutionary organisational and tactical framework developed chiefly by Lenin, and the practical experience of Communist parties in power, most notably the CPSU under Stalin. The specific emerged as Kim's own life experiences coloured and then dominated efforts to apply this body of knowledge, as he understood it, to the concrete conditions of divided Korea and to the goal of a united Korea under his leadership. The traits that emerged from this process – militarism, isolation, extreme centralisation and mobilisation, personal autocracy, cult of personality leadership and hereditary succession – are obvious enough, but accounting for them is a far from straightforward process. In this work we have considered a number of influences on the life-experience and outlook of Kim Il Sung, and while noting in passing the influence of the Japanese occupation and promotion of the Emperor cult, we have emphasised the role in the development of Kimist ideology played first by Kim's early life and experiences as an anti-Japanese guerilla and then by his practical experience of Stalinist state building. As we revisit and re-examine these influences in the light of the events described in the preceding chapters, we begin by placing them in the generic context of Leninist revolutionary movements in Russia, China and elsewhere.

Typically, Leninist revolutionary movements start as small study groups and cells led by young intellectuals. Their political strategies and tactics vary depending upon the political environment in which they operate, but common to the early period of all movements is the initiation of predominantly young revolutionaries into prolonged, almost constant political warfare against hostile authority. The pre-revolutionary period is a time when the leaders lay down the foundations of the Party's ideology and revolutionary mythology. The atmosphere of conspiracy, danger, political violence and ideological ferment has a profound impact on the revolutionaries' political values and personal lives, and imparts an intensity to their relationships and experiences that often acquires considerable significance if the movement gains power.

Isolation from the general population – 'the people' – is a further issue of considerable significance within the movement. Physical isolation occurs because of the pattern of illegal activities and this may impact strongly on their normal patterns of socialisation, removed as they often are from the experience of daily working-class life. More fundamentally, though, a self-inflicted form of intellectual isolation emerges because of the creation of a reimagined people, one innately receptive to the ideology of the movement as representing their interests, but hindered from recognising this primarily by 'false consciousness'. Meanwhile, the elitism of the leadership core, the exclusive, revelatory nature of Party ideology, the pattern of illegal underground activities, and the ever-present factor of state repression develop the revolutionary movement's organisational framework as a highly disciplined, conspiratorial political combat team. In turn, this combat shapes the later mythology of the movement, emphasising desirable qualities for followers such as loyalty, discipline, self-sacrifice, militancy and courage, and attributes of the leader such as perseverance, wisdom and prescience in securing the inevitable path to victory.

If the movement is successful in attaining power, it becomes subject to a further complex array of forces. The nature of its leadership – elitist, visionary, militant and monopolistic – becomes a major factor in shaping the revolution, as do the precise historical circumstances in which the Party first comes to power, the legacy of the pre-existing political culture, the stage of economic and social development reached under the previous regime, the models of other revolutionary traditions with which it identifies and the international environment at the time. In the light of these influences the Leninist party transforms itself from political combat team to promoter of socialist modernisation.

The Leninist blueprint, which above all else is a prescription for the seizure of power, has less relevance for the actual exercise of power, and so while Leninism remains a powerful ideological tool, the party is increasingly thrown back on more existential resources as it attempts to consolidate and institutionalise its rule. The concerted attack on existing state and societal institutions, the disdain for notions of bourgeois legality, the relative weakness of checks and balances, and the atmosphere of intense political and economic mobilisation bring to the fore cadres with exceptional willpower, organisational skills and psychological drives who are capable of forcing the movement through increasingly unfamiliar terrain, usually by applying strong levels of state violence and having little recourse to moral scruple, and at this point one member of the revolutionary elite typically assumes the role of a hero-leader and begins to exercise power on a personalistic basis with ever-diminishing reference to Party rules and procedures. This emergence may occur because by common consent the personage concerned possesses exceptional leadership qualities, but it may also often occur because other leading figures in the Party, many of whom are intellectuals pressed into the role of men of action, are taken by surprise, and find themselves with little option other than to fall into line behind the dominant leader, whether out of fear for personal safety, or concern that to do otherwise might imperil the Party. And so begins what we may term the Stalinist stage of the revolution, in which the new hero-leader is the dominant adjudicator in matters of ideology and state policy. Ideological debate – formerly the life-blood of the movement – becomes muted as the leader now only requires subservient cadres to carry out his orders.

However, such charismatic leadership becomes increasingly incompatible with the needs of the modernising state. The militant, visionary nature of Leninist party ideology sanctions the drive to seek monopolistic control over civil society, and the classic economic institutions and practices that evolve from this – central planning, heavy oversight of basic industrial development, workforce regimentation, collectivised agriculture, suppression of consumer demand, economic autarky, strong reliance on non-material incentives, restrictions on freedom of information and especially a pervasive security apparatus – give rise to elaborate bureaucracies. The hero-leader typically despises bureaucratism, whose concern with stability, precedent and routine runs counter to his pre-revolution life experience, thwarts his will and conflicts with his strong drive towards maintaining revolutionary mobilisation. Possessed of a strong ego, he may also feel psychologically challenged by the presence of bodies of specialised knowledge and practice beyond his ken, and may therefore launch lethal attacks on bureaucrats and technocrats, as did Stalin in the 1930s and Mao during the Cultural Revolution. However, despite extensive leadership intervention, a strong characteristic of Leninist polities is that the charismatic leadership of the revolutionary generation by a Lenin, Mao or Ho progressively gives way to institutionalisation, and its recurrence is blocked by the changing needs of the Party, and especially by the determination of leading cadres not to let this subversion of collective Party leadership occur again, for the experience of life under the charismatic leadership is usually as unhappy for them as it is for the general populace. Thus, when the charismatic transformer passes from the scene, he is not replaced and his personal achievement is swallowed up by far greater impersonal forces, whose emergence such rulers characteristically neither foresee nor understand.

As the era of charismatic leadership begins to pass, the focus turns more directly to social and especially economic development issues. Contrary to Marxist theory, Leninist parties have usually come to power in countries where the economic base is relatively low and must therefore gear the nation's economic life to rapid industrial transformation. Because of the low base and because the initial inputs are strong, the party usually achieves an initial breakthrough in the form of rapid, uneven economic growth. However, soon this process poses further dilemmas for the Party as its ideological control requirements and its reliance on a high degree of centralised planning become increasingly incompatible with the demands of a modernising economy. In particular, as the drive for monopolistic social control restricts information flows, it stifles innovation and initiative, inhibits the development of non-military science and technology, and obstructs the need for decentralisation and localised empowerment in specialised economic planning and decision-making.

In the context of seeking rapid economic transformation, external economic and political relations also assume greater significance. Such regimes typically define themselves in terms of a broader international struggle between imperialism and socialism, and regulate their foreign dealings accordingly. This process usually results in a substantial withdrawal from the international system, as well as stringent state control over any and all contacts with the outside world. But while Leninist doctrine rules out indefinite coexistence with capitalist states and predicts their downfall, this does not occur and tactical accommodations become necessary as the regime is forced to accept ever-receding time frames for the collapse of capitalism. The doctrine of the impossibility of continued coexistence with capitalist countries is then proven ironically valid as the continuing development of the country's socialist economic system increasingly forces planners into contact with capitalist markets and economies in search of investment capital and more advanced technology. Here its limitations and inefficiencies are exposed, often ruthlessly so, and the socialist economy becomes subject to increasing pressures for structural reform, partly generated from within and partly inspired by awareness of the comparative economic performance of capitalist economies. This further contributes to the dilution of the classic socialist centrally planned economy, forcing acceptance of more decentralised economic decision-making and reluctantly bringing into being a Second Economy, which trades in privately produced consumer items to meet a demand that the state-owned enterprise sector with its own set of priorities is endemically incapable of meeting. Nor can the repressive political system withstand comparison with more open systems. It cannot enforce sufficient isolation or ideological conformity and it loses its capacity to repress all non-approved political activity. The Leninist party becomes increasingly undermined by expedience and eventually falls completely or else, as has occurred in China and Vietnam, remains as the carapace for the new ruling class. The ideological rhetoric insists that the revolution continues, but to all intents and purposes the revolutionary phase is finally over.

The story of the DPRK follows much of this pattern, but to date it has offered a very different denouement, because some fifty years ago it became locked into the charismatic leadership phase and it has remained there. Kim Il Sung pursued a familiar path to domination over the ruling Leninist party, but then from 1967 on he intentionally destroyed as much of the Party and institutional infrastructure as he needed to in order to maintain a *suryong* system, or personal autocracy, whereupon further evolution along the lines described above fell away. Kim thus became far more than just an ordinary leader or policy arbiter, and his personal convictions defined an ideology that did not just legitimate political power in the DPRK, but that determined in stunning detail the daily basis on which North Koreans lived and died. These convictions were enforced throughout the society with exceptional intensity and brutality to the extent that the option of departing even marginally from his system has never been exercised by his successors, and so they have remained committed to preserving as much of it as they can despite widespread and on-going dysfunctionality.

As to how this came about, we have seen how Kim Il Sung's early years were marked by profound dislocations. He was born into and lived the first seven years or so of his life in a traditional Korean village almost entirely untouched by the modern world, save for the influence of a well-indigenised Christian faith on his family. He then passed into a life of flight, exile, orphan status, patchy education, underground Communist activity and finally guerilla warfare. From adolescence to the age of 33 he rarely saw, let alone lived in, any human settlement larger than a village. Moreover, he made his way among violent men within an esoteric, exclusivist armed political movement whose programme extended far beyond the mainstream cause of Korean independence to the huge, abstract cause of the defeat of the forces of global imperialism, a cause that often placed it on hostile terms with other branches of the Korean nationalist movement.

To physical isolation and social alienation, we may add Kim's self-inflicted intellectual isolation. Growing up in conditions of isolation and privation need not limit intellectual development, as the example of Abraham Lincoln among many others attests, but in Kim's case they did so glaringly. His grasp of Marxist–Leninist ideology was slight, and the same could be said for his grasp of the world of ideas in general, for though clearly intelligent and highly self-disciplined, personality drives intervened. Thus, throughout his life he displayed little intellectual curiosity or capacity for analysis, and he attacked these traits in others, tending instead to reduce all issues to simplistic, self-justificatory, often delusional formulae, while characteristically substituting the power of his own will for strategic thinking. In important ways, Kim never sensed any wider reality than adherence to the values of the guerilla community and he remained in thrall to them in such traits as the efficacy of a direct, centralised chain of command, an emphasis on unconditional obedience and loyalty, dismissal of the norms of civil society, an almost paranoid sense of threat, a hostile, predatory attitude towards external transactions, the promotion of violence and criminality as a means justifying the end, avowal of austerity and moral puritanism, and dissociation from family and from all private economic ties. In the Manchurian hinterland he developed such traits and thereafter applied them to the entire modern world as he encountered it. His instincts thus remained profoundly anti-modern, his mistrust of intellectuals and technocrats profound and his grasp of the processes of economic and social development limited. A self-made, self-reliant man, he found in his own life all he deemed necessary for the lives of others.

Isolation also affected Kim's exposure to, and understanding of, developments in the Korean cultural world during this era. After most Korean Communist activists had been driven out of Korea proper, many continued the struggle in cosmopolitan centres such as Shanghai and Tokyo, where they remained in contact with the broader cultural and political horizons which urban China and Japan provided. Moreover, within Korea itself, from the early 1920s on the broader world of Korean nationalism took on specific cultural orientations involving language, literature and the promotion of national identity by reclaiming what was felt to be a specifically Korean historical and cultural tradition (Robinson, 1988). Kim had little or no exposure to such movements and when he returned to Pyongyang in 1945, he was almost entirely ignorant of this world and, of course, he proceeded to wreak havoc on it, erecting in its place a bogus puritanist, militarist substitute that cut people off from their pre-1945 roots.

In addition to Kim's own inner drive to lead and dominate, his transition from nominal leadership of a Communist oligarchy to dominant leadership of the Korean Workers' Party and then to personal autocracy required further catalysts in the form of the Korean War, the death of Stalin and the workings of Leninist party political culture. During the Korean War, Kim came under strong attack as a defeated military commander of questionable competence, and similarly after the death of Stalin important elements within the KWP attacked his strong and continuing adherence to such Stalinist traits as cult of personality. Amid the ruthless, zero-sum struggles that defined the Communist oligarchy, Kim had little choice but to go on the offence against his detractors if he were to survive, and again, Leninist party culture was no more able in the DPRK than in Stalin's Soviet Union, Mao's China, Hoxha's Albania or Ceausescu's Romania to check the drive of an individual who was determined to subvert the party and establish personal rule, in each case seemingly for the same reason: his colleagues somehow believed this just wasn't meant to happen. And so in history we find people from Alexander the Great to Adolf Hitler who accomplish the seemingly impossible, the fantastic even, and whose success cannot be fully explained but for the dividend of disbelief on the part of their adversaries.

As dominant leader of the Party after 1958, Kim Il Sung proved ill-equipped by either training, experience, temperament or intellect to deal with the practical problems of governance. The period of post-war recovery until the mid-1960s is often perceived as something of a golden era for the North's economy, with often patronising tales of rapid socialist reconstruction under willing mobilisation and benevolent leadership, but whatever the degree of truth in this, it was no pointer to the future, for economic development as an end in itself was only minimally part of Kim's thinking, and so this period of regrouping was soon followed by a further great leap forward to the maximisation of the DPRK's military potential. In the process, his leadership style became even more marked by rigorous internal repression, by constant economic and political mobilisation campaigns, by intolerance for pragmatic or flexible solutions outside the ambit of his ideology and by further isolation from the outside world, including the Soviet Bloc. In the end, such campaigns and practices as the Chollima Movement, the Chongsanri Method, the Taean Work System, Equal Emphasis and later the Three Revolutions Team Movement attacked and successfully subverted the managerial expertise he needed to harness for effective government, but he did not view things that way, instead viewing such mobilisation as representing the very essence of collective social and economic life, and of course as essential to the reinforcement of his authority.

In analysing the inherent complexities of policy and motivation present in developing states, Chalmers Johnson's observation that a state's first priority will define its essence is a useful perspective from which to view the radical change in state policies that overtook the DPRK as the 1960s progressed (Johnson, 1982: 306). For Kim, the overriding priority was not to enhance the material well-being of DPRK citizens but to enhance the military's warmaking capacity with a view to reversing the verdict of the Korean War, a strategy as banal as that often attributed to generals that their favoured strategies often involve refighting their previous war. Kim's militarism was a matter of deep conviction, embedded in his own past, in his ideological role-models and in the Korean War experience. Like many nineteenth-century European leaders and their followers, and like the pre-1945 Japanese militarists, Kim held, albeit with greater intensity and far less sophistication, the belief that the primary purpose of the state, no less than the purpose of the guerilla detachment, was to wage war effectively. The purpose of the economy was to produce the means of waging war, the purpose of education was to produce soldiers for war and the purpose of ideology was to convince people of the social and historical inevitability of war. Foremost, war for Kim meant war to reunify Korea under the leadership of the KWP, but both his galling retreat before the force of Japanese arms in the early 1940s and then the role played by the US in Korea after 1945 appear to have caused him to embrace a highly literal interpretation of the Leninist–Stalinist worldview, and mandated a continuing anti-Japanese, anti-US, global anti-imperialist struggle.

Thus, while militarism had always been a major influence on the DPRK since its founding, after 1962 and the inception of the Equal Emphasis policy it became the dominant organising principle for both DPRK economy and society as the economy developed essentially as a war economy. We cannot precisely determine the full dimensions of DPRK military–industrial production, but the evidence of former Soviet officials and high-ranking defectors leaves little doubt that from the mid-1960s onward, the military in effect ran a separate economy responsible for up to half of all industrial production. It enjoyed priority access to raw materials, it determined a lopsided emphasis on heavy industry, it deployed the best available human resources, it had first call on the nation's power grid and transport infrastructure and it was not accountable to the Cabinet-level State Planning Commission. A number of factors contributed to the destitution of the DPRK, but the definitive organisation of economy activity in this manner was the crucial factor, and thus the DPRK case bears out handsomely Max Weber's observation during the First World War that the war economy, with its overwhelming sense of contingency and its rough, inefficient methods of resource allocation, inherently tends toward bankruptcy (Weber [1915?] 1964: 209).

This military fixation in turn fed a vision of the DPRK's destiny that was static, self-indulgent and retrospective. Thus, Kim's domination of the Party in the 1960s brought about the degeneration of ideology within the KWP and a decline in the intellectual life of both the Party and the country as a whole. Ideological truth became self-evident, to be accepted and acted upon with blind obedience by the people in an intimidatory atmosphere of incessant mobilisation and struggle in which emulation of the Manchurian guerillas became the dominant role-model. From the mid-1960s on, the ubiquitous Party slogan 'Live, work and study the way the anti-Japanese guerillas did!' was not just a vivid exhortation, but became the central tenet of a system whose claims on the allegiance of individual citizens grew proportionately more insistent and all-embracing as time passed and as the country's resource base diminished. By the early 1970s, Kim's near-deification had also produced a sinister twin – a profound belief in his own infallibility, for when one looks at the DPRK's pathological inability not just to change but to even minimally modify ruinous policies, we find that it *was* pathological, for it was rooted in the pathology of a man who had honestly concluded that his cause was immutably just, and so he could do no wrong in pursuing it, just as dissenters could only do wrong in not pursuing it. And who was there to disagree?

Kim's innate psychology and his socialisation in a harsh environment among ruthless and violent men crossed with his Leninist attraction to the necessity of revolutionary violence to develop an outlook that seems to have rendered him extraordinarily callous and indifferent to suffering. We see this in the harshness of his economic policies in the immediate aftermath of the Korean War, which even Soviet Bloc officials used to Stalinist methods at times found disturbing, and in the scale and rigour of the *gulag* system he constructed. Moreover, he ensured that such traits were enforced with sufficient force to become embedded in the system itself and to be passed on as part of his legacy. Thus, we observe the direct model for the policies of Kim Jong Il during the Arduous March famine, which accounted for the needless deaths of hundreds of thousands of people.

Yet another related facet of Kim's personality that compounded the stultifying effect of his ideology was his pervasive mistrust. Such mistrust or, if we wish to speculate, intellectual insecurity, caused Kim to view all other currents of Korean nationalism, socialism and communism as threatening, and so he found it impossible to share real power with any members of the post-war generations other than his son. He became known for his intimidatory tactics and did not cease to purge colleagues until he had surrounded himself with unconditional personal loyalists and sycophants from his guerilla days. The purges, the *gulags*, the *songbun* social classification system, the elaborate, multiple overlapping bureaucracies and security agencies, the continuing high levels of repression, the near-paranoid avoidance of all unnecessary foreign contact, the shrill insistence on unconditional loyalty and the daily torrents of self-righteous abuse heaped on a wide range of domestic and foreign 'enemies' institutionalised this mistrust, reflecting a worldview that discounted confidence, trust, equality, interdependence or win–win compromise as a viable basis for relations between individuals as well as nations.

In foreign relations too, Kim Il Sung's definition of the DPRK's place in the world and the foreign policy parameters that flowed from this also reflected rigid ideological underpinnings. To the North Korean people, Kim presented himself as a major international figure, but while the KWP adopted the rhetoric of proletarian internationalism, Kim clearly perceived the threat to his system posed by interaction with other socialist countries, let alone with the wider international economic and political system. He saw even less value – and more danger – in external contacts than Stalin or Mao ever did, and was successful in minimising them, effectively confining his entire population to base. This isolation in turn reflected strategic rigidity, broken only by occasional tilts at tactical expediency, and this is why the robust belief so often found among analysts that such a blunt instrument as Kim somehow managed to evolve a deft, subtle means of 'balancing' his relations with the Soviet Union and China does not survive closer examination. Instead, what we find is a constant pattern of unsophisticated, instinctive alignment with whatever forces Kim believed at the time were likely to oppose peaceful coexistence and thus aid his cause.

This strategic rigidity derived primarily from Kim's deep conviction of the historical necessity of continuing the anti-US, anti-imperialist struggle, and so when developments seemed to further this cause Kim welcomed them, but when they worked against it, he dismissed them as temporary aberrations. This in turn meant that when events and trends such as Sino–US rapprochement, Sino–Japanese rapprochement, ROK economic development, economic dynamism in the Asia–Pacific region and the collapse of the Soviet Bloc called into question the wisdom and efficacy of confrontationist and isolationist policies, the primitivism of Kimist diplomacy was displayed in his minimalist response. Typically, he portrayed all such trends as irrelevant in the face of his profound faith in the looming downfall of world capitalism, for here, truly, was a man who had no use for a Plan B.

The tide began to turn decisively against the DPRK in the late 1970s. There was no single event, nor was it immediately apparent to its adversaries that the customary danger presented by the DPRK would slowly abate. The factors in the DPRK's decline are clear in hindsight, but they were less clear at the time, partly obscured by the DPRK's curious state of aggressive denial, in which both rhetoric and policies remained unchanged. Internationally, the final ascendancy of Deng Xiaoping in 1977 announced the impending definitive reshaping of China's diplomatic and domestic economic agenda and the final extinction of any hope of Chinese support, but it was within the DPRK that the rot set in. Domestically, the creeping exhaustion of economic inputs now reached tipping point and in the early 1980s it began to become clear that the Kimist economy could not live within its means. The 1980s therefore became a pivotal decade in which the drive for war preparation slowly tipped over into a drive for nuclear-backed survivalism. Again, the change was disguised by unchanged strategies and triumphalism rhetoric, with the clearest indication of what had occurred being the inception in the early 1980s of the nuclear programme at Yongbyon to produce weapons-grade plutonium. Elsewhere, half-hearted tinkering occurred around the fringes of the economy, but Kim was incapable of thinking further than this and with his continuing alienation from the modern world, his policy compass unerringly swung back to the one input he did understand – human labour. And so, as the national wealth declined, the burdens fell increasingly on ordinary people as they now had to give the state more for less, more of their labour at state-assigned jobs, at 'loyalty' volunteer work and as contract labourers in the timber camps and mines of Siberia, all for fewer rations and fewer health and social services until, in the mid-1990s, the state had nothing left to give them.

Thus, in 1994 Kim Jong Il inherited a broken country, a state of affairs for which he, of course, bore considerable responsibility. His subsequent achievement can only be assessed meaningfully in accordance with his own objectives, and here we find that he gradually restored Kimist fortunes in a manner that virtually no one predicted at the time. The confronting truth is that, like Stalin during the Second World War, he drew on immense reserves of strength and perseverance, and evinced a strong work ethic and strong intellect that he deployed to achieve the survival of all he held dear, his indifference to people's suffering according with the inhumanity of his father's system. Also like Stalin, he retained a very fixed strategic vision and when the immediate crisis was contained, he returned to the old blueprint, making the best he could of it. Here he succeeded to the extent that by the time of his death in 2011, the DPRK was the sole historically Marxist–Leninist state not to have substantially reformed itself after 1991, while the transformation from righteous war-making state to nuclear-armed survivalist state was well advanced, the DPRK economy was for the moment viable and the state appeared safe from foreign military action.

What, then, enabled such a system to survive such a founder? The situation is unique, for this is the singular phenomenon of the successful dynastic transfer of autocratic power in an historically Marxist–Leninist polity, not once but twice. We can, of course, dismiss popular support as a factor, for as the fate of the Stalin and Mao cults remind us, such orchestrated displays of affection are hollow, and once such regimes cease to promote their leaders' cult of personality no popular movement emerges to take up the slack. It is therefore more fruitful to examine factors such as elements of Korean political tradition, the DPRK historical narrative and the intense socialisation process that feeds it, the continuing effective deployment of state coercion and violence, the specific ability of Kim Jong Il, elite solidarity founded on the belief that no other course is viable in a post-Leninist world, state-sanctioned corruption and isolation from foreign contact.

The contribution of Korean political tradition to this outcome is highly problematic. On one hand, there appear to be fruitful lines of enquiry, such as the organisational tendency of Koreans to form small, specific associative groups, which we noted in discussing the pre-1945 Korean nationalist movement, for this feeds the proposition that North Korean communist groupings were especially vulnerable and unable to form a united front against an individual or group such as the Kimists who were bent on their subjugation. We may also observe that a tightly organised, centuries-old monarchical and bureaucratic system is in the DPRK bloodline. More generally, though, citing such an amorphous, poorly understood factor as the Korean political tradition is likely to obscure more than it illuminates, since practically all basic DPRK traits, beginning with centralised authoritarianism, charismatic leadership, cult of personality and militarism are clearly the antithesis of this tradition (Buzo, 1999: 45–52). Moreover, these and other features cited in this way are usually not specifically Korean, but rather are generic features of 'traditional' societies, or else have entered the DPRK with solid Stalinist credentials, as is the case with the *songbun* ascriptive social status system, various other aspects of the punishment system and the specific contours of the cult of the fatherly leader.

By contrast, the influence of the DPRK's own historical narrative is clearly strong and, as previously noted, we ignore it at our peril, for eddying throughout the fraudulent Kimist version of this narrative is the genuine historical experience of a sizeable population of mobilised true believers whose allegiance was sealed by war and is still fortified by a race-based nationalism that casts their Baekdu state as the one true Korea. As near as can be guessed, citizens' allegiance to the DPRK state is not brittle, but is sustained by intense socialisation that begins practically from birth. This narrative is still what raises the DPRK above the level of the archetypal ephemeral, tin-pot variety of dictatorship, and it has been both a significant factor in the will of both elite and non-elite North Koreans to regroup and endure, and also a major reason why collapsist scenarios have been repeatedly confounded.

Of course, we must always return to state coercion and violence as a major factor in deterring regime modification. This is obviously the very darkest side of the DPRK's organisational abilities and only those who have experienced it can truly speak of its pervasive influence and effects, but for anyone who dealt with North Koreans in the Kim Il Sung era under any but the most formal, state-sanctioned conditions, fear was often palpably present. Now that the UN Office of the High Commissioner for Human Rights 2014 report on the DPRK has catalogued for international attention the full dimensions of the regime's systematic brutality, we may gain a deeper insight into this as a fundamental factor in the successful survival and transfer of Kimist power. Without this system and the will to enforce it, the Kimist state would have long since ceased to exist.

We then pass to the specific leadership attributes of Kim Jong Il and his performance as the Great Consolidator (Buzo, 2016). The debate on the relative contributions of subsequent Kimist leaders to the survival of the Kimist system will one day absorb scholars and when it does, the role of Kim Jong Il is bound to receive closer, more dispassionate attention. In pursuit of the Kimist cause and issuing out of strong continuity with the immediate past, his legacy has been the indefinite nuclear-backed survival of the Kimist state, a record of effective diplomacy in support of this objective, the extraction of billions of dollars in goods and services from his adversaries, acceptance of the necessity of forms of private market activity and containment of the threat this represents, the maintenance of elite solidarity and the smooth succession of his son, with the latter achievement standing in stark contrast to his own protracted struggle within the Party. These outcomes were by no means guaranteed when he entered office, but were all pursued carefully and calculatedly with no sign of vacillation, and while we don't know what drove strategic thought and policy deliberations in Pyongyang during his years, we can be assured that they were far more sophisticated and wide-ranging than could ever have been possible under Kim Il Sung.

To some extent, though, isolating the factor of leadership in DPRK state survival is misleading, for we also need to contend with the factor of the discipline and solidarity still evident among the wider elite, for which leadership cannot take all of the credit. Deconstructing the psychology of the several hundred thousand predominantly Pyongyang-dwelling elite and their dependants who enjoy substantial Party, military and bureaucracy rankings is a speculative task. However, high-level defectors to the South have remarkably similar stories to tell of the intensity and singularity of their lives, backed up by access to levels of wealth and privilege that have amazed many of their interlocutors. Their defections are often because of political or business connections gone wrong, rather than ideological disaffection, and most see next to nothing that attracts them in the South, viewing their present circumstances more as exile than release. It is clear that an intense, durable web of mutual obligation and reward is now in place, and as long as members of this elite continue to be subjected to the sundry disciplines of the regime and in turn to draw substantial rewards from this system, they will survive as a kleptocratic class and constitute an important pillar of the Kimist state.

The high level of endemic state corruption that has resulted is thus a significant factor in elite solidarity and hence regime survival. The scale is enormous and the sums are staggering, enough to place the DPRK at the very bottom of every reputable international league table of corruption, and since it remains publicly unacknowledged except in generalities, and since it has been allowed to grow to this level, it is clear that such corruption is an entrenched, sanctioned part of DPRK economic life. One need not repeat all the reasons why this vandalises the economy because for now this does not really matter, for as we have repeatedly stressed, the DPRK is not interested in following any path to economic development that would mandate strong anti-corruption measures. Corruption therefore has its immediate uses, for it both seals elite solidarity and also enables a degree of pragmatism to prevail in daily transactions that is otherwise proscribed by dysfunctional ideology. It is, therefore, a perverse agent of stability.

Finally, the high degree of isolation from the international community was another lesson Kim Il Sung learned from Stalinist practice. According to some, beginning in the 1990s the regime appeared to be taking baby-steps to modify its traditional policies of physical isolation and economic autarky during the 1990s. Border trade, the proclamation of the Rajin–Sunbong FETZ, the construction of the KEDO light-water nuclear reactors, dealings with a wide variety of international aid donors in responding to the famine, and production on consignment for ROK textile, clothing, footwear and electronics firms in the Kaesong Industrial Zone, all led to periodic and sometimes euphoric predictions that the DPRK was changing its isolationist ways. However, this was and continues to be illusory, for where such activity did not simply entail the plucking of low-hanging fruit, ultimately those forms of contact that appeared to break the traditional mould were either countermanded or else brought firmly under central control. Careful control of foreign contact has thus continued and remains as a powerful contributor to survival.

The net effect has been a so far successful survivalist strategy, but while this may be grounds for relief and even hope for the future in Pyongyang, it can scarcely be a source of gratification, for the North surveys failure by all metrics except survival. And after all, they were meant to be triumphantly in Seoul decades ago. Now the new reality is that state policies in the DPRK necessarily remain encased in Kim Il Sung's singular policy calculus, and this continues to be enforced by his heirs and successors. With the passage of time, this has allowed the widespread normalisation of the abnormal and, especially, it has allowed an economic system in which an ideologically well-armed population still performs its allocated primary role of supporting a huge military establishment and a military–industrial sector capable of producing a wide array of armaments. Kim Il Sung never encountered conditions in which he could confidently go to war again, but he remained convinced that this was due to ephemeral factors such as restraining hands from within the socialist bloc or the levels of deterrence offered by the US and the ROK, with their powers of massive retaliation. Nevertheless, he persisted because he persuaded himself that a time would come when these inhibitions might no longer apply, and in any case he knew no other way of life. His son and his grandson have not been so deluded, but they also have believed they have nowhere else to go.

What, then, of the future of Kimism? Neither theory, conventional wisdom or the extrapolation of current trends and data have proved to have very much predictive power in the past and are probably of limited use now. It is still far too early to predict how the Kim Jong Un regime will ultimately fare, although the evidence after some years is that whatever window for change putatively existed when he took over has now been tightly shut. The man-bites-dog narrative of incipient reform and change will continue to receive international play, as will tales of terror, purges and chronic instability, but domestically Kim's chief energies appear to be devoted to maintaining and pursuing the policy matrix determined by his father and grandfather. Intellectually and systemically, he and his advisers are probably not capable of charting any other course, even if they were so inclined. Meanwhile, the factors cited above will continue to operate and people will continue to serve the system he presides over in the name of survival and fear of change, even as this system continues to offer little material or spiritual fulfilment to most North Koreans.

Substantial intended reform is therefore no more likely now than at any other time in the past, unless we are witnessing the death-rattle of the regime. In the DPRK there is no avenue for such change, for consideration of the key people involved suggests that they are products of long, intense ideological training, and as long-standing incumbents are prey to the phenomena of creeping normalcy and groupthink. This intensely circumscribes the extent to which they could even conceptualise, let alone implement a process of reform, for they cannot induce what they themselves do not know, and even if they could, the institutions of state and Party have degenerated to the point where they are foremost instruments for exalting the incumbent genius-leader system. The vision imputed to Chang Song-t'aek of greatly expanding Chinese economic inputs while ostensibly retaining this system has represented the only discernible attempt to find a practical alternative to this state of affairs, but for now it has been anathematised. If we are looking at baby-steps, then gradual de-emphasis of Kimist ideology, reining in the *suryong* system, restricting the role of the Party, empowering the organs of government beginning with the Cabinet, advancing a leadership-backed, publicly proclaimed programme of reform beginning with agricultural decollectivisation and generally countering corruption with a modicum of rule of law would be a start, but of course none of these tendencies are currently in evidence.

The big unknown remains the long-term effect of current levels of private economic activity on the state. Such activity is already broad and diverse, and the potential for further growth is substantial due to the China factor, even though its higher end appears to be firmly controlled by the elite and their compradors in ways that strengthen Kimist political authority. Received wisdom is that if such activity continues to grow, it must eventually threaten and ultimately destroy the ideological foundations of Kimism, but this will not happen unless the elite allows it to happen, and of course so far they have prevented this from happening with singular tenacity. And so, after twenty years during which most North Koreans have owed their daily survival to such activity, the government still successfully pursues threat containment strategies and it is likely to do so into the indefinite future. Economically, then, the broader picture for ordinary North Koreans remains one of contained, not open-ended marketisation, with its social and political effects continuing to extend their impact on broader events at glacial pace.

Hopes are also perennially held for a cumulative subversive effect stemming from the breaches in the DPRK's information firewall, including access to South Korean popular culture chiefly by video, and also the exposure of significant numbers of young adult North Koreans to current Chinese business practices through transborder commerce. However, not only is it arrogant to assume that North Koreans will automatically embrace South Korean consumerism, but it is naive in the extreme to believe that the circulation of such prohibited materials will of itself be an agent of change, for while it may cause forms of cognitive dissonance as North Koreans compare such materials with what they are told about the South, a significant number of North Koreans, especially among the elite, have long been aware of the mendacity of official propaganda and in all likelihood are by now inured to it. Alongside the daily concerns of physically and politically surviving and caring for their loved ones, dwelling on such matters is probably not a widely practised pastime, and even if it were, people act upon such awareness at their extreme peril. Similarly, being exposed to more advanced foreign technologies is not necessarily subversive unless avenues exist for such experience to influence relevant policies and institutions, and this is not the case in the DPRK. The limit appears to be the creation of a possibly better, more efficient, productive version of the existing system, not its substantial modification.

Could outside pressure contribute to change? To date, the DPRK's major adversaries have not been able to find a foothold, in no small part because of misplaced perceptions of the challenge involved and poor resultant strategies. The Kimist DPRK is clearly confronting and intellectually challenging as a state that believes its survival depends on its rogue status, and it is the very essence of Kimism to place state policy beyond outside influences, as the fate of KEDO definitively showed. For this reason, overt pursuit of the goal of a denuclearised, interdependent Kimist state in return for economic and security guarantees is currently highly unrealistic, not the least because given the present success of the DPRK's survival strategy, it is by no means clear what the international community could offer the DPRK ruling class over and above what it already has, and hence it is also unclear what pressure it could apply to achieve the end of substantial regime transformation.

Military action to end the DPRK regime has at times been contemplated, and at times, such as in 1994, the US has been attracted to this option, but notwithstanding DPRK brinkmanship, careful calculations have prevailed in Pyongyang, as well as Seoul and to date Washington, and so far the peace has held. The rather discomforting option of hoping that time will bring about a change continues to hold sway, but the argument in favour of direct action will probably remain on the table for a number of reasons: first, the advocates of violent regime change may come to believe that such an infinitely risky course of action is less risky than the indefinite prolonging of the existing situation in which the DPRK's strategic position is continually strengthening and its threat potential is growing. Second, such advocates may also be able to convince themselves that they have a clear and contained view of what a post-DPRK North Korea would look like, thus avoiding their major mistake in Iraq. Moreover, the DPRK poses a peculiar type of challenge to US beliefs about its power and reach, which makes it hard for Washington to accept counsels that doing nothing might be better than doing something. Here we must also observe that despite the presence of experienced hands at senior levels of the Trump administration, questions will persist as to its capacity to pursue and maintain a steady, well-structured strategic course. Should all these inherently unpredictable factors somehow acquire critical mass, then we will enter unchartered waters, but meanwhile the DPRK appears safe from foreseeable external threat.

In the meantime, not all international trends are necessarily unfavourable to the DPRK. In recent times, China has evinced reluctance to support the DPRK, but when all is said and done, both parties know that they need each other, and since China will not connive at the DPRK's downfall, especially as US–China relations are now moving through their current cooling phase, the DPRK will continue to enjoy vital economic benefits irrespective of international sanctions. More broadly, the on-going fraying of the US-led international order, Russia's increasingly rogue status, on-going dysfunctionality in the Middle East, and the weakening of defences against transnational crime, especially cybercrime, offer the DPRK significant economic and strategic opportunities.

Moreover, while dialogue with the DPRK is currently a low priority for its major adversaries, there is an underlying predisposition to put the case for DPRK exceptionalism – that is, negotiating with the DPRK despite the fact that its policies and practices pose a fundamental challenge to key elements of the international order, ranging from the NPT to the Universal Declaration of Human Rights. Since the DPRK has manoeuvred itself into a position of strategic advantage, whereby its adversaries now want more from Pyongyang than Pyongyang wants from them, negotiations on the basis that talking is better than not talking lay the groundwork for Pyongyang to again extract the type of substantial economic concessions that it extracted from the Agreed Framework, the Sunshine Policy and the Six Party Talks.

Thus, while many possibilities existed for North Korea in 1945, what they ultimately got was Kim Il Sung. Sometimes the hubris of individual leaders brings mixed fortunes upon nations. Napoleon left France in ruins, but he also left behind the code of law that still bears his name, and some are still prepared to defend significant aspects of the legacies of Stalin and Mao. However, in the case of Kim Il Sung and his successors, the legacy is unredeemable. Large sections of the population are destitute, malnourished, exhausted and cynical. Their education is profoundly inappropriate to the modern world, the regime has done enormous damage to the national psyche, they have no sense of legal rights as a citizenry, they are subject to a brutal and pervasive punishment system, they continue to be indoctrinated with a harsh, fearful, utterly mendacious view of the modern world outside the DPRK's frontiers, and there is no end to this in sight.

The Party-based elite, despite its extraordinary incompetence and irresponsibility on many levels, still insists that its survival is inextricably linked with the survival of the Kimist state, and only abysmal failure on the part of Kimist leadership of a type that threatens this survival could change this. But if Kimist leadership were to falter and an enough-is-enough moment is reached, then a more humane, pragmatic course that nevertheless remains under elite control might gradually bring the country into a more reassuring, more international orbit. Scenario building of this type, though, is of course purely speculative, but what is not speculative is that the human cost of the Guerilla Dynasty will continue to be felt for years and years to come.

References

Buzo, Adrian (1999) *The Guerilla Dynasty: Politics and Leadership in North Korea*. I.B. Tauris: London.

Buzo, Adrian (2016) North Korea under Kim Jong Il, in *Routledge Handbook of Modern Korean History*, Michael J. Seth (ed.), pp. 221–33.

Johnson, Chalmers (1982) *MITI and the Japanese Miracle, 1925–1975*. Stanford University Press: Stanford, CA.

Robinson, Michael Edson (1988) *Cultural Nationalism in Colonial Korea, 1920–1925*. University of Washington Press: Seattle, WA.

Weber, Max ([1915?] 1964) *The Theory of Social and Economic Organization*, Talcott Parsons (ed). The Free Press: New York.

Index

Afghanistan: impact of Soviet invasion 82, 106, 108
Agreed Framework (1994) 134–5, 174–80; assessment of 178–80; and Korean Peninsula
Albania 153
Albright, Madeline 183
Arduous March famine (1994–7): causes 165–6, 193; food aid 167; government response 166–9

byungjin policy framework 240, 243

Carter, Jimmy 134
Chang Song-t'aek 207–8; Chinese connections 237; purged 236–7
China: relations with the ROK 108–9, 129–30
Ch'oe Yong-hae 208, 232, 239–40
Chollima 43–5, 95
Cho Man-sik 8, 9, 22–3
Cho Myong-nok 183, 240
Chongsanri Method 44, 95
Chun Doo-hwan 94, 102–3, 125–6
Comintern 5–6, 9
Communist Party of the Soviet Union (CPSU) 8, 10–11

Democratic People's Republic of Korea (DPRK): arms trading 123; comparison to other Marxist–Leninist states 274; Constitutional changes (1998) 159; effect of Soviet Bloc collapse 117–18, 121, 137–8; militancy towards the ROK 49–51; militarism in 47–8; politics in the 1970s 70–2; shaped by Kim Il Sung 1, 275ff; strategic reversals in the 1970s 84–6, 109–11; survivalist policies 152–3, 279, 283 *see also* Supreme People's Assembly *and* National Defence Commission
DPRK economy 16–17, 42–3, 85, 110, 214–16; agriculture sector 14, 34–5, 58–9, 249–52; autarky 35; corruption 173–4, 282; economic decline and collapse 120, 142, 152, 162–5; economic policies post Korean War 33–6, 55–6; economic policies under Kim Jong Un 247–52; economic trends in the 1970s 76–8; economic trends in the 1980s 98–102; Equal Emphasis policy 46–7; First Seven–Year Plan (1961–7) 48–9; foreign debt issues 77–8, 98–9; foreign trade 99–101, 246–9; illicit international trade 117–18, 163; industrial sector 14, 44–5, 251–2; Joint Venture Law (1984) 99–102; July 2002 Measures 169–72, 211ff; November 2009 currency readjustment 213–14; private economic activity 164, 284; Public Distribution System (PDS) 162, 165–6, 212–13; resistance to reform 99–102, 111, 117, 119–25; Six–Year Plan (1971–6) 76–7
DPRK foreign relations 54, 65, 71, 84–5, 94–5, 110–11, 118, 204
DPRK relations with China 53–4, 80, 82–3, 108–9, 217, 238, 254; cross–border trade 124, 213, 225; effect of Sino–Soviet split 52–4

DPRK relations with Japan 132, 146
DPRK relations with the Non-Aligned Movement 82–3
DPRK relations with the ROK 69–71, 94, 254–6: economic disparity 124–5; military build–up during 1970s 81; negotiating strategy 79–80; negotiations 71, 79–80, 102–6, 126–8; ROK Six Point Declaration (1988) 126; Summit meeting (2000) 183; Sunshine Policy 180–7; trade 122, 142
DPRK relations with the Soviet Union 52–3, 81–2, 106–8, 117; effect of Sino–Soviet split 52–4; *perestroika* 128–30, 144
DPRK relations with the US: talks with the DPRK 130–2, 145 *see also* Agreed Framework (1994) *and* Six Party Talks
DPRK society: anti–modern features 43–4, 226; effect of the Arduous March famine 154–5, 172ff; effect of the Korean War 32; human rights 252–4; isolation 284–5

Energy Development Organization (KEDO) 176, 179
Equal Emphasis policy (1962) 46–9; revived under Kim Jong Un 63, 240–1, 262

famine *see* Arduous March famine

Ho Ka-i 32
Hyundai: Kumgang-san Tourist complex 185

International Atomic Energy Agency (IAEA) 133–4

Japan 50, 71; influence on Kimist ideology 18–19; Japanese colonial era in Korea 3–4, 21, 24–5
Juche 41–2

Kaesong Industrial Zone (KIZ): 186, 238–9, 242
Kim Dae Jung 180–1, 183–5
Kim Il Sung: as military commander 57; consolidation of power (1945–58) 19–20, 29–37, 55–7; death of 151, 187; early life and career 1–2, 6–7, 17–19; effect of Korean War on 29–30, 54–5; establishes personal autocracy 51–2; foreign policy management 54; formative influences and worldview 13, 17–20, 30, 119, 140–1 275ff; guerrilla career 6–7; life in the Soviet Union 7; nationalist credentials 56; personality traits 19–20, 59, 275ff; relations with Kim Jong Il 120, 141–2; relations with Soviet occupation authorities 7, 13, 19
Kim Jong Il: assessments of 157, 187–90, 221–4, 280–2; consolidates power 151–2; culture and arts activities 74; early career 73–6; enters Politburo 75; ideological writings 97–8, 119–20, 141; policies and strategies 153–4, 155–7, 203–4, 206–7, 210–11; relations with Kim Il Sung 120, 141–2; role as designated successor 93, 97–98, 99, 120; succession planning for Kim Jong Un 206–7; suffers stroke (2008) 206; worldview 119–20
Kim Jong Un 206, 208; accession 231–2; consolidates power 232ff; policies 237ff, 256–8; purges Chang Song-t'aek 236–7; relations with the military 234–5, 240, 242–3
Korean communist movement: domestic Communist faction 9, 33; Manchurian guerrilla faction 11–12; pre–1945 activities 4–7; relations with Comintern 5–6; relations with Soviet occupation authorities 9–17; Soviet Korean faction 10–11, 23, 35–6; Yan'an faction 10, 32–3, 36
Korean Communist Party 4–6
Korean nationalist movement 2–4
Korean political tradition 280–1
Korean War 16, 30, 31, 57
Korean Workers' Party (KWP): effect of death of Stalin 35–6; erosion of support after 1994; Fifth Party Congress (1970) 72–3; First Party Conference (1958) 42; Fourth Party Congress (1960) 45; Organisation and Guidance Department (OGD) 74,

155; post–Korean War reconstitution 31–2; rise of Kim Jong Il 73–6; Second Party Conference (1966) 51–2; September 1956 crisis 36–7; Seventh Party Congress (2016) 242–6; Sixth Party Congress (1980) 93, 95–7; Third KWP Party Conference (2010) 209–11; Third Party Congress (1956) 36

Land reform 14

Manchuria 2; guerrilla movement 4, 6, 18; Manchurian guerrillas post–1945 role 11
Marxist–Leninist movements: generic features 271–4
Militarism in the DPRK 47–8, 158–62, 277–8
Military and terrorist incidents: Blue House assault 50; infiltration operations 50, 176; KAL bombing 125; Panmunjom axe killings 89; *Pueblo* seizure 50; Rangoon bombing 103 see also Northern Limit Line
Moscow Agreement (1945) 12
Mu Chong 32–3

National Defence Commission 159–60, 207–8; renaming 245
Northern Limit Line (NLL) 182, 184, 196; *Cheonan–ho* sinking 220; Yeongpyeong–do shelling 220–1
North Korea 1945–8: agriculture collectivisation 14; society 15; Soviet occupation policies 8–13; state formation 1945–8 13–16; war preparations 16–17
Nuclear weapons program 118, 219; background 133; crisis in 1994 134–5; DPRK strategy 135–7, 258; highly enriched uranium production 177, 227 see also Agreed Framework (1994) *and* International Atomic Energy Agency (IAEA)

O Kuk-ryol 95, 96, 119, 161, 207

Pak Ch'ang-ok 35, 59
Pak Hon-yong 4, 16, 29, 35; purged 33
Park Chung-hee 94, 102–3
Party Centre of the KWP 74–5

Rajin–Sunbong Free Economic and Trade Zone 118, 123–4, 143
Roh Tae Woo 125
ROK relations with the DPRK see DPRK relations with the ROK

Seoul Olympiad 94, 118, 125
Six Party Talks (2003–9): 204, 216ff, 226
son'gun 158–162; reaffirmed under Kim Jong Un 233–4, 235–6
Soviet Union: Cuban missile crisis 46; post 1945 occupation policies in North Korea 8–16, 19, 22; Sino–Soviet split 52–4; Soviet Bloc collapse 117–18
Stalinism in the DPRK 12–13, 15–16, 37–41
State Affairs Commission 245
Supreme People's Assembly of the DPRK 159, 205

Taean Work System 44, 95
Ten Principles on the Establishment of the Monolithic Leadership of the Party 87, 241
Three Revolutionary Fronts strategy (1964) 49, 69
Three Revolution Teams movement 75–6
Tripartite talks proposal 103–4

United Nations: joint Korean entry 132–3
United States: China policy 78; relations with the ROK 50; relations with the Soviet Union 106

Vietnam War 50, 70–1

Yi Tong–hwi 21
Yi Yong–ho 234, 259

Helping you to choose the right eBooks for your Library

Add Routledge titles to your library's digital collection today. Taylor and Francis ebooks contains over 50,000 titles in the Humanities, Social Sciences, Behavioural Sciences, Built Environment and Law.

Choose from a range of subject packages or create your own!

Benefits for you
- Free MARC records
- COUNTER-compliant usage statistics
- Flexible purchase and pricing options
- All titles DRM-free.

Benefits for your user
- Off-site, anytime access via Athens or referring URL
- Print or copy pages or chapters
- Full content search
- Bookmark, highlight and annotate text
- Access to thousands of pages of quality research at the click of a button.

REQUEST YOUR FREE INSTITUTIONAL TRIAL TODAY

Free Trials Available
We offer free trials to qualifying academic, corporate and government customers.

eCollections – Choose from over 30 subject eCollections, including:

Archaeology	Language Learning
Architecture	Law
Asian Studies	Literature
Business & Management	Media & Communication
Classical Studies	Middle East Studies
Construction	Music
Creative & Media Arts	Philosophy
Criminology & Criminal Justice	Planning
Economics	Politics
Education	Psychology & Mental Health
Energy	Religion
Engineering	Security
English Language & Linguistics	Social Work
Environment & Sustainability	Sociology
Geography	Sport
Health Studies	Theatre & Performance
History	Tourism, Hospitality & Events

For more information, pricing enquiries or to order a free trial, please contact your local sales team: **www.tandfebooks.com/page/sales**

 The home of Routledge books

www.tandfebooks.com